JAPAN AND RUSSIA IN NORTHEAST ASIA

Partners in the 21st Century

Edited by
Vladimir I. Ivanov and Karla S. Smith

Under the Auspices of the
Economic Research Institute for Northeast Asia

Forewords by
Alexander G. Granberg, Makoto Nobukuni, and
Robert A. Scalapino

Westport, Connecticut
London

Library of Congress Cataloging-in-Publication Data

Japan and Russia in northeast Asia : partners in the 21st century /
    edited by Vladimir I. Ivanov and Karla S. Smith, under the auspices
    of the Economic Research Institute for Northeast Asia ; forewords by
    Alexander G. Granberg, Makoto Nobukuni, and Robert A. Scalapino.
        p.   cm.
    Includes bibliographical references and index.
    ISBN 0–275–96382–9 (alk. paper)
       1. Japan—Foreign economic relations—Russia (Federation)
    2. Russia (Federation)—Foreign economic relations—Japan. 3. East
    Asia—Foreign economic relations—Forecasting. 4. Twenty-first
    century—Forecasts. I. Ivanov, Vladimir I. II. Smith, Karla S.
    III. Economic Research Institute for Northeast Asia.
    HF1602.15.R9J36   1999
    337.47052—dc21   98–33618

British Library Cataloguing in Publication Data is available.

Library of Congress Catalog Card Number: 98–33618
ISBN: 0–275–96382–9

First published in 1999

Praeger Publishers, 88 Post Road West, Westport, CT 06881
An imprint of Greenwood Publishing Group, Inc.

Printed in the United States of America

The paper used in this book complies with the
Permanent Paper Standard issued by the National
Information Standards Organization (Z39.48–1984).

10 9 8 7 6 5 4 3 2 1

Contents

Illustrations

TABLES

FIGURES

Preface

This book is the result of a lengthy process of seminars and roundtable discussions organized by the Economic Research Institute for Northeast Asia (ERINA) from April 1995 to July 1997 and called ERINA-Russia Forum. The volume represents the main outcome of this process. The forum was organized as an informal network of academics and practitioners. Its working meetings and public seminars served to discuss issues and problems in Japan-Russia relations and their relevance to Northeast Asia. By the end of 1996 the number of people involved in these working meetings and public lectures and seminars grew and the subject area covered by the forum expanded.

On July 29 and 30, 1997, several key members of this project participated in a concluding workshop "Japan and Russia in Northeast Asia: Building a Framework for Cooperation in the 21st Century" supported by ERINA and the Japan Foundation. The workshop was a productive event, and the participants were encouraged by the speech delivered by Prime Minister Ryutaro Hashimoto to the Association of Corporate Executives (*Keizai Doyukai*) on July 24, 1997, in which he mapped out key directions in Japan's policy with regard to the United States, Russia, and China proposing that Japan's diplomacy in the Asia-Pacific region be complemented by a proactive Eurasian diplomacy. A report summarizing the key findings of the workshop was published and distributed in early October 1997, a month before the Yeltsin-Hashimoto informal summit in Krasnoyarsk.

The goals we pursued in the activities of the ERINA-Russia Forum and the workshop that are reflected in this volume were to identify new directions for Japan-Russia relations and envision their impact on stability and economic development in the Northeast Asian subregion. The aim of the project was, first of all, to examine progress in Russia's economic reform, prospects for development of its Far Eastern region, and the new political foundations in Moscow-Tokyo relations that support Russia-Japan economic cooperation and political engagement in Northeast Asia. Moreover, despite differences in approaches and views among the participants of the project, all contributors to the volume strongly believed that positive changes in Japan-Russia bilateral relations need a comprehensive assessment and conceptual framework. This volume attempts to contribute to the development of such a framework.

Part I of the book underscores the extent to which history and domestic issues impinge on the foreign policies of Russia and Japan and on this bilateral relationship. Particular emphasis is placed on events and changes from 1991 to 1998. Contributors to this section review main domestic political, economic, and institutional shifts in Japan and Russia and evaluate progress in Russia's economic stabilization and reform with special attention to the role of the government in new businesses creation and lessons that Russia can learn from Japan in this realm. This part also addresses some fundamental changes in the international relations surrounding Japan and Russia and reviews key foreign policy issues in historical perspective and recent changes in Moscow-Tokyo bilateral dialogue, including Japan's economic assistance to Russian reform.

Part II deals with the problems of international and regional politics and covers important changes in foreign policies of Japan and Russia and their long-term strategic outlooks. The new political foundations in Moscow-Tokyo relations support not only progress in Japan-Russia economic ties but also facilitate economic and political cooperation in Northeast Asia. The contributors to this part focused their attention on the influence of U.S. policies and strategies on Japan-Russia relations, the phenomena of China's rise as a regional economic and political power, and instability on the Korean peninsula that negatively affects the overall situation in Northeast Asia. A new multilateral mechanism for crisis prevention in the subregion is discussed and a proposal made to incorporate Japan and Russia as major regional players in such a mechanism.

Part III concentrates on economic relations between Japan and Russia and provides an analysis of progress, opportunities, and barriers to bilateral cooperation. The contributors to this part of the book cover problems and prospects for Japan's economic links with Far Eastern Russia, the situation in the eastern regions of the Russian Federation and its expanded economic contacts with the Asia-Pacific region, prospects for Japanese investment in the energy resources development projects, bilateral trade in fishery, and trade and investment issues.

Finally, Part IV looks at Japan-Russia links in the context of Northeast Asian subregional cooperation and economic development. It covers the converging interests of Japan and Russia in Northeast Asia, including the prospects for the Sakhalin oil and gas resources development and transcontinental railway transportation between Northeast Asia and Europe. This final part also examines specific areas for cooperation within a multilayered relationship that includes cooperation in infrastructure development; prospects for Russia-China-Japan trilateral cooperation in border-crossing projects, particularly in modernizing and using the Zarubino port; problems of fishery and environmental protection; and prospects for multilateral subregional cooperation in Northeast Asia.

The chapters of this section demonstrate how the Japan-Russia bilateral agenda is expanding and includes issues significant for Northeast Asia. On the contrary, the list of problems covered in this concluding part of the volume also demonstrates that both editors and contributors were working with a moving target as new developments in Japan-Russia dialogue were taking place. The two informal summits held in Krasnoyarsk, Russia, in November 1997 and in Kawana, Japan, in April 1998 introduced more data related to both new issues and old problems, such as the territorial dispute.

Foreword

Robert A. Scalapino

Is there light at the end of a long, dark tunnel? After a century of relations ranging from hostility to indifference, can Russia and Japan open a new era of cooperation both bilaterally and within a meaningful multilateral framework?

There remain ample obstacles. Until recently, Japan assigned a relatively low priority to providing the economic resources and Russia has been slow to furnish the legal structure necessary if genuine cooperation is to unfold. Rhetoric has greatly outdistanced concrete action. Public opinion in the two nations also has not been of assistance. Foreignness rather than compatibility has dominated attitudes in both countries, with a negative history still remembered.

Russia's major difficulties in shifting from socialism to a market-oriented economy and the special problems of the Russian Far East have retarded progress, as has the propensity of Japan's business community to be very cautious with respect to risk-taking, perhaps understandable after earlier experiences. The significant challenges to the Japanese economy in recent times represent an additional obstacle, as does the special problem of the Northern Territories.

Yet there are signs that a more positive future for Japanese-Russian relations lies ahead. Despite continuing uncertainties, it seems likely that Russia will remain on the path of market-oriented economics and political openness. Thus, closer interaction with neighboring nations, including those in Northeast Asia, can take place in an atmosphere of greater compatibility and with threat removed.

In this setting Japan is a prime candidate for more positive interaction, especially with respect to the Russian Far East. Given its technological and managerial expertise, its resource requirements, and its intensive interest in environmental protection, Japan has much to offer and much to gain in a new relationship with Russia.

One hopes the Krasnoyarsk and Kawana meetings held in November 1997 and April 1998 signal the future course. Naturally, progress will continue to be dependent upon domestic trends in both countries. Moreover, enlightened governmental policies must be accompanied by closer interaction in the private sector. Further, it is essential that trust be developed through regularized bilateral and multilateral dialogues that cover the fullest range of issues including those in the security realm. Recent military contacts are a promising sign. One also hopes the pledge to seek a peace agreement by the year 2000 will be realized, with the thorny island issue handled successfully.

Further military reductions together with greater transparency in security matters must involve the United States and China as well as Japan and Russia. Indeed, in all spheres — economic and political — bilateral and multilateral relations will continue to be closely intertwined. Thus, at some point a Northeast Asia economic security forum may be established, a forum concentrating on the one region in the world where the major nations of the present and future come together closely.

In that fashion, a concert of powers could coexist with a balance of power. On a widening range of issues, including such difficult matters as that of the division on the Korean peninsula, cooperation could be enhanced. Moreover, the problems and the advantages of intensified economic interdependence could be examined, with concrete steps taken to provide for the new era we are entering.

The chapters in this volume present a range and depth of data and evaluation regarding Japan-Russia relations that warrant careful study. Moreover, the context is always the Northeast Asian subregion, with extensive attention given to the role of the United States and China in many of the studies.

There are no easy answers to the problems that we face in this transitional era. We are in the midst of a global revolution that in scope exceeds anything mankind has ever known. Moreover, the meaning of time has changed dramatically. Events are instantly known, with responses often required in minimal time. For leaders and citizens alike, leisure is a luxury seldom affordable.

Because Japan and Russia represent two prominent actors in the current drama, their ability to move toward a relationship greatly different from that of the past will be an important test as to whether the 21st century can inaugurate a protracted period of peace and mutual prosperity.

Let us hope that the optimists are correct, and let us urge governments and nonofficial bodies to take the steps that will strengthen their
position.

N/A

BK Title: # Foreword

Alexander G. Granberg

There is a growing interest within the political, business, and academic circles of Japan, China, Korea, and the United States in developing closer ties with Eastern Russia, particularly its Far Eastern region. These countries lead the way in Far Eastern Russia's external trade; investment cooperation; and academic, scientific, and humanitarian exchanges. This natural interest fully corresponds with Russia's own interests and international aspirations.

Eastern Russia serves as a testing ground for Russia-Japan business cooperation in such areas as oil and gas resources development, timber resources development, and fishery. Japanese officials have more than once proposed that at least half of the official credits and loans to Russia should be utilized in the Far Eastern region. However, this proposal has yet to be seriously considered and practically implemented by the Russian government, which needs to use the opened credit lines to the maximum extent possible. Japan maintains close and active relations with Russia through the subcommittee on the Far East of the Japan-Russia Committee for Economic Cooperation. Moreover, within the Russia-Japan Inter-Governmental Commission on Trade and Economic Cooperation a separate subcomission was set up to discuss economic cooperation between Japan and the Far Eastern region of Russia. Regular meetings among the governors of the Russian Far Eastern provinces and the prefectures of Japan also take place. Last, but not least, it was Prime Minister Ryutaro Hashimoto who proposed to hold a "no necktie" summit at some location in Eastern Russia to Russian President Boris Yeltsin.

Considerable attention in Japan was given to the Federal Program for Economic and Social Development of the Far Eastern and Trans-Baikal Regions. The draft of this program was, in fact, for the first time publicly presented in Tokyo in March 1996, before the program was officially launched by the Russian government. The entire text of the program was translated by the Economic Research Institute for Northeast Asia and published in Japanese. Our Japanese counterparts also made a number of useful proposals related to the program and urged the Russian side to incorporate the Zarubino Port development project into the program.

The current administration of the United States views the Far Eastern region as a priority area for cooperation with Russia. A special working group to facilitate business links between the Russian Far Eastern provinces and the Pacific West of the United States was created under the auspices of the Inter-Governmental Commission that became widely known as the Gore-Chernomyrdin Commission. This group's activities gained support from the U.S.–Russia Business Cooperation Fund, and a number of projects that improve the investment climate, such as a computerized system of advance notice customs clearance, create new opportunities for trade and investment.

Specialized institutions to promote business contacts with Eastern Russia were also created in China, the Republic of Korea, the Democratic Peoples Republic of Korea, and Mongolia. For example, a standing working group was created within the Russia-China Inter-Governmental Commission to discuss prospects for cooperation on the regional level and cross-border cooperation. An Association for Cooperation with Siberia and the Far Eastern Region was created in the Republic of Korea. Regular conferences are also taking place on the level of provincial administrations in Russia, China, Japan, and the Republic of Korea, and the resolution was adopted to establish an Association of Regional Administrations of the countries of Northeast Asia.

Russia's Pacific neighbors pay growing attention to the multilateral development projects in Eastern Russia, including a well-known development plan in the Tumen River area in southern Primorskiy Krai (that also involves border regions in northeastern China and North Korea); gas pipelines and electricity transmission projects that can link Eastern Russia with Mongolia, China, and Korea; and modernization and improvement of infrastructure facilities, including Russian ports and the Trans-Siberian Railway, that can be used for cargo transportation between East Asia and Europe.

In general, external political and economic conditions for the development of the eastern regions of Russia improved significantly. This contributes to a new geography and geometry of economic links emerging in Northeast Asian and Northern Pacific regions, with a growing participation of the neighboring provinces and regions of the states of this part of the world. Russia's eastern regions and provinces are involved in this process even though Moscow has yet to confirm that the Asia-Pacific region is a priority dimension in its foreign policy and economic plans.

The fact is that Russia's mutually beneficial linkages with other Asia-Pacific economies require economic recovery of its Far Eastern region, improvement of the investment climate, and development of efficient and competitive communications with Western Russia and Europe. Therefore, official declarations that the Asia-Pacific region is vitally important for Russia must be firmly linked with proactive domestic measures that will support the Far Eastern region's economic and social stability and development.

N/A

Foreword
Makoto Nobukuni

This book presents the views of experts who have collaborated in the Economic Research Institute for Northeast Asia (ERINA)-Russia Forum. Its aim is to send a twofold message to the world community: a call for actions by public entities for the construction of a historically legitimate international community and a call for engagement in business practices for establishing an empirical proof of the possibility and rationality of multilateral cooperation in Northeast Asia, particularly in the Russian Far East.

The book as a whole calls attention to development opportunities, identifies problems to be tackled, assesses economic rationality, provides prescriptions for policy implementation, and analyzes prospects for Russia-Japan cooperation.

The ERINA-Russia Forum, launched in 1995 by ERINA, Niigata, Japan, had been a part of the would-be broader scheme for the institute's mission to support economic development of this subregion. The mission was based on the concept of constructing a historically legitimate subregional community in Northeast Asia that will be aimed at prevention of regional disputes through preemptive economic development measures and construction of interdependent systems to anchor the Northeast Asian subregion as a stable system and secure its long-term development prospects.

Certainly, Northeast Asia has both political reasons and economic potential to accommodate this ideal. Having been burdened with the negative legacy of the cold war, this subregion had been shut off from the miraculous development of East Asia in the last two decades. The subregion was under the pressure of adverse economic environments of transitional economies, inadequate provision and management of economic laws, poor infrastructure, and, above all, lack of mutual confidence among the constituent countries.

Once mutual understanding and confidence have been established, this subregion could develop into one of the best stages for a new world community that embodies the concept of development-cum-interdependent systems.

The ERINA-Russia Forum intended to supplement the insufficiency in the density, frequency, and extension of then ongoing communications among political leaders, policy makers, business practitioners, and academics, both across national borders and within the respective countries. With the view to a broader Northeast Asian Forum incorporating, in addition to Japan and Russia, the People's Republic of China, the Republic of Korea, other Northeast Asian countries, and the United States, the ERINA-Russia Forum, although small in size, took up the challenge of building confidence among the concerned people across borders.

In a period of two years, the forum, as an action-oriented medium, was involved in providing support for various forms of communication and meetings ranging from workshops on the investment environment in the Russian Far East to direct policy dialogues with Russian authorities and facilitation of dialogues between Japanese business entities and the Russian economic and trade representatives.

Fortunately, many people spontaneously responded to the spirit of the forum and expressed strong interest in its objectives, such as opportunities for multilateral development projects and international joint ventures, some not even explored before 1996. In particular, regarding the Russian Far East, specific economic frontiers were diligently discussed with a special focus on Russia-Japan economic relations.

Although this book provides a comprehensive analysis of many subjects, there are important issues, however, that were not studied in the framework of the ERINA-Russia Forum. One among such issues is a strategy for developing Northeast Asia as a whole. Could a build-up of piecemeal bilateral cooperation lead to a rational subregional framework, or would it prolong the construction of a reliable multilateral system in this subregion? Would natural resources in Eastern Russia cause instability rather than security in this subregion?

These assets, if properly managed for maximizing economic prosperity and enhancing political stability, can serve as a factor of economic cooperation and goodwill between the constituent countries, while pursuit of national interests in a narrow sense may render the security of this region vulnerable. In this respect, a reliable multilateral framework can help to facilitate bilateral cooperation, including the Russia-Japan joint development projects discussed in this book.

It is hoped that the discussions in this book will kindle wide ranging interest among people who want to explore the political and economic potential of the Northeast Asian subregion, not only for the constituent countries but also for the world community as a whole. Most of the contributors to the ERINA-Russia Forum expressed their support for the idea of expanding the forum to a more integrated Northeast Asian Forum that will be able to explore prospects for a multilateral framework formation in addition to bilateral links.

In the long-term perspective multilateral cooperation in Northeast Asia will inevitably emphasize the collective interests and values of this subregion above any bilateral or unilateral interests. As a matter of fact, as other recently created subregional groupings demonstrate, a multilateral framework for Northeast Asia can bring with it many potential advantages.

First, there is the emerging and ever increasing need to cope with the so-called new threats, such as deterioration of the global environment, international crime organizations, illegal international trade, diffusion of drugs, the potential danger of nuclear hijacking, terrorism, and proliferation. The countries that form the Baltic Sea subregion and the Black Sea area have agreed to deal with these problems on a multilateral basis that will complement individual or bilateral efforts.

Second, such a multilateral framework will ensure a greater degree of flexibility in formulating collective subregional interests. The conflict of local and short-term interests can in many cases be resolved in a broader framework, as was observed in the Zarubino Port development project introduced in this book.

Third, as was evidenced in recent years, bilateral summit talks between any of the countries, including Russia, China, the United States, Japan, or the Republic of Korea invited a certain discomfort on the part of the others, thus limiting a movement toward a more secure and stable Northeast Asia. After all, international stability and security demand predictability in the behavior of the players involved, which, in turn, requires transparency in most of the areas related to modern international relations. In this respect, bilateral linchpins such as the newly expanding Russia-Japan economic cooperation extensively discussed in this book could serve as building blocks for future regional harmony.

viii

Acknowledgments

As editors of this volume and on behalf of the other contributors, we express our appreciation to Hisao Kanamori, chairman of the Economic Research Institute for Northeast Asia (ERINA); Shuntaro Shishido, director of ERINA; and the Japan Foundation for their support. From the inception of this project Makoto Nobukuni, former director of ERINA's Research Division, was enthusiastic about the idea to envision Japan-Russia improved relations that could lead to their partnership in the 21st century. This idea was shared by Robert A. Scalapino, Robson Research Professor at the University of California at Berkeley; Nobuo Shimotomai of Hosei University; Nodari A. Simonia of the Institute of World Economics and International Relations; Konstantin O. Sarkisov of the Institute of Oriental Studies of the Russian Academy of Sciences; and Alexander G. Granberg, chairman of the Council on the Location of Production Forces, a part of the Ministry of Economy of the Russian Federation. We extend our sincere thanks to these people for their generosity and knowledge, which have been crucial to the success of the project and publication of this book.

Finally, we express our sincere appreciation to the authors for the quality of their submissions, their enthusiasm for their work, and patience during the process of revisions of the draft of the manuscript. A note of special appreciation is also owed to Machiko Takahashi for her extremely thoughtful and effective coordination of the project from its inception and to Robert Valliant and Gregory Alan Dick for reading the draft of the manuscript and making valuable comments and suggestions. We also thank Dmitriy Sergachev for maps and graphics production for the manuscript. Although updating their chapters was the responsibility of the authors, any remaining inaccuracies or lack of clarity are the responsibility of the editors.

Introduction
Vladimir I. Ivanov

For about five years prior to large-scale financial meltdown in Russia in late 1998, Moscow and Tokyo demonstrated that they can start a new relationship with old disagreements about old problems and control emotions to overcome the mutually wounding history of their relations. New policy issues and economic opportunities with the elements of common interests were generated and discussed instead. The relationship turned around, supported by domestic changes in Russia, an improved international environment, a nuclear build-down with dismantlement and disposal of nuclear weapons in the North Pacific, bilateral defense exchanges, and initial steps in envisioning a cooperative approach to security issues in Northeast Asia.

Russia and Japan were getting closer through cooperation within the Group of Seven (G-7) and, from 1997, Group of Eight frameworks, increased people-to-people contacts, adjustments in security perceptions, nuclear weapons dismantling efforts, nonproliferation policies, and a shared interest in regional stability and economic development. Russian commitment to democracy and economic reform served as a factor that led Japan to change its perceptions.

The role of the United States and its cooperation with Japan in keeping Northeast Asia a stable region are essential.[1] Russia is gradually becoming a part of the multilateral process in the region and is now being perceived by other major powers as a partner or a potential partner. For example, in April 1996, in the Japan-U.S. Joint Declaration on Security, "Alliance for the 21st Century," the two governments stated that they will continue to work together and with other countries of the region to further develop multilateral regional security dialogue and cooperation mechanisms. With regard to Russia, a view was expressed that the ongoing process of reform contributes to regional and global stability and merits cooperation and encouragement provided that "full normalization" of Japan-Russia relations based on the Tokyo Declaration is achieved.[2]

Indeed, by virtue of epochal political shifts the Russia-Japan-U.S. relations became linked to the future of democracy in Russia, prospects for stability in Europe, and global security. Since 1991 U.S. and Japanese policy makers have dealt with two main issues: how to adjust the U.S.-Japan security and political partnership to the realities of the post–Cold War world without a Soviet threat, ideological competition, and a global nuclear standoff and how to make Russia a cooperative member of the international community.

From the Russian perspective, after 1992 the primary goal in relations with the United States and Japan was to secure external support for economic reform and domestic political restructuring, to preserve Russia's status in the international community, and to find ways to reconcile Russia's position with the U.S.-Japan security treaty. There was another relatively peripheral yet significant task for Russia: to be recognized as a participant in the Asia-Pacific regional process.

It seems that toward the end of the 1990s these expectations came to fruition for both sides. Changes in Moscow's relations with the United States and Western Europe encouraged the Japanese government to modify its policy toward Russia and to adjust Japan's interests in Northeast Asia. According to the Japanese government, its economic policy toward Russia is now based on three major principles: creation of a market economy, democratization and demilitarization, and the early conclusion of a peace treaty. Tokyo has become actively involved in programs of technical, humanitarian, and trade assistance to the former soviet republics, including Russia. Moreover, with the support of Japan, Russia was invited to join the Asia-Pacific Economic Cooperation summit in 1998.

Today, a major impediment in bilateral economic relations is the limited constituency in Japan that is able to influence both the perceptions of and the policies toward Russia. Moreover, since 1991, massive nonpayments caused by the depletion of gold reserves and partially by the dissolution of the Soviet Union have virtually undermined the position of those experts in Japan who were speaking in favor of more trade and investment links. In 1995 the Russian side owed Japan $1.3 billion in unpaid trade bills. In 1992 nine Japanese trading companies converted $330 million worth of unpaid bills left by the former Soviet Union into a collective financial claim through Japanese commercial banks, but the actual settlement could take many years. However, beyond the debt issue, the very concept of bilateral economic relations required reassessment.

The assumption that a high degree of complementarity between the two economies will be translated into expanding trade and investment relations between them appeared to be inadequate and misleading. In their bilateral economic ties Russia and Japan have to overcome a situation in which there is almost no horizontal trade among their manufacturing industries. Japanese major corporations, motor car exporters, and electric and electronic equipment producers are skeptical about their prospects in Russia and even prefer to channel their supplies to the Russian market through third countries.

Traditionally, Soviet-Japanese trade has been dominated by a small number of large Japanese trading companies. Their views toward Russia and interests reportedly coincided with those of the government, and business people in general were reluctant to challenge bureaucratic power or debate policy issues. However, by 1998 about 200 commercial and industrial companies, cooperatives, and associations participated in bilateral trade and investment relations with approximately 60 representation offices opened in Moscow and more in other major cities. Some large contracts have been negotiated by Mitsui Company, Sumitomo Corporation, KDD, Nippon Electric, Fujitsu, and Sinnihon. Japan's four major steel makers, including Nippon Steel Company, Sumitomo Metal Industries, NKK Corporation, and Kawasaki Steel Corporation, have reached an agreement with Russia to supply gas pipes and construction equipment.

Grants provided by the Ministry of International Trade and Industry supported these and other activities, as well as oil production projects as a part of the G-7 assistance package to help Russian oil production recover. The Japanese government has pledged $4.5 billion to Moscow within the multilateral economic assistance framework. As was suggested by G-7 in July 1993, Japan moved ahead trying to help Russia rely not only upon its natural resources, but other economic assets. In November 1994, using the model of the Gore-Chernomyrdin commission, Ryutaro Hashimoto, then head of the Ministry of International Trade and Industry, launched his own program called the Japanese Plan for the Promotion of Foreign Trade and Industry of Russia. A computerized database covering 106 Russian and Japanese enterprises was created to reveal potential Russian exporters and to inform potential Japanese importers about the products they need. In November 1996, an exhibition of Russian advanced technologies took place in Tokyo.

However, in the late 1990s both nations' agendas were dominated by internal problems. The reshuffle of the government in Russia in March and April 1998 and in August and September 1998 has revealed both the scale of unsolved economic problems and a potential for political instability. Taking place just weeks before the second informal summit between Prime Minister Hashimoto and President Boris N. Yeltsin at

Kawana and Prime Minister Keizo Obuchi's first official visit to Russia these domestic crises indicated that, in addition to deep changes in its economic system and political structure, Russia is undergoing a profound crisis of political leadership and a generation change. This triple transition combined with severe problems in Japan made bilateral dialogue an uncertain process. Otto Lambsdorff, former German minister of economics, referring to Japan's domestic problems, mentioned that economic reform cannot succeed without political reform and "Japan is in need of a change in its social and political paradigm, perhaps as fundamental as the Meiji Restoration has been."[3] An unsettled territorial dispute constitutes another impediment.

By the time of the summit in Krasnoyarsk in November 1997, it was basically understood (and tacitly accepted by diplomats on both sides) that a movement toward a peace treaty will not occur as a single dramatic event, but will take the form of a process that will be based on mutual trust and respect for the differences in positions. It was also understood that positive developments at the micro, not only macro, level and the focus not on the past but on the future are needed. The concept of joint development proposed by Moscow in November 1996 enabled Japan and Russia to replace traditional demand-refuse bargaining as the mode of dispute resolution with a concept of mutual benefit.

This new approach was based on the assumption that the implementation stage be viewed as an important goal in itself, one that would lead to increased confidence and trust, as well as consensus building both between and within Japan and Russia. It seems that a similar view was offered by Hashimoto in his speech delivered on July 24, 1997, at the Association of Corporate Executives. Therefore, a new, rather than traditional, vision of the territorial problem was advanced and a partnership-in-dispute-settlement approach began to take shape fueled by an understanding that a blend of different cooperative initiatives and interests, must replace rigid proposals advanced by conflicting sides and implying a winner and loser.[4]

Notwithstanding this progress, the question looms large whether the upward movement in relations will remain uninterrupted in the coming years, mostly because of the inability of politicians to handle the territorial issue under the changing circumstances. The fact of the matter is that this problem was formally reintroduced in the vastly changed agenda of bilateral relations as a result of Yeltsin's improvised proposal to sign a peace treaty before the end of the year 2000 during the summit in Krasnoyarsk.[5]

It is in the context of this self-imposed commitment that a concern was created that an admirable resolve to speed up a peace treaty process could become a time bomb threatening the improved relationship. To implement this plan it is very important to clarify that both parties are dealing with the same issue and share an understanding of how the settlement can be reached, and where to draw a final demarcation line between northeastern Japan (Hokkaido) and southeastern Russia (Sakhalinskaya Oblast). This, unfortunately, does not seem to be the case. In both Japan and Russia, there lingers an illusion that a peace treaty can be achieved merely by a political compromise.

The scope of this compromise, however, is seen by the two sides differently. In some quarters in Moscow there is an opinion that a handover of Shikotan and the Habomais, as was agreed by the two sides in 1956, can be a part of a peace treaty package. In Japan, the government views the return of all four disputed territories (that is, a transfer of title, even if the transfer of the islands is postponed) as a precondition for a peace treaty.[6]

These differences were confirmed in the statement made by Yeltsin's spokesman Sergei Yastrzhembskiy upon his arrival in Yuzhno-Sakhalinsk directly from Kawana to brief local administration on the results of the summit. Yastrzhembskiy's statement on the universality of the Russian Constitution Law was well received by the Russian public but in Japan created an impression that Moscow does not really view the territorial dispute in terms of compromise or, even worse, is interested in maintaining status quo camouflaged by a dialogue.

It seems that scenarios existing on both sides of the dispute can invite criticism from extremist groupings and politicians, leading, in the case of the presidential elections in Russia in the year 2000, to a new political situation. Russian conservatives will find even limited concessions unacceptable; Japanese hardliners and nationalists will call them inadequate and equally unacceptable. In both Tokyo and Moscow, legislators have generally little clout in foreign affairs, yet they remain relatively independent from the bureaucrats and must endorse any international agreement of the scale of a peace treaty with another state. Before they can do so, they must be given an opportunity and time to develop at least a general understanding of what is at stake.

Therefore, the idea to speed up a peace treaty process created a significant potential for disillusionment, particularly on the part of the Japanese. Disillusionment on the part of the Russian leaders cannot be ruled out as well, and there is no guarantee that in 1999–2000 domestic issues, including parliamentary and presidential elections, will not dominate Russian foreign policy, thus making Yeltsin's behavior with regard to Japan less compassionate and predictable.[7]

For both countries, the partnership process is a new phenomena compared with Moscow-Washington relations during the Soviet era and after 1991, or Russia's summit level dialogues with other G-7 members. Although in relation with Japan an orientation toward the future was basically formed, the image of a new relationship was created but only on the level of concepts and positive expectations. This image is yet to be rooted in practical ties, business-to-business and people-to-people contacts beyond the bureaucratic channels. The bilateral relations must become less a function of personal ties between two leaders and more vigorous on both the grassroots and institutional levels.

Although each party faces its own dilemmas, their respective motives to continue cooperative political dialogue are now better defined. This improves conditions for more trade and investment in the future. The "no necktie" summit at Kawana, for example, led to an agreement to set up an investment company to encourage Japanese companies to invest in Russia, thus adding an important tool to the implementation of the Yeltsin-Hashimoto plan of economic cooperation adopted in Krasnoyarsk.

At Kawana, two leaders agreed to set up a joint committee for space development and to conduct joint feasibility studies for 20 projects designed to improve Russian energy efficiency. In 1998 Japan agreed to provide $600 million out of a $1.5 billion untied loan from the Export-Import Bank of Japan. The Russian president called for Japanese automakers to set up a production line in Moscow. He reiterated his proposal to jointly construct fish-processing facilities on the disputed islands, and the Japanese prime minister offered to study a possibility of providing residents of the disputed islands with diesel power generators.

Both sides discussed prospects for cooperation in peaceful uses for nuclear energy,[8] business training for Russians in Japan, and the cleanup of oil spills. They agreed to continue to promote exchanges and high level dialogue on security and defense issues and to carry out a joint search and rescue exercise between Russian and Japanese forces. Moreover, the two leaders welcomed Japan's decision to hold a Japan Culture Festival in Russia in 1998–99, and add cultural, academic, and technical specialists to the list of Japanese allowed to visit the disputed islands on a visa-free basis.[9] Finally, a proposal was further discussed on how to make a peace treaty more comprehensive and cover a broader range of issues of economic and cultural cooperation.

For the Russian president, however, bad domestic news soon overshadowed both the "no necktie" summit at Kawana and another occasion to talk with Hashimoto during the Group of Eight meeting in Birmingham, England. On May 17, 1998, to the dismay of the powerholders in Moscow, former General Alexander Lebed was elected governor of Krasnoyarskiy Krai — an industrial and natural resources stronghold that occupies one-seventh of the Russian territory. The same week, in Kemerovskaya Oblast, the neighboring region to the west of Krasnoyarsk, coal miners who were demanding an end to several months-long delays in wage payments besieged the Trans-Siberian Railway in protest.

Compared with Krasnoyarskiy Krai and Irkutskaya Oblast, the position of some provinces that belong to Far Eastern Russia could become even more difficult. Economic reform abruptly changed the Far East's economic status. The administrative power and influence of Moscow has receded, coinciding with the end of the era of state-led economic development. Fewer subsidies contributed to the rising costs of living and transportation and badly affected population and enterprises. Capital investment spiraled down. Significant cuts in defense spending and downsizing of the military force limited the flow of financial resources to the area even more. Fewer defense contracts threw the entire machine-building industry of the region into collapse. Despite rising salaries and wages, purchasing power has declined because of inflation, chronic delays in payments, and a cost of living much higher than the national average.

Both Krasnoyarskiy Krai and Irkutskaya Oblast, that separate Kemerovskaya Oblast (a hotbed of coal miners' protests and Trans-Siberian Railway blockades) from the Far Eastern economic region, are better off than some of the Far Eastern provinces in two major respects: the population's dynamics and the cost of primary energy.

From 1991 to 1997, the Far Eastern and Trans-Baikal regions' populations decreased by almost 1 million. In 1996 alone, the population shrank by 93,300 people. People appeared to be less affected by worsening economic and social conditions in the southern provinces of the region, while northern and island provinces of the Far East were losing comparatively more inhabitants. However, it is difficult to expect that a steady population growth (typical for the region before 1991) can be easily restored because of rising unemployment (219,000 people) and a limited number of jobs (13,500 vacancies), particularly in the developed and urbanized areas.

The situation in the energy sector — one of the most troubled areas of the regional economy — also remained difficult, and the electricity tariffs in Sakhalin were twice as high compared with Irkutskaya Oblast; in Kamchatka the difference was four-fold. The region's high dependency on coal and the inefficiency of many local mines necessitated the long distance deliveries of coal from Eastern Siberia and that, in combination with other factors, makes the electricity tariffs in the Far East the highest in Russia. Although the energy sector of Far Eastern Russia was given priority by both the federal government and regional authorities, the key energy-related projects were delayed or stalled by lack of investment.

On the investment front, the federal government ignored its own promises given to the Far Eastern provinces. On April 15, 1996, the *Federal Program for Economic and Social Development of the Far Eastern and Trans-Baikal Regions for 1996–2005* was adopted to ensure a sustainable development of the region. The plan was declared by Yeltsin as a presidential program a week later. However, in 1996–97 the government fell short of its own targets. Although the program was not entirely neglected and the federal budget kept its percent share in the available investment resources, both federal and local budgets were too tight to help the implementation of the program, while the Russian private sector was still too weak to play a major role in the process. Moreover, because of flaws in the administrative mechanisms, a program directorate (an executive body) was not formed as was planned. No decision was made, either, on the creation of the regional fund for reconstruction and development.

Unlike the energy rich provinces of Siberia, the key Far Eastern provinces are maritime and better positioned for foreign trade. The dependence of the Far Eastern economy on exports became more obvious and its relations with the rest of Russia weakened. Although growing trade volumes were not sufficient to balance the destructive consequences of rising transportation and electricity costs and declining living standards, the Far Eastern provinces benefited from finding new sources of supply in Northeast Asia to substitute for sources in Western Russia.

These long-term economic reorientations in combination with the protests by Siberian coal miners, the blockade of the Trans-Siberian Railway, and Lebed's political reincarnation as the governor of Krasnoyarskiy Krai demonstrate how fragile the Russian Federation could become under the strains of economic crisis, social unrest, and political uncertainty.

For the Japanese, domestic political changes proved even more dramatic. Hashimoto's party's poor performance in the upper house elections in July 1998 forced him to resign. Russian Prime Minister Sergei Kiriyenko, invited by Hashimoto to visit Japan, came to Tokyo only hours after the resignation became effective. Kiriyenko had a brief meeting with Obuchi, who was later confirmed as the new prime minister. This took place only weeks before his Russian counterpart, Foreign Minister Yevgeniy Primakov, became chairman of the Russian government in September 1998. It remains to be seen whether new political actors in Russia and Japan can stay the course of cooperative bilateral relations and positive interaction between the two countries in Northeast Asia.

NOTES

1. Considering this broader political context, the project participants were working on the assumption that a trilateral approach to Japan-Russia relations that involves U.S. experts can be useful in practical terms and in expanding the range of professional expertise and making the project more comprehensive and productive.

This book can be seen as a follow-up of the project supported by the United States Institute of Peace, which in May 1993 convened a trilateral conference in Washington, D.C., followed by a collective monograph entitled *"Northern Territories" and Beyond: Russian, Japanese, and American Perspectives*, published by Praeger in 1995.

2. See "Prospects for International Cooperation in Northeast Asia. A Multilateral Dialogue," *Political Issues*. New York: Asia Society–Japan Institute of

International Affairs, 1996, p. 11.

3. Otto Lambsdorff, "Lessons Shared Between Germany, Japan," *The Japan Times*, April 21, 1998.

4. According to the editorial article published by *Asahi* newspaper on July 25, 1997, a Japanese official involved in negotiations with Russia said "It was easy to justify and insist on Japan's position. What was difficult was a question of how to leave room for the other party to satisfy its domestic audience."

It mentions that "in 1955 and 1956, negotiations to normalize diplomatic relations between Japan and the Soviet Union became a political football amid the turmoil in Japan, which led to the merger of two major conservative parties and more confusion amid U.S. pressure. As a result, Japan's original claim to two islands in the Northern Territories was changed into a demand for four islands. This eventually led to the never-ending territorial problem."

5. See Stanislav Kondrashov, "Yeltsin-Hashimoto: Without Neckties but with a Load of Problems," *Izvestia*, April 16, 1998. Ironically, the idea of setting a concrete deadline for a peace treaty conclusion was aired by Lebed, who visited Japan in fall 1997. According to Keizo Nabeshima, an editorial writer for Kyodo News Service (see his article in *The Japan Times*, January 26, 1998), Yeltsin's initiative to set the 2000 deadline for treaty negotiations came as a pleasant surprise to the Japanese side.

6. In his New Year's Day (1998) press conference, Hashimoto was expressing the confidence that Japanese sovereignty over the Northern Territories — "an integral part of Japanese territory" — will be confirmed when the treaty is signed and that Japan cannot sign a peace treaty unless the border is established. He also mentioned that Japan will pay close attention to remarks to be made by Yeltsin about the bilateral territorial issue in a speech to the Russian Parliament in May 1998. See *The Japan Times*, January 26, 1998, and April 24, 1998.

7. See a commentary by Viyatcheslav Nikonov, "Whether the Kawana Skies Are Clear?" in *Izvestia*, April 14, 1998. The author said that, although for Japanese people a peace treaty equals the return of the disputed islands, for Russian politicians and citizenry these are different subjects, because the majority of Russians consider these islands as belonging to Russia — "justly and legitimately" — because Japan, according to the Allied nations' joint agreement, was punished for its acts of aggression on the side of Germany and Italy during World War II.

8. Cooperation in environmental protection, in addition to a common understanding, can also be seen as a part of the nuclear disarmament and dismantlement effort. Japan's role in helping Russia to build a treatment facility for low-level radioactive waste reprocessing and construction of the storage facility can be extended to disposition of nuclear materials (plutonium and highly enriched uranium), consuming them at Japanese nuclear power plants, collaboration in building a joint storage facility, and joint research and development programs that will help convert formerly secret nuclear research and production centers into civilian and commercially viable enterprises. These issues were addressed in an article by Neil J. Numark carried by *The Japan Times* on April 17, 1998.

9. Under a cabinet agreement reached in October 1991, only former residents of the islands, members of groups working for the return of the islands, and mass media people have been allowed to participate in a mutual visa-free visit program formed as a result of the proposal made by Mikhail Gorbachev in 1988.

I

HISTORY AND DOMESTIC ISSUES

The late 1990s present a unique situation pointing to a new era in Japan-Russia bilateral relations. Japan and Russia entered this decade with no consistent or continuous progress in dialogue; they continued to look at each other over their shoulders. A few years later, however, these two countries, estranged for more than a century, are entering a new stage of reconciliation and accommodation. This historic repositioning seems to be more than a result of skillful diplomacy or friendly personal contacts among politicians. Rather, this change reflects major shifts in national interests and long-term priorities.

The main reason for change was the transformation of Russia, its democratization and economic reform. Changes in Russia's system allowed Japan and Russia to speak the same political language. A second reason for change was a realization on both sides that relations could remain stalemated indefinitely if more innovative policies were not sought.

Despite optimistic assessments, sustained improvement in relations is uncertain. The long history of antagonism and conflict may again project itself onto current relations. Domestic concerns also now exert a greater influence on the diplomacy of these two countries. Therefore, how the two countries manage to come to terms with the past, with lingering negative perceptions, and with domestic exigencies and crises will test whether this is indeed a new era.

The eight chapters in this part underscore the extent to which history and domestic issues impinge on the foreign policies of Russia and Japan and on this bilateral relationship. As Tsuneo Akaha points out, "domestic structures and processes will become a more dominant factor influencing the external behavior of both Russia and Japan." Will Russia's domestic economic exigencies create a need for policies that encourage closer economic cooperation with Japan? Or will they ferment nationalistic sentiments that preclude this? Will Japan's political and bureaucratic systems exhibit enough flexibility to respond to Russia's painful reform and aid its transition? Or will it succumb to bureaucratic inertia and exhibit only occasional changes in tactics (not of strategy) in its policy toward Russia?

Akaha compares the situation of Russia in the 1990s to Japan's postwar economic development. He is uncertain, however, that Russia can mimic Japanese development, noting that Japan's export-driven economic growth was possible because of assistance from the United States and its open market. He is hopeful that economic relations between Japan and Russia can be improved and that this will help to ensure that Russia continues on the path toward a market economy. The greatest potential for bringing the economies of the two countries together is Japanese assistance for Russia's reform and development of the Far Eastern region. However, Akaha emphasizes that only strong policy commitment on both sides will make this possible.

Hisao Kanamori in his opening chapter reviews changes in the Japanese economy compared with the period of the 1970–80s. In the 1990s, its rates of economic growth became the lowest among the main members of the Organization for Economic Cooperation and Development. There were mistakes in economic policy, and it was possible for Japan to achieve higher rates of economic growth in the 1990s. However, by restraining demand, the government of Japan did not allow the economy to grow. Since the early 1990s there were also shortcomings in the management of the financial sector that led to the accumulation of bad loans, and it is not easy now to solve the problem of these loan repayments. Finally, there are structural problems that restrain economic growth and Japan finds itself at the crossroads. Will it be possible to make right choices at this turning point in Japanese history?

Nodari A. Simonia asserts that Russia is now part of the capitalist world. The nature of political power in Russia rests not in a single political party but with a new moneyed ruling class of capitalist bureaucratic managers and technocrats. Simonia proposes that political contests in Russia, such as the presidential election of 1996, may appear to be about ideology, but in reality they represent struggles for influence over economic management and the direction of economic reform. The main contenders in this struggle are three main factions that can be distinguished by their close links and interests in either export-oriented extracting industries, commerce and finance services, or the industrial complex (particularly defense-related enterprises).

From 1991 two of these factions (extracting industries and commerce and finance services) joined forces virtually to control the Russian economy. They succeeded in doing so by securing the support of the International Monetary Fund and other international organizations. The third faction, however, proved during the 1996 elections that it can challenge this control. Simonia interprets Alexander Lebed's temporary integration into government as an expression of Yeltsin's need to respond to the demands of the faction of industrialists and economic nationalists, and questions whether the concentration of economic power in these factions will eventually allow Russia to modernize and diversify its economy and improve its long-term prospects for foreign investment and trade relations with Japan and other countries.

In his chapter, Nobuo Shimotomai traces Japan-Russia relations from 1991 to 1996. He emphasizes that during this period Tokyo and Moscow dialogue represented a "matrix of domestic factors." He supports Simonia's view of competing factions or clans and elaborates further on the implications of this on foreign policy. In its early years, the Yeltsin administration embraced an assertive and proactive approach toward Japan in an effort to stimulate economic cooperation. However, progress was hindered by opposition in Russia and by a tepid response from Japan. In Shimotomai's view, Japan was too slow to respond to the collapse of the Soviet Union and the massive changes that took place in Russia during 1991–96. He also suggests that policy makers in Japan and Russia underestimated the influence of domestic considerations on foreign policy.

Shimotomai is sanguine, however, about the prospects for closer Japan-Russia relations. He sees Russian policy toward Japan from 1996 as pragmatic and realistic but concedes that, although Japan's new policy of a multidimensional approach toward Russia is ambiguous, it represents an important departure from the previous policy of balanced expansion. This departure may provide an opportunity to set new goals in bilateral relations that are not "rigidly linked to the formal solution" of the Northern Territories dispute.

"On the Way to Economic Deadlock," Ivan S. Tselitschev's chapter, offers a more sobering analysis of economic affairs in Russia than his title suggests. Tselitschev believes the Russian economy is in a trap: The government's deflationary policy, which is critical for macroeconomic stabilization and to restore investor and consumer confidence, hinders economic growth and industrial output. The only way out of this trap is to remove the structural impediments that preclude growth without inflation. These structural impediments, Tselitschev explains, are combined with protectionism and a misallocation of resources, barter and "quasi money" transactions, a lack of incentives for companies to restructure and government subsidies, the government's budget deficit, and tax evasion and rent-seeking.

Tselitschev also explains that the Russian taxation system and legal framework for foreign investment remain a problem, as does the fact that the Russian government has failed to adopt strategies to promote manufacturing exports, knowledge intensive ventures, and small- and medium-sized business. He is encouraged, however, by the wider public and political support for stronger economic ties with Japan.

Douglas Barry provides a deeper analysis of the importance of small business development in Russia. He goes as far as to say that if Russia can improve a nurturing environment for new small enterprises, its economy may not only recover, but flourish. Barry's analysis of the factors that frustrate new business creation and performance echoes Tselitschev's list of structural impediments. Barry is somewhat pessimistic about an improvement of conditions mostly because the Russian "economic and political elite" does not consider small business development a priority.

Business development in the Russian Far East, however, may be promoted through large foreign investments, particularly in Sakhalin oil and gas. Although obstacles to investment will still need to be removed, these major projects provide opportunities for businesses throughout the region in terms of subcontracts and technology transfers through joint ventures with foreign partners. Another potential advantage of the Russian Far East lies in the eventual conversion and privatization of the military industrial complex. In regard to assistance from the United States and Japan, Barry concludes that technical assistance that supports small business should play a key role in promoting the Russian economic transition.

Like Akaha, Andrei I. Kravtsevich also compares the approaches to economic modernization of Russia and Japan. He examines the lessons that can be drawn from Japan's postwar experience and explains how this experience can be adapted to Russia's situation. Of particular interest to Kravtsevich is what he terms a nationwide "super-idea" that is based on "healthy and enlightened national interests." He sees this as a means to unify a nation and believes it to have been key to Japan's success. He also suggests borrowing from Japan's *shingikai* or consultative committees system for political and economic decision making and from Japan's experiences in securing public support for governmental policy and small and medium enterprises promotion.

The conclusion Kravtsevich draws from his comparison is that the key difference between the situations of Russia and postwar Japan is that Japan had to correct market mechanisms, while Russia must form new mechanisms. This precludes a direct borrowing of methods and development approach. Nonetheless, Kravtsevich concludes that Japan's "comprehensive approach" to solving economic problems is valuable and that the implementation of particular policies may be applied to the Russian economy.

Konstantin O. Sarkisov goes back to the early 18th century to trace the history of Japan-Russia relations. In his retrospective, Sarkisov proposes that bilateral relations can be divided into four periods: geopolitical rivalry, nationalistic and ideological antagonism, Cold War confrontation, and transition.

At the end of the third period, Sarkisov reflects a slight improvement in relations that is carried over to the fourth period: transition. He describes this period as one "marked by the abatement of rivalries." He then provides an analysis of the Northern Territories issue and its legal, historical, political, geostrategic, economic, and psychological aspects. As other authors in this part, Sarkisov notes that the domestic situation in Russia and the "emotional burden" in Japanese politics will continue to influence dialogue on the territorial dispute making it difficult to pursue a pragmatic policy. He cautions, however, that the dispute must be seen not only in terms of Japan-Russia bilateral relations but also in the context of Northeast Asian stability. He proposes that if the positive momentum of relations between 1996 and 1998 can be maintained, the two nations may be poised to enter a fifth period in their history.

053

1

Japan in the 1990s

Hisao Kanamori

In the 1990s, the Japanese economy changed dramatically compared with the period of the 1970s and 1980s. Until the late 1980s rates of economic growth were at a record high, and in that respect Japan was ahead of other industrialized countries. However, in the 1990s the rates of economic growth became the lowest among the main members of the Organization for Economic Cooperation and Development (OECD). It is important to understand the reasons behind this change in performance. There are three main contributing factors.

First, there were mistakes in economic policy and measures of supporting economic growth. It was possible for Japan to achieve higher rates of economic growth in the 1990s. However, by restraining demand, the government of Japan did not allow the economy to grow. Second, since the early 1990s there were shortcomings in the management of the financial sector that led to the accumulation of bad loans, and it is not easy now to solve the problem of these loan repayments. Third, there are structural problems that restrain economic growth. In a sense, Japan is at the turning point of solving these structural problems.

MISTAKES IN ECONOMIC POLICY

In nominal prices Japan's gross domestic product (GDP) grew 15 percent from 1990 to 1997, from ¥439 trillion in 1990 to ¥505 trillion in 1997. In real terms the growth was about 10 percent during this period. However, this rate is very unsatisfactory for the Japanese economy. In 1976–80, the rate of economic growth was 4.6 percent, in 1981–85 it was 3.3 percent, and in 1986–90 increased to 4.8 percent. This means that in the Japanese economy, average rates of economic growth were maintained at the 4 percent level. However, in 1991–95 the rate of growth decreased to only 1.2 percent.

The recent rates of economic growth are the following: 2.9 percent in 1991, 0.4 percent in 1992, 0.5 percent in 1993, 0.6 percent in 1994, 2.8 percent in 1995, 3.2 percent in 1996, and it was estimated that the economic growth was negative (–0.5 percent) in 1997 (Table 1.1).

Obviously the rates of economic growth were decreasing, but the slowdown in the Japanese economy cannot be accurately assessed and understood on the basis of these figures alone. In 1987–90, there was considerable investment in capital equipment, and this mainly explains the high rates of economic growth. By 1991 there was excessive equipment accumulated in almost every industry. The overall economic slowdown began.

In 1992–94, investment in equipment was falling, causing stagnation in wages, employment, and consumption. In theory, during periods of stagnation in private sector demand, the government sector demand should be expanded. However, in 1991 government investment was not sufficiently increased. In 1992 and 1993, the investment volume in the public sector also grew, but, again, this increase was inadequate. In 1994, the government continued to restrain investment in the public sector.

In 1995 and 1996, there were some signs of recovery in private sector investment in equipment. However, the public sector investment was restrained in 1996, and its volume lowered in 1997. This demonstrated that the government had no clear-cut policy of public spending; this policy was not actually responding to the economic fluctuations. At some points this policy was expansive, but when there was a need to support positive developments in the private sector the government backed off fearing the accumulation of a budget deficit.

In fiscal year 1996, for example, the budget deficit was ¥37 trillion, which is 7.3 percent of GDP. According to estimates by the ministry of finance, by the end of fiscal year 1998 the accumulated public debt of the national and local governments will reach ¥529 trillion, which will exceed the GDP of Japan. Therefore, the government is attempting to reduce the budget deficit by ¥9 trillion by increasing the consumption tax, abolishing tax reduction schemes, and increasing the burden of social security.

At the extraordinary session of the Diet in fall 1997 the national government proposed to enact a new law to reform the financial system. This law stipulated the reduction of public investment for the next three years. This seems to be a mistaken policy. Compared with the ability to supply, the demand generated by the Japanese economy is relatively low.

TABLE 1.1

Japan's Real Gross Domestic Product Growth Rate

(in percent, compared with the previous year)

	1990	1991	1992	1993	1994	1995	1996	1997ᵃ	1998ᵃ
Gross domestic expenditure, nominal	8.0	5.6	1.9	1.0	0.4	2.2	2.8	0.4	0.7
Gross domestic expenditure, real	5.5	2.9	0.4	0.5	0.6	2.8	3.2	-0.5	1.2
Private final consumption	4.2	2.8	1.2	1.7	1.5	3.1	2.8	-1.2	1.8
Private housing investment	4.9	-12.3	-3.5	4.9	7.6	-6.7	13.7	-21.0	-7.1
Private capital investment	11.3	2.7	-7.2	-10.4	-2.5	7.4	9.1	1.7	-1.7
Private inventory increaseᵇ	-0.1	0.3	-0.7	0.0	-0.2	0.2	-0.1	0.1	-0.2
Government's final consumption	2.2	1.4	2.1	2.4	2.9	2.7	1.0	-0.2	0.2
Public fixed capital formation	4.6	7.2	16.6	12.6	-1.1	7.9	-2.7	-8.1	6.6
Public inventory increaseᵇ	0.0	-0.1	0.0	0.0	0.1	0.0	0.0	0.0	0.0
Export of goods and services	6.5	5.3	4.4	0.5	5.9	4.6	5.1	10.2	1.7
Import of goods and services	3.7	-1.6	-1.6	1.5	10.5	15.2	8.7	-2.9	-1.1
Domestic demand contributing ratio	5.2	2.2	-0.2	0.6	0.9	3.8	3.5	-2.2	0.8
External demand contributing ratio	0.3	0.7	0.6	-0.1	-0.3	-1.0	-0.4	1.6	0.4
Gross domestic product deflator	2.3	2.5	1.5	0.6	-0.2	-0.6	-0.3	0.9	-0.5
Real gross domestic expenditureᶜ	5.3	3.0	0.7	0.3	0.6	2.9	3.5	-0.5	1.1
Mining industry production indexᵈ	5.0	-0.7	-6.4	-4.0	3.2	2.0	4.0	1.8	-3.3

Notes:

ᵃestimates

ᵇcontributing ratio to real gross domestic expenditure

ᶜgross national expenditure total of all expenditures of all kinds within the economy, both public and private. It is usually different from gross domestic product because expenditures on imports are included, but those on exports are not.

ᵈin calculating the mining industry production index the level of production for 1990 was estimated at 100 percent

Source: Economic Planning Agency, *Annual Report on National Accounts* (1990–98, annual issues) (Tokyo: Government of Japan); Ministry of International Trade and Industry, *Trade and Industry Statistics Handbook* (1990–98, annual issues) (Tokyo: Government of Japan).

According to OECD estimates, in 1997 the gap between demand and supply was about 3 percent of GDP, which places Japan next to Switzerland among the OECD economies.

The government has, therefore, to increase public investment and to reduce the gap between demand and supply. When this gap is large the government should avoid decreasing public investment. If the government ignores this principle, GDP will not grow, taxable income will decrease, and the fiscal imbalances, therefore, cannot be corrected. It is also possible that the current account balance will expand. In reality Japan's GDP shrank in 1997 and the current account balance exceeded 2 percent of the GDP. The Japanese government should implement a policy to stimulate demand, instead of adopting the policy of fiscal deficit reduction before the economy recovers.

FINANCIAL FACTOR

It might be wrong to blame only the weak demand for low growth in Japan. The environment of high rates of economic growth after 1987 allowed Japanese banks to extend huge loans that later became nonperforming assets. Compared with 1990, the GDP of Japan is about 10 percent higher in 1997, but stock prices have declined to about 40 percent at the 1990 peak, and land prices contracted to about 30 percent. Therefore, even though the GDP volume has grown, the value of assets dramatically decreased and the banks that have huge outstanding loans cannot really compensate their losses considering that their collateral has sharply contracted in market value.

According to a report issued by the ministry of finance in January 1998, Japanese banks' bad loans were estimated at ¥76 trillion, which equals 12 percent of the total amount of outstanding loans of ¥624.9 trillion. Among these nonperforming loans, ¥2.7 trillion cannot be recovered, ¥8.7 trillion are doubtful with regard to their recovery potential, and ¥65.3 trillion need individual risk management. Declining prices of stock and land strongly affected banks, security companies, and construction companies. In 1997, Sanyo Securities, The Hokkaido Takushoku Bank, Yamaichi Securities, and The Tokuyo City Bank collapsed. Some medium-sized construction companies also went out of business.

CHANGING INDUSTRIAL STRUCTURE

Even during the phase of economic stagnation, the process of change in the industrial structure in Japan has continued. Therefore, industrywise, the composition of the GDP was changing (Table 1.2).

The share of material production in the GDP was decreasing, while the service sector relative weight was growing. This trend was particularly

TABLE 1.2
Gross Domestic Product: Composition by Sector
(percent, in nominal prices)

	1990	1995
Agriculture, forestry, and fisheries	2.5	1.9
Mining industry	0.3	0.2
Manufacturing industry, including:	28.2	24.7
Textiles	0.6	0.4
Petrochemicals	2.2	2.1
Steel	1.6	1.3
General machinery	3.7	2.9
Electric machinery	4.5	3.9
Transport equipment	2.7	2.5
Precision machinery, equipment, and instruments	0.5	0.4
Construction	10.1	10.3
Electricity, gas, and water supply	2.6	2.8
Wholesale and retail trade	13.6	12.7
Finance and insurance	5.9	4.8
Real estate	10.9	12.9
Transportation and telecommunications	6.6	6.5
Service sector	14.8	17.0
Public service sector	7.6	8.1
External private service sector	2.0	2.3
Total GDP, including errors	100.0	100.0

Source: Economic Planning Agency, *Annual Report on National Accounts* (Tokyo: Government
of Japan, 1998), p. 139.

visibly reflected in the share of the manufacturing sector. In fact, the decrease of the share of electric machinery in the GDP stemmed from the reduction in prices caused by rapid progress in technical innovation. In physical terms, the share of this group of industries is growing. However, the share of the service sector in the GDP has increased dramatically. In this sector, the services provided by the public sector, companies, and individuals have increased their respective contribution to the GDP.

EXTERNAL ECONOMIC RELATIONS

In the 1990s the Japanese economy was strongly affected by other countries' economies. The exchange rate of the Japanese yen is the best illustration of this new situation. In January 1985, one U.S. dollar was traded for ¥254 on the Tokyo foreign exchange. After the 1985 Plaza Agreement the Japanese currency became much stronger and by May 1988 the value of the yen vis-à-vis the dollar doubled. By April 1990, the dollar rose to ¥158, but after that the yen became stronger, and by November 1994 the value of the dollar declined to the ¥98 level. At that time the Japanese export industries experienced major pressure and the government did not expect the yen to rise much in value.

By March 1998, the Japanese currency became weaker, declining in value vis-à-vis the dollar to the ¥125 level. At this exchange rate it is easy for the export-oriented industries to compete internationally. Although the Japanese economy was in a prolonged period of stagnation, many exporting companies boosted their overseas sales. In general, changing exchange rates influenced the Japanese economy very much and the economic policy of the government became confused by the exchange rate fluctuations.

In 1997, the total amount of Japanese exports increased to ¥51 trillion from ¥43 trillion in 1991. The volume of exports to the leading industrial countries did not grow much: ¥24.6 trillion in 1997 compared with ¥23.8 trillion in 1991. However, exports to developing countries increased from ¥16.9 trillion in 1991 to ¥25.7 trillion in 1997. Moreover, over this period Japan's exports to the United States were on the same level, and the significance of the countries of Asia was growing. There were similar changes in Japan's imports. Imports from Asia, including office equipment, semiconductors, and electronic components, increased.

With regard to the trade with Russia, Japan's exports decreased to ¥122.7 billion in 1997 compared with ¥285 billion in 1991. During the same period, imports from Russia increased somewhat from ¥447.6 billion to ¥481.5 billion. However, as the latest developments reveal, Japan's trade with Russia, both its exports and imports, is steadily growing.

In export sales to Russia the share of such categories as motorcars, electronic goods and appliances, and general machinery is growing. At the same time, Japan imports from Russia, such as fish and marine products, timber, and aluminum are growing in numbers. Considering the development of the resources of oil and natural gas in the Sakhalinskaya Oblast, it can be expected that Japan will export more capital goods and industrial equipment.

In 1986 Japanese foreign direct investment, modest before 1985, rapidly increased because of the rising value of the yen and its purchasing power. In 1990 the annual outflow of foreign direct investment reached its peak level of ¥9.6 trillion, and after that the average annual level was about ¥5 trillion. The number of subsidiaries of Japanese companies in foreign countries has increased rapidly and, reportedly, in 1996 their total production volume became larger than the total value of Japanese exports. The annual inflow of foreign direct investment in Japan stood at a relatively low level (¥500 billion in 1996, or 10 percent of the annual foreign direct investment outflow), but it is growing.

In the 1990s there was a massive surplus in the current account balance. In 1997 it reached more than $130 billion or about 2.6 percent of GDP. This fueled sharp criticism of Japan by its trading partners, who indicated that Japan imports less than the size of its economy allows.

LIBERALIZATION

In September 1993 the Hosokawa cabinet announced 94 different criteria for liberalization to stimulate the Japanese economy. The reason behind this initiative was that foreign countries were focusing their criticism on the Japanese system of domestic laws and regulations that effectively prevented foreign competition or introduction of new businesses in Japan and stimulated higher domestic prices.

The Hosokawa cabinet was too weak to achieve real liberalization. However, in March 1995, the Murayama cabinet announced its own plan on how to deregulate the Japanese economy. As a result of this effort, the distribution system, information and telecommunications sector, and temporary labor were reformed.

Important steps were taken to amend the Large-Scale Retail Store Law in 1990, 1992, and 1994. Because of these amendments the average enterprises in retail business have grown in size allowing the reduction of costs and prices. Also, the selling of cosmetics, pharmaceuticals, and alcoholic beverages was liberalized. Deregulation in the information and telecommunications sectors (along with the contribution of high technologies and innovations) allowed the reduction in prices and tariffs. The liberalization proceeded in areas such as land ownership, housing, temporary labor, and imported petroleum products.

In April 1998 a drastic reform called "Big Bang" was introduced by the Hashimoto government to liberalize the financial sector. It will allow the financial, security, and insurance companies to diversify into the neighboring areas of the financial sector, thus enhancing competition (it will also make possible mutual penetration of these three businesses). Comprehensive liberalization of financial derivatives will be ensured. Finally, the foreign exchange operations will now be open for business entities other than authorized foreign exchange banks. According to the estimates by the Economic Planning Agency, by mid-1998 these measures stimulated an ¥8 trillion increase in domestic demand (equivalent to 1.6 percent of the GDP).

CONCLUSION

In the 1990s Japan has experienced low rates of economic growth. However, in 1997–98 the Japanese government recognized that the economic policy based on restrictions was mistaken and that a new economic policy of expanding demand must be promoted. The government has decided to allocate ¥30 trillion to protect individual account holders of the troubled commercial banks and to support some of these banks. In 1998 the government introduced an income tax reduction plan estimated at ¥4 trillion, and a ¥16-trillion program to stimulate public works.

These measures were designed to help the restructuring of the financial sector, to smooth the concerns of its entities, and to stimulate domestic demand. Moreover, technological innovations in such sectors as information and telecommunications will continue to progress, and the government policy of liberalization must be continued. It is likely that by the end of the 1990s, the Japanese economy will be revitalized and will recover at about a 3–4 percent growth rate annually.

2 $P20$

Russia's New Ruling Class
Nodari A. Simonia

Despite considerable euphoria, the 1996 presidential elections in Russia did not really symbolize the final turnaround in the struggle between communism and democracy. Communists failed long before the elections. From August through December 1991, they ceded their ideology-based bureaucratic authority to economic managers and technocrats. After unprecedented economic liberalization and commercialization of the state-owned economic assets this ruling group has consolidated its power and formed a new capitalist-bureaucratic class. This is Russia's new ruling class, which took full advantage of the economic liberalization introduced by Yegor Gaidar's government in 1992, paving the way for the economic collapse of late 1998.

POLITICAL EQUATION

From the outset this group was diverse, and the three main factions had their roots in the main sectors of the postcommunist Russian economy, including export-oriented extracting industries; commerce, finance, and related services; and manufacturing, particularly defense-related enterprises. Despite numerous nuances, such as regional differences and size and wealth of the provinces and territories, it is safe to assume that the first two major factions successfully allied themselves and were able to keep Russia under their control until 1998.

In the meantime the military-industrial lobby, however, was gaining more power, represented from 1993 to 1996 by Vice Premier Oleg

Soskovets and other influential men in Boris Yeltsin's entourage including Alexander Korzhakov, the head of the presidential security service. Soskovets was in charge of industrial policy, defense industries and their partial retooling, the machine-building sector, transport, steel making and nonferrous metal smelting and refining. This group attempted to gain control of some segments of oil production and banking with limited success.[1]

The industrial lobby was speaking mostly the language of economic nationalism, while the two ruling factions were more positive toward the West and were able to secure the support of the International Monetary Fund (IMF) and other international organizations. Using their access to the president, these people were trying to persuade him that the managers of industrial enterprises would be unable to implement structural changes and ensure the international competitiveness of the Russian manufacturing sector. In the domestic political standoff they did not fail to stress similarities in the position of the industrial lobby and the political platform of the Communist Party of the Russian Federation and their potential to restore the old economic system. However, the main questions were not about ideology or restoration of communist rule in Russia but mostly about wealth redistribution, leadership in top political management, influence of the state over economic matters, and the direction of economic reforms. Political maneuvering was rather common.

Shortly before the 1996 election Yeltsin's rating was rather low. In an attempt to enlarge his political base, Yeltsin decided to free the government from the very unpopular privatizer Anatoliy Chubais and authorize the establishment of the ministry of defense industry, promising more financial support to this sector.[2] Yeltsin was still unable to secure a solid majority during the first round of the presidential election race. The threat of losing his political power pushed him into an alliance with retired General Alexander Lebed at the expense of Minister of Defense Pavel Grachev.

Shortly before the elections Yeltsin also had to make a choice between the Soskovets-Korzhakov group and the influential people who supported Chubais. As a result both Korzhakov and Soskovets were ousted, and the Chubais lobby prevailed. By gaining support from the two leading factions and forming an alliance with Lebed, Yeltsin made a powerful comeback and won the second round of the election.

Lebed's temporary incorporation into the ruling elite as a secretary of the security council and assistant to the president on security issues should be interpreted as a recognition of the growing influence of opposition leaders who questioned the economic policy of the government led by Prime Minister Victor Chernomyrdin. Lebed's pronouncements about a new and strong Russia as well as his main slogan "honesty and order" appealed to many of those who voted both for him and Yeltsin.

However, the promise to arrest corruption in domestic affairs and put Russia's national interests first in foreign and economic policy was not supported by the new ruling class, particularly by people linked with export-oriented extracting industries, finance, and commerce.

Lebed's economic views were in line with those nationalists who warned that Russia is losing its industrial and technological base and sliding into the position of a mineral resources enclave. Industrialists and economic nationalists failed shortly after the elections when Yeltsin prevented Lebed from interfering with economic security issues and strategic matters of economic policy. Moreover, the newly created defense council coordinated by Chernomyrdin weakened the role of the security council and further undermined Lebed's administrative influence and political role. The president withdrew his support when Lebed complained about the role of Minister of Interior Anatoliy Kulikov in the unfolding drama in Chechniya. Even though the former general was able to find a way to stop an open military conflict in the northern Caucasus, he was isolated, stripped of his official duties, and forced to quit the administration. Less than two years later, in May 1998, he was elected governor of Krasnoyarskiy Krai in Eastern Siberia.

ON THE ECONOMIC FRONT

Global financial upheavals that followed soon demonstrated that Russia has become a part of the capitalist world. The nature of political power in the country rests in neither ideology nor a single political party. The power of money, however, in combination with the systemic transition that Russia is experiencing, has created numerous problems, including growing corruption, organized crime, an illegal export of capital, and a shadow economy estimated at 30–40 percent of the gross domestic product (GDP).

The short-term internal debt of the federal government has skyrocketed leading, in August and September 1998, to a default and devaluation of the ruble. Moreover, efforts to refinance it have left the industry almost without any hope of receiving new investment. The tight monetary policy, insolvency crisis, various tax concessions to large enterprises, such as Gasprom and Norilsk Nickel, exacerbated the problem of tax collection and put the government on the brink of a major financial crisis. In 1996 the total amount of all unpaid debts, including taxes, wages, default payments to suppliers, and repayment of commercial credits, was estimated at $90 billion or 21 percent of the GDP. In 1997, according to Chubais, the volume of unpaid debts grew almost 50 percent reaching $127 billion.

Despite the obvious irregularities in economic policy of the federal government, the IMF continued the monthly financial transactions (out of the February 1996 $10.2 billion loan). In addition, the IMF agreed to raise the ceiling for the federal budget deficit from 4 percent to 5.25 percent. Only in July 1996 was there an attempt by the IMF to restore the rules of the game and the issue of tax collection was reemphasized anew.

THE CRISIS

From 1996 through 1998, the government and the country were facing a profound economic and social crisis. Income inequality was growing as well as social stratification. The industrial sector was undergoing a sharp decline and it bore the primary responsibility for a stagnating GDP volume and massive unpaid taxes.

Only about 17 percent of business entities pay their taxes on time. The largest 1,600 companies were responsible for two-thirds of all unpaid taxes. A special governmental commission has been created to deal with the problem of collecting $13 billion in tax arrears. There was also an announcement by the minister of finance that all election campaign promises will be put on hold, saving the government about $9 billion. In opposition, large companies, particularly those from the energy sector, claimed that their support for Yeltsin during the election campaign deserves some reciprocal actions by the reelected president.

The tax pressure was high, and industrial enterprises were responsible for about 70 percent of all taxes, although their share in the GDP is 43 percent. Their debt to federal and regional budgets has reached $12.5 billion, but the debt of the government to the enterprises totaled $6 billion. In contrast, Gasprom's debt to the federal budget was estimated at $2.8 billion, and its tax breaks and other privileges were equivalent to about 2–3 percent of the Russian GDP.

Industrial restructuring has been delayed and there was little support from the federal government to the national industry in reverting the current trend toward deindustrialization. It is estimated that without such supporting measures and reallocation of significant financial resources by 2005 the absolute size of the Russian manufacturing sector may shrink to about one-fourth compared with 1992.

The government's inability to revive real sector economy and to collect taxes led to delayed and unpaid salaries and wages for civil servants, military personnel, teachers, medical workers, coal miners, and others. Subsequently, the number of enterprises affected by labor strikes and other organized actions of protest increased from 514 in 1994 to 8,856 in 1995 and 8,278 in 1996. From 1997 through 1998 labor protests proliferated further. All this made the domestic political situation in Russia highly unstable and socially explosive.

CONCLUSION

The attitudes of Western countries toward Russia are complex. Yeltsin as president of Russia is perceived by many in the West as a main counterbalance to communists. Being in favor of the capitalist transformation, the West, particularly the United States, seems to be interested in a specific type of capitalism in Russia that will not compete with the industrial economies but will complement them as a resource base, an economy dependent on energy resources extraction and export.

For example, according to the top executives of the IMF, the Russian government should further liberalize its foreign trade and cut import duties from the current 30 percent average level to 20 percent and avoid tax incentives (at the expense of Russian taxpayers, they say) for the Western auto makers willing to invest in Russian local production. Indeed, the Russian economy is becoming increasingly dependent on the production and export of raw materials, minerals, and fuels. The share of energy resources in Russian exports exceeds 47 percent with an additional 23 percent coming from the exports of iron and steel, nonferrous metals, and lumber.[3]

Despite the gloomy realities of a postcommunist transition and profound economic difficulties, the majority of Russian people hope to see their country internationally competitive and its wealth based on a strong, efficient, modernized, and diversified economy. However, the dramatic increase in the concentration of corporate power in the hands of few 19th century-type barons raises concern over whether these dominant groups will turn out to be the positive long-term force that most Russians and foreign investors would have wanted. Another question is whether the Russian government will be able to unite competing factions finding a proper balance for economic growth and investment inflows, comprehensive development of the economy, and a healthy social environment that will ensure effective integration of Russia into the global economy.[4]

NOTES

1. In January 1996 Soskovets launched the Russian Association of Financial and Industrial Groups, which included more than 60 commercial banks and 642 large industrial enterprises from various regions of Russia. After he left the government he was elected president of the association.

2. See the interview of Minister of Defense Industry Z. Pak, *Deloviye Ludi*, No. 67, May 1996, pp. 24–27.

3. "Foreign Trade of Russia in 1997," *Economika i Zhisn*, no. 7, February 1998, p. 26.

4. These and other important goals were declared by Yeltsin in his annual address before the Federal Assembly on February 17, 1998.

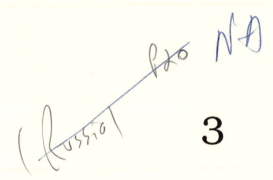

3

The Yeltsin Factor

Nobuo Shimotomai

The events that took place between the time the Tokyo Declaration was signed in 1993 and the political upheavals in both Russia and Japan in 1998 demonstrated that the Tokyo-Moscow dialogue represents a matrix of various domestic factors in both Japan and Russia. After the demise of the Soviet Union in December 1991, the role of domestic policy issues in Russia on bilateral relations drastically increased.[1] This was followed by what foreign observers have called a "political revolution" in Japan, referring to the July 1993 collapse of the 40 years' dominance by the Liberal Democratic Party. Although the change to a new coalition government led by Morihiro Hosokawa had little implications for Japan's foreign policy, Russian diplomacy toward Japan underwent a series of adjustments under the fluid conditions of Russian domestic politics.

YELTSIN'S DIPLOMACY

President Boris Yeltsin's diplomacy toward Japan was in line with Russia's general policy of cooperation with the international community, especially Western countries. The Russian leadership aspired to become a part of the international system, including the Group of Seven and other key international institutions. Some members of Yeltsin's team advocated a proactive reconciliatory approach toward Japan to be able to benefit from its international economic power and influence. Yeltsin initially seemed to be determined to make progress where his predecessors had failed.

Yeltsin's letter to the Russian people dated November 16, 1991, stated that the current generation of Russians is not responsible for the political adventurism of the country's former leaders. He did indicate, however, that it is the responsibility of the new Russian administration to find solutions for the problems inherited from the past in order to build normal relations with the international community. The main principle of the foreign policy of the new, democratic Russia and the foundation of its international legitimacy should be, in Yeltsin's words, respect for international law, justice, and human rights.

Foreign Andrei Minister Kozyrev together with State Secretary Gennadiy Burbulis (he was acting as First Deputy Prime Minister, 1992–93) were responsible for Yeltsin's first state visit to Japan planned for September 1992. Georgiy Kunadze, a political scientist trained as a Japanologist and Kozyrev's first deputy at that time, directly advised Burbulis on the concept of the visit and reportedly pushed for a decisive resolution to the territorial dispute.

However, domestic developments and the complexity of relations with Tokyo put the brakes on the initial optimism and determination on the Russian side. Yeltsin's political position was not strong enough to pursue the proposed proactive scenario. His administration encountered mounting criticism and opposition and the economic situation was very bad. Emerging nationalistic sentiments were strong, and opposition to the Kunadze-Burbulis approach to the territorial dispute with Japan was heard from various quarters. Finally, those who opposed a proactive reconciliatory policy toward Japan succeeded, and the president's official visit to Japan scheduled for September 1992 was canceled.

Yeltsin's rescheduled visit of October 1993 was motivated by a wish to catch up in relations with Japan and stimulate economic cooperation that would support domestic economic reform. The result was the Tokyo Declaration. This visit, however, took place just weeks after a dramatic confrontation with the opposition in parliament led by Vice President Aleksandr Rutskoi and Speaker of the Supreme Soviet Ruslan Khasbulatov. This confrontation resulted in the bloody clash between the executive branch and the legitimate legislative body.

The Tokyo Declaration, however, represented only a partial success for Russian reformers, who had expected more substantial changes in Japan's policy. The results of the December 1993 parliamentary elections in Russia added new concerns on the part of Japan because Victor Chernomyrdin's ruling political group lost a number of seats in the parliament to Vladimir Zhirinovskiy's ultranationalistic Liberal Democratic Party of Russia.

Moreover, Zhirinovskiy received support in border regions, including those of Far Eastern Russia, particularly Sakhalin and Primorskiy Krai.[2] Russian regional elites, including Far Eastern governors, did not seem to

be interested in cooperation with Japan at the cost of territorial concessions. Some of them feared that Russia's Asian neighbors would penetrate
the Far Eastern region economically and influence local markets. Thus,
the rise of Russian nationalism was coupled with protectionist pressure.
The radical reformers, including Burbulis and Yegor Gaidar, were either
dismissed or lost influence.

The State Duma elections of December 1995 and the presidential election of 1996 proved hard victories for Yeltsin and the governmental party.
In fact, Chernomyrdin's faction secured only 10 percent of the seats in the
December 1995 parliamentary election. Yeltsin's policy between 1994 and
1996 aimed to consolidate his regime on the basis of consensus among the
old and new elites. Under these circumstances several factions and clans
competed for influence over Yeltsin. Conservatives, such as Alexander
Korzhakov and Oleg Soskovets, were important power brokers. After the
1996 presidential election Anatoliy Chubais returned to influence and
Boris Nemtsov rose as another newly appointed first deputy prime minister charged with the coordination of economic relations with Japan.

It appeared, however, that both Japanese and Russian policy makers
underestimated the fact that post-soviet Russian politics were more influenced by domestic considerations and economic and social problems. In
this environment consensus became more important for Yeltsin than
Gorby-style radical foreign policy initiatives. Thus, from mid-1994
through 1996 expectations for radical changes in Russia-Japan relations
proved to be an illusion, and radical diplomacy gave way to pragmatism
and realism in Russia's international posture.

CHANGES IN JAPAN

To a lesser extent, Japanese politics also were shaken by a sudden political change in July-August 1993 that resulted in political fragmentation.
The conservative Liberal Democratic Party government collapsed, and
Hosokawa's coalition government was formed. Hosokawa's Japan New
Party, the newly born conservative party Shinseito led by Ichiro Ozawa,
the religiously inclined Komeito, the Social Democratic Party, and several other smaller factions joined in a coalition government.

Ambassador to the former Soviet Union and Russia Sumio Edamura
(1990–94) and his successor Koichi Watanabe (1994–96)[3] were not Russian
experts, but they were experienced diplomats. Because of their expertise
and strong influence in Tokyo, Japanese policy toward Russia was modified and the main emphasis was put on the reconstruction of the Russian
economy.

However, Japanese foreign policy toward Russia continued to be made
by the ministry of foreign affairs' Russian desk and was based on the concept of expanded equilibrium adopted in 1988. For decades Russia-Japan

relations meant a coupling of politics and economics. Because Japan had little political leverage to use with the Soviet Union, Tokyo relied on its economic resources to attain political goals. After the demise of the Soviet Union, Japanese policy remained essentially unchanged, and a recognition of Japan's sovereignty over the southern Kurils was still a prerequisite for support of Russian reforms. Moreover, the Japanese business community was not very enthusiastic about Russian economic recovery.

This concept of expanded equilibrium proposed an expansion of economic contacts with Japan in exchange for political flexibility on the part of Russia in the territorial dispute. It took many years before this concept was replaced with a new multidimensional approach toward Russia. According to this formula, which remains ambiguous, the territorial issue should be solved along with other bilateral and multilateral problems.

The Japanese stance toward Russia is being further modified. Japan has recognized de facto Russia's claim over southern Sakhalin and the Kurils to the north from Etorofu. In other words, Japan changed the nature and scale of its long standing claim on the territorial issue in line with the Tokyo Declaration, which refers to only four islands as an issue for peace treaty negotiations between the two countries. Thus, the territorial dispute became "an issue" rather than "the issue." Moreover, debate over the territorial dispute with Russia was overshadowed in the late 1990s by heated discussions over disputes with other regional neighbors, China and Korea. In 1996, Japan's territorial disagreements with these two countries flared while relations with Russia over the Northern Territories remained relatively calm.

PRIMAKOV'S DIPLOMACY

For decades the Northern Territories issue was the only main subject between Japan and Russia that acted as an appeal to the importance of development in relations. Toward the end of the 1990s the tendency to consider relations from a new perspective has gained momentum. A shared interest in Japan and Russia to establish a new set of goals not rigidly linked to the formal solution of the territorial dispute has become evident. However, it was difficult to expect that such a solution can be found without a shared and clear vision of the future.

Unfortunately, Tokyo's official relations with the Russian top leadership remained weak. As former head of Japan's Ministry of International Trade and Industry Prime Minister Hashimoto had developed a working relationship with First Deputy Prime Minister Soskovets, who had extensive links with the Russian steel-manufacturing and machine-building industry. With Soskovets' dismissal in June 1996, shortly before the presidential election, Japan lost one of its few key connections. After Kozyrev stepped down, Yevgeniy Primakov was appointed foreign minister, which helped to restore channels of communications.

This also made Moscow's foreign policy more pragmatic and cautious. Primakov's agenda seems more realistic than his predecessor's idealistic commitment to the strategic alliance with the West, which did not gain bipartisan consensus. The enlargement plan of the North Atlantic Treaty Organization was the final blow to Kozyrev's bias toward Atlanticism. Primakov appeared to have more bipartisan support and thus a more solid influence on decision making. He has embraced a "look East" policy. Thus, Russia has turned its attention and diplomatic initiative to the East. In September 1994, Chinese President Jiang Zemin visited Moscow. This was followed by official visits by President Yeltsin to Beijing in April 1996 and November 1997. Central Asian leaders were also invited to Shanghai in April 1996 to join a confidence-building agreement between Russia, China, Kazakhstan, Kirgistan, and Tadjikistan. The new Russia-China relations are described as a strategic partnership.

By mid-1996 slow progress in Japan-Russia dialogue prompted a successful visit to Moscow by Foreign Minister Yukihiko Ikeda. He met with his Russian counterpart Primakov and President Yeltsin. Ikeda and Yeltsin reaffirmed their commitment to the 1993 Tokyo Declaration, and Primakov stressed Russia's commitment to the demilitarization of the disputed islands. Furthermore, a working group on the Northern Territories was reactivated, and an agreement was reached to expand the scope of areas for a loan initially slated for humanitarian purposes.

In April 1996, Hashimoto visited Moscow to attend the Group of Seven summit on nuclear safety. During this visit the two sides agreed to revive talks on the disputed islands. This was followed by the first ever visit to Russia by the director of Japan's National Defense Agency. The visit resulted in an agreement on cooperation between the defense establishments. Finally, Primakov visited Japan in November 1996 proposing joint development of the disputed islands. This visit coincided with the fortieth anniversary of the 1956 Joint Declaration that restored diplomatic relations between the two countries. It seems likely that the political dialogue can be further developed if Primakov is able to retain and consolidate his position as prime minister to which he was elevated in September 1998.

NOTES

1. The dynamics of Japan-Russia bilateral relations up to October 1993 when Yeltsin visited Japan were analyzed in the book *"Northern Territories" and Beyond: Russian, Japanese, and American Perspectives* (Praeger, 1995), pp. 119–26. The goal of this chapter is to analyze Japan-Russia relations after the Tokyo Declaration of October 1993, in which Yeltsin and Hosokawa agreed to conclude a peace

treaty by solving the issue of sovereignty over the Northern Territories (Kunashiri, Etorofu, Shikotan, and Habomai Islands). Special attention is given to new developments in bilateral relations that emerged after Yeltsin's presidential election victory of June and July 1996.

2.   Both Primorskiy Krai and Sakhalinskaya Oblast were regarded as pro-reform areas. In the 1991 presidential election Yeltsin was leading and Zhirinovskiy's popularity was marginal. However, in the 1993 election, the Liberal Democratic Party of Russia received almost 39 percent of votes in Sakhalin and 23 percent of votes in Primorskiy Krai. By contrast, Gaidar's party received only 14 percent of votes in Primorskiy Krai and 9.7 percent in Sakhalin.

3.   Japanese diplomats from the so-called Russian school were on the whole too attached to cold war politics and perceptions of Russia. During the 1990–96 transition these two Japanese ambassadors to Russia were able to change the nature of the dialogue with their Russian counterparts and were highly respected in Moscow for their positive role in changing bilateral relations.

4

On the Way to Economic Deadlock

Ivan S. Tselitschev

It is well known that Russian economic reforms were accompanied by a deep economic crisis and fundamental changes in the economic system that the reformers themselves did not anticipate and were ill prepared to deal with. In August 1996, however, consumer prices in Russia fell by 0.2 percent for the first time since the beginning of economic reforms in 1992. In 1996 inflation was brought down to 21.8 percent and in 1997 to 11.1 percent on an annual basis.[1] Curbing inflation was critical for the macroeconomic stabilization and was considered a basic precondition for restored confidence on the part of investors and consumers.

MONETARY AUSTERITY

Deflationary policy pursued by the government was accompanied by a fall in the volume of production and declining economic activity. The volume of gross domestic product (GDP), industrial and agricultural production, and investment activities became hostages of the tight monetary policy aimed at macroeconomic stabilization. Compared with some other transition economies Russia was 2–3 years behind in restoring the pattern of economic growth. However, the third stabilization attempt in 1995 set some preconditions for recovery. The ruble was strengthened by restrictions imposed on the exchange rate fluctuation and more or less persistent deflationary policy. This improved conditions for inflow of foreign capital. The central bank's discount rate went down from 160 percent in December 1995 to 46 percent in December 1996 and 28 percent in

December 1997 (then it was raised again in early 1998 because of strong downward pressure on the ruble in the wake of the Asian financial crisis).

By 1998 speculative financial transactions became less attractive and financial institutions seemed to show more interest in the production sector. Banks became more active in acquiring shares of mining and manufacturing enterprises and some of them set up special departments for production investment. Financial institutions and trading companies that profiteered from high inflation found themselves in a less favorable environment. Reorganizations, mergers, and tie-ups opened the way to the invigoration of this sector.

In 1997, for the first time since the beginning of reforms, the Russian economy grew, albeit at slow pace (the GDP increased 0.4 percent, and industrial production was up 1.9 percent).[2] Unlike in 1996, improvement was registered not only in export-oriented industries but also in transportation equipment production, medical instruments and pharmaceuticals, personal computers, electronic and electrical appliances, and other areas of the domestic market.

However, these initial improvements did not largely affect production investment, which continued to shrink because of political uncertainties, weak institutional and legal preconditions, and poor financial performance of the vast majority of producers. Moreover, the improved position of the ruble did not much affect its attractiveness vis-à-vis the dollar. Prospects for future sustainable growth are better than before but still uncertain because of unsolved structural problems on the supply side and a mixed picture on the demand side, because no major segment of the final demand, such as public and private investment, consumption, or exports, demonstrates an expansion (Table 4.1).

Tight monetary policy created a shortage of money. Indeed, the M2/GDP ratio has been frozen at a very low level of 12–15 percent compared with 60–100 percent in developed economies. The money shortage has become a problem for producers and an obstacle to increased production and investment activities. It also aggravated the problem of payments among companies, and by the end of 1997 cumulative bad debts in mining and manufacturing alone amounted to more than 18 percent of the GDP.[3] Delayed wage and salary payments as well as barter and quasi-money transactions became a routine practice across the nation.

In other words, the Russian economy appeared to be in a kind of trap: Deflationary policies helped to keep inflation under control, but inadequate money supply put the brakes on economic growth and industrial output. The government was under strong pressure to allow the money supply to grow. However, the opinion prevailed that inflation must be kept under control to form conditions for sound economic growth. The fear was that loosening the money supply would provoke inflation and undermine producers' adaptation to the market demand, thus ruining the

TABLE 4.1
Russia's Main Economic Indicators, 1992–97

(in percent, to the previous year)

	1992	1993	1994	1995	1996	1997
Gross domestic product	85.5	91.3	87.3	95.9	95.1	100.4
Mining and manufacturing	82	86	79	97	96	100.9
Agriculture	91	96	88	92	94.9	100.1
Fixed capital investment	60	88	76	90	81	95
Foreign trade volume	83	97	117	122		100.6*
Exports, $ billion	53.6	59.6	68.1	81.3	88.4	78.2*
Imports, $ billion	43.0	44.3	50.5	60.9	61.5	59.9*
Retail sales	97	102	100	93	94.2	103.7
Consumer price index	2,610	940	320	230	21.8	11.0
Unemployment	4.7	5.5	7.4	8.8	9.3	9.0

*for January through November

Source: Russia in Figures, 1997 (Moscow: Goscomstat, 1997); Socioeconomic Position of Russia, 1997 (Moscow: Goscomstat, 1997), no. 12.

macrostabilization strategy. Therefore, by the end of 1997 the Russian government proved that it can control inflation under the conditions of economic decline but appeared unable to promote non-inflationary growth.

STRUCTURAL PROBLEMS

Among the structural factors that create a hidden inflation potential in Russia are the unprofitable companies that prevent the transfer of resources to competitive enterprises. For example, the Bankruptcy Law effective since 1993 was not enforced.[4] On the contrary, the government and regional administrations frequently opted to support troubled enterprises and avoided their reorganization.

One of the biggest Russian auto makers, ZIL, was taken by Moscow city administration under its financial protection. The company was suffering big losses and its debt was growing. The Moscow authorities pledged to purchase 1,000 trucks and requested the federal government to reschedule or write off the debts and to place more orders. In this and other cases the federal government agreed to postpone a substantial part of tax payments.

Another issue is that inter-company transactions continue even under conditions of nonpayments for orders and materials. Barter deals and various kinds of quasi money (certificates of tax payment deferrals, promissory notes without a proper guarantee, state guarantees for commercial banks, and so forth) were in circulation. Employees were often paid wages in food coupons, company products, and other surrogates. Obviously, these instruments had little or no liquidity compared with money. The quality of the entire financial system was questionable and the inflationary pressure was camouflaged by these and other irregularities.

Many ailing enterprises were also protected by import duties and tariffs. For example, in the case of imported autos, custom duties together with value-added tax and other fees have reached 70–90 percent of the initial price. Protectionism in a transitional economy may be needed to allow some breathing space for industrial restructuring. This, however, does not seem to be the case in Russia, because existing programs of modernization were lacking funds and the implementation was delayed. As a result the competitiveness of national producers was low and import restrictions were used to protect the domestic market.

Lack of incentives for companies to restructure aggravated the problem of excessive labor resources, which was another factor of hidden inflation. Some companies were trying to streamline their personnel structures and save money by shortening working hours and reducing work days, enforcing long vacations without compensation, and delaying wage payments. However, many enterprises avoided rationalization that involved personnel cuts. As a result excessive labor resources were preserved. It is also true that the low mobility of labor in Russia inhibits its transfer to competitive enterprises and industries.

In contrast, more than 1,000 companies were receiving government subsidies. Ironically, wages and salaries paid by some companies in the red were higher than those paid by enterprises making profits. In most cases, labor motivation was low and wages were not used as an incentive to increase productivity. Productivity measured as GDP per employee declined about 20 percent between 1992 and 1997.

BUDGET VERSUS INVESTMENT

Yet another factor of hidden inflation is the government's failure to curb the budget deficit. On the one hand, the level of spending remained high; on the other hand, there were chronic problems with revenue collection. According to some estimates, from 1993 through 1997 total spending (federal and local budgets, special funds, payments in surrogate money) reached at least 50 percent of the GDP. The level of state consumption was estimated at 24–26 percent of the GDP, while in China these ratios were estimated at 29 and 9 percent correspondingly.

For 1997, for instance, the government projected the budget deficit at 3.3 percent, but independent sources estimated the deficit at 13 percent of the GDP. Moreover, public funds sometimes were misused and directed to all kinds of speculative financial transactions. Meanwhile, funds promised to the enterprises by government agencies were often unavailable or only partially available, thus destabilizing production plans.

Finally, as far as revenues and tax collection were concerned, the government failed to fulfill its own plans, and only 60–70 percent of taxes were actually available to finance budget spending. Tax rates remained excessively high and tax systems too complicated, affecting investment activities and provoking tax evasions.

The government covered the budget deficit through bond issues and loans from the International Monetary Fund and other international financial institutions. Servicing the debt became a major problem and one of the largest items in government spending, reaching about 25 percent of federal budget spending and about 4 percent of the GDP. In October 1996, it was even decided to set up an emergency committee on tax collection. At the same time, the public investment segment of the GDP was falling from 20 percent at the end of the 1980s to only 3.9 percent in 1996. The role of the government in research and development activities, education, and health care dropped.

In other words, the economic impact of government spending was diminishing and its ability to stimulate economic growth was falling. The growing national debt exerted strong pressure on interest rates, relocating available financial resources from the private sector to the state and from investment purposes to short-term financial operations. For example, the ratio of the total value of government bonds and financial obligations to the value of stocks and bonds issued by private companies was estimated as 10 to 15, while normally in other countries it does not exceed 20–60 percent.

During 1996 and 1997, Russian state bonds absorbed about 80 percent of the total amount of bank lending, leaving little for loans to companies and investment in the production sector. The situation improved somewhat as decreasing government bond yields induced banks to increase short-term loans to enterprises, enabling them to fill the gaps in circulation funds. In the second half of 1997 the share of loans went up to 65 percent, but in early 1998 the government raised the rate of returns for state bonds, thus redirecting the capital flow away from the private sector, particularly production enterprises.

OUTCOMES AND PROSPECTS

Under Prime Minister Victor Chernomyrdin the government achieved visible progress in bringing about macroeconomic stabilization. At the same time the federal debt was growing and social tension was escalating, including large-scale strikes by coal miners and electric power industry workers, particularly in Primorskiy Krai. Moreover, having shifted from inflationary to non-inflationary methods of financing the budget deficit, the government was slow in dealing with a soaring public debt and working out a sound fiscal policy. The economic system failed to ensure equal starting conditions for producers. Special relationships between the government or local authorities, on the one hand, and selected companies, on the other hand, were becoming a major feature of the business climate.

In the meantime, some structural adjustments were taking place spontaneously, rather than because of government efforts. For example, small and medium enterprises, as well as joint ventures and foreign-affiliated companies, that is, producers most adaptable to the conditions of the market economy, were the main contributors to a modest growth in the GDP volume, but big companies (particularly those with a long production cycle) still dependent on state support lagged behind.[5] The number of bankruptcy cases taken to court in 1996 reached 2,500 or six times more than in 1994.

Until the October 1997 Asian economic crisis, stock market trading volumes were growing rapidly, supported by a demand for Russian blue chips by foreign investors. More people were looking for new and additional employment opportunities. Many were trying to start their own businesses despite the prohibitive tax system, complicated administrative regulations, and the threat of the Mafia. The number of registered small enterprises grew from 560,000 in 1993 to 896,900 in 1995 but dropped to 877,100 in 1996 and further to 844,400 in 1997. These developments showed that millions of Russians were working and acting more and more in line with market rules.

The unemployment rate increased from 4.7 percent in 1992 to 9 percent in 1997, also reflecting a newly formed supply-demand equilibrium in the labor market and growing competition from foreign producers. However, it was obvious that the government had to play a more proactive role, adopting more radical reform measures and combining efforts aimed at macrostabilization with the policy of structural adjustments, therefore withdrawing state support and putting more pressure on enterprises to restructure. However, the government was doing too little and too late in promoting competition or boosting the new companies, including small and medium private enterprises. Many good plans and programs were left unrealized and promises were dropped. There was no strategy to promote knowledge intensive venture enterprises, encourage small scale businesses, support labor mobility, promote exports, or improve the environment for foreign investment. The taxation system and legal framework for foreign investment, including guarantees, property rights, and other institutional measures, remained a problem.

NEW PROSPECTS FOR JAPAN

Doubts about political stability, personal safety, and other irregularities have not altogether disappeared, and Russia still has to do a lot more to restore long-term economic confidence and attract foreign investors. However, even under the present environment there has been a substantial increase in the volume of foreign investment, especially in 1997. The total amount of foreign investment increased from $2,797 million in 1995 to $6,506 million in 1996 and $10,500 million in 1997, including about $3,700 million in foreign direct investment.[6]

Foreign investors became more interested in manufacturing, including high value-added products and research and development projects, in addition to financial sector, distribution, and natural resources extraction. For example, Pratt & Whitney invested $120 million in the Perm Motors Company to produce engines for the new generation of Russian passenger aircraft, Fiat invested $850 million in a joint venture with Russian auto makers, and Stollwerck of Germany put $35 million in a baking factory near the city of Vladimir.

However, the share of investment from Japan is falling as U.S. and European firms invest more in Russia. In 1995, Japan was the eighth largest investor in Russia with a share of 2.7 percent of total accumulated foreign direct investment, but in 1996 and 1997 it dropped from the leading ten countries list.[7] Yet, some Japanese companies have started or plan to invest in important projects in Russia. Also, Sakhalin-1 and Sakhalin-2, the Neva Telecommunications Systems joint venture in St. Petersburg with participation of NEC, Mitsui Bussan, and Sumitomo Shoji is picking up. Asahi Glass in cooperation with the European Bank for Reconstruction and Development plans to invest in glass production in Russia.

In general, the Japanese government has adopted a proactive posture with regard to joint economic projects and other forms of economic cooperation. In addition, the Asian financial crisis demonstrated the vulnerability of Japan's foreign investment strategy, which is too dependent on one region. With Asian fever faded among the business leaders the need for a more diversified and regionally balanced structure of the foreign assets of Japanese corporations has become obvious.

At the same time, as leading Japanese manufacturers go global in their production networks, management, sales, and research and development activities, Russia's place in these global strategies deserves clarification. In the medium- and long-term perspective Japanese investment links with Russia can be visualized as a four-layer structure.

Natural resources projects will constitute the first level of this structure with special emphasis on certain geographical areas, such as Far Eastern Russia and Siberian provinces with their unique energy and mineral wealth. In view of that Russia can be a long-term strategic economic partner for Japan and other Asian economies.

The second level can contain the material-producing industries, thus filling a structural gap between extraction of resources and value-added refining and production of the final products, which is typical for Far Eastern Russia. The development of refinery industries in the Far Eastern region can be beneficial for the enterprises, their potential customers, and Russia and Japan as a whole.

The third level can be comprised of assembly production in such areas as auto and electronics; it can be organized at the defense factories under conversion, as the example set by Toyota demonstrates. As such ventures develop, parts and components production can be gradually relocated to Russia.

Finally, the fourth level promises mutually beneficial links in high-tech areas, including nuclear energy, space research, and many other fields in which Japanese technical and research and development power can merge with Russian expertise and technologies.

This idea is not new. However, since it was first formulated about 20 years ago, major political and economic impediments have disappeared opening opportunities for experiments in biotechnology, environmental protection, health care, and other key areas. As some Japanese companies set up globally diversified research and development networks, Russian research organizations, design bureaus, and manufacturing companies can be integrated into these networks. New ideas have to be put forward on how to facilitate and expand such cooperation and make it efficient. Russia-Japan science parks and technopolises could possibly become one among possible directions for cooperation in the field of advanced technologies and new product development.

NOTES

1. *Socioeconomic Position of Russia, 1997* (Moscow: Goscomstat, 1997), No. 12, p. 7.

2. Ibid.

3. Ibid., p. 37.

4. A modified version of the law was enacted in March 1998.

5. *Russia in Figures, 1996* (Moscow: Goscomstat, 1997), p. 34 [in Russian]; *Socioeconomic Position of Russia*, p. 283.

6. *Foreign Investment in Russia*, No. 2 (1998) p. 11 [in Russian]. During the first half of 1997 the federal budget ran a deficit of 51.3 trillion rubles (4.2 percent of the gross domestic product), using the Ministry of Finance definition. The broader International Monetary Fund definition, which includes interest payments on short-term government debt, was 8.1 percent of the gross domestic product. See *Russian Economic Trends, 1997*, No. 3 (London: Whurr Publishers, 1997), p. 9.

7. *Russia in Figures, 1996* (Moscow: Finansy and Statistika, 1996), p. 245; *Russia in Figures, 1997*, p. 252; *Socioeconomic Position of Russia, 1997*, p. 132.

5

Small Business Development in Russia

Douglas Barry

We hoped for the best but things turned out as always.
— Victor Chernomyrdin, former Prime Minister

If Russia can improve the climate for new and newly privatized businesses, the Russian economy may start to flourish early in the next century. The purpose of this chapter is to describe the current state of private small businesses in Russia, noting in particular the problems that cause Russia to lag behind other faster reformers in small business creation. In addition the chapter will examine some of the ways in which official policy in both the United States and Japan can help the Russian private sector develop at a faster rate, particularly in the Russian Far East where small businesses face an unusual array of problems and opportunities.

Some of the preconditions for economic growth in Russia are in place. The country has a democratic government, a highly educated work force, vast natural resources, and some political stability. It has made substantial progress with the three essential steps of economic liberalization: removal of most price controls, privatization of perhaps 50 percent of state-owned enterprises, and lower inflation. An extra bonus of a credible commitment to reform (as yet mostly unrealized in Russia) is faster integration into international economic institutions, foreign direct investment inflows, and external technical assistance.

However, Russia has been less successful in providing a nurturing environment for its small businesses. In most transition economies in Eastern Europe and elsewhere new business formation has been the engine of economic growth.[1] A general failure to create employment by expanding the *de novo* private sector could ultimately threaten the course of economic and political reforms in Russia.

WHAT IS SMALL BUSINESS IN RUSSIA?

Small businesses in Russia range from "mom and pop" shops to sophisticated software firms. Some are self-financed sole proprietorships, while others are partnerships whose shares are publicly traded. The average number of employees is 7.3.[2] Some of the businesses provide minimal wages and benefits, while others follow a more traditional Russian corporatist model and furnish meals, continuing education, even housing.

Small private businesses are evident throughout Russia, but the conditions for supporting them vary enormously. Variables for the creation of small business include local government policy, availability of credit, proximity to natural resources and transportation, population, foreign investment, and perhaps even the availability of foreign technical assistance.

Business of all kinds and sizes tends to be equated both inside and outside Russia with the term "New Russian." Many New Russians are relatively young, ambitious people who have embraced private enterprise wholeheartedly and whose penchant for conspicuous consumption tends to generate a mixture of loathing and envy from other Russians. The challenge facing Russia is how to create more New Russians.

A number of factors bedevil efforts to create more New Russians and account for Russia's stunted private business creation performance. Perhaps not surprisingly, some are unique to Russia. Communism lasted for more than 70 years in Russia, compared with 40 years in Eastern Europe. This longevity has negatively affected production structures, human capital, economic diversity, and a competitive spirit. To recreate the potential for wealth is far more difficult than merely redistributing wealth.

Another factor was the extraordinary emphasis on the military sector of the economy. The resulting economic bias came at the expense of other sectors, including the service sector. Although the emphasis on defense industries created many advanced technologies, it continues to serve as a drag on needed diversification and to divert funds away from investments that might yield much higher returns. This is especially true in the Russian Far East, where the concentration and economic importance of large defense-related enterprises is greater than in other regions of the country.

A third impediment for small business in Russia is a civil bureaucracy with a penchant for autocratic and interventionist management styles. The unbridled nature of government discretion, the inefficiency of government regulations, and the lack of strong parallel non-government institutions raise costs for new enterprises as they struggle to establish themselves.

A fourth factor is the growth, especially in the last few years, of a phenomenon perhaps partly linked to cultural and historical factors, referred to as oligarchic capitalism. This is an economic system characterized principally by the domination of giant business conglomerates and a handful of wealthy tycoons who enjoy a symbiotic relationship with the state. This model resembles present day South Korea and the powerful banks of postwar Germany. It has also been compared to the seven boyars, or noblemen, who took over the state after the overthrow of a Russian monarch at the beginning of the 17th century.

Critics of this development argue that the mostly Moscow- and St. Petersburg-based tycoons and their copycats in other regions want to dominate markets by eliminating all competition, not by inventing new mousetraps, but by slicing and dicing formerly state-owned assets that the tycoons have acquired at fire sale prices, often using free state money to make the purchases. Because Russia's fledgling capital markets are a kind of Jurassic Park, dominated by big dinosaurs, there is little investment capital (domestic or foreign) for smaller enterprises.

The role of the Russian government in creating a climate in which small enterprises can flourish figures prominently in an array of other issues and dilemmas. According to official government rhetoric, the Yeltsin economic team supports the middle class and family businesses. Boris Nemtsov, the first deputy prime minister, states that he is in favor of "people's capitalism." In contrast, Irina Hakamada, the Russian government's small business chief, states glumly that the people are getting the short end of the stick. "I can tell you openly that in the system of priorities among the economic and political elite in Russia, small business occupies the last place."[3]

Next I present a general overview of some additional issues and practical problems that might explain why some people think small business, including the forms that it takes in Russia's Far East, is in last place and unlikely to change its status anytime soon. Is this perspective excessively bleak, stemming as it may from an understandable impatience with the often tortured path of reform?

BUSINESS CLIMATE

Capital markets, especially private commercial banking, are underdeveloped in Russia, and businesses have great difficulty obtaining funds. For example, Russian bank assets were $155 billion in 1996, but only $9 billion were lent to enterprises. Credit is tight because bank funds are used to buy Russian treasury bills that pay relatively high rates of return. Private banks in Moscow and St. Petersburg are growing and increasing their commercial loans, but lending to small businesses is less developed in regional and smaller city centers.

Another issue is more basic. The presence or absence of trust among people and between people and their public institutions has been related to economic development. One study suggests that high trust societies enjoy higher rates of growth.[4] Widespread distrust is certainly not unique to Russia, and whether Russian people are more distrustful than people in other societies at comparable levels of economic development is a debatable point. However, in Russia, trust or lack of it looms large in the absence of reliable legal structures for protecting private property and enforcing agreements.

The lack of an efficient legal system in Russia means that disputes go unresolved and the costs of doing business become very high because of excessive levels of risk. Respect for the concepts of ownership and private property is largely absent in the value systems of many people. There has been progress on civil law reform and the development of a new commercial code that took effect in 1995. However, many of the provisions are excessively complex, and enforcement is inconsistent. In addition, legislation has been adopted to regulate monopolies and security markets. A law guaranteeing the independence of the central bank also was passed in 1995. Bankruptcy laws are now on the books. However, some of the provisions are badly constructed and official enforcement remains a problem.

As unpaid debts mushroom many firms that have issued vouchers but lack the benefits of effective private owners are slowly sliding toward bankruptcy. The potential volume of bankruptcies would overwhelm the already inadequate court system, and in any event widespread liquidation poses potentially huge social and political problems. However, within this destructive situation exists the means to promote necessary restructuring.[5]

Crime is a problem for small business because it adds costs. Increased crime in Russia has many causes, among them the breakdown of government police enforcement and the general weakening of central oversight systems. Much of the economic crime that is plaguing Russian citizens is committed by government entities as well as by private enterprises.

Bribed government officials can also lower a firm's costs by reducing the burdens of excessive regulation or by speeding access to licenses and approvals. There are significant costs as well. Substantial efficiency is lost because of payments and time wasted by the bribed and briber in getting around licenses and fees. Second, the bribed officials share benefits arising from lower costs of the businesses they favor, paradoxically and perversely creating incentives to increase the regulatory burden. In general, organized bureaucratic crime captures for private pockets proceeds that might otherwise go to the state budget.

Another kind of organized crime that gets far more publicity in the United States and Japan is the so-called Mafia crime, which involves money laundering, drugs, extortion, murder for hire, and other criminal activity. Organized business crime, bureaucratic crime, and the unorganized crime that includes robbery and murder have increased the costs of doing legitimate business, created contempt for some government bureaucracies, and eroded confidence in the legitimacy of the legal system that may take years to reverse. Economic crime has confused public attitudes about legitimate versus illegitimate means for making money, and created in the minds of some people a nostalgia for earlier times.

The complex, unduly burdensome nature of the Russian tax system has resulted in large scale tax evasion and contributed to the creation of a massive unofficial economy. Taxes currently comprise the largest chunk of a company's budget. It is said that if taxes are paid honestly, it is unlikely that firms will be able to survive.[6]

One business owner ticked off 27 or 28 taxes, which have since been reduced to 19 under new, streamlined legislation.[7] In addition companies are taxed for providing other kinds of benefits, including an extra 41 percent for health benefits. Also, companies cannot write off many travel expenses or the costs of business cards. Advertising is taxed, discouraging companies that want to launch new products or services. Another problem is the way value-added taxes are calculated. The tax rate is applied to gross revenues, not profits.

Tax authorities have a vast array of tools for collecting taxes. Incentives are high to audit returns and assess fines. The budget of the tax police comes in part from revenues from fines. Because of the import duties local firms importing foreign parts and technologies become less competitive in both local and international markets. Businesses complain that some 20 new government documents explaining and supplementing taxation law are received each month.

By law, businesses are required to keep abreast of new laws and forms even though some of the information is extremely difficult and sometimes impossible to find. Lack of coordination among the different taxing authorities can, in some larger cities, cause business owners to scramble from office to office filing paperwork for the pension fund, social security fund, statistical offices, financial administration, other government offices, and banks. For small enterprises, this interagency bounce can be a huge problem, necessitating the hiring of special fixers and sometimes full-time accountants to run around town and feed the paper mill.

Profit taxes are also levied at the local level. For example, in Khabarovsk 22 percent of total profit taxes are collected by the regional administration. The local authorities argue that they desperately need this revenue to pay for social services that are no longer covered by the federal budget or former state-owned enterprises. Local governments, however, can and do provide tax holidays as a means of helping small companies survive the critical first few years of existence.

The problem for the government is that companies will not operate officially (paying registration and other fees, as well as taxes) unless their net costs are lower than the net costs of operating unofficially. Therefore, tax rates should be designed in such a way that the overall burden on the enterprise is lower than that of operating unofficially. It would also be helpful to end tax breaks for the politically well connected. Doing so could add an estimated $28 billion annually to government coffers, a huge sum for a nation whose annual budget is $96 billion.

SMALL BUSINESS IN THE FAR EASTERN REGION

At the start of reforms the Far Eastern provinces enjoyed a situation that was more favorable than in many other parts of Russia. Initially rapid growth of foreign trade buoyed production and business development, but output began to fall first in 1992, then rapidly in 1993, and drastically in 1994–95. Investment was about 20 percent of pre-reform levels, and 42 percent of all firms were making losses by 1997, compared to an average of 26 percent for all Russia.[8] Manufacturing, food, and forest products output were all down.

However, some regions, including Kamchatka and Sakhalin, showed output improvements in 1996–97, primarily because of increased exports. The government announced a stabilization program in 1996, but by early 1998 federal payments for regional wages were substantially in arrears, inter-firm arrears ballooned, and there were frequent work stoppages protesting unpaid wages. Strikes by coal miners and others followed. To make matters worse, serious fuel shortages have gripped the region for the past several years, hurting the business sector by limiting output and adding costs.

Many of the assets of former non-military state enterprises have already transferred to leech companies, private firms that receive the state enterprises' assets. Privatization of mining has not made much progress, except gold mining.

Foreign investment is credited with helping regions of the Russian Far East boost their exports. More than 2,200 foreign affiliated companies, most of them with local Russian business partners, are registered in the region, with the greatest concentration in Primorskiy Krai. However, it is believed that only one-third are actually in operation. A poll of Russian specialists in Primorskiy Krai concluded that growth in the territory is impossible without foreign investment.[9]

Foreign investors, who seek advantages in being the first to operate in what is hoped will be a sizable future market, have stakes in both small and large enterprises. They invest in the skills of Russian personnel and transfer cost-effective technologies and management know-how to Russian partners.

Many of these investors appear willing to invest relatively modest sums of money for small projects with the intention of investing more in the future. However, the small scale of investments, at least from the U.S. side, suggests that the gains from investment to both parties will remain unrealized until Russia succeeds in putting into place the key institutions of a market economy.

However, assuming major obstacles to investment can be removed and the Far East in general becomes more welcoming to foreign money, particularly in the energy and other natural resource sectors, prospects for the Far East and its businesses could improve quickly. The various oil and gas schemes on Sakhalin Island could, for example, in the medium-term, create 22,000 jobs and attract $27 billion in total investment.

Local hire and content rules assure that Russian companies (small and large) throughout the region will get a major piece of the business, and foreign firms wanting a slice will have to offer to transfer technology to their Russian partners, which could make the Russians more domestically and internationally competitive in the future.

THE ROLE OF GOVERNMENT

Federal, regional, local, and even foreign governments are attempting to provide seed capital in the form of grants and loans for smaller enterprises. The funds, their size, and the rules for borrowing the capital vary widely, and not all regions have funds to offer. Those governments with funds to loan have had widely different experiences. The Sakhalin government has created a development fund that will grow to more than $100 million over the next few years. In addition, 1 percent of the annual budget will be used to support Sakhalin's newly created entrepreneurship fund.

Magadanskaya Oblast was one of the first regional governments to create a regional fund (in 1993). Entrepreneurs submitted mostly vague proposals to government bureaucrats. Priority was given to proposals that improved the production and distribution of food, especially in rural areas. An evaluation of the program's first few years indicates that few of the entrepreneurs who received the funds were still in business in 1995 and that some of the funds have disappeared.[10] Subsequent changes in the program included limiting funding to equipment needed by new enterprises. This change was based on the assumption that the regional government authorities could repossess the hardware if the enterprises failed to meet their obligations or if they went bankrupt. In addition, government authorities now require detailed business plans from entrepreneurs seeking support and have received training on how to evaluate them from business development specialists in nearby Alaska. Eventually, Magadanskaya Oblast would like to create a semi-autonomous fund authority with a board of directors specifically charged with making sure that loans and grants are not steered toward the friends, family members, or patrons of government. The value of this local fund in 1997 was about $200,000.

There is evidence that these efforts have launched some successful local enterprises. Russian government data indicate that unemployment in Sakhalin and Magadanskaya oblasts is relatively low, while output of small enterprises per worker is among the highest in the country. Is there a link between local government policy, small business formation, and unemployment? Is there a link between small business formation, unemployment, and small business technical assistance provided by foreign governments? In any case, the role of a local government as a lender of first and last resort is one of the few hopes these communities presently have for creating new jobs, products, and services, as well as for developing business expertise.

THE ROLE OF THE UNITED STATES AND JAPAN

One positive indicator of the Russian economic reform process is that the country is receiving some external assistance, especially from the United States and Japan. This assistance comes not only in the form of loans and grants but also in technical advice and other kinds of know-how. Providing this assistance should be a major priority for the governments of the United States and Japan at both the national and local government levels. The U.S. government's Regional Investment Initiative, including risk-sharing partnerships with local Russian banks, is an example of a promising policy shift. Experience shows high rates of loan repayment by small enterprise clients.[11] Japan is also targeting assistance on a regional basis, as is the case with the Export-Import Bank's loan to the Sakhalin Oblast.

Technical assistance and education services appear to be valued by Russian recipients. In these training efforts more emphasis should be placed on lessons drawn from other countries in the midst of economic transition. In addition to Russian business people, training should be expanded to include federal and local government bureaucrats, a group that maintains strong influence over the business environment but whose thinking remains largely out of sync with the changes buffeting the country. Attrition during the next ten years will give whatever government is in power a chance to jettison one of the biggest drags on the pace of economic and political reform.

Beyond natural resources extraction, the Russian Far East has a second potential advantage in its military industrial complex. Some of these military hardware factories and concentrations of highly capable specialists are still off limits to the private marketplace, but this will eventually change. Privatized spin-offs of these large ex-conglomerates, with shares offered for purchase to present managers and workers, could create dozens of small, lean enterprises organized into the Far East's first high-tech industrial parks.

Assistance efforts from U.S. and Japanese national governments should be coordinated with the efforts of sub-national entities, such as those in the U.S. Pacific Northwest and Japan's Sea of Japan rim area. More regional forums for official conversation, such as the American West Coast–Russian East Coast Working Group under the Gore-Chernomyrdin Commission and the Northeast Asia Economic Forum, should be encouraged. Such forums serve not only as catalysts for regional cooperation but also provide valuable information on how national policies affect regional and local business, economic, environmental protection, and other interests.[12]

CONCLUSION

Russia is a far different place than it was even a few years ago. Indications are that it is gradually becoming a normal country with all the imperfections and diversity that the concept entails. The problems facing the private sector, especially small business, are daunting. Policy makers in the United States and Japan cannot by themselves create a Russia that is stable and prosperous. They can, however, design programs and offer incentives that will help keep the reform process headed in the right direction.

NOTES

1. At the end of 1995 Poland had approximately twice as many small, private businesses as did Russia. Even allowing for additional unregistered businesses operating in the unofficial economy, Russia is still far behind Poland.

2. Statistical data compiled by Alexander Pilyasov, Institute on Problems of the North, Moscow.

3. Quoted in David Hoffman, "Big Tycoons Squeeze Out Small Business," *Washington Post*, December 28, 1997, p. A22.

4. Stephen Knack, "Low Trust, Slow Growth," *Financial Times*, June 26, 1996.

5. For a useful approach to rethinking enterprise restructuring see David Ellerman, *Spin-offs as a Restructuring Strategy for Post-Socialist Enterprises*. Washington, D.C.: World Bank, 1995.

6. D. Barkan, G. Sannikova, and E. Timofeeva, *How the Russian Entrepreneur Operates*. Moscow: USAID/Center for Business Information, 1995.

7. Ibid., p. 15.

8. Judith Thorton and Nadezhda N. Mikheeva, *Surveying Foreign Assisted Businesses in the Russian Far East and American Northwest*, Foundation for Russian American Economic Cooperation, (Seattle: September 1996), pp. 52-53.

9. *The Case for Russia's Pacific Far East: Investing, Trading, Partnering*, Middlebury, Vt.: Geonomics Institute, 1995, p. 3.

10. *The Russian Far East News*, University of Alaska, Anchorage, December 1996.

11. See David Ciagne and Jo Anne Steel, "Banking on Small Business in Vladivostok," *BISNIS Bulletin*, September 1997, p. 3.

12. For a comprehensive summary of government and non-government relations between Alaska and the Russian Far East, see Victor Fiesher, "Alaska-Russian Far East Connection: Experiments in the Development of Local Governance," in Douglas Barry and Kazuhiko Okuda, eds., *Development Issues and Prospects in the North Pacific Region* (Anchorage: University of Alaska, 1996).

6

Traditions, Institutions, and Lessons

Andrei I. Kravtsevich

Russians appear eager to receive Japanese investment. However, until recently the economic and legal environment in Russia discouraged even domestic investors from putting their money in Russian enterprises. In fact, the rapidly declining volume of investment represented one of the most serious negative by-products of the reform process. After the severe crisis unfolded in Russia in August and September 1998, the question was raised whether Russia should explore some alternative approaches to economic modernization and apply some modifications to its newly born economic system.

In the early 1990s some economists in both Russia and Japan suggested that the Russian government could borrow from the Japanese economic experience.[1] This could help the economic recovery and would probably make Russian enterprises more attractive to Japanese and other foreign investors. However, the Japanese postwar experience of economic reconstruction and management reveals significant institutional differences between Japan and Russia. These disparities seem to complicate the understanding of the Russian reform process on the part of Japanese business people, affecting their perceptions of Russia and the predominant attitudes toward closer economic contacts with Russian enterprises.[2]

DIFFERENCES AND SIMILARITIES

The direct borrowing of methods and practices can be dangerous. After the end of World War II, Japanese experts studied the Soviet system of

central planning, but the practical applications of their findings complemented market economy mechanisms. Similarly, in the former Soviet
Union some economists studied and analyzed Japanese postwar economic methods and industrial policy, but the Russian version of a market
economy is far from the one adopted in Japan. Whether Russia moves in
the direction of so-called industrial policy its economic model still needs
to be fine tuned to ensure steady development and efficient restructuring
of the manufacturing industry to restrain its heavy reliance on natural
resources exports.

Compared with Japan in the 1960s and 1970s, Russia has some important components for economic success, including liberalized trade and
financial markets, human capital and technologies, a relatively high savings rate, and low unemployment. What is missing is the market-friendly
government policy to promote growth. The main problem Russian government economists now face is how effectively to combine market incentives, administrative instruments, and fiscal and other measures to
encourage new investment. In essence, the issue is the role of the Russian
government not only in the macromanagement of the economy but also
in taking responsibility for creating or facilitating a reliable market environment that will bring visible changes at the enterprise level.

What lessons can be drawn from Japan's experience that have relevance to the contemporary economic situation in Russia?

First, the idea of mobilizing the entire nation to leapfrog to the status
of a world power was a key element in Japan's economic success. This
idea helped to mobilize the spiritual energy of a nation, it helped the people to withstand economic hardships and the psychological burden of the
U.S. occupation, and it allowed the consolidation of intellectual potential.
However, political leaders, including Prime Minister Shigeru Yoshida,
demonstrated flexibility and managed to create a rather ideologically
unbiased but effective team of highly professional experts, including
Marxists, socialists, and followers of Keynesian and liberal schools of
thought. Ideological differences among experts did not prevent the government from involving them in drawing economic policy or from
appointing them to key posts in the Economic Stabilization Board.

In Russia, as in postwar Japan, political pluralism is taking root, thus
encouraging national consolidation. However, the process of formation of
a unifying national idea is not over yet, and national goals are yet to be
established.

Second, in Japan special emphasis was placed on securing public support for the economic plans and policies in the early stages of their development and implementation. Japan's success in economic modernization
was stimulated by various linkages between the policy-making process
and the public. During 1946–47, the government employed all means,
including information and propaganda, to get public endorsement of the

first five-year plan. The main purpose of the plan was to restore the pre-war volumes of industrial production. However, the major goal of the plan was the achievement of a pre-war consumption level.

In the case of Russia, the opposition in the State Duma plays an important, although not always constructive, role in analyzing and correcting the plans of the government. The Federation Council (an upper house) of the Federal Assembly also performs a useful check-and-balance function with regard to economic plans and laws. Mass media coverage of various economic issues is extensive, and competing views can be heard. However, it is important that the federal government provide timely and adequate information on key economic issues to the public and avoid unrealistic targets.

Third, there is a fundamental difference between Japan and Russia with regard to social security policy and safety net measures. In Japan, a system of social security was created step by step; in Russia it is gradually being dismantled. In the 1950s and 1960s the government tried to stimulate the expansion of economic activity, intentionally boosting household incomes and constraining social programs.

The Japanese government officially declared the social orientation of the economy only in 1990. Obviously, the Russian government faces many difficulties in managing an unusually difficult transition in social affairs, including the reform of the pension system, housing reform, and changes in education and health care systems.

Fourth, Japan has succeeded in adopting a modern and relatively efficient legal system that supports both market mechanisms and state-private business relations. Understanding that assembling an entirely new system of rules and laws will require many years, Japanese leaders decided to adopt the legislation of an advanced country (Germany was recognized as an acceptable model), and then translated these laws and regulations. As a result Japan managed to introduce a proven and integrated legal system. Although not all the elements of this system worked equally well, the Japanese constantly amended them to suit Japan's social and economic conditions.

In Russia, post-soviet legislation is being gradually developed, too, including a new constitution, tax code, civil code, and many other major acts, including those critically needed for civilized market relations. However, it is widely known that legal regulations are inadequate and that the lack of efforts to enforce them undermines conditions for economic and social development, leads to a spread of criminal economic activities, allows capital flight, and complicates the situation for foreign investors interested in Russia. There are also numerous contradictions and conflicts between the soviet-time legislation and the new laws and legal acts.

Fifth, the decision-making process in Japan can be studied also, particularly the system of *shingikai* or consultative committees.[3] In Japan these consultative bodies have played a very significant role in preparation, elaboration, and adoption of all major policies and decisions. These consultative committees represent not just advisory bodies, whose opinion the government can adopt or ignore, but the principal tool of the political decision-making process. All elements of this system (consultative committee creation, the definition of the policy concept, and the formulation of recommendations) are legally institutionalized. In terms of membership, the process usually includes the representatives of all concerned parties: government, private businesses, trade unions, academics, the mass media, and consumers. This combination allows a compromise of interests.

Shingikai proved to be very effective not only for collecting, processing, and disseminating information but also for the implementation of policy. The comprehensive composition of these bodies made them an instrument of public control over the governmental policy-making process.[4] Many governmental policy initiatives were brought into advisory committees by ministerial bureaucrats, others were initiated by business circles. As one of the prominent critics of Japan's bureaucracy, R. Komiya, notes, "it is absolutely not certain that the opinion of officials always prevails. Therefore, advisory committees can be called a place for settlement of various interests. It is possible even to say that the system of advisory committees represents a concrete form of post-war democracy in Japan."[5]

Considering the current shape of the Russian bureaucratic system, the lack of professionalism, tradition, and experience, the development of a system of consultative committees could be useful not only for the management of major national, regional, or local problems but also to gain support for democratic principles in decision making. In Russia there are a number of similar advisory bodies functioning within the administration of the president, central government, and legislative offices. However, they have no official legal status and the issued recommendations are non-binding.

Finally, Japan always was very attentive to its small and medium enterprises. This served political and economic goals, supported job creation, and helped to ensure political and social stability. This policy was implemented by the government's Small and Medium Business Agency. A special legal base, credit institutions, tax concessions, depreciation rates, and a nationwide network of consultative support were applied in a comprehensive manner.

In this segment of economic reform Russia is lagging quite far behind despite some recent actions and plans to support small and medium private businesses. Scattered elements of such policy are adopted in Russia, but so far they have had limited impact on the economic situation. Real progress can be achieved only on the basis of a comprehensive, long-term strategy for encouraging and nurturing small and medium businesses. Of course, the processes that are taking place in contemporary Russia differ fundamentally from those in Japan in the postwar years. It is enough to point out the key difference in the situation of these two countries. Japan had to correct the market mechanisms; Russians are facing the challenge of forming new mechanisms proceeding from a predominantly non-market environment.[6]

Unfortunately, as one can see from the presidential and other elections, the Russian political elite (both the ruling group and the opposition) overlook the urgency of national consolidation. A nationwide super-idea is needed based on healthy and enlightened Russian national interests.[7] Real lessons from the experience of Japan can be taken not so much from a positive estimation of its economic success but rather from Japan's process of finding effective methods and adaptations of the economic system to the specific priority needs of the country.[8] The logic presented by the government to the ordinary Japanese was based on a rather simple scheme: Economic growth of your company $\Rightarrow$ expansion of the national economy $\Rightarrow$ growth in the standards of living. At the same time, political leaders in Japan never committed themselves to unrealistic targets.

RUSSIAN REALITIES

The history of capitalism demonstrates that countries like Japan, Germany, and Russia (sometimes called economic latecomers) with a so-called catch up pattern of economic development, relied more on the economic role of the state compared with the developed economies of individualistic capitalism, such as Britain and the United States. The central authority in these catch up economies was compelled to compensate for the weaknesses of market institutions and to supplement and correct market mechanisms.

Various instruments were applied in the process, including administrative and fiscal measures, support for state-owned enterprises, and efforts to promote new industries. This economic model was far from liberal. For example, Japan approached the stage of economic liberalization in the beginning of the 1980s, but this process continues in the 1990s, gradually affecting banking, insurance, the securities market, and the wholesale and retail sectors. In Germany this process was faster and was influenced by European integration.

In Russia between 1994 and 1998 the federal government was unable to propose any set of measures to arrest the decline in industrial output or to offer long-term economic and industrial priorities. According to some estimates, in 1996 about one-third of Russian enterprises were in the red and 17 percent of them did not make investment. Moreover, compared with Japan and Germany, Russia can be seen as a late latecomer to the group of highly institutionalized and internationalized developed economies, and this raises the question of whether its catching up with this group is possible at all.[9]

Many Japanese experts believe that in order to join the group of leading industrial democracies Russia needs the active economic role of the state.[10] However, intensive academic and political debate that is going on in Russia demonstrates the enormous complexity of this issue. Principally, despite all the differences among various approaches to economic reforms in Russia, the majority of analysts do not describe the reforms as a success.

Unlike Japan, China, or the newly industrialized economies of East Asia, Russia had to break decisively with a rather well-established soviet system of values and social, economic, and political organization. Unlike in China, the mechanisms of totalitarian or authoritarian rule were abandoned, allowing regional, economic, and ideological forces to compete. The confrontation between the executive branch and the legislature at some point made economic stabilization a secondary goal.

Moreover, the entire system of centralized investment ceased to exist and the market value of fixed capital assets substantially decreased along with the value of human resources because of their strong educational and professional linkages with the industries that declined or appeared internationally noncompetitive. In addition, unreasonably high taxes have discouraged normal economic activities and stimulated tax evasion. The government is unable to collect all the taxes and has defaulted in payments for state orders. It appears unable to ensure that salaries and wages in the state sector are paid on time. The second phase of privatization (mortgage tender type) was unfair and unjustified. Incomplete, uncertain, and fairly loose legal regulations stimulated capital flight and prevented foreign investment inflows. Russia is a federal state, but this federation is evolving with both central and regional authorities defining their roles and sharing responsibilities, not without friction. Finally, the war in Chechniya, the president's long illness, and confrontation with the opposition in the parliament along with other political, social, and economic complications have made the transition from the old economic and political order an uneven and painful process.

On the positive side, inflation is now under control, the shortages of food, consumer goods, and services have eased and the program of privatization, particularly in the municipal housing sector, has allowed rapid changes in the system of ownership. Despite a sharp decline in industrial output the level of personal consumption did not shrink dramatically; more durable consumer goods became available to ordinary people. The rapid pace of privatization was dictated by pragmatic (economic and political) reasons, including confrontation with the old ruling class and communist opposition on the federal and local levels.

Russia made outstanding progress in establishing new institutions. For example, the central bank appears to be an independent, professional, and efficient body. The stock market is slowly developing. Civil code and other legislation acts have created a better basis for a new legal environment and an improved investment climate. According to some estimates, Russia is lagging one year behind successful (albeit smaller) economies in transition in curbing inflation, and two to three years behind in moving to positive growth rates. There is more room for entrepreneurial initiative, there are significant changes in the structure of the gross domestic product, and some Russian enterprises compete in international markets.

The Russian domestic market appears to be huge, and competition on the part of foreign producers forced many Russian companies to compete more aggressively in sales promotion, prices and quality, and economic, financial, and technological modernization. There is also a trend toward a restructuring in the chain of relations between stockholders-owners, managers, and capital lenders. Their interaction under the conditions of scarce investment resources requires more transparency, flexibility, and accountability.

CONCLUSION

In Russia's case Japan's reconstruction experience can be useful in two main areas. First, it is valuable from the point of view of a complex approach to the solution of vital economic problems. Second, it provides a manual for the implementation of particular economic policies. It seems that in the Japanese experience of economic reconstruction there were some mistakes and miscalculations as well. However, the country was able to draw long-term plans for economic and social modernization and had enough political will to implement these plans. This unique ability to execute national strategies supported by the majority of Japanese across political, ideological, regional, and economic differences needs to be carefully studied, and perhaps some of the findings can be applicable to the current and future needs of Russia.

NOTES

1. As a student of the Japanese economy I analyzed this problem at the Research Institute on the National Economy of Japan during 1993–95.

2. In the late 1980s in the former Soviet Union special attention was given to Japan's postwar experience of economic rehabilitation. Many Japanese experts were supportive of this effort and saw the applications of the Japanese model as an opportunity for Russia to make the transition less painful.

Among published examples is the digest (in Russian) by Hideo Inaba and Seiji Tsutsumi (eds.), *The "Japanese Miracle" and Soviet Economic Reforms: Japan's Recommendations for Reforming the Soviet Union's Economy* (Moscow: Silk

Road Research Center, 1991) and a collective monograph (in Japanese) by Noria-ki Yonemura and Yoshiaki Nishimura (eds.), *Russia Transition to the Market Economy: Japan's Experience and Intellectual Assistance* (Tokyo: Saimaru Shuppankai, 1992). See also another publication (in Russian) of the Research Institute of Foreign Trade and Industry, *Problems of the Systemic Economic Reforms in the Countries of the Former USSR: What Can Be Taught from Post-War Japan's Experience* (Tokyo: RI/MITI, 1992).

3. British scholars S. Wilks and M. Wright studied the *shingikai* system and came to the conclusion that consultative committees in Japan "amalgamate technical analysis." The forum for discussions and consultations and the mechanism of achieving consensus, (and also) the mechanism of mobilization and coordination of a wide spectrum of organizations are seen by these authors as a desirable direction of development. See Stephen Wilks and Maurice Wright (eds.), *The Promotion and Regulation of Industry in Japan* (London: Macmillan, 1991), p. 16.

4. R. Komiya, M. Okuno, and K. Suzumura, *Japan's Industrial Policy* (Tokyo: Daigaku Shuppankai, 1984), p. 482 (in Japanese).

5. Ibid., p. 20.

6. See Andrei Kravtsevich, *The Problem of Applying Japan's Post-War Economic Rehabilitation Experience to Russia,* (Tokyo: Institute of Industrial Policy, Research Institute on the National Economy, 1995), (in Russian).

7. In English, it is difficult to draw the line between the name of the country (Russia) and the name of the main nationality (the Russians). However, there is a principal distinction in the Russian language: the name of the country is *Rossiya* and its citizens are called *Rossiyane*. *Rossiyane* is inclusive of all nationalities living in *Rossiya* (the Russian Federation), that is, not only the largest and the core ethnic group *Russkiye* but also other groups and minorities.

In this particular context I would emphasize the meaning *Russkiye*. The significance of the Russian national idea probably will not be questioned by non-Russian groups, because in very many cases their elites emphasize national identity, which supplements their belongingness to the Russian Federation. Moreover, many educated people in Russia, who belong to other ethnic groups but live in the Russian cultural and social environment, associate themselves more with Russian culture than with their original ethnicity.

8. Juro Teranishi and Yutaka Kosai (eds.), *The Japanese Experience of Economic Reforms* (New York: St. Martin's Press, 1993), pp. 18–19.

9. For example, P. Gregory of Houston University mentions that not more than 20 percent of the world population (including the economies of Southeast Asia) enjoy modern standards of living based on well-established legal, social, and institutional foundations. See his article on Russian economic reforms (Did Russian reforms prove so unsuccessful?) in *Voprosi Economiki*, No. 11, 1997, p. 20. In his opinion, countries like the United States, New Zealand, or Germany are rather exceptional, while Mexico, Philippines, Egypt, Turkey, or Pakistan can be described as more typical societies. Therefore, the standards of evaluating Russian reforms can be artificially high. However, factors like the size and geography of the country, its population, leading economic role in the former Soviet Union, military and nuclear strategic potential, political influence, membership in the Group of Eight process, and rich natural resources make Russia a far more important regional and global entity to apply lower Western standards.

10. Tsuneaki Sato, *Transition in Market Economy: Lessons from the East European Experience.* Synopsis of the paper prepared for the conference on "Asian Transitional Economies: Challenges and Prospects for Reform and Transformation," Osaka, October 30–31, 1994, p. 7.

7

Potentials and Realities
Tsuneo Akaha

The era of conflict in Japan-Russia relations seems to be over,[1] and a new era is in the offing. Both powers are redefining their national interests and engaging in a geopolitical repositioning vis-à-vis one another.[2] By improving their relationship Russia and Japan can contribute to the establishment of a post–Cold War peace world and regional order. They can facilitate each other's global aspirations and regional interests. Russia supports Japan's efforts to obtain a permanent seat in the United Nations Security Council, and Japan has agreed to accept Russia into the Group of Seven and has endorsed Moscow's membership in the Asia-Pacific Economic Cooperation forum. Tokyo and Moscow are seeking mutual accommodation and discussing prospects for cooperation, not in the sense of harmony of interests but in the sense of mutual adjustment of policies based on each country's basic interests.[3] However, mutual accommodation and cooperation will be possible only if Russia becomes a democratic society with a market economy. Russia's sustained transition toward a market democracy and Japan's assistance in this process should be seen in this light.

INTERNATIONAL CONTEXT

In describing recent global trends, many analysts have referred to "the end of history," "the end of the Cold War," and "the end of geography."[4] It is asserted that the end of the East-West ideological conflict has marked the victory of liberal capitalism over socialism and communism, and the disappearance of the Soviet threat has ushered in an era of global cooperation. It is also claimed that the logic of liberal economics and the imperatives of modern technology are creating a borderless world economy.

Northeast Asia — the region of immediate concern to both Russia and Japan — has been affected only marginally by these global trends. The regional powers remain suspicious of each other politically and unable to remove national barriers to international economic transaction. The end of the Cold War has raised the specter of major power shifts and realignment in Northeast Asia, and consequently heightened Russian and Japanese roles in the region. The decline of U.S. hegemony, the rise of China as a major political power and a compelling economic factor, the potential instability in the Koreas, and the uncertainties of Russia's transformation complicate the structure of international relations in Northeast Asia.[5]

Russia has a deepening concern over its declining influence in the region and is attempting to shore up its regional profile through bilateral improvements with the United States, China, South Korea, and Japan. Russia's economic assets are limited, but Moscow is attempting to establish itself as a legitimate Asian-Pacific player.[6] Russia remains a potentially powerful military power in the region,[7] and Japan watches Russia's improving relations with its Northeast Asian neighbors with a mixture of relief and anxiety.[8] Japan's own future is a matter of growing uncertainty as well. Central to this uncertainty is the imbalance between the nation's outwardly aggressive economic policy and its relatively reactive foreign policy and a defense posture interdependent with that of the United States.

On the economic front, the gap between Russia and Japan is conspicuous. During the 1991–96 period the Russian and Japanese economies moved further apart in terms of wealth production and accumulation. The real gross domestic product growth rate for the 1991–96 period was –9.1 percent for Russia and 1.3 percent for Japan, with the two countries' per capita gross domestic product in 1996 standing at $2,461 and $40,897, respectively.[9] Japan's global economic position is evident in the fact that its exports represent almost 10 percent of the world's total exports and 6.5 percent of global imports. Japan's position among the Asian-Pacific economies is even more pronounced, with its exports and imports within the Asia-Pacific Economic Cooperation region representing almost 75 percent and 70 percent, respectively, of total regional trade. In contrast, Russia's international economic role is much lower. Its world exports in 1997 amounted to $84.8 billion, and its imports stood at $52.5 billion.

Although the global context of Russia-Japan relations improved in the aftermath of the Cold War, their regional environment remains uncertain and complicates policy options. Their bilateral economic relations are also not developed enough to contribute to regional economic integration. There is a glaring gap between their impact and dependence on economic relations

within Northeast Asia, thus differentiating their incentives and contributions for regional economic cooperation. These disparate foundations of
national power between Russia and Japan do not make for a common
strategic calculus. Naturally, differences abound between their domestic,
regional, and global priorities.[10]

DOMESTIC FACTORS

As the legacies of prewar history and the impact of the global Cold War
wane, as they eventually will, domestic structures and processes will
become a more dominant factor influencing the external behavior of both
Russia and Japan. It is important, therefore, that in exploring the possibilities of bilateral cooperation, we pay closer attention to the differences
and similarities in the two countries' internal developments.

Politically, Russia is a nascent democracy dominated by a powerful
president and a divided legislature, often unleashing unpredictable policy shifts. Japan, on the other hand, is a bureaucracy-driven democracy
with a weak political leadership, characterized by a stable and predictable
policy trajectory. Both systems, however, exhibit common symptoms of
excessive concentration of power, ineffective opposition, porous public
oversight, and public corruption.

Economically, Russia is a transition economy struggling to introduce
market principles. Japan is a global capitalist superpower with efficient
productive capacity. However, both systems also share a degree of simi-
larity in the overbearing power of central administrative bureaucracies. In
both countries there are marked disparities in economic development
between the highly industrialized and urbanized centers of economic
power and relatively neglected provinces. In both countries there are also
growing local and provincial initiatives for bilateral and regional economic cooperation. However, historically both countries were dependent
on an administration from the center and it is likely that their new national priorities will overshadow local interests.[11]

A related issue is the role the state plays in national development. The
political and economic development of the czarist and soviet empires was
almost entirely controlled by the prerogatives of one dictatorial ruler or
party that essentially was the state. Postcommunist Russia is entrusted in
the president who, in spite of all the attempts by legislative opposition,
yields enormous power in law making and policy formulation, if not in
enforcement and implementation.

Since the 16th century, Japan has been a highly state-centric political
system, and its modernization since the 19th century has been led by the
developmental state with powerful central bureaucracies in control of the
basic direction of national economic development.[12] Although the Japanese economy is increasingly liberalized and its private sector is growing

in power, the system's essential elements are still heavily regulated by the powerful central bureaucracies.

Russia's liberalization of trade and investment policies and consequent exposure to external economic processes is reminiscent of Japan's postwar economic development, in which international trade and foreign investment played a crucial role. Russia is discovering the growth potential of export activities in its strategic industries, including primary commodities and military production, and it is becoming dependent on foreign investment and capital goods import, not to mention the important role international economic assistance plays in stabilizing Russia's economy. In this respect, Russia can learn much from Japan's experience in postwar economic development.

Following its disastrous defeat in World War II, Japan consistently and persistently followed an industrial policy focused on public investment in basic and strategic industries and export-driven growth. The lesson has not been lost on Moscow, which in February 1997 adopted a development budget and established a federal economic development agency for the purpose of development of basic and strategic industries.

A striking difference exists, however, between Japan's postwar experience and Russia's current situation. Japan's export-driven economic growth could be sustained only because of the United States' strategic assistance and its open market, as well as the liberal international trade regime. Japan's membership in the General Agreement on Tariffs and Trade, the International Monetary Fund, the World Bank, the Asian Development Bank, and other multilateral institutions was very important. In contrast, Russian exports continue to be severely restricted by export controls carried over from the Cold War era and Russia's membership in international economic institutions is still conditioned on the pace of its domestic economic reform. Removal of export controls and acceleration of domestic reform must, therefore, be priority items for Russian-Japanese cooperation.

Finally, it is often observed that there is a substantial degree of complementarity between the economies of Russia and Japan, the former as a source of energy and other natural resources and the latter as a source of capital and industrial technology.[13] However, the complementarity remains largely a potential — not a reality — and integration of Far Eastern Russia into regional trade and economic networks is at an early stage.[14]

The growing trade between Far Eastern Russia and Japan is due largely to the natural resources exports to Japan and the imports of consumer and capital goods from Japan. However, the exchange is not contributing to the modernization of industrial production or economic restructuring in the Far Eastern territories. Given the absence of market forces strong enough to bring the Russian and Japanese economies closer together, it is obvious that policy commitments to change this situation are in order.

Especially important in this context is Japanese assistance for Russia's economic reform and development.

BILATERAL CONTEXT

The Russian people's view of Japan is informed by the memory, predominantly in the form of written history, of Russia's humiliating defeat by Japan in the war of 1904–5, which resulted in the loss of the southern half of Sakhalin Island; Japan's intervention in Siberia in 1918–20; and the U.S.–Japan alliance. From their perspective, Japan's claims to the southern Kurils are unjustified in view of its unconditional surrender in 1945.

In spite of this, many Russians, particularly those in the Far Eastern provinces, hold a generally favorable view of Japan. A 1992 survey of public opinion in southern Primorskiy Krai revealed that Japan was the second most popular country after the United States with which the local residents wished to establish close and friendly relations. The same survey also showed that almost half of the respondents named Japan as the country from which they wished to receive experience and assistance in economic development.[15]

On the Japanese side, sources of negative views of Russia include the declaration of war before the expiration of the neutrality pact of 1941, the Japanese prisoners of war treatment in Siberia, and the soviet military presence in Northeast Asia during the Cold War era. Moreover, from the viewpoint of many Japanese, Russia continues to occupy the Northern Territories. According to an opinion survey conducted by the Japanese prime minister's office in October 1995, only 9.9 percent of the Japanese in the poll had friendly or somewhat friendly feelings toward Russia, in comparison with the 86.4 percent who felt either somewhat unfriendly or unfriendly.[16]

Japan has been criticized for a seeming lack of interest in assisting Russia in its economic reform. Nonetheless, Japan's assistance to Russia is by no means negligible. By January 1996, Tokyo had pledged $4.4 billion. In total assistance for Russia, this made Japan the third largest provider of aid after Germany and the United States. For its part, Tokyo has correctly raised the absence of legal and institutional infrastructure and accountability for the disbursement of international assistance in Russia as important obstacles to a more effective and timely transfer of Japanese assistance.

There are four areas in which Russia and Japan can advance cooperation and improve their mutual perceptions: Japanese assistance to Russia in economic reform and development, bilateral cooperation in environmental and resource conservation, military confidence-building, and expansion of non-governmental contacts. Goals and objectives of Japanese assistance programs are stated as support of Russia's transition to a market economy, support of its democratization, and establishment of diplomatic relations based on "law and justice," a reference to the settlement of the territorial dispute over the Northern Territories.[17] Tokyo emphasizes technical assistance for human resources development in support of market economy development, and priority is given to Far Eastern Russia.[18]

Tokyo has pledged $200 million in Export-Import Bank of Japan loans to support the modernization of communication links between Moscow and Khabarovsk, and $50 million for the establishment of a regional enterprise fund targeted for small- and medium-sized enterprises in Eastern Siberia and the Russian Far East. In addition, about $500,000 in humanitarian aid was extended to the residents of the southern Kurils in the aftermath of the earthquake on October 4, 1994. Tokyo provided additional humanitarian assistance, including the setting up of a temporary clinic on the island of Shikotan in October 1995. Tokyo also extended about $1 million in humanitarian assistance to Sakhalin in the wake of the devastating earthquake in the northern area of the island on May 27, 1995.

Japan has also been willing to extend cooperation and assistance to Russia in curbing environmental problems in the Russian Far East.[19] The most visible program is for the management of radioactive wastes. Following Moscow's acknowledgment in 1993 that from 1959 to 1992 the Soviet Union had dumped radioactive wastes in the North Sea and the Far Eastern seas and the Russian Pacific Fleet had dumped radioactive waste material in the Sea of Japan in 1992, Russia, Japan, South Korea, and the International Atomic Energy Agency jointly studied the environmental impact of these activities.[20]

Japan is also cooperating in the construction of radioactive material treatment facilities in Bolshoi Kamen near Vladivostok, as part of bilateral cooperation in nuclear weapons dismantlement. The facilities will have an annual capacity to dispose of 7,000 cubic meters of liquid radioactive wastes. Additionally, in the aftermath of the disastrous oil spill in the Sea of Japan by the Russian tanker *Nakhodka* in January 1997, Russia, Japan, Korea, and China met in Toyama in July to discuss ways to prevent this kind of accident in the future.

In the area of military confidence-building, Russia-Japan cooperation is at the very beginning stages. In 1992, Russia-Japan policy planning consultations were organized by the two countries' foreign ministries. The year 1993 saw the beginning of a defense research exchange between the two countries. During President Yeltsin's visit to Tokyo in October 1993, the two countries concluded an agreement on maritime accident prevention. However, serious bilateral defense dialogue had to wait until April 1996, when the Japanese Defense Agency director general visited Moscow.

In July 1996 a Japanese maritime self-defense force escort, the *Kurama*, called in Vladivostok for the first time in 71 years. This was reciprocated by a Russian destroyer's visit to Tokyo in June 1997. Another event of note is Japan's advance notification to Russia of the joint U.S.–Japanese military exercise in the Sea of Japan in November 1996.

Finally, increased people-to-people contact is an essential part of the equation. In this context, the growing interest in mutual communication and cooperation among many local and provincial communities on both sides of the Sea of Japan is encouraging. Also welcome are the various programs of technical assistance initiated by the Japanese government, technical centers, the Regional Venture Fund, dispatch of experts and training programs in Japan, as well as the Ministry of International Trade and Industry's Support Plan for Russian Trade and Industry.[21]

Another indication of bilateral interest in promoting human contact is the agreement announced in March 1997 to expand the non-visa mutual visits by the citizens of both countries involving the disputed islands and Hokkaido to include not only the former Japanese residents of the Northern Territories and reporters but also technical experts in agriculture and education. Although these are still limited in scope, Japanese government assistance programs will contribute to expanded human contacts between Russian and Japanese people, as will private level technical cooperation and non-governmental humanitarian assistance. In November 1993 Japan opened consulate offices in Vladivostok and Khabarovsk, and in 1997 it opened a branch of its Khabarovsk consulate general in Yuzhno-Sakhalinsk.

CONCLUSION

The above analysis points to several sources of potential change in relations between Russia and Japan:

growing local and provincial interest in cooperation;

economic complementarity;

Japanese assistance to economic reform;

Russia's interest in expanding economic ties with the Asia-Pacific region; and

shared interest among Russia, Japan, and the United States in maintaining regional stability.

The end of the Cold War has changed the relative weight of global versus subregional factors in favor of the latter.[22] Regional and subregional developments now impinge more directly on the shape of global affairs. However, the Asia-Pacific region is in a state of flux, neither a bipolar nor a multipolar pattern dominates the scene, and the different foundations of national power complicate the international relations of the region.

If removing uncertainties and eliminating anxieties in the world in general and in Northeast Asia in particular can contribute to an improvement of Russian-Japanese relations, there has never been a better opportunity than today. Russia and Japan must start by removing the legacies of their past relationship and developing a mutually compatible relationship. This will be in their national interest both from the perspective of their bilateral relationship and in terms of their respective places in the world.

NOTES

1.   Wolf Mendl, *Japan's Asia Policy: Regional Security and Global Interests.* (New York: Routledge, 1995), p. 52.

2.   For a recent examination of the prewar history of Russian-Japanese encounters, see G. Patrick March, *Eastern Destiny: Russia in Asia and the North Pacific.* (Westport, Conn.: Praeger, 1996), pp. 69–90, 159–84, 211–28. For a recent study of Soviet-Japanese relations since the 1970s, see Joachim Glaubitz, *Between Tokyo and Moscow: The History of an Uneasy Relationship. 1972 to the 1990s.* (Honolulu: University of Hawaii Press, 1995).

3.   For this definition of cooperation, see Joseph Nye, *After Hegemony: Cooperation and Discord in the World Political Economy.* (Princeton, N.J.: Princeton University Press, 1984), p. 12.

4.   The "end of geography" means the emergence of a borderless world economy through transnational interdependence of national and regional economies.

5.   For a detailed exploration of the uncertain balance of power in Asia, see Paul Dibb, *Toward a New Balance of Power in Asia,* Adelphi Paper 295 (London: International Institute for Strategic Studies, 1995).

6.   See Tsuneo Akaha, "Russia in Asia in 1994," *Asian Survey,* 35(1) (January 1995): 100–10; Tsuneo Akaha, "Russia and Asia in 1995," *Asian Survey,* 36(1) (January 1996): 100–108.

7.   Mendl, *Japan's Asia Policy,* p. 61.

8.   For a Japanese defense analyst's view of the changing Sino-Russian security relations, see *Higashi-ajia Senryaku Gaikyo, 1996–97* (East Asian Strategic Review, 1996–97). (Tokyo: National Institute for Defense Studies), pp. 102–3, 114–18.

9.   *Japan 1997: An International Comparison.* (Tokyo: Japan Institute for Social and Economic Affairs, 1997), p. 17.

10.   Tsuneo Akaha, "Japanese-Russian Economic Relations and Their Implications for Asia-Pacific Security." In *Power and Prosperity: Economics and Security Linkages in Asia-Pacific,* edited by Susan L. Shirk and Christopher P. Twomey. (New Brunswick, N.J.: Transaction, 1996), pp. 197–212.

11.   For an exploration of this theme more generally in the entire Northeast Asian region, see Tsuneo Akaha, "Northeast Asian Regionalism: State-directed Economic Interdependence?" *The Sejong Review,* 3(1) (November 1995): 81–112.

12. See the seminal work on this theme, Chalmers Johnson, *MITI and the Japanese Miracle: The Growth of Industrial Policy. 1925–1975.* (Stanford, Calif.: Stanford University Press, 1982).

13. See, for example, Kazuo Ogawa and Kinji Hishiki, *Kan-nihonkai Keizaiken to Roshia Kvokuto Kaihatsu* (The Japan Sea rim economic zone and the development of the Russian Far East), (Tokyo: JETRO, 1994); Kazuo Ogawa and Takashi Murakami, *Mezameru Soren Kvokuto: Nihon no Hatasu Yakuwari* (The awakening Soviet Far East: The role Japan should play). (Tokyo: Nihon Keizaihyoronsha, 1991); Evgenii B. Kovrigin, "Problems of Resource Development in the Russian Far East." In *Proceedings: Seminar on Integrating the Russian Far East into the Asia-Pacific Economy*, October 20–22, 1994. Monterey, California, edited by Tsuneo Akaha. (Monterey, Calif.: Monterey Institute of International Studies, Center for East Asian Studies, 1995), pp. 62–71. For a more cautious view, see Tsuneo Akaha and Takashi Murakami, "Soviet/Russian-Japanese Economic Relations." In *Russia and Japan: An Unresolved Dilemma between Distant Neighbors*, edited by Tsuyoshi Hasegawa, Jonathan Haslam, and Andrew C. Kuchins. (Berkeley: University of California International and Area Studies, 1993), pp. 161–86.

14. Viktor Ishaev, "Foreword." In *The Russian Far East: An Economic Survey*, edited by Pavel A. Minakir and Gregory L. Freeze. (Khabarovsk: Institute of Economic Research, 1996), p. 7.

15. The survey was conducted by the Institute of History, Archaeology, and Ethnography in Vladivostok. Nikolai G. Shcherbina, "The Reaction to the Foreign Presence in the Primorsky Region," a report prepared for the Monterey Institute of International Studies' Center for East Asian Studies, 1994, pp. 7–9.

16. Sorifu Kohoshitsu (ed.), *Seron Chosa* (Tokyo: Okurasho Insatsukyoku, 1996), pp. 27–34.

17. The following description of Japanese assistance to Russia is based on information provided to Sorifu Kohoshitsu by the Japanese Ministry of Foreign Affairs, including Japan's Assistance to the New Independent States. (Tokyo: Secretariat of the Cooperation Committee, Ministry of Foreign Affairs, 1996).

18. For this purpose, Tokyo has funded the establishment of "Japan Centers" to provide corporate management and other training. One center has opened at the Plekhanov University of Economics in Moscow, another is being developed at Moscow State University, and a third in Vladivostok.

19. For an examination of the environmental situation in Russia's Far Eastern regions and its implications for international cooperation, see Tsuneo Akaha (ed.), *Politics and Economic in the Russian Far East: Changing Ties with Asia-Pacific.* (London: Routledge, 1997), pp. 120–34.

20. See Japanese-Korean-Russian Joint Expedition, "Investigation of Environmental Radioactivity in Waste Dumping Areas of the Far Eastern Sea Areas: Results from the First Japanese-Korean-Russian Joint Expedition 1994," Tokyo, July 1995 (unpublished, data collected in 1994).

21. Ministry of Foreign Affairs, Secretariat of the Cooperation Committee, "Japan's Assistance to the New Independent States," Tokyo, March 1996, p. 5.

22. Aaron L. Friedberg, "Ripe for Rivalry: Prospects for Peace in a Multipolar Asia," *International Security*, 18(3) (Winter 1993–94): 5–33.

8

A Retrospective View: A Fifth Period?

Konstantin O. Sarkisov

The study of Russia-Japan bilateral contacts, conflicts, and dialogue calls for a retrospective approach that can help identify the obstacles to improved relations. If we follow the main developments since the initial Japan-Russia contacts and look at their predominant pattern, the whole history of bilateral relations will be clearly divided into four periods mostly dominated by tensions, mistrust, and confrontation.

There was an era of geopolitical rivalry (beginning of the 18th century until 1917), one of nationalism and ideological antagonisms (after the Russian Revolution), and one of Cold War strategic confrontation (1945–91). The fourth and current period, which began after the dissolution of the Soviet Union, may be termed a "transition period" because it is not one of true confrontation, but rather a time when the past is receding although its legacy of nationalism and misperceptions lingers.

THE FIRST PERIOD

The first period spans the 18th and 19th centuries — the era of great power territorial expansions. By the time of Catherine the Great, Russia's territorial gains included all of Siberia, the Far Eastern territories, Kamchatka, Alaska, and some of the northern Kurils. Japan, in contrast, exercised a self-imposed policy of isolation (however, Hokkaido, or Ezo, as it was known, was colonized after the Matsumae domain was taken under control by the Tokugawa shogunate).

This 200-year period includes the discovery of the Kuril Islands and the first contacts there with Russians, who made attempts to engage Japan in trade. Adam Erikovich Laxman visited Nemuro in 1792 and Matsumae in 1793, where he unsuccessfully negotiated the opening of trade relations. Russia's strategy toward Japan was determined by Catherine II, who was reluctant to proceed with excessive territorial expansion and gave priority to trade relations. Efforts to open Japan continued under Alexander I, and in 1804 Russian envoy Nikolai Petrovich Rezanov visited Nagasaki (the same year Novoarkhangelsk, now Sitka, became the center of Russian power in Alaska, shortly after Ivan Kruzenshtern began his exploration of the Northern Pacific Ocean). Rezanov, too, was unable to reach an agreement with the Japanese. When efforts to open Russia-Japan relations failed, Alexander I issued an order not to move southward of Urupp Island. It was not until January 26, 1855, that the two countries signed a treaty that divided the Kuril Islands between them and provided for joint possession of Sakhalin Island.

However, Russia's changing geopolitical interests soon required new efforts to engage Japan. During the reign of Nicholas I, Sakhalin gained special strategic importance, because it was located opposite the mouth of the Amur River. The center of Russian geopolitical interests shifted from the Pacific to the mainland and China, thus affecting policy toward Japan. The notion that the "one who holds Sakhalin commands the river"[1] brought to the forefront the debate over Sakhalin's sovereignty and dictated relations with Japan. In 1875 Japan and Russia concluded the Treaty of St. Petersburg, in which Russia regained control of all Sakhalin Island, and all of the Kurils were reverted to Japan.

However, these first contacts and treaties between Japan and Russia ended in tension. During the Sino-Japanese War Russia acted as China's protector. After the war ended in 1895, Russia and China signed a mutual defense treaty against Japan in 1896 and Russia was granted the right to construct and hold an 80-year lease on the Chinese Eastern Railway that connected Chita and Vladivostok through Manchuria. In 1898 Russia was able to lease Liaotung Peninsula, including Port Arthur, and the Chinese Eastern Railway company was granted a concession to construct a southern Manchurian rail line from Harbin to Port Arthur.

In 1898 Russia signed an accord with Japan that recognized Japan's special interests in Korea. However, the conflicting strategies of the two countries and their ambitions to expand influence over northeast China and Korea led to an era of conflict. In 1903, after Japan's "special rights" in Korea were supported by England, Russia-Japan relations deteriorated and led to a major war after the Japanese fleet launched a surprise attack on Port Arthur on January 26–27, 1904.

On August 23, 1905, the Treaty of Portsmouth was negotiated with the mediation of President Theodore Roosevelt. Under that treaty Russia ceded Port Arthur, the southern portion of the Manchurian railway, and the southern half of Sakhalin Island to Japan. The treaty was seen as a diplomatic victory for Moscow because there was a real danger that it would lose all of Sakhalin and have to pay war reparations. In 1907 the two powers signed another accord that established their spheres of influence encompassing northern Manchuria and Outer Mongolia for Russia and southern Manchuria and Korea for Japan.

The 1904–5 war was a result of the expansionist policies of both Russia and Japan. The war ended with a peace accord and normal relations were restored, but this first period of geopolitical rivalry provided a fertile ground for the future conflicts and tensions that punctuated Russia-Japan bilateral relations.

THE SECOND PERIOD

Both the civil war and communist revolution in Russia had a great impact on bilateral relations. The emergence of ideological confrontation did not imply the disappearance of geopolitical rivalry. Russia's weakened condition and civil war encouraged foreign powers to try to extort the Russian Far East from its mainland. The Japanese were among those who invaded the Russian Far East, and they were the last to withdraw from Vladivostok.

The Japanese occupation of Northeast China also contributed to long-standing geopolitical tensions with Russia. The Russia-Japan rivalry intensified, as it became both geostrategic and ideological. The result was armed conflicts. First was the border conflict in Primorie at Lake Khanka from July 29 to August 11, 1938. Then from May 11 to September 15, 1939, Soviet and Japanese forces clashed in Mongolia at Khalkhin Gol River.

Although Russian forces scored two victories in these armed conflicts, on April 13, 1941, Japan signed a Pact of Neutrality with the Soviet Union. This treaty guaranteed borders in the Far East but was unilaterally abrogated by Moscow before the end of World War II. The political aspect of Stalin's decision was his obligations as part of a coalition of powers fighting against Germany and Japan. The Soviet Union's territorial claims were supported by allied powers in Yalta in February 1945, because President Franklin Roosevelt wanted Soviet troops to be involved in the war against Japan to exert more pressure on Tokyo to surrender and to limit U.S. losses.

In the context of Russia-Japan bilateral relations after World War II, three important factors were to preclude the restoration of normal relations: abrogation of the neutrality treaty (and military activities against Japanese troops), the territorial losses of Japan, and the imprisonment of 660,000 Japanese prisoners of war in Soviet labor camps. The lessons from the second period are that ideology and nationalism aggravated the geopolitical rivalry, but it was the second major war that created insurmountable obstacles for future relations.

THE THIRD PERIOD

Following the war, the world divided into two economic and politicomilitary blocks with their own spheres of influence and power centers. Ironically, the divisive borders were, in general, defined at Yalta in February 1945. Postwar relations between Moscow and Tokyo were greatly influenced by the San Francisco Peace Treaty and the U.S.–Japan Security Treaty signed on the same day in September 1951. These documents laid out a political, legal, and psychological framework for very close relations between Japan and the United States. Furthermore, the subsequent Yoshida doctrine of Japan (in reference to Prime Minister Shigeru Yoshida) became in essence a strategy that concentrated all national resources on economic resurgence and delegated strategic decisions and security issues to the United States.

Stalin, however, refused to sign the San Francisco Peace Treaty; as a result there is no peace treaty between Japan and Russia. Among Stalin's reasons for not joining the treaty may have been a belief that the communist victory in China would affect other parts of Asia and a peace treaty with Japan based on Anglo-American conditions represented an obstacle to greater communist success. The territorial issue between Russia and Japan became much more complicated because the San Francisco Peace Treaty clause on sovereignty over southern Sakhalin and the Kurils was ambiguous; the question over to whom they belong was left open to interpretations. This in itself has placed the territorial issue at the center of any peace treaty.

In October 1956 diplomatic relations were restored after Japan and Russia signed the Joint Declaration as a substitute for a peace treaty. This document includes a clause specifying that "as a sign of good will," Russia would hand over Shikotan and Habomai islands to Japan after a formal peace treaty is concluded. Nikita Khrushchev's policy toward Japan was less rigid, but it was controversial and very much in the spirit of the harsh ideological and geopolitical confrontation of the times. His erratic policy toward Japan was replaced by the consistently hard diplomacy of Leonid Brezhnev's era. In East Asia, the Soviet Union was primarily concerned with China, particularly after the Sino-American reconciliation and subsequent establishment of diplomatic relations between Japan and China. For Japan, foreign policy priority was then placed on the United States and China. Naturally, the U.S. military presence in Japan focused even more on Far Eastern Russia and the conventional and strategic forces deployed there.

A new window of opportunity for better relations between Russia and Japan was not opened until Mikhail Gorbachev transformed soviet foreign policy. The new diplomacy advocated substantial improvements in Moscow's relations with Washington and its Western European allies. On the other hand, the new "look East" policy declared in Gorbachev's Vladivostok speech was aimed at reconciliation with China and later led to the diplomatic recognition of South Korea. All these events dramatically changed international relations, particularly in Asia. Gorbachev's visit to Japan was not a breakthrough, but it was a historic step forward in bilateral relations and a gesture toward a reconciliation encapsulated in the Joint Declaration signed on April 19, 1991.

This document included new elements in Russia's attitude toward Japan, a recognition of the existence of a territorial dispute, acknowledgment that the solution to this question is a prerequisite for a peace treaty, establishment of a visa-free regime for Japanese visiting the southern Kurils, and a promise to withdraw troops from the disputed islands. Gorbachev made all possible steps toward Japan except promising to yield territory.

The lesson from the third period is that the Soviet attempt to construct positive relations with Japan on the basis of anti-Americanism was doomed to fail because close relations between Japan and the United States matched Japanese interests. However, Gorbachev's image and his new political thinking helped bilateral relations by changing public opinion in Japan and subsequently beginning a process of finding a mutually acceptable way out of the stalemate.

THE FOURTH PERIOD

The fourth period is marked by the abatement of all three previous types of rivalries based on geopolitical interests, nationalistic and ideological tensions, and strategic conflict. After the collapse of the Warsaw Pact and the breakup of the Soviet Union, Russia improved relations with all industrially advanced democracies, including Japan.

Boris Yeltsin, before rising to the Russian presidency, had traveled to Japan and studied the territorial question. At that time he came up with the idea of a five-stage resolution plan that basically defers the solution to the next generation. As president, however, Yeltsin was confronted with the complexity of the territorial issue, and more importantly, the interaction between the territorial issue and domestic politics. This led to the abrupt decision to cancel his first state visit to Japan.

The visit eventually took place only one year later in October 1993, when the Tokyo Declaration was signed. This document recognized the existence of the territorial issue and the need to conclude a peace treaty.

Yeltsin also apologized for the detention and mistreatment of Japanese soldiers in Siberia and other parts of Russia after the war.

Russia, however, will likely continue to pursue the strategy of taking small steps toward a peace treaty. These efforts have encountered unexpected obstacles as a result of Russia's prolonged transitional difficulties. Two events in 1997 that damaged bilateral relations are rooted in Russia's political and economic turmoil, as well as in some unfortunate accidents: the spill of crude oil from the Russian tanker *Nakhodka* into Japanese waters, a huge blow to Russia's image, and the abrupt cancellation of then First Deputy Prime Minister Victor Ilyushin's visit to Japan in April 1997 (he was scheduled to attend the inter-governmental commission on trade and economic issues).

On the Japanese side, Tokyo has oscillated between a soft and hard attitude toward Russia. Hardliners believed that Russia would yield only under pressure. Softliners doubted that Japan could even apply real pressure on Russia and that incentives would be more effective on a huge but ailing Russia where political leaders are working under the pressure of domestic problems and in a complicated international environment. Indeed, under these circumstances the territorial issue with Japan became not only an annoying impediment to pragmatic foreign policy needs but also an emotional burden in terms of domestic politics. It was, therefore, very important to de-emotionalize the issue, to put it on a pragmatic track of small but steady steps forward.

To analyze the territorial issue, it should be divided into six parts: legal, historical, political, geostrategic, economic, and psychological. All are essential elements of the whole; they are intertwined and interrelated. The legal aspect is crucial because the new Russia claims to be a good international citizen that espouses international law as a fundamental principle. The historical aspect is also essential because unbiased examination of history provides both sides with a sense of justice. The psychological aspect, in contrast, is closely linked with national identity; any proposed solution should avoid a perception of national humiliation and should work to enhance national dignity.

The importance of the political factor is clear. Any solution to a territorial dispute depends on the decision makers on both sides, on their inclinations and abilities. Only high level and friendly political relations, reliable channels of communications, confidence, and mutual trust will create needed political conditions and the personal will on both sides to reach a solution. The political formula for the resolution of the dispute will entail economic interests and potential economic losses. Can these losses be compensated, and how will the agreement promote economic exchange and provide benefits for both countries and the local communities involved?

If the economic situation in Russia improves, further reforms will affect the military, the system of retirement benefits, housing, ownership of land, and so forth. The short-term effects of these reforms for the domestic political situation in Russia are difficult to predict. This uncertainty is related to the question of who will be elected the next Russian president. What will be the composition of the Federal Assembly? What kind of relationship will emerge between Moscow and the provinces?

Geostrategic considerations are also essential because any change of borders can affect security. The solution to the territorial dispute, therefore, requires arrangements that will enhance the security perceptions of both sides. The effects of the enlargement of the North Atlantic Treaty Organization extend beyond Europe and they may impinge on Russia-Japan relations. Agreement with the North Atlantic Treaty Organization can lead to different long-term consequences. The compromise may help long-term accommodation with the West, including Japan. Conversely, Russia may be trying to minimize its perceived losses by strengthening its relations with China.

The main lessons to be drawn from the fourth period of Russia-Japan relations are that democratic changes alone do not produce immediate, positive results. Ironically, Soviet rulers could have settled the territorial dispute without losing political control, but they did not want to compromise. Conversely, current Russian politicians may wish to reach a settlement, but they are too vulnerable.

Another lesson is that Russia sees relations with Japan in a broader context than the one in which Japan sees its relations with Russia. Both Russia and Japan are more concerned with their relations with the United States, Europe, and China. Thus, a solution to the territorial dispute with Japan must be seen not only in terms of Russia-Japan bilateral relations but also in the context of global stability and security and cooperation in Northeast Asia.

THE FIFTH PERIOD

In 1996 there were major changes in the high-ranking staff in charge of Russia's foreign affairs. This marked the second phase of Yeltsin's period in Russia-Japan relations, a period characterized by a new strategy of gradual but steady and consistent progress through concrete positive deeds. New Russian Foreign Minister Yevgeniy Primakov's visit to Japan in November 1996 was a successful demonstration of this strategy.

Among the achievements of this visit were a proposal for joint development of the disputed islands, an agreement on the enlargement of visa-free travel, and confirmation of the president's decision to reduce and finally withdraw Russian troops on the islands.

In general, the Japanese reaction to new Russian steps was positive. In January 1997, Japanese diplomats came up with a new concept, the multilayered approach to relations with Russia, to replace the previous concept of balanced expansion. The appointment of Alexander Panov as ambassador to Japan was well received. One of Panov's significant achievements was the first ever visit to Japan by a Russian minister of defense.

Japanese Minister of Foreign Affairs Ikeda put Japan's multilayered approach to practice during his visit to Russia in May 1997. During this visit, Japan and Russia agreed to replace the "7 plus 1" formula with a "G-8" composition, and they signed an agreement to open a Japanese consulate general branch office in Yuzhno-Sakhalinsk. This was a significant decision and a sign of Japanese flexibility, because, according to the Japanese interpretation of the San Francisco Peace Treaty, Sakhalin along with the Kurils does not have clearly defined sovereignty.

These positive developments paved the way for Prime Minister Hashimoto's informal visit to Krasnoyarsk City in eastern Russia on November 3–4, 1997, the first visit of this kind since October 1973, when Kakuei Tanaka met Brezhnev. The results surpassed the expectations even of the most optimistic observers. The Yeltsin-Hashimoto plan of economic cooperation was adopted. The leaders agreed to exert all efforts to conclude a peace treaty before the year 2000. The meeting was very friendly and constructive.

An immediate result of the Krasnoyarsk informal summit was the energetic support by Tokyo of the Russian application to the Asia-Pacific Economic Cooperation forum. Consultations on Russia's membership in the World Trade Organization are progressing as well. A joint committee on the problems of the peace treaty was established. The agreement on fishery in the area of the Russian territorial waters off the southern Kurils was signed in early 1998. This agreement may be a harbinger for future agreements on joint development and resource exploration of the disputed islands.

The diplomatic initiatives of 1996–98 demonstrated that Russia and Japan may be entering a fifth period in the history of their relations. Time will tell if this will be a different and dramatically positive new phase or if the two nations will continue the current transitional phase of dialogue, waiting for better political conditions or more difficult times.

NOTE

1.   In the "Secret Instructions to Admiral Putyatin by Nicholas I, 1853," Central Archive, St. Petersburg, unpublished.

II

INTERNATIONAL AND REGIONAL POLITICS

For almost a century the dramatic currents in the world and regional politics effectively kept Japan and Russia apart as adversarial powers. Mutual suspicions and mistrust were high, expectations and confidence low. These respective postures began to change only with the end of the Cold War and dissolution of the Soviet Union.

The new era of massive geostrategic repositioning involved first post-soviet Russia and the United States, major European powers, as well as China. Japan-Russia dialogue continued as usual for some time, but neither Japan nor Russia was able to withstand the new currents in global politics and regional relations.

The U.S. policy toward Moscow, its interests and involvement in Europe and Asia, and overall strategy with regard to democratic and economic changes in Russia and other post-soviet states have provided a general framework for both Russian and Japanese diplomats and politicians, sending them signals and words of encouragement and concern. Russia's new relations with the Group of Seven and significant involvement of the international financial institutions in the Russian economic transformation deepened Japan's involvement as well, at first more on a multilateral basis than through bilateral channels.

Economics was not a primary driving force in new developments in Moscow and Tokyo. Japan's primary interest in relations with China and rapid progress in Beijing-Moscow relations were the two main factors making Russia a more attractive partner for Tokyo, both in global and regional terms. Japan's wish to join the United Nations Security Council as a permanent member, Russia's wish to be more fully integrated into international economic arrangements, and both countries' concern over the situation in the Korean peninsula have served as incentives for dialogue and policy coordination.

The chapters included in Part II review these and other issues relevant to Japan-Russia bilateral relations, their foreign policies, and long-term strategies. This part opens with an excellent analysis of changes in U.S.–Japan and U.S.-Russia relations by Robert A. Scalapino. In the post–Cold War world the "only superpower's" global and regional policies and interests are centered on containing violence, promoting economic openness and market-oriented systems, and supporting political freedom. This chapter reflects the primacy of the Asia-Pacific region for the United States and indicates that Japan and China will continue to be critical in Washington assessments of U.S. interests in Northeast Asia, with marginal players to watch. A Russian foreign policy that is more closely linked with domestic needs and aimed at closer relations with China makes the United States more interested in building stronger links with Russia across the Pacific, but it also raises concern over a Moscow-Beijing link in a strategic partnership. However, recently new opportunities for U.S.-Russia relations opened up through multilateral institutions such as the Asia-Pacific Economic Cooperation and the Asian Regional Forum. This improves prospects for the emergence of a Northeast Asia security dialogue, one that could possibly evolve toward consensus on a range of important issues.

Jiro Kodera's main attention is on Japan's relations with Russia. It is an encouraging attempt to expose misunderstandings regarding Japan's official policy. This chapter clearly focuses on Japan's first and foremost intention to support Russia's reform. Its second priority is radical progress in bilateral relations by settling the territorial issue. This chapter reveals how Japan's approach to this issue has changed since 1992 and why Russia is now considered a partner in the Asia-Pacific region. Kodera explains that Russian reform complements Japan's national interests and that both countries have entered a new stage in relations that includes identifying shared interests, creating human networks, developing diversified bilateral relations, and expanding cooperation through the United Nations, the Group of Eight, and the Asia-Pacific Economic Cooperation.

Evgeniy V. Afanasiev and Vladimir I. Ivanov look at the regional situation and discuss Russia's role and interests in Northeast Asia. They also provide a brief account of Russian views on the United States, relations with China, and Japan. After 1992 Russia's role and interests in the region were downplayed by Russians and ignored by their key international partners. However, Russia's diplomatic posture in the region, political concerns, and economic priorities began to change, particularly after

Yevgeniy M. Primakov became foreign minister. Moscow's greater interest in East Asia is linked with the expansion of the North Atlantic Treaty Organization, Russia's virtual exclusion from multilateral dialogue on the Korean Peninsula, and the strategic importance of closer and mutually beneficial relations with China. The authors contend that the negative elements have been removed, significantly changed, or faded, and that the territorial dispute is no longer the main point of departure for bilateral discussions. Improvement in relations with Tokyo closely corresponds with Russia's prime attention to economic issues, the economic recovery of the Far Eastern provinces, and the new economic opportunities associated with closer relations with neighboring countries in Northeast Asia.

Tsuyoshi Hasegawa reviews Japan-Russia relations as well as U.S.–China-Japan-Russia relations in the context of Northeast Asia. He points out that unresolved problems, such as the Japan-Russia territorial dispute, fluid security perceptions, and the changing interests of the four major powers in Northeast Asia could derail the process of forging a stable international order in the region. The preferable strategic choice for all major powers in this region is to pursue omnidirectional friendliness. However, Hasegawa insists that as long as the Northern Territories issue remains unresolved, Japan will be unable to follow this policy line. In the case of China, a growing economic potential transformed into military power in combination with nationalism may pose a serious threat to the stability of the region. Hasegawa also believes that Russia is a nuclear superpower with sizable strategic force, and that the strategic competition with the United States may not be entirely over. This may have a continued effect on U.S.–Japan defense cooperation and the territorial dispute. He also sees Japan's policy toward the Northern Territories as ambiguous, preventing full fledged support for Russia. Hasegawa suggests that a change in priorities is needed and that by approaching Russia through the Pacific the United States can facilitate the creation of a regional system of stability, security, and cooperation.

Georgiy D. Toloraya tackles the issue of instability in the Korean Peninsula. The roots of conflict between the two Koreas have not been eliminated and the concentration of military power on the peninsula remains one of highest in the world. Toloraya believes that it is unlikely that the two sides will be able to resolve the conflict by themselves and that the constructive participation of external players, such as China, Russia, and Japan, in addition to the United States, will be important for crisis prevention and conflict resolution. Worsening economic conditions in North Korea and extreme food shortages have added a new dimension to the Korean standoff and created an unknown potential of instability both in North Korea and its posture vis-à-vis South Korea. South Korea's own economic crisis has suddenly weakened its ability to provide food to the North, thus eroding incentives for North Korean leaders to deal with

Seoul directly. However, Kim Dae Jung's administration has opted for a softer approach to the North and proposed a six-party formula in February 1998, opening the door for the participation of Russia and Japan in multilateral dialogue. Toloraya analyzes in detail Russia's views on the Korean situation and proposes a crisis prevention mechanism that includes Russia's active participation. He also proposes that Russia and Japan work together in monitoring uncertainty and enhancing stability in Northeast Asia.

Hajime Izumi also makes a proposal for Japan and Russia policy coordination. He writes that Japan and Russia should consider taking the initiative in food aid to North Korea provided that North Korea ensures transparency in the food supplies, embarks on agricultural reform, and provides guarantees to observe these conditions in the future. Japan and Russia may also call for a multilateral policy on food aid to North Korea and cooperate with South Korea and other countries in this endeavor. In the opinion of Izumi, even though Japan and Russia are showing a positive attitude toward food and humanitarian aid to North Korea, they should act more proactively and promptly to help avert a humanitarian disaster. The real issue, however, is that even with some hints of changes in North Korean diplomacy, the ability of Pyongyang to act consistently and constructively may be limited due to internal political constraints and a struggle for political power within ruling circles. The current status of the North Korean regime and its interlinkage with the food crisis are also analyzed.

Steven Rosefielde's chapter looks at the future regional power and geoeconomic equation both in global and regional terms. His chapter provides a thought-provoking outline of mega-trends in economic development of the Asia-Pacific region and the role of the United States as a main guarantor of economic prosperity and security. Rosefielde presents future prospects for five major systems: the United States, Japan, Europe, Russia, and China. He proposes a scenario in which the ranking of these systems may change particularly vis-à-vis Russia with its current deficiencies. Along with Russia, Japan and Europe are showing signs of an economic deceleration creating an anticipation of a relative decline compared with the United States and China. However, U.S. economic and military dominance could be called into question as well, considering not only its gradually flagging gross domestic product per capita growth but also its extreme inequality and social strife. These changes can lead to a reconfiguration of global power and China's rise to a dominant position in the Asia-Pacific region. Rosefielde wonders whether the losers will passively accept their declining role and winners will be content with their affluence.

Robert Valliant reviews in detail the main events of a new era in Japan-Russia bilateral relations. This chapter contains a year-by-year account of the main highlights between 1993 and 1998, including domestic developments and bilateral events. Valliant believes that both governments drifted in their policies toward each other. Japan continued to augment its economic aid to Russia, and toward the end of the decade the economic relationship has gradually come out of the sharp decline experienced in 1992–94. Political dialogue between Japan and Russia has moved ahead, including new areas such as military-to-military exchanges. Ryutaro Hashimoto's rise to power in 1996 and close contacts between Yevgeniy Primakov and Yukihiko Ikeda and later Keizo Obuchi paved the way to a major change in the format of bilateral discussions traditionally dominated by the territorial problem. The bilateral agenda rapidly expanded and mutual understanding and trust in diplomatic contacts positively affected the relationship at the top level. Contacts at the local level were developing as well, helping to move some economic projects. The Denver Group of Seven summit, Yeltsin-Hashimoto informal meetings in Krasnoyarsk and Kawana, and other important developments have helped to build a new type of relationship.

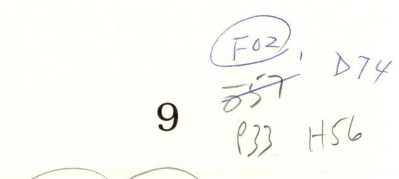

9

Japan, Russia, and the U.S. Role

Robert A. Scalapino

In the aftermath of the Cold War the foreign policies of the United States evoke three very different images. The first is that of a fire fighter, dashing out to quell brush and house fires when the alarm bell rings. The second is that of an accountant, totting up balance sheets and dunning delinquents for late payments, sometimes assessing heavy interest. The third is that of a missionary, intent upon saving souls and preaching to sometimes unreceptive audiences on the virtues of freedom and democracy.

U.S. FOREIGN POLICY PREMISES

For nearly a decade U.S. foreign policy has lacked a single overriding strategy. Perhaps such a strategy is neither possible nor necessary in this era. Putting the matter differently, one goal must be to contain violence, especially when it threatens order in a vital region or subregion of the world. The issues of whether, when, and how to intervene become critical.[1]

If it is perceived that U.S. national interests are immediately and vitally involved, a range of options can be considered, not excluding unilateral action. If national interests are involved in a less compelling manner, risk and cost sharing, whether through international organizations or existing alliance structures, is certain to be pursued.

To be sure, escape routes for those in peril can be fashioned, and economic sanctions applied against miscreants, but soft intervention of these types is not likely to be decisive in determining the outcome. Even when the decision is for soft intervention, the United States has repeatedly found itself confronting the task of seeking to create an effective ad hoc coalition attuned to the specific situation at hand. No truly effective peacemaking or peacekeeping organization exists at present, including the United Nations.

In recent years, the accountant role has generally been more appealing to U.S. leaders. In this role they can reach the American people quickly and often, with useful political effect. The U.S. story, put in simple terms, is one attractive at home: for decades after World War II, the United States, being a wealthy, global power, took the lead in rehabilitating the war-ravished societies of West Europe and East Asia, including former enemies. The combination of substantial economic assistance and largely open markets enabled the rise of such societies as Japan, and subsequently, the young tigers. Until recently, most Asian societies were showing great economic dynamism except for the few that stubbornly clung to autarkic policies. Yet our major Asian trading partners retain excessive protectionism and economic structures that preclude genuine competition. Their unfair practices wreak damage on the U.S. economy, producing extensive trade imbalances and totally inadequate protection of intellectual property rights.

The complete picture, of course, is more complex and includes U.S. faults and shortcomings, but in its basic outline, this is the U.S. story. In the United States it is a powerful story, because economics drive U.S. politics at present. Market-oriented economies have triumphed over socialism, but how do such economies, coming from different cultural heritages, at different stages of development, and employing different economic strategies, prosper together and peacefully coexist?

The acceptance of multilateralism in the economic sphere grows stronger. However, time is of the essence, and at this point, bilateralism is generally the more expeditious route. In no sphere are domestic and international politics so deeply intertwined as in the economic realm. This is an arena, moreover, in which the United States has considerable leverage. Its huge domestic market, its rising overseas investments, its technological prowess, and its influence on international financial agencies cannot be taken lightly. Clearly, there are risks involved in pursuing hard line economic diplomacy, and recent returns for the United States have been spotty. However, until and unless organizations like the Asia-Pacific Economic Cooperation (APEC) and the World Trade Organization (WTO) grow more effective in both rule-making and rule-enforcing, a strong element of bilateralism will remain in U.S. economic policy, and U.S. leaders will have to answer before Congress and the public as to the results.[2]

If national interests were the only consideration dominating U.S. foreign relations, perhaps priorities could be more easily established and maintained. However, from early times the American people have demanded that moral commitment be interwoven with national interest in creating and maintaining U.S. foreign policy. It is of course true that when national interest and moral commitment appeared to be in conflict, the former often prevailed.

The aforegoing analysis suggests that the strategy underwriting U.S. foreign policy today rests on three pillars: providing security and repelling violence in crucial global zones; promoting economic openness and market-oriented policies; and supporting maximum political freedom, with democracy the goal. This program confronts two basic challenges, one international and one domestic. Abroad, various countries at various times assert that the United States is interfering in their domestic affairs or seeking to implant its rules and values upon them, the region, or the world.[3]

The domestic challenge lies in the increasing concern of the American people with the problems of a post-modern society, problems that are often intensely local — education, crime, housing, and the family structure. Thus, isolationism in various forms has reappeared with substantial if far from majority support for the first time since World War II. With respect to the domestic challenge, it can be met only when U.S. leaders, including the president, convince the American people that an effective, goal-oriented foreign policy and the domestic well-being of the United States are inextricably interconnected. It is not logical to view foreign and domestic policy in an either-or framework, and it is the task of leadership to make that fact clear.

THE PRIMACY OF THE ASIA-PACIFIC REGION

It has long been commonplace to assert that the 21st century will be the Asian century, but it would be more accurate to define the region of primacy as Asia-Pacific. The vast ocean between East Asia and the western hemisphere contains resources that will be in ever greater demand in the years ahead. Moreover, although the power of the United States will decline in relative terms in coming years, it will remain a nation in which the combination of multiple strengths and fewer weaknesses than most rising powers will continue to provide it with regional power and influence.

The sources of power in the Asia-Pacific region lie first in the economic dynamism characteristic of the region, a dynamism that will continue, albeit with periodic crises such as are now occurring, and a declining rate of growth in most places. Further, economic developments have fostered the emergence of Natural Economic Territories (NETs) cutting across political boundaries.

In the social sphere, the heritage of cohesive nuclear units and effective community structures together with the high premium placed on education provide a basis for uniting stability and development. Political stability will be relatively strong for most of the region. With some exceptions, the political effect of both secular ideology and religion has been moderated in this region, thus reducing the type of conflict endemic in our late 20th century world.

It would be very misleading, however, to rest with a recitation of the strengths of the Asia-Pacific region. A number of formidable weaknesses or challenges also exist. Crony capitalism has to go, with sounder financial-banking policies and reduced corruption. Markets must be opened and competition, both at home and from external sources, must be allowed.

Serious demographic issues also lie ahead. The population-resource ratio, already under strain, will grow much more severe in the decades ahead. A combination of rising living standards and increasing populations will make energy and food foremost issues, likely to engender crises both within societies and among them.[4]

Environmental degradation will also be a mounting problem and another issue that will demand far greater interstate cooperation than currently exists. In addition, for some societies such as Japan, the rapid aging of the population will require major adjustments of a difficult nature. Migration flows, especially within states like China, will create the type of social problems associated with rapid urbanization. When these flows spill over national borders, both intensified domestic reactions and interstate crises are likely.

In the strategic realm, it seems likely that in the name of military modernization, virtually all Asia-Pacific nations will continue to upgrade their military capacities after brief delays caused by budgetary constraints. Arms sales will be a valued source of exports for nations like the United States, Russia, and China, further stimulating arms expansion.

In the meantime, territorial issues will remain unresolved, including those of divided states. Although the boundary issues between Russia and China, and China and India have been reduced to negligible proportions, such issues as China-Taiwan and North–South Korea promise no immediate solution. Such issues are connected with a much broader, more complex issue, relating to history and the legacy of lost empires. Each of the major Asian-Pacific nations had de jure or de facto control over a much larger territory in the not distant past, and the memory of that fact remains.

Accompanying the above issues is an overarching political condition of great consequence. Three different political systems now exist in the region — Leninist, authoritarian-pluralist, and democratic.[5] This may well continue, although there are signs that Leninism is faltering, with societies like China and Vietnam slipping into the authoritarian-pluralist category. In any case, however, with the appeal of ideology having declined, it no longer represents the rigid barrier to contact that was true a few decades ago. However, we are witnessing a new phenomena, namely, the simultaneous intensification of internationalism, nationalism, and communalism.

To some extent, nationalism represents a substitute for the declining appeal of ideology. Note the degree to which it has swept over societies like China and North Korea, virtually removing the internationalism of Marxism-Leninism in the effort to make the prevailing system "Chinese" or "Korean." Nationalism has also risen in such non-socialist countries as South Korea, Japan, Russia, and the United States. It is ironic that at a time when nation-state sovereignty must be melded with the requirements of multilateral economic and security agreements and institutions, the call is made in certain quarters for the maintenance of state sovereignty in absolute terms.[6]

Meanwhile, another equally significant trend is underway, namely, the reversion of authority to the subregion and community. When the rapidity of change threatens each individual's moorings, the search for identity often takes localist or special community directions, sometimes in the form of stronger affiliation with one's ethnic group, religious community, or subregional culture. Thus, the nation-state must adjust not only to the rise of regionalism and internationalism above it, but to a variety of subnational appeals below it.

JAPAN AND THE UNITED STATES: NATURAL PARTNERS?

Against the broad canvas set forth above, how do two key Asia-Pacific actors — Japan and Russia — fit into the U.S. vision of the future, and, in turn, how do they view their relationship with the United States? Let us commence with Japan. Despite the physical devastation of Japan in 1945, this nation did not start from ground zero in its upward climb. It had earlier become the first industrial Asian nation, and it had had extensive experience with state-managed, market-oriented economic policies. Japan also had a highly educated people and a civil bureaucracy. Nonetheless, the initial assistance of the United States was of great importance, as aid giver, market, and sponsor on the international stage. Within three decades Japan had begun to show its economic prowess, and by the 1980s it had evolved from aid recipient to strong competitor with the United States.

The Japanese system was based upon close interaction between the government and large-scale business, with a cluster of government-supported enterprises holding extensive market share, especially in financial services and public works. In effect, the Ministry of International Trade and Industry and the Ministry of Finance were a part of the economic planning and production process, with resources and income distribution heavily government-controlled. The *keiretsu* system whereby sub-contractors were tied permanently to primary producers, the deep cross-penetration of corporate funding, and lifetime employment further solidified the system. This system effactually precluded genuine market-based competition or the entry of foreign investment. Thus, surpluses in trade balances mounted. Combined with a high savings rate and low interest charges, capital was extensively available. The Japanese miracle was based on this system, and it was widely heralded as a model for other developing Asian societies.[7] Viewed from the United States, Japan stood ten feet tall, and thus represented a threat, very different from that previously posed by Russia, but aimed at the vital center of the United States: its economy.

The Structural Impediment Initiative talks that were conducted between the United States and Japan during the Bush administration enabled both sides to present their views: Americans insisted that broad market-opening measures via the removal of both tariff and non-tariff barriers by Japan were essential. The Japanese urged that the U.S. savings rate be improved, the budget deficit tackled, and U.S. industry concentrate upon becoming more competitive. There followed intensive bilateral negotiations during the opening years of the Clinton administration.

During this period the appropriate relationship between the economic and security aspects of the U.S.–Japan relationship was widely discussed and debated on both sides of the Pacific. Some argued that these two elements could and should be separated, because they spoke to different aspects of national interests. The economic issues, moreover, were primarily bilateral in character, whereas the security issues were regional and even global in their implications. Others insisted that sooner or later, unresolved economic issues would inevitably affect the degree of trust and bonding necessary for a meaningful security relationship. As this debate continued, the economic picture changed. Japan entered a prolonged recession, with growth rates dropping sharply, unemployment rising, and a serious banking crisis because of the mountainous bad loans, primarily based on over-inflated property. Japan became testimony to the fact that no economic strategy is appropriate for all times.

As a result the internal pressure for fundamental reforms including deregulation, the restructuring of the financial system, and greater flexibility in all aspects of the industrial structure grew. The business community, the media, and even elements within the government, such as the Ministry of International Trade and Industry, increasingly spoke of the indispensable need for change if Japan were to remain competitive.[8]

As the Japanese recession lengthened and various challenges made themselves felt, the U.S. attitude toward Japan was affected. Japan was no longer the seemingly invincible giant that threatened the U.S. economy. The positive aspects of the U.S.–Japan economic relationship received more attention. Meanwhile, the U.S. public and private sectors had begun to face up to those aspects of the U.S. economy that were threatening the domestic and global picture. Belatedly, the budget deficit became a central issue in Washington, with pledges for a reduction timetable enacted by the Congress. Moreover, U.S. industry, not without some painful measures, took steps to become more competitive.

As these developments in Japan and the United States were unfolding, a new agency, the WTO, emerged to replace the General Agreement on Tariffs and Trade, and the APEC forum acquired stronger foundations, with the goal an open trading system for the entire Asia-Pacific region by the year 2020. A new premium was thus placed upon using multilateral channels in trade disputes.

The future picture for both economies is disputed. Bolstered by a weakening yen, low interest rates, and stimulus measures, the Japanese economy achieved some growth in 1996 but stagnated in 1997. Pessimists point to the loss of momentum of corporate profits, the high federal budget deficit (steepest percentage-wise among developed nations), and the 3.3 percent unemployment (steep by Japanese standards).[9] Hashimoto has pledged that a far-reaching reform of the Japanese financial system will be in effect by 2001 to increase the competitiveness of Japan's financial and capital markets, and that throughout the economy, deregulation measures will promote incentives to innovate, with domestic producers competing for state-of-the-art technology. Many observers are skeptical, noting the strongly entrenched bureaucratic opponents of reform and other obstacles.

Looking ahead, Japan faces certain formidable problems. By the year 2015, one in four Japanese will be 65 or older. The work force, it is estimated, will drop by 4.6 million; thus, it will be necessary to use human resources more efficiently. The greater problem, however, will lie in the heavy burden of taxation and the social security costs of an aging society.

The gravity of the problem for the U.S. economy in the future does not appear to be as serious. Yet the challenges are not easy. To maintain and advance its economy, the United States must raise the low savings and capital formation rates, sustain balanced budgets, and rectify the educational system at the primary and secondary levels, while making available substantial funds from both public and private sectors for research and development so as to remain foremost in the technological sphere. Moreover, U.S. society is also scheduled to age, albeit at a somewhat lower rate than Japan, and reform of the social security and welfare systems is imperative.

Given the Asian currency depreciations, the United States will continue to run high trade deficits with Asia for the foreseeable future and can be expected to insist upon greater market openness, the monitoring of agreements already reached, stricter enforcement of intellectual property rights, and appropriate measures to curb dumping. The concentration, however, will no longer be on Japan. A wide range of countries will be involved: South Korea, Taiwan, Thailand, and above all, China.

It is too early to predict with certainty the future course of U.S.–Japan economic relations, but there are reasons to worry about the near term. Despite extensive pressure from the United States and others, the Hashimoto government has refrained from taking bold measures to stimulate the domestic market. If it seeks to export its way out of the current malaise, trouble with the United States and others lies ahead. One must hope that the reform measures earlier pledged are sustained and strengthened, and that Japan and the United States accept responsibility for assisting less developed Asian nations to move forward. It seems virtually certain that both countries will become increasingly involved in the regional Asia-Pacific economy, with Japan setting the pace.[10] One may anticipate a Sea of Japan (Eastern Sea) NET and closer interaction with Sakhalin, especially in terms of its gas deposits. The continued flow of Japanese investment abroad, especially in Asia, can also be forecast. In sum, Japan will remain a major economic actor in the Asia-Pacific region despite, or perhaps more accurately, because of domestic transformation.

The United States is also scheduled to internationalize, with both the North American Free Trade Agreement and APEC as symbols of the future. The United States is a prime investor at present in China, and U.S. enterprises are showing increased interest in some of the countries of the Association of Southeast Asian Nations. A portion of the Asian community in the western United States is building economic ties with the region, and correspondingly, the flow of Asian investment into the United States shows no signs of declining.

In this setting and with unexpected as well as anticipated changes likely, regularized economic dialogues between the United States and Japan on economic issues should be inaugurated or strengthened. Either separately or in some combined form, these must include business representatives and economists as well as government personnel. General forecasts for both economies should be carefully analyzed with appropriate actions reviewed. Reports on governmental and private sector initiatives should be presented with various alternatives discussed. Interaction with APEC and the WTO should be made a part of the agenda.

Turning to the political and security realms, the United States and Japan have numerous common interests and certain common problems. In recent times, the two nations have displayed the difficulties engendered by rapid modernization: money politics and corruption in official circles; public cynicism or indifference to politics; the greatly increased employment of hype by the media to attract an audience; the adverse balance of rewards and punishments for public life, and the resultant shrinking pool of top talent willing to make politics a career.

Neither society faces a regime-threatening situation, but Japan in particular is in a transitional period in terms of party politics.[11] Will it return to the old one-and-one-half party system when one party was always in power, the others always in the opposition? Or will a two party system eventuate? Or a continuance of coalition politics, with accompanying weakness?

In the United States also, party loyalties on the part of the citizenry are less firm, as recent elections have indicated. The trend is toward centrism, but without clear programs that anticipate the changes that the 21st century will bring. Under these circumstances, the United States and Japan should engage first in some in-depth, continuous joint studies at the non-official level on the issues and challenges confronting modern democracies. At the same time strategies relating to human rights in the international arena should be regularly reviewed, with coordination sought.

The United States should support the admission of Japan and Germany as permanent members of the United Nations Security Council. In addition, Japan should be encouraged to take an active role in Asia-Pacific relations. In the recent past, Sino-Japanese relations have been delicate, although improvements may be en route. Beijing has criticized Tokyo for a variety of reasons: the Daiyu (Senkaku) Island controversy; the Yasukuni Shrine issue, and more generally, the perceived reluctance of Japan to apologize for wartime actions; the upsurge of ultra-nationalist activities and supposed signs of renewed Japanese militarism.[12]

Thus far, Japan's response to these criticisms has been moderate and low key. Japanese investment in China continues on the upsurge and loans have been resumed with relaxed conditions. In addition, on February 4, 1998, Japan and China agreed to strengthen bilateral defense exchanges, including top-level visits between defense officials as well as naval vessels.

In the recent past, some Japanese have worried that the United States is shifting its primary attention to China and without sufficient consultation moving in such a fashion as to make this bilateral relation the key to its Asian policies. In reality, however, the Sino-American relation is destined always to be complex, with elements of cooperation matched by those of difference edged with wariness. Similarly, fear in certain quarters of a Sino-Japanese entente is without foundation. Intrinsic to this relationship is a strong element of competition, sharpened and made more negative by the history of the past century. Thus, as has been pointed out by several observers, the U.S.–Japan–China triangle is likely to be isosceles and not equilateral, with the United States and Japan the closer partners. However, both the United States and Japan have a great stake in a China that is deeply engaged with the rest of the Asia-Pacific region, increasingly interdependent economically, and playing an important role in fashioning regional economic and peace-keeping institutions. Hence, their policies should be directed toward that end.

Relations between Japan and Russia have recently taken an upturn. An improvement in Japan-Russia relations can only be of benefit to the region as a whole, not only in economic but in security terms. The United States should encourage Japanese assistance to such projects as the Tumen River Delta Program and to the economic revival of the Russian Far East.

Meanwhile, the basic issues of U.S.–Japan security relations and Japan's future security policies have assumed enhanced importance in recent times, highlighted by the Clinton-Hashimoto communiqué of April 1996 calling for a review of the earlier guidelines for Japanese security policy. This announcement provoked China to wrath, with the allegation that it was being made the enemy and that Japanese military activities were scheduled for extensive expansion. These charges were swiftly denied in both Washington and Tokyo.

The complexity of the situation lies in the fact that Japan is inhibited by its U.S.-sponsored constitution from the type of full-fledged military activities available to other powers. By successive reinterpretations of Article 9 of that constitution, a Self Defense Force of some 160,000 has been declared constitutional, and that force has undertaken a variety of functions. The restrictions upon the Self Defense Force, however, make it impossible for Japan to be a full-fledged military ally of the United States, and its response to a range of possible crises — from another Korean conflagration to an explosion in China-Taiwan relations — remains unclear. Many Japanese and a larger number of other Asians support the U.S. defense treaty as an umbrella over Japan, and one that produces relatively minimal risks and prevents high posture Japanese military policies in the region.[13]

The dilemma for the United States is clear. It, too, wants to keep Japan non-nuclear and within a cooperative security framework. Japan's military budget is not negligible, and it covers approximately 70 percent of the costs of the U.S. occupation forces. Its current commitment is to a smaller but more modern military force of some 150,000, equipped with the highest grade weaponry. Reportedly, it is also prepared to undertake joint research with the United States on a ballistic missile defense program. Yet the burden of serving as guarantor of peace in Asia-Pacific falls heavily upon the United States.

Is there a growing disposition among Japanese to consider revision of the constitution to enable Japan to become a normal nation? The issue of constitutional revision is obviously one for the Japanese people to determine. If military modernization programs continue throughout Asia, as seems likely, the external reach of a number of countries will be lengthened, and arms control made more difficult. In a context where certain crucial territorial issues remain unresolved, dangers may well be heightened. Current indications are that although sentiment in favor of constitutional revision may have garnered some additional support, it is far from majority opinion at present. Only a combination of two events — a greatly increased perception of threat and a U.S. strategic withdrawal from the region — would be likely to produce a rapid shift in Japanese public opinion.

It is essential, therefore, that the United States retain its security commitments in Asia-Pacific, specifically to Japan and the Republic of Korea.[14] Technological changes in modern warfare, however, make possible modifications in past security policies.[15] It is premature to withdraw all U.S. personnel from Asian bases, and total withdrawal may never be wise in some instances. The type of problem engendered by the overuse of Okinawa can be avoided in the future without jeopardizing the security commitment.

One possibility that would be satisfying to both the United States and Japan would be the emergence of a Northeast Asia security dialogue, one that could possibly evolve toward consensus on a range of issues, such as greater transparency with respect to defense policies; regulations regarding arms sales; enhanced safety measures, including those relating to nuclear materials storage; a nuclear-free zone; and arms reduction. By contributing its expertise and its funds to such programs, Japan would be playing the type of role for which it is ideally suited.

It is possible to be optimistic about the future of U.S.–Japan relations. Our alliance is not only crucial for our two countries, but for the region of which we are both a critical part. Moreover, despite occasional signs to the contrary, this fact is recognized by virtually every Asia-Pacific nation. It is natural for U.S.–Japan relations to evolve with the times, including changes in the two societies. On balance, however, the gradual shift from clientism to partnership will give the relationship stronger foundations. The task remains to build more knowledge and understanding into our relationship, thereby providing a firmer psychological-political foundation for our extensive mutual interests.

Meanwhile, each nation faces an overarching challenge in the foreign policy realm. The supreme challenge for Japan lies in the fact that it has remained basically an inward-looking, introverted, homogeneous society while economic and security trends project it ever more intensely onto the international stage. For the United States, the central challenge lies in remaining internationalist and managing enormously complex domestic issues without reverting to an isolationist past that would be wholly anachronistic in our times.

THE UNITED STATES AND RUSSIA: OPPORTUNITIES AND UNCERTAINTIES

On the perimeters of the Asia-Pacific region lies another major society, with its eastern section forming a part of Northeast Asia. The Russian Federation continues to go through its second massive revolution in this century. The partially unwilling initiator of this revolution was Mikhail Gorbachev, whose desire was to reform socialism, not overturn it. He lost control of events, however, and in the aftermath of his departure from power, a turn toward liberalism and looking West ensued. Under individuals like Deputy Prime Minister Yegor Gaidar, the effort was undertaken to create a market economy rapidly. In this period (roughly 1991–92) U.S. influence was extensive, and momentous changes in the direction of deregulation and privatization took place.

In retrospect, many observers argue that the actions of this period took insufficient account of the capacities of the Russian economy, attempting too much, too soon, without adequate preparations. In any case, mountainous inflation, precipitous production declines, serious unemployment, and other manifestations of an economic disaster unfolded. Corruption was rampant and the activities of Mafia bands widespread, with a huge second economy emerging upon which most Russians depended.[16]

Naturally, these developments had a political impact. Spokesman for the Left in the person of Communist leader Gennadiy Zyuganov and for the Right in Vladimir Zhirinovskiy arose to challenge the Yelstin administration. In general, moreover, two broad trends could be observed: First, a retreat from the extensive emphasis on westernization took place, with increased attention to relations within the Commonwealth of Independent States and with the East. Accompanying this was a resurgence of nationalism, a call to appreciate Russia's history, culture, and contributions to the world. As the 21st century approached, future leadership and the institutional structure remained uncertain.[17]

In its policies toward Russia in the recent past, the United States has had several cardinal objectives: to support Russian democracy and a market-based economy, capitalist in nature; to seek strategic agreements that would reduce weapons of mass destruction by both parties; and to bring Russia into harmonious relations with its neighbors and active participation in the international community.[18]

Whether U.S. policies have always been conducive to these objectives, however, can be debated. On the economic front, although the United States has supported assistance to Russia through the World Bank and the Group of Seven, U.S.-Russia trade and investment are restrained by a lack of legislative support for extensive investment in the oil sector, concern about protection of intellectual property rights, and a host of other problems.

In any case, the economic situation in Russia dampens the enthusiasm of most U.S. investors. The bureaucracy remains extremely powerful and heavily corrupt. Old managers of the state-owned enterprises have no new ideas, and have frequently ended up the beneficiaries of the privatization program. The legal system remains fragile and incomplete. On a structural level, the traditional relationship between the center and the regions is largely defunct, but intra-regional relations are weak, and key regions like the Russian Far East have had enormous problems in seeking economic rehabilitation.[19] There are some bright spots. Inflation, once running at more than 2,000 percent per annum, has been reduced to 10 percent. More than 70 percent of Russia's old state enterprises are now privately owned. Trade is rapidly rising. Perhaps most importantly, sufficient change has taken place to preclude a return to the old economic order.

Generally speaking, however, the United States remains peripheral to the Russian economy except in a few select fields. The crucial bilateral relationship lies in the strategic realm, and here progress is currently stalled. As 1997 closed, the State Duma had refused to ratify the Strategic Armaments Reduction Treaty signed by Bush and Yeltsin in January 1993 and ratified by the U.S. Senate in January 1996. Further, in the autumn of 1996, the two countries failed to reach an agreement on appropriate regional missile defenses, required if an anti-ballistic missile treaty is to be effectuated.

One critical issue that emerged was the expansion of the North Atlantic Treaty Organization (NATO).[20] All NATO members supported such action, with Hungary, Poland, and the Czech Republic leading initial candidates. The move had bipartisan support in the United States, making its achievement virtually certain. As might have been expected, sentiment among Russian leaders, including Yelstin, was strongly negative. At the end of 1996, Defense Minister Igor Rodionov, rejecting the invitation to exchange military liaison officers with NATO, warned that enlarging the Atlantic alliance eastward could return Europe to the "bad old days" of the Cold War, forcing Russia to take "certain appropriate actions."[21]

Not all Western observers were favorable to NATO expansion. It was argued that the move was certain to have a destabilizing effect on European security and especially on U.S.-Russia relations. Whatever accommodation it ultimately made, Russia would eventually be more rather than less prone to adopt a protective, big power policy toward those countries on its western borders. The NATO aim, in which the U.S. government concurred, was to work with Moscow in negotiating a document spelling out Russia's relations with NATO in such a fashion as to encourage a cooperative rather than antagonistic relationship. Such a charter was concluded in 1997, at the same time as the formal NATO expansion took place. However, skeptics assert that sooner or later, a redivided

Europe will result in the type of big power rivalries reflective of the earlier 20th century. Russian nationalism in its more xenophobic and anti-Western manifestations has been given additional strength, they argue, and the process of democratization made more difficult.

This debate will continue, with no determination of the accurate appraisal possible in the near term. Meanwhile, however, a more extensive Russian foreign policy is emerging, directed by Foreign Minister Yevgeniy Primakov. The broad objectives are these: to make foreign policy a source of support for domestic needs, economic and security; to pursue an omnidirectional course, with improved relations especially in the Middle East and East Asia; to avoid any alliance, but to reassert Russia's status as a major power, fully prepared to participate in global councils with a strong voice.[22]

Thus, Russia has been actively expanding its relations with the newly independent Transcaucasus states and also strengthening its ties with Iran, Iraq, and Libya. At the same time it has been making major efforts to improve its relations with the key nations of East Asia, especially those in Northeast Asia.[23] The greatest strides have been made recently in Russia-China relations. At the time of the visit of Prime Minister Li Peng to Moscow at the end of 1996, Yeltsin called for the establishment of "a strategic partnership" between the two nations that would help "create a multi-polar world."[24] Were these words aimed at the United States? Russia indicated that it might furnish China with several nuclear power units. Yeltsin asserted that the two countries could cooperate in energy, manufacturing, space, transport, and military technology. The goal is to reach $20 billion in bilateral trade by the year 2000.

Russia is currently the largest arms supplier to China. Moreover, the border demarcation was essentially completed in 1997, and agreement on border troop reduction was reached, aided by frequent summit meetings. Few seasoned experts, however, fear a return to a China-Russia alliance of the type that existed briefly after 1945. The ideological glue is gone, together with the sense of isolation from the capitalist world. Perhaps both Russia and China will benefit in bargaining with the United States by showing that there are other partners with whom to dance, but intimacy is not in prospect.

With the other major power in the region, gains have also been made, albeit of a less far-reaching nature. Primakov's November 1996 visit to Japan resulted in a Russian proposal for joint development of the disputed Northern Territories (South Kurils), and as 1998 opened the prospects for joint development seemed good.[25] Separately, a U.S. $10 billion joint oil development agreement relating to Sakhalin and vicinity has been reached. Further, in late February 1998, at a meeting with Yelstin in Moscow, Foreign Minister Obuchi expressed Japan's readiness to provide Russia with $1.5 billion in loans from the Export-Import Bank of Japan.

Earlier, in their meeting at Krasnoyarsk in November 1997, Hashimoto and Yelstin agreed to conclude a peace treaty by the year 2000, based on the 1993 Tokyo Declaration, and preliminary discussions have begun.

An effort to establish a genuine two-Korea policy is also underway. The Russians hope to remedy the extremely low level to which relations with the North fell after 1990, but without sacrificing their growing economic and cultural relations with the South. Similarly, although prizing the improved relations with China, at the close of 1996 a Russian office was set up in Taipei, staffed by a retired foreign service officer. In addition, Russia has become a participant in APEC as well as the Asian Regional Forum and has proposed the creation of a Northeast Asia security structure. In sum, after a period of low posture, Moscow is gradually returning to the status of major power in the Asia-Pacific region and on the international stage.

In general, the expanded Russian foreign policy should receive U.S. support. The United States wants peace and prosperity in East Asia, and to obtain these conditions a cooperative, participating Russia is essential. Further, that portion of Russia known as the Russian Far East has every reason to interact with the nations around the Sea of Japan (East Sea) as a part of a vital NET that could benefit all participants.

Although various challenges remain to be overcome, the long-term future of Russia, as indicated, is one of reemergence to major power status. Moreover, Russia — like the United States — will have an interest in both Europe and Asia. Given the enormous importance of oil, its attention, like that of the United States, will be directed to the Middle East as well. In sum, a combination of geopolitics and economic capacity dictate that the United States and Russia will retain a global perspective. This fact argues strongly for a multifaceted U.S.-Russia relationship far more sensitive to each other's needs than has recently been the case. The U.S.-Russia relationship will be a crucial variable in determining the future international course of both nations and of the world at large.

Japan and Russia together with China are the key nations of the 21st century for the United States. In each case, close bilateral relations will be required to resolve or contain specific issues. The closest security relationship will continue to be with Japan. One hopes that both Japan and Russia will retain an open political system broadly compatible with that of the United States and conducive to an exchange of views on how to strengthen the democratic system. As China moves further away from Leninism and into an authoritarian-pluralist phase, the ideological component will be further reduced on that front as well. For each of these countries, however, nationalism will replace the old ideological barrier as the force to be watched.

Thus, the internationalist component in our mutual relations must be assiduously cultivated at both the regional and global levels.

Multilateralism does not hold all the answers to problems, present and future, but it must be strengthened if we are to live up to the challenges of the 21st century.[26]

NOTES

1.   Recent perceptive analyses of the international environment and U.S. interests are contained in Desmond Ball (ed.), *The Transformation of Security in The Asia/Pacific Region.* (London: Frank Cass, 1996); Han Sung-Joo (ed.), *The New International System — Regional & Global Dimensions.* (Seoul: Ilmin International Relations Institute, 1996); Young Whan Kihl and Peter Hayes (eds.), *Peace and Security in Northeast Asia — The Nuclear Issue and the Korean Peninsula.* (Armonk, N.Y.: M. E. Sharpe, 1996); Kent E. Calder, *Pacific Defense — Arms, Energy, and America's Future in Asia.* (New York: William Morrow, 1996). For articles expressing diverse views, see Robert A. Manning and Paula Stern, "The Myth of a Pacific Community," *Foreign Affairs,* Nov/Dec 1994; Yoichi Funabashi, "The Asianization of Asia," *Foreign Affairs,* Nov/Dec 1993; Harry Harding, "Asia Policy to the Brink," *Foreign Policy,* Fall 1994, pp. 57–74; David Shambaugh, "Growing Strong: China's Challenge to Asian Security," *Survival,* Summer 1994; Robert A. Scalapino, "The U.S. and Asia: Future Prospects," *Foreign Affairs,* Winter 1991/92.

2.   For different views on the economic dimension of Asia-Pacific relations and the economic dimension of U.S. policy toward the region, see *Prospects for International Cooperation in Northeast Asia — Economic Issues.* (New York: The Asia Society 1995); Dwight Perkins, Andrew MacIntyre, and Geza Feketekuty, "Trade, Security, and National Strategy in the Asia Pacific," *NBR Analysis,* 7(3) (1996); Jane Khanna, "Asia-Pacific Economic Cooperation and Challenges for Political Leadership," *Washington Quarterly,* 19 (Winter 1996): 257–75. A discussion of the economic issue in recent U.S.–Japan relations is Kurt W. Tong, "Revolutionizing America's Japan Policy," *Foreign Policy,* (Winter 1996–97): 107–24.

3.   China has been especially vehement in denouncing U.S. interference. Foreign Minister Qian Qichen in his statement to the UN General Assembly on September 25, 1996, outlined the usual Chinese charges as follows: "the Cold War mentality still dies hard and hegemonism has repeatedly raised its ugly head. Interference in other countries' internal affairs under various pretexts and indulgence in sanctions-wielding or even the use of force are trampling on the purposes and principles of the UN Charter and all accepted norms of international relations, thereby threatening and undermining world peace and stability." *Embassy of the People's Republic of China Press Release,* Washington, D.C., no. 1, September 26, p. 2.

4.   See *Toward a Pacific Rim Food System — Forum on U.S. Agriculture and Food Trade Policy in APEC.* (Seattle: Washington State University, National Center for APEC, 1996).

5.   Robert Scalapino sought to analyze these political systems in *The Politics of Development — Perspectives on Twentieth Century Asia.* (Cambridge, Mass.: Harvard University Press, 1989).

6.   See Jane Khanna and Chang-Jae Lee (eds.), *Economic Interdependence and Challenges to the Nation-State — Economic Cooperation in the Yellow Sea Rim.* (Seoul:

The Korea Institute for International Economic Policy, 1996). For an example of a traditionalist view, see Qian Wenrong, "United Nations and State Sovereignty in Post-Cold War Era," *Foreign Affairs Journal*, 42 (December 1996): 1–10.

7.   See E. F. Denison and W. K. Chung, *How Japan's Economy Grew So Fast: The Sources of Post-War Expansion*. (Washington D.C.: The Brookings Institution, 1976); Hugh Patrick and Henry Rosovsky (eds.), *Asia's New Giant: How the Japanese Economy Works*. (Washington, D.C.: The Brookings Institution, 1976); K. Yamamura, *Economic Policy in Postwar Japan*. (Berkeley: University of California Press, 1967). For more recent works, see Tokue Shibata (ed.), *Japan's Public Sector — How the Government is Financed*. (Tokyo: University of Tokyo Press, 1993); Shigeto Tsuru, *Japan's Capitalism: Creative Defeat and Beyond*. (Cambridge: Cambridge University Press, 1993); Edward Lincoln, *Japan Facing Economic Maturity*. (Washington, D.C.: The Brookings Institution, 1988); Richard J. Samuels, *The Business of the Japanese State*. (Ithaca, N.Y.: Cornell University Press, 1987); Hugh Patrick (ed.), *Japan's High Technology Industries — Lessons and Limitations of Industrial Policy*. (Tokyo: University of Tokyo Press, 1986).

8.   See Atsushi Suemura, "Japan Inc. Needs To Adapt to True Market," *Nikkei Weekly*, November 25, 1996, p. 6; Haruo Shimada, "For Economy to Work, Labor Rules Must Be Reformed," *Nikkei Weekly*, November 11, 1996, p. 7; Kazuhito Ikeo, "Japan Needs User-Friendly Financial System — Fast," *Nikkei Weekly*, November 8, 1996, p. 7.

9.   One of many gloomy reports of the Japanese economy was Takahiko Ueda, "Analysts Pessimistic about the Economy," *Japan Times Weekly* (International edition), September 23–29, 1996, p. 14. For the potential short-term adverse effects of the "Japanese Big Bang," namely, the reforms projected by the Hashimoto government, see "Japanese Stock Plunge Signals Painful Fallout of Deregulation Trend," *The Wall Street Journal*, January 10, 1997, pp. A1, A5.

10.   See Yoichi Funabashi (ed.), *Japan's International Agenda*. (New York: New York University Press, 1994); Richard D. Leitch, Jr., Akira Kato, and Martin E. Weinsten, *Japan's Role in the Post-Cold War World*. (Westport, Conn.: Greenwood, 1995); Peter F. Cowhey and Mathew D. McCubbins, *Structure and Policy in Japan and the United States*. (New York: Cambridge University Press, 1995).

11.   An interesting analysis of contemporary Japanese politics is found in Ichiro Uchida, "What Does the Result of the General Election Mean?" 1996, unpublished.

12.   A sampling of recent Chinese press comments is as follows: Lu Naicheng, "U.S., Japan Create Instability," *China Daily*, October 2, 1996, p. 4; Xiao Lu and Da Shan, "Japan Urged To Value Trade Ties," *China Daily Supplement*, November 11, 1996, p. 1; Zhu Jian Rong, "Leave the Senkakus Alone," *Japan Times Weekly* (International edition), December 2–4, 1996, pp. 10–11.

13.   For Japan's current defense program and various views concerning the future, see *Japan's New Defense Policy*. (Tokyo: Japan Defense Agency, 1996); *A New Era in Defense — Compact, Effective, Flexible*. (Tokyo: Boeicho/Jieitai, 1996); Michael Armacost, *Friends or Rivals, The Insider's Account of U.S.-Japan Relations*. (New York: Columbia University Press, 1996); Andrew K. Hanami, *The Military Might of Modern Japan*. (Dubuque, Ia.: Kendall/Hunt, 1995); Richard L. Armitage, "Modernizing the U.S.-Japan Security Relationship," *Tokyo Report*, 21(10) (November 1996); Kumao Kaneko, "Japan Needs No Umbrella," *Bulletin of the Atomic*

Scientists, (March/April 1996): 46–51; Ryukichi Imai, "Japan's Nuclear Policy: Retrospect on the Immediate Past, Perspectives on the Twenty-First Century," IIPS Policy Paper 169E, November 1996 (Tokyo: International Institute for Policy Studies); Toshiharu Kato, "East Asia as a New Hanseatic League — Japan's Strategy," 1996, unpublished.

14.   For two perspectives on U.S. strategic policies, see Andrew J. Goodpaster, "When Diplomacy is Not Enough — Managing Multinational Military Interventions," a report to the Carnegie Commission on Preventing Deadly Conflict, New York, Carnegie Corporation, July 1996; Ralph A. Cossa, "The Major Powers in Northeast Asian Security," McNair Paper 51. (Washington, D.C., National Defense University, 1996).

15.   For an analysis emphasizing the role of technology in the reshaping of U.S. strategy, with particular stress on improved information systems, see Brian R. Sullivan, "The Reshaping of the US Armed Forces: Present and Future Implications for Northeast Asia," *Korean Journal of Defense Analysis*, 8(1) (Summer 1996): 129–52.

16.   For one view of recent development in the Russian economy, see Clifford G. Gaddy, *The Price of the Past — Russia's Struggle with the Legacy of a Militarized Economy*. (Washington, D.C.: The Brookings Institution, 1996).

17.   One perspective on the Russian political scene at the outset of 1997 is David Remnick, "Can Russia Change?" *Foreign Affairs*, (January/February 1997): 35–49.

18.   An insightful article on U.S.-Russia relations is Alvin Z. Rubinstein, "Agenda 2000 — America's Stake in Russia Today," *Orbis*, (Winter 1997): 31–38.

19.   At an informal roundtable under the auspices of the Asia Foundation for Governor Victor I. Ishayev of the Khabarovskiy Krai in San Francisco, January 10, 1997, points were made that the Russian Far East constitutes 40 percent of the land area of the Russian Federation, but has a population of only 8 million. Hence, it has a total of only 24 deputies out of 450 in the Russian Duma.

20.   Support for NATO expansion is voiced in the editorial, "Russia's Growl at NATO," *Christian Science Monitor*, December 20, 1996, p. 20. See also Edward L. Rowny, "A New START With Russia," *The Wall Street Journal*, December 11, 1996, p. 14. For two critical views, see Michael Mandelbaum, "Don't Expand NATO," *Newsweek*, December 23, 1996, p. 33; David Fromkin, "Hidden Danger In a New NATO," *New York Times*, December 18, 1996, p. 34. A negative Russian view is presented by Alex Alexiev, "Expanding NATO — The Folly of Retrofitting an Outdated Alliance," *Los Angeles Times World Report*, December 15, 1966, p. 7.

21.   "Russia Reject NATO Offer to Exchange Liaison Officers," *Korea Times*, December 5, 1996, p. 4.

22.   Stephen J. Blank, "Russia's Return to Mideast Diplomacy," *Orbis*, (Fall 1996): 517–35.

23.   See Herbert J. Ellison and Bruce A. Acker, "The New Russia and Asia: 1991–1995," *NBR Analysis*, 7(1) (June 1996).

24.   See "Sino-Russian Summit Planned," *China Daily*, December 28, 1996, p. 1.

25.   For details on Primakov's visit to Tokyo, see "Japan, Russia Take steps Toward Closer Ties," Tokyo, Reuters, November 15, 1996. Papers on Russian-Japanese relations are Tsuyoshi Hasegawa, "Russia and Japan: Old and New

Issues," prepared for the National Bureau for Asian Research's conference, Washington, D.C., October 5–6, 1996; Donald C. Hellman, "Power, Passivity and Stalemate: the Paradox of Japan's Relations with the New Russia in Asia," prepared for the National Bureau for Asian Research's conference, Washington, D.C., October 5–6, 1996.

26. In addition see Nicholas Eberstadt and Ralph Cossa, "Multilateralism and National Strategy in Northeast Asia," *NBR Analysis*, 7(5) (December 1996).

D74

10

Status and Perspectives: A Dialogue

Jiro Kodera

In much of the West, in Russia, and even in Japan there is much misunderstanding regarding Japanese governmental policy toward Russia. This chapter aims to expose misperceptions, clarify Japan's current policy, and provide an analysis of issues that will affect Japan-Russia relations. The misperceptions or misunderstanding of Japan's policy can be summarized as follows: For Japan, there is only one important issue in relations with Russia: the Northern Territories; because of this pending issue, Japan is not supporting Russia's historic transformation. In other words, while the international community faces the enormous task of helping Russia reform, Japan is selfishly pursuing narrow interests without extending due assistance to Russia. Japan will not allow any improvement in relations with Russia until progress is achieved in the territorial issue, even if this intransigent attitude contributes to stagnated relations between the two countries. These perceptions, although widely shared, do not correspond to the actual policy of Japan.

POLICY PRIORITIES

Japan's current policy toward Russia is based upon two main objectives. These are to support Russia's present reform and to achieve radical progress in relations with Russia by settling the territorial issue. However, the latter objective is not a precondition; there is no clear linkage between the two objectives. Japan fully supports Russia's historic transformation into a democracy and market economy. Japan's assistance to

Russia already amounts to $4.6 billion. This makes Japan the third largest contributor after Germany and the United States. Large-scale economic assistance would not have been possible were there a policy link with a resolution to the territorial dispute. Since the birth of the new Russia, relations between Japan and Russia have steadily improved.

Two government initiatives illustrate Japan's policy. First, it was Japan, as a Group of Seven member, that in the spring of 1993 proposed a package of economic assistance for Russia. This initiative was materialized at the Tokyo Summit in June of the same year. Second, the Japanese government invited President Boris Yeltsin to pay an official visit to Japan despite the fact that Yeltsin had abruptly canceled a planned visit the previous year and blamed Japan for the cancellation.

NORTHERN TERRITORIES

In postwar Japan-Russia relations, the Northern Territories issue has indeed played a key role. The official position of the Japanese government has always been that the Northern Territories are historically and legally Japan's; therefore, they are illegally occupied by Russia. Thus, it is only natural for Japan to seek the return of its territory. The questions are, how should Japan seek their return? What should be the procedure and timetable? How can a favorable environment be created for the return of the territories? What leverage does Japan have? What kind of relations should Japan maintain with Russia until the return of the disputed islands? In theory, there are many possible answers to these questions, and it is the task of policy makers to find the right ones.

Until the collapse of the former Soviet Union the position of the Japanese government was to seek an immediate and unconditional return of all four islands and to firmly link politics and economics. This means that economic cooperation with the former Soviet Union was directed toward and contingent on progress achieved in finding a solution of the territorial dispute. This policy was adopted against a background that included the former Soviet Union's denial that a territorial issue existed and the division of the international community into two rival camps.

However, the current situation is markedly different. The Soviet Union has collapsed and the Cold War is over. The new Russia clearly has denied the communist system that governed the Soviet Union for more than 70 years, and it is no longer considered an enemy of the West. Russia is now a partner. Russia's attitude toward the Northern Territories issue has also changed; it now recognizes the existence of a dispute and it has begun to discuss the issue. Therefore, the factors that determined the modalities of Japan's policy toward the Northern territories have changed.

RUSSIA AS A PARTNER

In accordance with this, the Japanese government has adjusted its policy toward Russia. Examples of this policy include the accepted concept of balanced expansion of relations and Japan's assistance to Russia. Still it is important to question whether the Japanese government has made enough adjustments, taking into account the changes that both Russia and the international community have undergone. Three factors must be taken into consideration when formulating relations with Russia. First is the direction and significance of Russian reform, second, the nature of the current international community, and third, the role that Russia can play in the Asia-Pacific region.

The main goal of Russia's foreign policy has become the establishment of a favorable environment for its economic recovery. In fact, economic recovery has become Russia's first priority. As a result, in Japan the perceived threat from Russia has been greatly reduced (although the military in the Russian Far East remains a source of some concern). This threat reduction is a positive change not only for Japan but also for the international community. Russia's current reform process clearly suits Japan's national interests; therefore, supporting the reform process benefits Japan.

The result of the Russian presidential elections in July 1996 were in fact a rejection of the old communist regime and, to a certain extent, showed popular support for reforms. However, this does not necessarily translate into bright prospects for reform and democracy. If the reform fails, there is a real danger that chauvinistic nationalism may gain public support. Should that happen, Russian policies of cooperation with the United States and other Western countries may change. What is worse, a failure to reform may also lead to the weakening of governance in Russia and a chaotic situation may develop. If the situation in Russia — with its large arsenal of weapons of mass destruction and its ability to produce yet more — became chaotic, the implications for the world would be serious indeed. This scenario certainly contradicts the national interests of Japan.

Russian reform is the business of Russians themselves; however, there are many reasons for Japan to lend assistance. The ongoing Russian reforms make it impossible for Japan to regard Russia as an enemy of the West. How could Japan continue to regard Russia as a potential enemy when Russian reform complements Japan's national interests and the international community is welcoming Russia as a partner? The territorial issue alone would not be enough to justify such a position.

SHARED INTERESTS

The world is becoming increasingly interdependent, not only economically but also in many dimensions. An increasing number of critical problems require international cooperation for their solution. Disarmament, terrorism, environmental issues, and drug trafficking are among them. For any international cooperation effort to be effective, it is essential to secure cooperation from major countries, including Russia. Without Russian cooperation, many of these problems will not be solved. Moreover, Russia's rich heritage of natural and human resources portends its revival as a major power. In the future Russia will certainly become a key player in the international community. It is in Japan's national interests that Russia abide by international rules and maintain good relations with Japan.

Peace and stability in the Asia-Pacific region serve as the foundation for the prosperity of Japan. Japan pursues this by maintaining strong U.S.–Japan relations based upon a bilateral security treaty. This policy will and should be maintained in the future. Here Russia can also play an important role. Sound U.S.-Russia and Japan-Russia relations would greatly contribute to the continuation of peace and stability in this region. By forging good relations with Russia and engaging Russia in the Asia-Pacific region, Japan will enhance its own security and gain more room to maneuver in its diplomacy. Indeed Japan's diplomatic weight might be enhanced with Russian backing.

However, Russia's interests seem to lie primarily in Europe. Asian interests are secondary and mainly economic. Despite repeated statements otherwise, the Russian central government neglects its Far Eastern region. As long as this situation persists, Asian countries, including Japan, will continue to have doubts about Russia's intentions of becoming an active partner in the Asia-Pacific region. If Russia is truly interested in the Asia-Pacific region, it must first devote more attention to its own Far Eastern provinces. Russia's economic interest in the Asia-Pacific region should serve as a sign to Japan that Russia does not intend either to pose a military threat or seek hegemony in this region. Engaging Russia in the Asia-Pacific region, therefore, will not create a new security problem, it may in fact enhance stability.

PROSPECT AND GOALS

There is still much room for improvement in Japan-Russia relations. Therefore, it is useful to consider the reasons for this and the measures to further relations. First we must consider the psychological and emotional factors that affect them. Japan-Russia relations lack mutual trust. Although foreign policy should be formulated on national interests rather than emotion, it is not easy to gain support for a policy that contradicts the general feeling of the people. In October 1993, when President Yeltsin visited Japan, he apologized for the internment of Japanese prisoners of war in Siberia after World War II. This greatly helped to alleviate the sense of mistrust that ordinary Japanese feel toward Russia. However, other events, such as the dumping of radioactive waste into the Sea of Japan, fueled Japanese mistrust.

From the Russian standpoint, Japan's policy toward Russia might appear too focused on the territorial issue, and there seem to be fears that Japan is trying to exploit Russia's current weakness to its advantage. That perception probably breeds mistrust toward Japan. To improve this situation, both countries must take bold measures designed to eliminate mistrust and adopt policies based on national interests rather than emotions.

To enhance trust, Japan and Russia must promote dialogue and exchange. As major powers, they share responsibility for the maintenance of international order. To live up to this responsibility, discussions between them on many issues are necessary. Discussions should be more frequent and take place at various levels, including the highest. The success of political dialogue should not be evaluated by whether there is progress in the territorial issue, because political dialogue has its own merits, and by deepening mutual understanding Japan and Russia may lay the foundation for a relationship based on trust.

The expansion of dialogue and exchanges should extend to the military, especially the military in the Russian Far East. Confidence-building measures are also important. When the Russian Army considers security in the North Pacific region, it must take into account the U.S. naval presence in the region. Because of that, in expanding exchange with the Russian army, it may be better for Japan to consider trilateral cooperation among Japan, Russia, and the United States.

Besides exchanges at the governmental level, other exchanges such as parliamentary and youth exchanges need to be expanded. Youth exchanges are particularly important; they will form a basis for the future of Japan-Russia relations. Various programs should be initiated for students at different levels to study in Japan. In this connection, Japan and Russia should cooperate to simplify the present visa procedures. Current procedures hinder closer cooperation and exchange. Japan can also provide Russia with further technical assistance in the fields of crime prevention, taxation, and judicial reform. The environment is another area of cooperation that offers mutual benefits.

It is in Japan's interest to constructively engage Russia in the Pacific and to maintain good Japan-Russia relations. Japan, therefore, supported Russia's membership in the Group of Seven and the Asia-Pacific Economic Cooperation. This not only helped to foster trust among the two countries but also the participation in these processes itself encourages

Russia to play a constructive role in the international community, and it may also aid domestic reform.

CONCLUSION

For Russia the best way to gain the trust of the Japanese people is to take a step forward in the solution of the territorial issue. True trust will be difficult to achieve without the settlement of this dispute. Without this step forward, the best we can hope for is a marriage of convenience. Japan–U.S. relations and the mutual benefits that the two countries have reaped by creating a true friendship may serve as an incentive for Russia. A Japan-Russia friendship would also see great mutual benefits.

It is only natural for Japan to seek a return of the Northern Territories. At the same time, it is important for Japan to promote good relations with Russia and to encourage it to play a responsible role in the Asia-Pacific region and the world. Until recently it was almost impossible to achieve the two objectives at the same time — to have negotiations with Russia (the former Soviet Union) on the return of the Northern Territories and to improve relations. The former Soviet Union even denied the existence of the problem and refused to talk about it.

The Tokyo Declaration of 1993 brought new possibilities. The Tokyo Declaration is a remarkable and important document: it recognizes the existence of the territorial dispute; it acknowledges that the territorial dispute is over claims to four islands: Habomai, Shikotan, Kunashiri, and Etorofu; it states that the issue should be resolved based on relevant agreements and documents, "law and justice," and legal and historical facts; and it reconfirms the validity of all the agreements, including those concerning the territorial issue, concluded between Japan and the former Soviet Union.

Thus, the Tokyo Declaration laid the foundation for further negotiations. The task for Japan in the immediate future is to build on this momentum and take the necessary measures to show Russia and its people that the return of the four islands to Japan is in their own national interest as well. To do so Japan must address the following issues: how to make the Russian people aware of the benefits that the improvement of relations between the two countries will bring them; how to make Russia aware that by continuing to ignore the principle of "law and justice" it may tarnish its international image, and that it prevents the development of friendly relations with Japan and thus potential benefits; and how to make sure that the inhabitants of the Northern Territories will not suffer from the return of the islands to Japan.

NOTE

The views expressed here are the author's own and do not necessarily reflect the views of the Japanese government.

11

Making a Comeback in Asia

Evgeniy V. Afanasiev and Vladimir I. Ivanov

Unlike any other European country, Russia has not only an Atlantic but also a Pacific coastline, an immeasurable advantage for developing close economic ties in Northeast Asia and the Asia-Pacific economic area.[1] No matter how objective and timely this observation may be, in reality, after the breakup of the Soviet Union new Russia was mostly concerned about a strategic partnership with the West and allowed European affairs to dominate Russian foreign policy. In the aftermath of the Soviet Union's dissolution, Russia's role in Pacific Asia and its legitimate interests in the region were downplayed and largely ignored by their key international partners.

This situation was unfair and basically unhealthy because the new Russia was a primary source of positive regional developments. In 1990–92 Russia experienced difficulties in its relations with North Korea and established diplomatic relations with Seoul. In 1991–93 Russia advanced relations with China, and in 1993 progress was made in relations with Japan with the signing of the Tokyo Declaration. Russia's foreign policy and defense posture in the Far East changed dramatically while domestic issues moved to the forefront.

RUSSIA'S NEW POSTURE

The diplomatic and political losses that Russia suffered in the Far East did not endanger its vital interests, territorial integrity, or military security. However, economic security was imperiled and expectations of a breakup of the Russian Federation and separatist trends in Siberia and the Far East were widely reflected in lectures and seminars, research papers, and articles by Western experts. Fortunately for Russia, the domestic situation in the eastern provinces was tolerable (by Russian standards), and the regional environment in Northeast Asia and the North Pacific area became more relaxed.

After several years of economic decline and diminishing political posture in Northeast Asia, Russia's posture in the region is improving. Its position in Northeast Asia began to change after Yevgeniy M. Primakov replaced Andrei Kozyrev as foreign minister in early 1996. Primakov's unique experience in working closely with two presidents and intimate knowledge of Asia helped to restore partially Russia's presence in East Asia, and its symbolic return to the region was encapsulated in the invitation to join the Asia Pacific Economic Cooperation forum.

New Russia's concerns are largely with such issues as illegal immigration in the Far East, poaching in the Russian special economic zone and territorial waters, coordination of national and regional development programs, and multilateral problem-solving efforts. However, only a combination of unilateral efforts, bilateral improvements, and multilateral initiatives can help to protect national interests. Russia's long-term goals in the Asia-Pacific region can be summarized as follows:

to protect territorial integrity, economic interests, and the maritime economic zone;

to maintain and strengthen Russia's role in the regional military equation;

to participate in a balanced manner in regional economic cooperation;

to ensure regional security, mainly by political means;

to participate in conflict prevention efforts; and

to prevent illegal immigration.

Moscow still proposes to discuss regional security issues in a multilateral setting to promote confidence building, ensure transparency of military doctrines, and limit military activities in the area. Whether these proposals are realistic depends on Russia's partners in the region, but Moscow does not seem to be excessively interested in pushing these ideas to the forefront of its regional agenda. Moreover, the agenda itself has become more inward looking and bilaterally oriented.

Although the Far East of Russia is a relatively small and troubled part of the Russian economy, it is likely to be an important part of Northeast Asia's economic dynamism and an economic contact zone between Russia and Japan, Russia and China, and Russia and other Asia-Pacific countries. Obviously, the trade and investment links with the region will be of much higher importance for the Pacific provinces, where the economic opening is in progress and democratic institutions are being created through a devolution of administrative power and the growing autonomy of local administrations.

THE UNITED STATES

From 1992 to 1997 Washington was in no hurry in accepting the Russian Federation as a participant in various regional dialogues, and some people in Washington did not even consider Russia a regional entity.[2] In November 1993, Russia was not even mentioned in President Clinton's address given in Seattle during the first Asia-Pacific Economic Cooperation summit meeting. This discriminatory exclusion stemmed partly from the nature of U.S. foreign policy in general and from U.S. policy toward Asia in particular during Clinton's first term in office. Some in the West who remained interested in or concerned about eastern Russia were mostly busy trying to figure out what kind of dividing lines may be drawn through the map of the Russian Federation so that "a Far Eastern Republic" would be a part of a loosely confederated Russia.[3]

Democrats in Washington dismissed the potential of a post-communist Russia as an Asian, even Northeast Asian, regional player more bluntly than their predecessors had. In the 1993 State Department outline for East Asia Russia received a little more attention than Mongolia but less than Vietnam — a considerable departure from the Republican views on the Soviet Union's potential role in the "emerging architecture" of East Asia and the Pacific.[4] North Korea and China moved to the forefront of U.S. policy in Northeast Asia and completely eliminated Russia from Washington's Asian agenda both as a source of threat and positive expectations. This was quite in harmony with Tokyo's views, because until 1996–97 Japan never really considered the Soviet Union or Russia as playing a role in regional affairs.

There were impulses originating both from regional political changes and bilateral dialogues that prompted Moscow to become concerned over Russia's declining status in East Asia. There was a feeling that excessive hopes were invested in improved relations with the United States. The isolation of Russia from the Korean Energy Development Organization and the four-party talks on the Korean situation and the little interest shown in the proposal to discuss the Korean problem in a multilateral setting were hard to swallow. Finally, the expansion of the North Atlantic Treaty Organization urged Russian policy makers and diplomats to reassess their European and trans-Atlantic experiences and stimulated Moscow diplomacy in Northeast Asia. The multipolarity of the post–Cold War international system was adopted as official foreign policy concept.

THE CHINA FACTOR

From the Russian standpoint close relations with China can solidly guarantee its independent role in such a system of multipolar international relations. The interests of Russia and China in economic development and international affairs are quite similar, their economies are complementary, and they cannot afford to be at odds. It is quite natural that Russia and China will differ in their approaches to certain problems, but this should not preclude efforts in strengthening peace, security, and economic cooperation.

Russian foreign policy aims to ensure an independent role for Russia in regional affairs. Currently there is no power or an alliance of powers that presents a threat to Russia's national interests. The improvement of Russia-China relations complements the shift in Russian foreign policy toward a partnership with the United States and other Western countries and radically improves the security of Russia in the North Pacific and Northeast Asian regions. These two factors help Russia to open up economically to the Asia-Pacific region, make possible Russia's participation in regional institutions, facilitate a market access, and contribute to the development of eastern Russia.

China-Russian relations are seen as one of the pillars of stability in Asia, and in fact they may mark the end of the era of triangles in Asia, which existed during the Cold War. Russia-China political relations were recently called an equal and cordial partnership aimed at strategic cooperation in the 21st century. The concrete examples of such partnership are agreements on mutual non-targeting of missiles, non-use of nuclear weapons, confidence-building measures, and the reduction of armed forces in border areas between Russia, China, Kazakhstan, Kirgizstan, and Tadjikistan.

The long-standing territorial dispute between China and Russia has been successfully resolved. The 4,300-kilometer-long border between China and Russian eastern provinces was agreed in full detail, leaving only three islands (two on the Amur River near Khabarovsk and one on the Argun River in Chitinskaya Oblast) for future negotiations. This agreement with China, signed in Beijing in November 1997, may be more than a treaty; it may be the beginning of an era of stability in Northeast Asia.

RELATIONS WITH JAPAN

One of the most important goals of Russian diplomacy is the improvement of relations with Japan. Fortunately, Moscow and Tokyo are showing an interest in advancing political and economic contacts. Compared with the early 1990s, negative elements have been removed from the dialogue, significantly changed, or faded away. Both sides are expressing a readiness to be closer and better neighbors.

The territorial dispute is no longer the point of departure for bilateral discussions. The quality of bilateral engagement is changing mostly on the political and diplomatic fronts, not in trade and investment or in public perceptions. Economic cooperation and people-to-people contacts are the two major areas for bilateral engagement in the absence of adversarial military intentions, third party threats, or ideological differences. However, two basic questions remain unanswered. What kind of bilateral relationship do the two countries want? and how will they achieve it?

Prime Minister Ryutaro Hashimoto's speech to the Association of Corporate Executives on July 24, 1997, was an impressive step forward in this respect. Through his Eurasian diplomacy concept and the three principles that apply to Russia (mutual confidence, mutual benefits, and a long-term approach) a window of opportunity was opened. It provides an exit from the stalemate over the Northern Territories and raises hope that both parties can act together to reach a positive sum solution. The speech symbolizes a major shift in political attitudes and encourages the two countries to move from a phase of post–Cold War political accommodation to one of cooperative engagement. Russian leaders are speaking the same political language; they have invited Tokyo to participate in the development of the disputed territories and the economic reconstruction of Russia.

In November 1997, at the informal summit meeting in Krasnoyarsk between President Boris Yeltsin and Hashimoto, an agreement was reached to try to sign a peace treaty before the year 2000. However, it is clear that both nations need to develop relations in various fields, creating and strengthening mutual confidence and expanding economic and political cooperation in order to solve this most difficult problem.

Years ago it became clear that power diplomacy in dealing with the territorial issue will not bear fruits for either side. There is no forceful or quick way to settle the dispute. Both parties must act together to work out a positive sum solution based on mutual benefits and cooperation. A new level of bilateral relations can create new conditions for the settlement and show future alternatives and direction to both politicians and the populace. The issues that test the new policy are the cooperative fishery agreement (that transcends the problem of sovereignty) and how Russia's proposal for joint development of the Northern Territories or South Kurils will be realized. New approaches to the border disputes can facilitate an expanding dialogue with Japan, and there is a modest hope that the problem of the disputed territories can be transformed into an area of cooperation and mutual economic benefit through joint development.

PRIMACY OF ECONOMICS

There were other crucial factors, probably more powerful than Moscow's own interest in being recognized as a part of the Asia-Pacific region. China was rather forthcoming in relations with its northern neighbor (and recent antagonist) in the attempt to balance the dominant influence of the United States and to satisfy certain economic, technological, and defense needs. On the part of the United States and Japan concern was demonstrated with regard to China and its future posture in Asia. In this fluid geopolitical environment Russia may be perceived by both these powers as a regional partner, with limited power but with some influence and a role to play.

Economic interests were also a factor. Russian public opinion, local administrations, and the business community are strongly in favor of developing closer economic ties with Northeast Asia. Russia, therefore, has opened up its market to neighbors, directing more trade to Asian markets. For example, the exports and imports of the Far Eastern provinces became far more aligned toward China, Japan, South Korea, and the United States. The regional market and investment opportunities of the Far East, particularly oil and gas resources development, have attracted close attention from the United States, Japan, China, and South Korea. Constituencies supporting closer relations with Russia have formed in neighboring countries.

Foreign investors, particularly U.S. companies, became involved in the Far East, and the Japanese government has shown an interest in assisting the economic development of this part of Russia. U.S.-based multinationals and Japanese corporations lead in the development of oil and gas fields in Sakhalin. U.S. companies are the largest foreign suppliers of food, consumer goods, machinery, and equipment to the Far Eastern cities; Japanese trading firms and consumers benefit from imports of fish and crab harvested by Russian fishermen. However, long-term economic links are yet to be built, particularly with capital-rich neighbors.

During the Krasnoyarsk informal summit between Yeltsin and Hashimoto new links were discussed that will include Japanese investment promotion in Russia, energy resources development (particularly in Sakhalin oil and gas fields), improvement of trans-Siberian transportation and telecommunication systems, fishery, and other important areas.[5] It is hoped that as a result of these and other efforts Far Eastern Russia will become a more hospitable place for foreign companies and interdependence with economies of the Asia-Pacific region, particularly Northeast Asia, will be promoted.

Meanwhile, the U.S. private sector has moved ahead even more dynamically, particularly within the framework of the Sakhalin projects. By 1996 there were more than 100 representation offices of U.S.

companies established in the capital cities of the Russian Pacific provinces, including ABB, Alaska Airlines, AT&T, DHL, IBM, Mobil Oil, Apple Computers, Chevron, Caterpillar, Exxon, Amoco, Marathon, McDermott, Price Waterhouse, and Deloitte & Touche, as well as three offices of the American Business Center.

In the United States and Japan, attitudes toward Russia and its role in Northeast Asia are changing. Russia's recovery is now perceived by many Americans and Japanese to be important to regional stability and economic dynamism. This change in attitudes makes trade and investment ties between Russia and Northeast Asia compatible with U.S. and Japanese interests. Moreover, Russia's economic transformation creates markets for capital and consumer goods, as well as demand for investment and technologies.

There are new opportunities for large-scale export-oriented projects. Russia and China reconfirmed their commitment to develop close links in the energy sector focusing on the Kovyktinskoe natural gas field near Irkutsk and a pipeline project. It seems that Russia, which plans to build a nuclear power plant in China, considers this neighbor a huge market for Russian high-tech products, including advanced military equipment.

CONCLUSION

In the few years elapsed since the dissolution of the Soviet Union Russia has learned a great deal about the main trends in the Asia-Pacific region. Not only diplomats and politicians but also the first generation of Russian business people, particularly those who have traveled to East Asia, have had an opportunity to compare, reflect, and make pragmatic analyses regarding the current status of Russia in the world and the region. Findings about Pacific Asia are mixed, and feelings and attitudes differ significantly. However, Moscow's diplomacy is becoming increasingly Asia-Pacific and trade- and investment-oriented. This reflects the fact that Russian foreign policy in the region and its security thinking toward East Asia are now better coordinated with domestic interests and pragmatic economic concerns and development plans.

Although economic links with immediate neighbors are the most significant force for integrating Russia into the region, it is too early to expect strong currents toward integration in Northeast Asia. Certainly, key bilateral relations between Russia and China or Japan and China are developing with relatively good prospects for more economic interdependence. However, as far as Russia's relations with Mongolia and North Korea are concerned we can see a considerable weakening of economic ties.

However, Russia still belongs to the group of major powers that has begun to form a new framework for post–Cold War relationships in the region. With Russia recovering from economic difficulties and because of its improved diplomatic posture in Northeast Asia, the concept of a multipolar world is becoming more closely linked with real politics in the region. From the Russian perspective, new regional relations must be organized on the following principles:

harmonization of interests among the regional states,

coordination of national economic programs,

coordination of efforts with regard to the main regional problems,

mutual restraint in military exercises,

promotion of confidence-building measures, and

settlement of disputes through mutual concessions and compromises.

Confidence-building measures, including limited and non-provoking military activities and transparency of military doctrines and strategies, are the important elements of new regional relations. Regular consultations on these and other problems now take place. The post-ministerial meeting dialogues of the Association of Southeast Asian Nations may be used as a model for Northeast Asian dialogue. In this rare moment in history this region is free from open regional rivalry and conflict. Unless something goes terribly wrong — a violent crisis in Korea, for example, which would force major powers to take sides — interdependent economic relations will provide a new pillar for security, stability, and regional cooperation.

NOTES

The views expressed in this chapter are solely the personal views of the authors.

1. Richard Layard and John Parker, *The Coming Russian Boom: A Guide to New Markets and Policies.* (New York: Free Press, 1996), p. 282.

2. On U.S. policy toward Russia since 1992 see Vladimir Ivanov, "Russia and the United States in Northeast Asia and the Russian Far East: Economics or Defense?" in *Politics and Economics in the Russian Far East: Changing Ties with Asia-Pacific*, edited by Tsuneo Akaha. (London: Routledge, 1997), pp. 137–43, 151–52.

3. See Zbignev Brzezinski, "A Geostrategy for Eurasia," *Foreign Policy*, 76(5) (September–October 1997): 56, 60 (map).

4. Richard Solomon, "Asian Security in the 1990s: Integration in Economics, Diversity in Defense," address at the University of California in San Diego, October 30, 1990, pp. 245–46, 247.

5. In its relations with the Association of Southeast Asian Nations, for example, the Japanese government pledged to apply "most preferential" low-interest loans to cross-border infrastructure projects such as the construction of roads between two or more countries. See *Japan Times*, December 17, 1997, p. 1.

12

The Northeast Asian Dimension
Tsuyoshi Hasegawa

According to Foreign Minister Yevgeniy Primakov, Russia's chief foreign policy success in 1997 was to avoid confrontation. Indeed, even Russia-Japan relations are emerging from a stalemate despite the inability to resolve the Northern Territories dispute. Given complex historical roots as well as psychological and political impediments on both sides, it is unlikely that this dispute will be resolved soon. The question is: Does this matter? The attitude taken by the major powers involved (Russia, Japan, and the United States) is that Russia-Japan relations are basically normal and unlikely to cause a serious crisis. The Russian threat in Asia has largely disappeared, and Russia is no longer a major player in the region. Therefore, the territorial dispute is basically an irritant of bilateral relations without greatly influencing international relations in Northeast Asia. However, the potential impact of a slide back to a stalemate goes far beyond bilateral relations and could derail the process of forging a stable international order in Northeast Asia.

NEW CONFIGURATION OF POWER

International relations in Northeast Asia are in a state of flux. The old order characterized by strategic triangle, patron-client relations, and alliances has disappeared, but a new order has not emerged. After the collapse of the Soviet Union, none of these four powers in Northeast Asia (Russia, Japan, China, and the United States) faces a primary adversary that vitally threatens their security in the immediate future. This gives a great opportunity, unprecedented in history, for forging a new international order based on cooperation. However, none of these powers can take others for granted as one's natural ally, giving future international relations an element of uncertainty.

Russia

In his perceptive essay, Steve Miller lists three broad strategic options in coping with the new security predicament: "go it alone" strategy, great power "balance of power" games, and omnidirectional friendliness.[1] If Russia is disillusioned by the West, it could choose a go-it-alone policy by reestablishing Moscow's dominance over its nearest neighbors — former soviet republics — and restoring military strength. However, in the post–Cold War world, the economy is in the driving seat, as Robert Scalapino[2] argues, dominating both domestic and international affairs. Russia's economic weakness, therefore, will inhibit bold foreign policy options; the go-it-alone policy is not an attractive option for Russia. However, there is an opportunity for Moscow to play balance of power games by pitting one power against the other in pursuit of its own national interests. The emergence of China as a geostrategic power helps Russia to be a critical player in the reconfiguration of power in East Asia. Positioning itself between China, on the one hand, and the United States and Japan, on the other hand, Russia could play a crucial role in tipping the balance. A third option would be to avoid creating enemies and forge good relations with all other major powers to maximize Russia's engagement with the outside world. Russia's strategic choices outlined by Miller are not unique to Russia but are common to all four great powers in Asia.

United States

Although it is unlikely, the go-it-alone option cannot be ruled out for the United States. The mounting cost of foreign commitment might force the United States to withdraw from engagement in Asia. Russia has ceased to be the United States' number one security problem, thus, the United States has an option of playing a balance of power game by cooperating with Russia against China or Japan. However, the balance of power option in its classical definition should be excluded from the U.S. option, because such a strategy entails maneuvering and a shift of alliances to maintain equilibrium. With the disappearance of the soviet threat, against which the U.S.–Japan security treaty operated, it is likely that future debate concerning the alliance will involve Russia. Therefore, the third and most desirable option for the United States is to pursue omnidirectional friendliness.

Japan

The most disadvantageous and, therefore, the most unlikely scenario for Japan is to adopt a go-it-alone policy. This would happen only if the U.S.–Japan security alliance collapsed. Like Russia, Japan is surrounded by neighbors who basically distrust it or with which it has serious historical or economic conflict. Japan's future is tied to the continuing stability and prosperity of the region; it is, therefore, in Japan's best interest to follow a policy of omnidirectional friendliness. Three factors, however, impede implementation of this policy.

Japan is plagued with weak governments, whose energy is concentrated on domestic issues. It is thus incapable of initiating bold foreign policy that clearly defines Japan's role in the international community. As the recent debate on history textbooks shows, Japan is not prepared psychologically, politically, and intellectually to overcome the legacies of colonialism, imperial expansion, and the Pacific War. As long as the Northern Territories issue is unresolved, Japan will be unable to follow an omnidirectional foreign policy, because its relations with Russia will remain uneasy. This also means that for Japan a balance of power game is limited to the United States and China.

China

In the 21st century an economically and militarily strong China will become a decisive factor in international relations. This has both positive and negative aspects. On the one hand, to sustain continued economic growth, China will have to follow a foreign policy designed to maintain stability in the region by avoiding conflict. On the other hand, economic power breeds military power. Because nationalism tends to supplant ideology in the post–Cold War world, militant nationalism in China may pose a serious threat to the stability of the region. To maximize its international position and to avoid isolation, China may rely on the balance of power strategy. Yet, one cannot exclude the possibility of either China's being forced to adopt a go-it-alone policy if faced by international isolation, or China's being induced to adopt an omnidirectional policy for the sake of ensuring stability in the region.

It is in the best interests of each power as well as of the region as a whole that all powers are induced to seek omnidirectional friendliness. However, a regression into a stalemate in relations between Russia and Japan could prevent quadrangle power relations from developing along this line of omnidirectional friendliness.

THE SECURITY DIMENSION

On the surface the Russian threat in Northeast Asia has disappeared. The number of troops in the region has been halved from the 1987 level; the budget cut and difficulties in fuel supply and maintenance have resulted in a considerable reduction of the Pacific Fleet. Two aircraft carriers, *Minsk* and *Novorossisk*, were sold to South Korea as scrap metal. The construction of a new carrier, expected to enter service in 1995, was stopped because of lack of funds. The time warships spend at sea was reduced by half. More than 100 nuclear submarines have been decommissioned, and by the year 2000 the Pacific Fleet plans to dispose of approximately 160 submarines with 300 reactors.[3] The situation of aircraft is no better. The lack of supplies of fuel, lubricants, and liquid gas forced air force command to reduce training missions to a minimum.

However, Russia continues to be a nuclear superpower, possessing a sizable strategic force. The strategic competition between the two nuclear superpowers may not be entirely over. Although the presidents of both nuclear superpowers can pledge that their nuclear weapons are no longer targeted at each other, the nuclear strategists in both countries still continue to calculate their nuclear force in terms of deterring each other. Eventually the military balance in Northeast Asia may be drastically altered by the Strategic Armaments Reduction Treaty process. Russia has committed itself to reducing the number of its nuclear warheads allowed on sea-launched ballistic missiles from the current 3,620 to 2,160 by the year 2000 and to 1,700 to 1,750 by 2003.

The questions are how the Russian military will achieve the necessary reductions and how the force will be deployed in the future. In 1992 the Russian Navy had 61 nuclear-powered strategic submarines (SSBNs), 37 based in the Northern Fleet in Murmansk and 24 in the Far East. According to Geoffrey Jukes, the Russians will have to reduce the number of existing SSBNs. Some experts argue that Russian military planners may choose to concentrate all SSBNs in the Kola peninsula and scrap SSBN bases on Kamchatka peninsula. If this speculation is correct, by the beginning of the next century the nuclear threat posed by the Russian strategic force in Asia will be eliminated. Yet, there are still others, particularly among Japanese defense specialists, who believe that Russia will maintain at least some of its SSBNs in the Sea of Okhotsk area. If so we can expect a more active force posture and deployment in the Pacific Fleet. Even if the Russian strategic force were withdrawn from the Far East, a sizable force is expected to remain in the region.

U.S. and Japanese defense analysts have not developed a coherent concept of the Russian military in the Far East after the collapse of the Soviet Union or a way to draw the Russian military into a constructive security arrangement in Northeast Asia. Noting that Russia does not figure prominently in important defense documents, such as the 1993 White House report *National Security Strategy of the United States* or the presidential report to Congress, "A Strategic Framework for the Asian Pacific Rim," Vladimir lvanov comments: "for American politicians and the public, the status of Russia in the Pacific remains one of irrelevance."[4] In contrast, Japanese defense experts (and some of their U.S. counterparts) continue to see the Russian military threat as a potential danger, although reduced, to security of the Asia-Pacific region. Traditional Cold War thinking is also evident on the Russian side. Among five possible threats to Russian security listed in military doctrine, none is concerned with the threat from the United States and Japan. Yet, when some military experts discuss the Northern Territories or a hypothetical global contingency, they point to the combined forces of the United States and Japan as the major threat to Russia in the Far East.[5]

FUTURE OPTIONS FOR JAPAN AND RUSSIA

Three factors make a slide back to a stalemate possible. Foremost, neither side can find a mutually acceptable formula for the resolution of the Northern Territories dispute. Second, the inability and unwillingness of either side to seek an acceptable solution to this problem is rooted in the dynamics of domestic politics. In Russia, the domestic political situation does not favor any concessions to Japan's territorial demand. In Japan, any solution short of a Russian pledge to return all four disputed islands may encounter substantial political opposition. Third, in both countries for too long the improvement of bilateral relations with each other was given low priority on the foreign policy agenda. It remains to be seen whether the current efforts to improve relations and to raise their importance to a high priority level will be sustained on both sides.

Nevertheless, a reversion to a stalemate will have serious negative consequences for the future stability of Northeast Asia. Russia's successful transition to democracy and a market economy will contribute to the stability of the Asia-Pacific region, which provides an important precondition for Japan's sustained economic growth. In the reconfiguration of major powers in Northeast Asia, the stalemate would impede the process of forging an international order based on cooperation by all major powers. Russia will not be able to seek omnidirectional friendliness if one of the powers is unwilling to reciprocate. Instead, Russia may be tempted to seek a balance of power policy designed to isolate Japan by exploiting U.S.–Japanese economic friction or by courting favor with China. Dissatisfied with the West, conservative political forces already look to China as Russia's partner.

It will serve Japan's best interest to improve relations with Russia. Nevertheless, there is little possibility that Japan will overcome the

Northern Territories syndrome and fashion a more imaginative, constructive Russian policy designed to achieve rapprochement by offering a mutually acceptable compromise to the territorial dispute.[6] This syndrome is too deeply rooted in Japan's collective historical memory to be expunged easily in a short time.[7] We must assume that the Japanese will continue to be preoccupied with the Northern Territories problem.

Despite its obsession with the territorial question, the Japanese government is adjusting its policy, albeit too gingerly, to the changing circumstances. If the Japanese government adhered to an inflexible exit approach until 1989, it gradually shifted its gear by adopting the policy of balanced expansion. After the cancellation of Yeltsin's trip to the summit in Tokyo in September 1992, Tokyo officially adopted aid to Russia's transition to democracy and a market economy as one of two pillars of policy toward Russia, together with the resolution of the territorial dispute. Nevertheless, the Japanese government and its Ministry of Foreign Affairs have been ambiguous about the priority of these two goals. This ambiguity has prevented Japan from pursuing full-fledged support for Russia. Every time its relations seem to move in a positive direction, the bony hands of the ghost of the Northern Territories dispute have sneaked in from behind, stealing the momentum for improvement.

The first measure by which Russia-Japanese relations can be prevented from reverting to a stalemate is, thus, to convince the Japanese government to reorder its priorities in Russian policy and to subordinate clearly the territorial issue to more important strategic objectives. Second, Japan should craft a more assertive, comprehensive policy toward the Russian Far East. This policy should include the elimination of barriers to official development assistance (or its equivalent) for the Russian Far East. Third, Japan should move forward with active efforts to incorporate Russia into the Asia-Pacific economy. Finally, Japan together with the United States should develop a broader security framework into which Russia can be incorporated.

We must take it for granted that the domestic political turmoil will continue, and that Russia's more important foreign policy priorities will be directed toward its relations with the United States, Western Europe, and China before being directed to Japan. This means that ultimate resolution of the Northern Territories dispute will be shelved until domestic political stability is restored and the Russian economy recovers.

Considering the enormous psychological, political, and economic difficulties, it is almost impossible to expect that the Northern Territories dispute will be resolved and a peace treaty will be concluded in the near future. For the time being, the best strategy for both Russia and Japan is to continue with practical improvements and gradually expand the realm of cooperation. By downshifting the gear of the Northern Territories issue and by elevating economic aid to the forefront, Japan and Russia can retain the momentum for improving bilateral relations and can aspire to the pursuit of omnidirectional friendliness in their foreign policy. The United States may play an important role in contributing to this momentum and aspirations or to derailing them.

NEW PRIORITIES

For the first time in 150 years an opportunity has opened to forge an international system in Northeast Asia based on cooperation and collaboration among all major powers. The United States may be the crucial actor in making this happen. First, the United States must start approaching Russia not merely through Europe, but also through the Asia-Pacific region. This requires coordination between the U. S. policy toward Russia through Europe and through the Pacific.

In security, force reductions are proceeding on both sides, but these reductions are neither regulated nor coordinated. The end of the Cold War does not immediately mean that the United States and Russia have suddenly become allies. Nevertheless, the choice for the United States is either "to remain passive concerning the Russian role in Asia" or "to adopt a more proactive policy, by engaging Moscow in a regular and comprehensive dialogue concerning Asia-Pacific developments and issues."[8] Such a comprehensive, consistent U.S. policy toward Russia in Asia will help Russia and Japan continue to ameliorate mutual hostility and engage in a constructive dialogue. However, by formulating such a strategy, the U.S. government may ultimately have to face the difficult dilemma of whether to support Japan's claim over the Northern Territories.

In view of the cardinal importance of its alliance with Japan and of the past partisan involvement of the U.S. government in the history of the Northern Territories problem, the United States may have little choice but to affirm eventually its support for Japan's position on this issue. However, even when supporting Japan's position on the territorial dispute, the United States should make it clear that it is deeply committed to Russia's transition to democracy and a market economy, and that this overall objective outweighs an essentially bilateral issue of territorial dispute. The U.S. sensitivity to the territorial issue should never deter it from what should be the U.S. priority: pursuing the more important task of creating a new international order that includes Russia as a constructive member.

For the first time in this century, all major powers have a vested interest in establishing a cooperative economic and security system in Northeast Asia. To quote Ambassador James E. Goodby, "The choice for policy makers is to be either reactive or proactive in shaping change . . . whether any democratic government today can negotiate change from the position of strength or whether it takes a major crisis to make these governments seize the opportunity to shape the future. The situation in the Asia-Pacific region is as serious as that faced by Truman and Acheson in Europe in the 1940s. What is missing is fear. What must take its place is imagination, persuasion, and persistence."[9] Will the United States, Japan, and Russia be blessed with leadership with such imagination, persuasion, and persistence?

NOTES

1.   Steven E. Miller, "Russia's National Interests," in *Damage Limitation or Crisis: Russia and the Outside World*, edited by Robert D. Blackwill and Sergei A. Karaganov. (London: Brasseys, 1994), pp. 103–5.

2.   Robert A. Scalapino, "Economic Dynamism and Political Fragility in Northeast Asia: Prospects for the 21st Century," *NBR Analysis*, 6(2) (1995): 19.

3.   See Alexei Zagorskiy, "The Post–Cold War Security Agenda for Russia: Implications for Northeast Asia," *Pacific Review*, 8(1) (1995); Geoffrey Jukes, "The Russian Military and the Northern Territories," *Acta Slavica Iaponica*, 12 (1994).

4.   Vladimir Ivanov, "Russia and the United States in Northeast Asia and the Russian Far East: Economics or Defense?" in *Politics and Economics in the Russian Far East: Changing Ties with Asia-Pacific*, edited by Tsuneo Akaha. (London: Routledge, 1997), p. 123.

5.   See B. Makeev, "Kuril'skaya problema: voennyi aspect," *MEMO*, No. 1 (1993): 54–59.

6.   See Tsuyoshi Hasegawa, "Soviet-Japanese Relations in the 1990s," in *Japan and the United States: Troubled Partners in a Changing World*, edited by Mike Mochizuki, James E. Auer, Tsuyoshi Hasegawa. (London: Brasseys, 1991), pp. 57–58; Tsuyoshi Hasegawa, Jonathan Haslam, and Andrew C. Kuchins (eds.), *Russia and Japan: An Unresolved Dilemma between Distant Neighbors*. (Berkeley, Calif.: International Area Studies, 1993), pp. 49–82; Tsuyoshi Hasegawa, "Continuing Stalemate," in *"Northern Territories" and Beyond: Russian, Japanese, and American Perspectives*, edited by James E. Goodby, Vladimir I. Ivanov, and Nobuo Shimotomai. (Westport, Conn.: Praeger, 1995), pp. 103–18.

7.   See Tsuyoshi Hasegawa, "Hopporyodo to sengo 50 nene" (The Northern Territories and post-war 50 years), *Chuokoron*, No. 10 (1995): 162–80.

8.   James Goodby, "Cooperative Security in Northeast Asia," in *"Northern Territories" and Beyond*, edited by James E. Goodby, Vladimir I. Ivanov, and Nobuo Shimotomai. (Westport, Conn.: Praeger, 1995), p. 297.

9.   Ibid., p. 311.

13

Crisis Prevention in Korea

Georgiy D. Toloraya

The improvement of relations between the Democratic Peoples' Republic of Korea (North Korea) and the Republic of Korea (South Korea) is an issue of crucial importance for crisis prevention in Northeast Asia. The Korean peninsula was the stage for the largest armed conflict in the region after World War II, and the roots of this conflict have not been eliminated. The two Koreas remain enemies with a conflicting ideology, incompatible political and economic systems, and military strategies aimed against each other. The concentration of military power on the peninsula remains one of the highest in the world: The quantitative and qualitative military power, including missiles and state of the art aircraft, would make an armed conflict a devastating one.[1]

The two Koreas have proven that they cannot resolve the conflict by themselves; contacts and dialogue in the 1970s and 1980s (including secret ones) led nowhere. The lack of progress during that period can be attributed to the Cold War and the inability of the two Koreas to accommodate each other because of superpower rivalry. The 1991 agreement on reconciliation, non-aggression, cooperation, and exchanges between North and South was largely left on paper despite the end of the Cold War.

BACKGROUND

The antagonism, however, continued after the end of the Cold War based on a deeply rooted intention to eliminate each other. The breakup of the Soviet Union, changes in China's policy, and collapse of the socialist community deprived North Korea of allies who would support its schemes for overcoming South Korea and led to severe economic difficulties. North Korea's economic decline also resulted in a military decay changing the balance of power in South Korea's favor.[2]

These changes and the death of Kim Il Sung led to a de facto reappraisal of strategy by the North Korean leadership. In the 1990s the primary goal became maintaining the status quo, that is, ensuring the survival of the regime. Accordingly, North Korea's diplomatic tactics and military buildup strategy were modified. A critical element of the latter became a nuclear weapons capacity, and the diplomatic dialogue with South Korea was downgraded.[3] Ironically, however, these new priorities that helped to open direct negotiations with the United States led to the framework agreement of October 1994. Pyongyang now believes that a bilateral dialogue with the United States could more effectively guarantee its security.

The South Korean government has also failed to formulate a coherent approach toward North Korea, and problems of an inter-Korean security regime and unification process remain unsolved. Former President Kim Young Sam tried to break with the past by taking a soft approach to North Korea. He officially moved from the goal of creating a unified state[4] to an announcement of a policy of peaceful coexistence, mutual exchanges, and cooperation in a spirit of friendship.[5] However, deeply rooted hostility toward the North, demonstrated during the nuclear crisis and in the wake of the death of Kim Il Sung, has prevailed, and contacts with North Korea were all but severed.

South Korea's strategic and long-time policy goal is national reunification.[6] Although North Korea still declares that reunification is its goal, too, it appears to prefer the status quo as a prerequisite for the regime's survival. A more recent concern is that the continued decay of North Korea and gradual strengthening of political influence and military capabilities of South Korea could compel Seoul to break the stalemate, should an opportunity arise. Another, and perhaps more potent, danger lies in the possibility of a military conflict caused by a miscalculation, border clash, or domestic crisis that could trigger a North Korean military attack.

Recently the domestic situation in both Koreas has worsened considerably. In the 1990s the North Korean economy experienced the worst crisis in its history with almost no hope for an effective recovery from mounting economic troubles. Worsening of economic conditions, particularly the food supply shortages, added a new, worrisome dimension to the standoff creating a threat of large-scale humanitarian disaster and raising the question of a need for outside involvement. A major consequence was a shortage of food in North Korea that, according to the United Nations Children's Fund, caused severe malnutrition for about 40 percent of North Korean preschool-age children.

SOURCES OF CONCERN

The cross-recognition scheme, once advocated by South Korea as the key method to ensure stability on the Korean peninsula, was completely abandoned by Seoul in the late 1980s, and the strategy of isolating the North was chosen instead. This new policy was later combined with a claim of special rights vis-à-vis other nations to manage North Korean affairs. Accordingly, North Korea's answer was more hostility and efforts to undermine South Korea's cooperation with its allies. As a result, the long awaited four-party talks proposed in April 1996 and initially seen by many observers as a mechanism to prevent crisis declined in importance. North Korea made it clear that relations with the United States are its primary goal. In the meantime, South Koreans have repeatedly said that they do not expect any swift results from these talks.

South Korea's trump card in its dealings with North Korea has always been its economic power. However, the South Korean economic crisis has weakened its ability to provide food and economic assistance, eroding incentives for North Korean leaders to deal with Seoul directly. The economic crisis in South Korea had major implications affecting inter-Korean relations. Seoul's partial loss of confidence and ability to provide economic assistance to the North may include crucial financial support for the light water nuclear power plant to be built in North Korea through the sponsorship of the Korean Energy Development Organization, which is comprised of both Koreas, the United States, Japan, and other countries. Moreover, widely debated scenarios of unification on the basis of South Korea's economic and financial resources became rather unrealistic simply because the country will not be able to afford the cost of North Korea's economic restructuring.

President Kim Dae Jung's administration had no other option but to soften inter-Korean relations. Kim Dae Jung was rather well known for his flexible approach to the problem, and his new power allows him to move toward dialogue. Limited economic options and a broader view of the divided Korean peninsula in the regional context led the new government to adopt a modified policy with regard to major powers participation in Korean affairs.

A six-party formula was proposed by Seoul in February 1998, and prospects for Russia's and Japan's direct participation in a multilateral diplomatic dialogue were opened. The question is what these two countries can do to help avoid a potential crisis in Korea that would imperil their interests as well.

A VIEW FROM RUSSIA

Russia views effective crisis prevention from the perspective of a comprehensive peace settlement. A homogenous people such as Koreans cannot be divided forever. Moreover, the eventual peaceful reunification of Korea is in Russia's national interests. Reunification will defuse a source of military tension and potential armed conflict near Russian borders. A unified Korea would become a bigger economic partner and export market for Russia, and regional cooperation in Northeast Asia will be more attainable with active participation of both Koreas or a unified Korea. Indeed, diplomatic relationships will be simplified for all parties involved, including Russia.[7]

However, Russia is unlikely to support a unification at all costs. Although the problems between the two Koreas, including coming to terms with each other and eventually reaching reconciliation, may be considered an internal matter of the Korean nation, the external parameters of the inter-Korean conflict are of immediate concern for neighboring countries, including Russia. Therefore, the prospect of a unification resulting from open conflict, turmoil, human suffering, and regional instability is unacceptable.

For Russia the Korean Peninsula will always be important. Likewise, Russia will remain important for the Koreas. No matter how much South Korea or North Korea change or diversify their policies, Russia is bound to remain of importance for them. Russia's policy vis-à-vis the two Koreas is one of constructive engagement with both sides until unification is achieved. It must never be perceived as a threat to the interests of either side.

There is no reason, however, to try to maintain a mechanical balance in practical matters. For example, Russia and South Korea adhere to democratic principles. High-level political dialogue is maintained. Their market economies create a broader opportunity for mutually beneficial cooperation, and the volume of trade with the South is more than ten times greater than that with the North.

In 1992 the relationship between Russia and South Korea was officially defined as a constructive partnership based on a complementarity of interests. By contrast, Russia's relations with Pyongyang have cooled after the diplomatic recognition of South Korea by Moscow and the breakup of the Soviet Union, which lead to the discontinuation of economic assistance to North Korea. Russia took steps to correct this situation through parliamentary delegations, high level government official meetings, and dialogue on economic issues. Preparation of a new bilateral treaty to replace the treaty of 1961 is underway. In general, an understanding is growing in Russia that more developed relations with

Pyongyang contribute to stability on the Korean Peninsula and enhance Russia's role in Northeast Asian regional diplomacy.

CRISIS PREVENTION

Historically, problems of the Koreas have a much stronger impact on public opinion and policy makers in Japan than in Russia. However, Russia, as a founding member of the United Nations and a permanent member of its Security Council, is naturally concerned about the events and developments that take or may take place on the Korean Peninsula. In the 1990s the Korean problem became an important topic in Russian foreign policy. The practical short- and mid-term goals of Russian diplomacy with respect to crisis prevention in the Korean Peninsula[8] can be summed up as follows:

developing a constructive partnership with the Republic of Korea;

maintaining good neighbor relations with the Democratic Peoples' Republic of Korea;

preventing the proliferation of weapons of mass destruction in the area;

creating a permanent peace structure in Korea to replace the armistice; and

facilitating dialogue, national reconciliation, and peaceful reunification.

Long-term objectives, it should be stressed, will be difficult to achieve unilaterally; they require a multilateral approach. Also, it seems that Russian key objectives coincide with those of Japan, making a coordinated approach possible and essential for the stability of Northeast Asia. It is necessary, for example, that both Russia and Japan participate in problem-solving efforts and support the enforcement of the solutions through the authority of international bodies.

The cross-recognition of two Koreas, initiated by the United States and South Korea, is yet to be completed. Although diplomatic normalization does not guarantee peace, the reluctance to recognize sovereignty undermines the existing framework that so far has allowed problem solving and conflict prevention through diplomatic efforts.[9] In this context the resumption of normalization talks between Tokyo and Pyongyang is significant. It important for Russia and Japan to act in coordination to address the Korean issue through existing multilateral mechanisms, such as the United Nations, the Asian Regional Forum, and other institutions.

A MULTILATERAL PROCESS

Experience shows that a multilateral approach to the Korean problem is an effective method of crisis prevention. A system of effective checks and balances to ensure regional stability can be created only with the participation of all major nations involved in Northeast Asian regional affairs. The four-party process was a useful start, but it did not meet this requirement because it excluded both Russia and Japan.[10]

The proposal made by Moscow in 1994 to convene an international conference on Korea was quite relevant, although the idea of such a conference is not new. In fact, the Armistice Agreement of 1953 recommended that governments of the countries concerned hold a conference to solve the problem of withdrawal of all foreign forces from Korea and a peace agreement conclusion. The idea of a six-party "consultative conference" raised during the forty-third session of the United Nations General Assembly was first proposed by South Korea and was supported by Japan.[11]

The problems to be discussed at the multilateral conference on Korea can include such topics as prospects and conditions for improvement of relations between the North and South, a replacement of the armistice agreement by a permanent peace agreement, confidence-building measures,[12] international guarantees for a nuclear-free Korean Peninsula, and normalization of diplomatic relations between the concerned participants.[13]

The prospects for Korean reunification can constitute a special topic for discussion. The principles incorporated in the Joint Declaration for the North and South of July 4, 1972, can serve as a basis for such a discussion. According to the declaration, the reunification of Korea should be achieved independently and without foreign interference, through peaceful means, and on the basis of "national consolidation."[14] An agreement reached by the North and South would be sealed by other participants serving as international guarantors.

The problem of nonproliferation of nuclear weapons and other weapons of mass destruction on the Korean Peninsula is now frozen, but it needs to be settled permanently. A multilateral format could allow dialogue on prohibiting production, deployment, or acquisition of chemical, biological, and nuclear weapons or long-range missiles both in the North and the South.

The United States could also confirm that there are no U.S. nuclear weapons in South Korea and pledge not to introduce them. The United States, South Korea, and North Korea could express their readiness to accept international inspections of military installations to verify the agreement. The two Koreas can ratify the convention on nuclear weapons and join the Missile and Missile Technology Control Regime.

CONCLUSION

Defusing potential crisis in Korea will probably be a lengthy process. With a new leadership in South Korea and prospects for improved inter-Korean relations, the next five years could well become a period of normalization between the two Koreas. That would pave the way for gradual integration of North Korea into the world community. The opportunity to enhance regional stability and promote a Northeast Asian regional economic cooperation network is among the potential positive outcomes of this process. Russia and Japan should work together to diffuse the crisis on the Korean Peninsula and to create such a unique opportunity.

NOTES

The views expressed are solely the personal views of the author.

1. The two sides are estimated to possess armed forces of more than 1.7 million troops, 5,800 tanks, 15,000 artillery pieces, and 2,000 aircraft. See *Defense White Paper, 1994–1995*. (Seoul: Ministry of National Defense, 1996), pp. 44, 80.

2. *Tongil Paekso* (White paper on unification). (Seoul: Ministry of Unification of the Republic of Korea, 1995), pp. 471–75 (in Korean).

3. See, for example, "U.S. Policy Toward the North Korean Nuclear Issue: A Case Study in Multilevel Bargaining," *IRI Review*, 1(3) (1996): 125–57. The United States is interested in the development of bilateral relations with North Korea not only because of security concerns but also from a broader political and economic perspective.

4. A three-phase unification process including reconciliation and cooperation, followed by the formation of a commonwealth, and finally leading to the establishment of a unified state.

5. *Korea Overseas Information Service*, Seoul, June 1993.

6. "The Challenges and Opportunities Facing Korea in the 21st Century," address at the Korean Society in New York, March 25, 1996, p. 2.

7. C. S. Eliot Kang, "Korea Unification: A Pandora's Box of Northeast Asia?" *Asian Perspective*, 20(2) (1996): 30.

8. V. I. Denisov, "Russia and the Problems of Korean Unification," paper presented at the seminar on Korean Unification Strategies for the 21st Century, Kyngnam University, Seoul, 1996.

9. Samsung Lee, "Building a Peace Regime on the Korean Peninsula: The Three-Step Concept for the Peace Process," *Asian Perspective*, 20(2) (1996): 121.

10. The idea of a political process that excludes Russia created an uneasy situation both for the Russian Ministry of Foreign Affairs and the political leadership and provided the opposition with an extra opportunity to criticize the government.

11. G. Toloraya, *Republic of Korea* (Moscow: Mysl, 1991), p. 45 (in Russian).

12. See Kang Choi, "Inter-Korean Confidence-Building," *Asian Perspective*, 20(2) (1996): 103–05; and *Arms Control on the Korean Peninsula* (Seoul: Institute of Foreign Affairs and National Security, 1990), pp. 116–20.

13.   Y. Afanasiev, "Russian Perspective and Politics," paper presented at the International Conference on the Korean Peninsula and Northeast Asian Security, Institute for Foreign Affairs and National Security, Seoul, November 26–27, 1996, pp. 15–19.

14.   *Tongil Paekso*, pp. 469–70.

14

North Korea and Japan-Russia Relations

Hajime Izumi

In 1997, three years after the death of President Kim Il Sung, an end to the three-year mourning period was declared. The focus of attention shifted to the question of when and how Kim Jong Il would assume the presidency of the Democratic People's Republic of Korea and the post of general secretary of the Workers' Party of Korea (WPK). In September 1973, Kim Jong Il was elected secretary of the party in charge of organization and propaganda and concurrently director of the party's organization and guidance department. On February 11, 1974, he was elected to the Political Committee of the party's Central Committee and became his father's heir apparent. In October 1980, when the sixth congress of the party was held, Kim Jong Il was elected to the Presidium of the Politburo and secretary to the Military Affairs Committee. On December 24, 1991, shortly after North Korea entered the United Nations and five rounds of the inter-Korea premiers' talks were conducted leading to a basic agreement on reconciliation, non-aggression, exchanges, and cooperation, Kim Jong Il became supreme commander of the Korean People's Army. On April 9, 1993, he was elected chairman of the National Defense Commission.

STATUS OF THE REGIME

Kim Jong Il assumed the WPK general secretary post on October 8, 1997, just two days before the day of the WPK's foundation and three months after the three-year mourning period for Kim Il Sung was

declared over. Long before that happened the sturdy ideological foundations for the transition of power were created. The Red Flag concept that
preaches absolute obedience to Commander Kim Jong Il began to invoke
him as a new god. This concept, announced in January 1996, represents
Kim Jong Il's own version of his father's ten major principles and will
probably be an important tool for the consolidation of his regime.

On February 14, 1974, Kim Il Sung announced the ten major principles
to the party leadership, thus forcing potential power rivals to accept his
"divinity, absolutism, and unconditionality" as was articulated in the
principles.[1] As a result, one may consider Kim Jong Il's control over North
Korea, at least for the time being, as absolute, because he has made it
almost impossible to openly advocate ideas directed against his father or
express discontent with the system.

Possible scenarios regarding an internal power struggle in North Korea
include speculation on whether the death of Choe Kwang, minister of the
People's Armed Forces (equivalent to a minister of defense) on February
21, 1996, followed by the death of First Vice Minister of Defense Kim
Kwang Jin on February 27, 1996, was a coincidence.

Moreover, on February 12, 1997, Hwang Jang Yop, party secretary of
the WPK in charge of international affairs, applied to the South Korean
Embassy in Beijing for asylum. Never before had such a high-ranking official long at the center of power in North Korea defected, thus revealing
cracks in Kim Jong Il's regime. Hwang Jang Yop did not simply abandon
North Korea, but set his hopes on South Korea, thereby sending a signal
to the international community that the South is superior to the North.
This had a very strong impact on North Korea's elite.

Although these and other events in their combination may reveal the
instability of the regime or a power struggle to secure control over North
Korea's military, a major shakeup of the ruling pyramid is highly unlikely. The issue, instead, is whether sprouts of reform that have begun to surface in recent years will be ripped up in the atmosphere of regime consolidation. For example, the sub-work team management system in agriculture, infamous for not being implemented despite being in place for
some time, was beginning to be transformed into something close to the
Chinese private contractor system. In other words, a reform policy for
farmers was being developed.

FOOD CRISIS

There is no doubt that North Korea is facing severe food shortages,
particularly after massive floods hit the country in July-August 1995
destroying crops, and after heavy rains damaged farmland again in July
1996. It is very difficult to assess accurately the scale of the crisis, because
Pyongyang remains unwilling to provide the international community

with objective projections on the food situation in the country, although in 1995 North Korea appealed for assistance to the United Nations.

According to a report issued in December 1996 by the United Nations World Food Program and the Food and Agricultural Organization, North Korea lacks at least 2.3 million tons of grain to maintain the minimum necessary norms of consumption. Moreover, the malnutrition may be more dramatic considering the differences between the regions, urban industrial and rural areas, and the disparities in food rationing among military forces compared with civilians. An internal report by China in fall 1996 estimated the shortfall at less than 1 million tons.[2]

Chinese experts believe that although the suffering is real, it is unthinkable that the regime will collapse any time soon because of a food crisis.[3] Their own experiences probably influence this conclusion. At least 20 million people died of starvation in China in 1959–61 after the Great Leap Forward policy failed. The chance that Pyongyang will experience a famine similar to the one in China is not necessarily high, considering Beijing's interest in the stability of North Korea and the growing role of international organizations in humanitarian assistance and food relief efforts in North Korea.

If China had had opponents of the same nationality singing the praises of prosperity just over the border, its regime may not have maintained control during the famines. When China experienced mass starvation, the outside world knew nothing of the situation. At least some information is available with regard to the food shortages in North Korea through ethnic Koreans living in China, the United Nation's food aid activities, and U.S. diplomats engaged in contacts with Pyongyang,

The shortage of food as a humanitarian problem, however, must not overshadow the possibility that the food crisis might slowly undermine the fragile stability on the Korean Peninsula, although there is not much potential for a regime crisis. The hope is that the outside world will know enough about the food situation to make emergency aid available.

NORTH KOREAN DIPLOMACY

When analyzing North Korean diplomacy, one cannot avoid the feeling that the country suffers from shrinking horizons. North Korean policy toward Japan, the United States, and South Korea since the end of 1996 supports this notion. A joint editorial published in *Rodong Sinmun*, *The Korean People's Army*, and *The Youth Front* on January 1, 1997, gained attention because it referred to the international environment, thus signaling a policy shift.

The editorial stated that the issue of Korean unification is a national problem that should be resolved by the Koreans themselves. At the same time, the editorial described the problem as an international issue that involves other nations, which should feel a responsibility for the division of Korea and extend cooperation. The joint editorial also called on the United States and Japan to change their postures vis-à-vis North Korea. Behind this shift may lie an ulterior motive: gaining food aid by advancing relations with both the United States and Japan. Unlike the years before 1997, when there was no mention of Japan, the editorial demanded that Japan abandon its hostile policy toward North Korea and refrain from actions that hinder Korean unification.

Japan considers North Korea's steady progress in adopting behavior appropriate for a member of the international community as a prerequisite for food aid. Without this kind of change in North Korea's posture, Japanese public opinion will not support government initiatives. For example, WPK Secretary Hwang Jang Yop attended an international seminar at the end of January 1997 in Japan but left the country without being able to meet Taku Yamazaki, head of the Liberal Democratic Party Policy Research Committee.

At that time in Japan suspicions that the mysterious disappearances of Japanese women 20 years ago had actually been kidnappings by North Korea returned to the spotlight, affecting Japanese public opinion toward the North. Under these conditions it was no longer possible for Japan to consider either food aid or improving relations with the Democratic People's Republic of Korea. North Korea, however, failed to understand adequately Japan's policy and alter its posture accordingly.

Eight rounds of diplomatic normalization talks between North Korea and Japan broke down on November 5, 1992. In February 1993 North Korea refused to allow inspections by the International Atomic Energy Agency of the two undeclared sites in Yongbyon, and on March 12 announced its decision to withdraw from the Non-Proliferation Treaty. However, on October 21, 1994, it signed a framework nuclear agreement with the United States and promised to freeze its nuclear development program. The Korean Energy Development Organization was established on March 9, 1995, and on April 16, 1996, the United States and South Korea proposed four-way talks with North Korea and China to finalize a permanent peace treaty for the Korean Peninsula.

Although North Korea does not seem to deliberately create tension in inter-Korean relations or in contacts with the United States and Japan, a certain degree of tension seems inevitable. The settlement worked out between the United States and North Korea at the end of 1996 in response to the incursion of a North Korean submarine into South Korean waters was conducive for creating a better political environment.

The settlement was a package deal in which North Korea agreed to issue a statement of regret. As a part of the deal, Washington agreed to issue permits for U.S. trading companies to export grain to North Korea. Following this agreement, a joint briefing was scheduled for January 29,

1997, and the United States issued permits for grain exports to North Korea totaling 500,000 tons. The U.S. promise was not to provide aid to North Korea, but to grant trading companies export permits.

Despite having fully understood this point, North Korea embarked upon a new game with the United States. It adopted the position that it would not be able to attend the joint briefings if it did not get 500,000 tons of grain in aid from the United States. As a result, the joint briefing scheduled for January 29, 1997, was postponed. However, in February 1997 North Korea permitted an inspection team from the Korean Energy Development Organization to enter the country. Moreover, on March 5, 1997, the North Korean representative attended a briefing session on the four-party talks, where for the first time he joined South Korean representatives in a public forum.

JAPAN'S RESPONSE AND RUSSIA

The first thing to address is the prevention of a military offensive launched by Pyongyang against the South. Should a Korean war break out again it would not only bring tragedy to both North and South Korea but would also inflict heavy damages and have an extremely severe impact on Japan and other nations in the surrounding area. Thus, Japan and Russia can also be counted among the involved parties when it comes to preventing war on the Korean Peninsula.

Providing a certain amount of food aid to North Korea is the first thing that should be considered as a concrete way to reduce the danger of war. As already mentioned, North Korea participated in a briefing session for the four-party talks among the United States, China, and the two Koreas on March 5, 1997. Until then, it had adamantly insisted that it would not make its position on the talks clear until it received food aid from the United States. Preparatory discussions for four-way talks were scheduled to take place in New York on August 5, 1997, and there were reasons to believe that North Korea would agree to a plenary session. It was suspected that North Korea's goal was simply the continuation of negotiations. Indeed, Pyongyang had no other venue for gaining sufficient food aid from the international community but the four-party talks that are linked with a resumption of inter-Korean dialogue.

Although Japan and Russia are showing a positive attitude toward food and humanitarian aid to North Korea, they should act on it promptly. Certainly, this aid would be more than a response to humanitarian problems and must be considered from a perspective of regional security and stability. Even if the possibility of famine in North Korea is small, it would inevitably increase the likelihood of the North sliding into a humanitarian disaster and the chances of North Korea using military force against South Korea as an act of desperation. Food aid will probably be the most effective method to avoid a crisis.

South Korea's response to Japan and Russia's decision to provide food aid to North Korea will probably be negative. Should this be the case, Japan and Russia should call for a multilateral policy on food aid to North Korea that includes South Korea. The cooperation of South Korea is extremely important when responding to the North. The most desirable policy would be to provide aid in concert with South Korea and other nations. However, should this fail to work out and South Korea remain negative about aid, Japan and Russia should consider taking the initiative by going ahead with food aid to North Korea even if South Korea opposes this.

However, it will be necessary to make the following conditions clear to Pyongyang before implementing aid measures.

First, North Korea must ensure transparency with regard to the state of the food supplies in the country. It must reveal what food resources are in shortage and make clear what percentage of this shortfall will be covered by aid from the international community. In addition, it will also need to be forthright about its own efforts to cover the shortages. There will also be questions about how food received from the international community will be distributed to the general public and whether North Korea is willing to allow Japan and Russia to monitor the distribution routes should it receive Japanese and Russian food aid.

Second, aid from Japan and Russia would only account for some of the food currently required by North Korea. More food aid than this will not be considered until Pyongyang at least acknowledges the failure of its agricultural policies and embarks on agricultural reform.

Third, Japan and Russia will not provide aid in food if North Korea refuses to meet the above conditions. They will suspend food aid if North Korea fails to live up to these requirements even after implementation begins.

Aid to North Korea with these conditions attached might serve to calm concerns that aid will not benefit the North Korean people but only strengthen the military and be linked to the perpetuation of Kim Jong Il's regime. Of course, seen from the opposite angle, aid under these conditions might be difficult for North Korea to accept. Should North Korea feel unable to accept aid under such conditions, we would be confronted with the danger of North Korean adventurism again.

Finally, in view of the four-party talks and the change of administration in South Korea, Japan and Russia should cooperate to expand the four-party talks and to join the framework as full members. The ultimate goal of the four-party talks is to see a peace agreement concluded between the North and South. The surrounding countries have to support this goal and encourage the sides to implement the agreement. An environment in which surrounding countries encourage North-South reconciliation can only be created when Japan and Russia are included. The current framework for the four-party talks is, thus, incomplete.

CONCLUSION

Japan and Russia should have a role to play, and the four-way talks should at some point become a six-party framework. Both Japan and Russia should go on with the matter, stressing this point in their contacts with other parties already involved in the process. Although the prospects of full fledged four-party talks look good in general, we must not overlook another element in the Korean situation: uncertainty over the future of North Korea itself. The country is mired in crisis and Hwang Jang Yop's defection has exposed a big rift in the Kim Jong Il regime, no matter how hard it was trying to minimize the shock. In the long run, a collapse of the regime cannot be entirely excluded from our calculations, and such disintegration can strongly affect North Korea and its society. If that is the case, neighboring powers should help find ways to cushion the crisis providing some framework for a softer landing.

We should also consider yet another possibility: What if North Korea starts pursuing some kind of reform and open-door policy? Notwithstanding how selective and half-baked that policy may be, it could ease the tension and provide the regime more breathing space. We should welcome such a development as long as it means stability for North Korea. For neighboring countries, the top priority is to see that peace prevails on the Korean Peninsula.

NOTES

1. See Suzuki Masayuki, *Kitachosen* (North Korea). (Tokyo: University of Tokyo Press, 1992), pp. 100–1.

2. See, on this point, "North Korea's Food Situation," (A research report commissioned by the Ministry of Foreign Affairs, FY 1996). (Tokyo: Japan Institute of International Affairs, 1997).

3. Interviews in Beijing with Chinese party and government officials.

15

Future Geoeconomic Equation
Steven Rosefielde

The East Asian region was a relatively poor, underdeveloped, and volatile region at the dawn of the postwar era, comprised of diverse countries and cultures seeking to cast off the yoke of colonialism and build modern societies on ideological principles that often exacerbated historical enmities. Although many states in the region were inclined to spread their gospel, settle old scores, and establish their own empires, they lacked the requisite economic and military capabilities. This made it relatively easy for the United States as a peripheral Asian Pacific power to fill the void. It was the world's preeminent economic and military power. It had defeated Japanese imperialism and imposed peace terms that precluded Japan from using force as an instrument of regional domination.

CHANGES IN THE REGION

Ideally, in accordance with its democratic and pluralist credo, the United States should have used its authority to dispel ancient animosities and promote regional harmony, freedom, cooperation, and rapid economic development. The Cold War made this impossible. The Soviet Union's conquest of the Northern Territories and the rise of communist revolutionary power in China, North Korea, Vietnam, Cambodia, Laos, and Malaysia compelled the United States to restrict its focus, serving principally as a defensive shield for Japan, South Korea, and Taiwan and a booster for capitalist free enterprise outside the communist zone of control.

U.S. policy within these confines was a great success, despite the annoyance caused by asymmetries in market access. The capitalist subregion flourished, and communism faltered because of its economic vulnerabilities. Had the soviet military and the state security police correctly appraised Gorbachev's shortcomings and chosen Romanov to succeed Chernenko;[1] had Deng Xiaoping lacked the courage of his convictions, Asian Pacific prospects in the 21st century would look today much like they did at the end of the 1980s, with the region fractured along ideological lines and Japan expanding its influence as the strongest economic power in the area. However, the collapse of communism has roiled the economic waters more profoundly than most analysts grasp, fundamentally altering the shape of things to come.

It has created a new, independent base for East Asian prosperity and introduced several untested market economic systems, including Russia and China. Also, the opening of China has created competitive problems for Japan, which have contributed to the fading of its economic miracle and its flirtation with liberal economic systemic reform. The Asia Pacific region thus stands on the threshold of a new beginning. Its colonial and communist past behind it, members can now start afresh to find a path forward beneficial to all.[2]

ASYMMETRIES IN POTENTIALS

In contemplating this matter it is advisable to pay careful attention to asymmetries in economic trends and systemic potentials, which are likely to have a profound effect on regional influence and power, as well as evidence indicating global growth retardation. Is it reasonable to suppose as development theorists hypothesize that the central global tendency is for economies to converge to a common high frontier and for growth to gradually accelerate, or should we anticipate a different pattern? Recent trends in per capita income and standard of living and also gross domestic product (GDP) appear to suggest a mixed outcome with the United States retaining its lead, Japan and Russia lagging behind, and China gaining ground, while worldwide growth slowly decelerates.[3]

The durability of U.S. economic leadership suggests the superiority of the democratic free enterprise model over its competitors and the possibility that other Asian systems may continue to lag behind. For a time it appeared as if Japan's managed capitalist system would be able to defy the odds and outperform the United States despite its anticompetitive policies, but as the advantages of postwar recovery and economic backwardness faded its per capita gross national product growth persistently decelerated, falling below the United States' and converging toward stagnation.[4]

Russian per capita GDP growth also appeared to outpace that of the United States during the early Cold War years, but recent advances in theory and reestimated purchasing power parities demonstrate that this was an illusion.[5] Russia undoubtedly lost ground under communism and has yet to demonstrate that it is successfully transitioning to a viable form of modern capitalism.[6] Its per capita GDP has been in free fall since December 1991, and its often heralded recovery is still only dimly in sight.[7]

Only post-Maoist China appears to pose a challenge to the superiority of U.S. entrepreneurial capitalism. Although the state owns most of the means of production and is unabashedly authoritarian, it has managed to sustain a remarkably brisk rate of per capita GDP growth since 1980 by opening its economy to massive direct foreign investment led by overseas Chinese businessmen, despite the persistence of pervasive socialist constraints.[8]

If the current model is retained with little further privatization, growth will doubtlessly decelerate as various experts predict,[9] but the pace of advance could remain extraordinary for decades as China's productivity converges to the norms set by the developed West from an extremely low base. The persistence of these trends to the year 2025 will have a profound impact on regional economic and military power.[10] The data in Table 15.1 and forecasts in Table 15.2 suggest that the gap between U.S. per capita GDP (computed at dollar purchasing power parity) and its East Asian neighbors will widen dramatically,[11] with the exception of China, which

TABLE 15.1
Great Power Per Capita Gross Domestic Product in the Asia-Pacific Region

Country	Base Dollars* 1992	Growth Percent 1993–96	Current Dollars* 1996	Index
United States	23,760	1.5	25,218	100
Japan	20,520	0.8	21,185	84
Russia	6,140	–5.0	5,051	20
China	1,950	10.0	2,855	11

* Figures in columns 2 and 4 are given in U.S. dollar purchasing power parity values.

Sources: United Nations, Human Development Report 1995. (New York: Oxford University Press, 1995), p. 203, Table 28, column 1; p. 178, Table 12; Economic Commission for Europe, Economic Survey of Europe in 1994–1996. (New York: United Nations, 1996), p. 11, Table 2.2.2; Economic Commission for Europe, Economic Bulletin for Europe, vol. 48. (New York: United Nations, 1996), p. 20, Table 2.2.1; Organization for Economic Cooperation and Development, National Accounts, Main Aggregates, vol. 1, 1960–95. (Paris: Organization for Economic Cooperation and Development, 1997), pp. 87, 96, 105; Organization for Economic Cooperation and Development, Economic Outlook, 60, (December 1996): 127–28.

will displace Russia from third place in the hierarchy. Russia's importance, moreover, may be further diminished by the enormity of the Chinese market, which because of its huge population, nearly dectuple Russia's, may well exceed $15 trillion.

TABLE 15.2
Projected Great Power Per Capita
Gross Domestic Product in 2025

Country	Base 1996	Growth Percent 1996–2025	Estimate 2025	Index
United States	25,218	1.5	38,835	100
Japan	21,185	0.8	26,692	69
Russia	5,051	0.5	5,837	15
China	2,855	5.0	11,752	30

Notes: The per capita growth rates for the United States and Japan are extrapolated from the trend 1993–96. The per capita growth rate for Russia assumes that after the economy stops declining, its recovery will be slower than elsewhere in Eurasia. The per capita growth rate for China assumes that the current pace is unsustainable and will decelerate by half.

Sources: United Nations, *Human Development Report 1995*. (New York: Oxford University Press, 1995), p. 203, Table 28, column 1; p. 178, Table 12; Economic Commission for Europe, *Economic Survey of Europe in 1994–1996*. (New York: United Nations, 1996), p. 11, Table 2.2.2; Economic Commission for Europe, *Economic Bulletin for Europe*, vol. 48. (New York: United Nations, 1996), p. 20, Table 2.2.1; Organization for Economic Cooperation and Development, *National Accounts, Main Aggregates*, vol. 1, 1960–95. (Paris: Organization for Economic Cooperation and Development, 1997), pp. 87, 96, 105; Organization for Economic Cooperation and Development, *Economic Outlook*, 60, (December 1996): 127–28.

REDISTRIBUTION OF POWER?

Should it not be anticipated that as Japan, Russia, and China emulate U.S. liberal economic principles, they will become more efficient and catch up with the front-runner because of the advantages of relative backwardness?[12] It seems reasonable to suppose so, but the facts do not always support the hypotheses. The Japanese and Soviet-Russian economies have been continuously liberalizing since the early 1950s, but their per capita GDP growth has steadily decelerated. Their experience is not unique. United Nations data show that 51 nations ranked from twenty-third to one hundred seventy-fourth in terms of human development experienced negative per capita GDP growth from 1980 to 1992.[13]

Most economists and politicians have convinced themselves that liber-alization forestalled more severe deterioration and, therefore, are unfazed by this inverse correlation, but there is little empirical evidence support-ing their logically well-founded conviction. From a statistical standpoint there are no grounds for rejecting the hypothesis that the performance of the Japanese and Russian managed economies will worsen, converging toward stagnation or turning negative despite liberalization.[14] Should this occur, it would suggest that these nations must do more than liberalize; they must adjust their cultures to facilitate technology-oriented entrepre-neurship.[15]

U.S. economic performance also may prove disappointing. Although historically low levels of involuntary unemployment have thus far fore-stalled the backlash building against austerity and pro-entrepreneurial liberalization,[16] widening income disparities and social polarization may soon sour the government's strategy of promoting affirmative action friendly, techno-entrepreneurship, and laissez-faire as the best approach to solving its social ills.[17] U.S. long-term economic growth adjusted for the peak in the current cycle also has been gradually flagging, so that no one should be stunned if per capita GDP growth slows perceptibly. Should this occur, U.S. economic and military dominance could be called seri-ously into question. Anemic per capita GDP growth, extreme inequality, and social strife will not seem especially attractive alternatives to Euro-pean social democracy or Japanese communal capitalism.

Although Japan and the United States probably will not diverge drastically from their secular trends, the variance in Russia and China could be enormous. Both could bite the bullet and transition to entrepre-neurial, techno-oriented free enterprise or succumb to the Russian disease (resource demobilization brought about by elite rent-seeking and asset-seizing).[18] The odds favor the latter outcome, transition euphoria notwith-standing.[19]

The prospects delineated above may seem unduly somber in the flush of capitalism's triumph over communism, but they are optimistic. The data driving the forecasts are drawn from a period of unparalleled eco-nomic expansion unblemished by the depressions that marred earlier capitalist performance. If the world economy (Russia aside) is at the crest of a Schumpeterian long wave judged by record high global capitalization levels and recent financial turbulence in Asia, all projections should be drastically pared. A scalar adjustment would lower expectations for future welfare and power, leaving the ranks intact. This is the likely out-come if the hypothesized global depression is mild and transitory. If the depression is more severe all bets are off, because the disturbances are apt to undermine the systems.

It follows directly from the core projections and their various permu-tations that the gay nineties will not be seen in retrospect as a prelude to the golden millennium[20] but as a euphoric interlude in the devitalization of Eurasia and the reconfiguration of global welfare and power. The United States appears well positioned to augment its standing in the new world disorder because of its techno-entrepreneurial culture, but as in all competitions it is prudent to underscore the full potential of long shots.

INTRIGUING CHINA

The most intriguing is China. The core per capita GDP estimate, which is computed on the assumption that Chinese growth will decline from the 10 percent rate clocked in 1993–96 to a compound average rate of 5 percent, indicates that by 2025 a standard of living may reach a third of that of the United States. However, suppose the anticipated deceleration does not materialize, and per capita Chinese GDP compounds at the trend rate for 29 years. China on this assumption will become the world's preeminent superpower with a GDP five times that of the United States with the globe's highest standard of living. In this scenario China would dominate the Asia-Pacific region and through it much of the planet.[21]

Japan also should not be taken for granted. It has repeatedly proved its adaptability over the past 14 centuries and clearly knows the drill. The Japanese media are abuzz with all the right slogans: liberalization, deregulation, government downsizing, and techno-entrepreneurship, but its economists and businessmen acknowledge that progress is less than meets the eye, because its group culture is better at task-setting than stimulating individual innovative initiative. The Japanese are also keenly aware that the Chinese are positioned to make rapid inroads into their traditional export markets, particularly the U.S. market. Perhaps this challenge will galvanize Japan's will to break with tradition and develop a vibrant techno-entrepreneurial culture.

Finally, Russia, the darkest of the dark horses, could live up to the expectations of its well wishers by using its abundant natural resources and foreign direct investment to finance its post–Cold War recovery. It might capitalize on its location, prospering as a Eurasian land bridge, or use its military-industrial know-how as a platform for techno-entrepreneurship. No one disputes Russia's resource and engineering potential; it is its entrenched systemic deficiencies and its predeliction for a rentier state that blight its prospects.

The likely reconfiguration in the structure of global welfare and power implied by the various scenarios considered raises disturbing questions about how the players are likely to respond to their altered international economic stature. Will losers passively accept their declining role, or compensate by forming alliances or expanding their armed forces? Will winners be content with their affluence, or will they be emboldened to dominate their neighbors?

CONCLUSION

Systems theory cannot provide general answers to these provocative questions but does shed some light on potentials. Mature, affluent nations generally are disinclined to divert resources from civilian to military use. Even though the leadership may harbor imperial aspirations, taxpayers are loath to pay the bill. This is likely to be especially true in the slow growth environment forecast for the United States and Japan in the core scenario as domestic factions struggle to preserve and expand their share of social outlays.

The very same logic implies that poor and faltering great powers like Russia, where the opportunity costs of militarism are lower, may be tempted to modernize their arsenals using capacities that would otherwise remain idle. This alternative has been forestalled for the moment because Russia's leadership finds it more advantageous to engage the United States in a joint military build down than to risk an arms race it is unlikely to win.[22] Russia's tycoons are also more interested in their personal enrichment than military confrontation and understand that Western aid and joint venture investment are more lucrative than potential conflict. However, the situation is volatile and could change abruptly if Boris Yeltsin's circle is replaced by neo-nationalists before the foundations for a viable mass consumption economy are firmly in place.

China as an aspiring superpower, resentful of its subservient colonial past, also may be inclined to flex its military muscle in the fast growth environment envisioned. If civilian and military activities increase proportionally at 5 percent per annum this should not be destabilizing, but faster growth, which could make China the world's preeminent military superpower, could be provocative.

The collapse of the Soviet Union and the decline of communism in the Asia-Pacific region have rekindled visions of a golden age of U.S. leadership secured by global liberalization and stabilizing economic growth. Events may unfold this way, but systems theory under a wide variety of assumptions and the factual record suggest otherwise. The world generally, and the Asia-Pacific region in particular, are much more likely to be buffeted by traumatic reconfigurations of global welfare and power than to sail tranquilly along the path of rapid complementary capitalist development scripted by the Group of Eight.

NOTES

1. Arnold Beichman and Mikhail Bernstarn, *Andropov: New Challenges to the West*. (New York: Stein and Day, 1983).

2. The economic systems of Vietnam and Cambodia also display a variety of special characteristics.

3.   Paul Krugman, *Peddling Prosperity: Economic Sense, and Nonsense in the Age of Diminished Expectations*. (New York: W. W. Norton, 1994); Paul Krugman, *Pop Internationalism*. (Cambridge, Mass.: MIT Press, 1997); Steven Rosefielde, "Dark Horses: Contemporary Challenges to American Leadership," unpublished manuscript, May 1998. Global per capita GDP growth was: 1960–80, 4 percent; 1980–92, 1.9 percent; 1993–96, 1.5 percent.

4.   Richard Katz, *Japan — The System That Soured: The Rise and Fall of the Japanese Economic Miracle*. (Armonk, N.Y.: M. E. Sharpe, 1998); Michael Hirsh and Keith Henry, "The Unraveling of Japan Inc.," *Foreign Affairs*, 76(2) (March–April 1997): 11–16; Scott Gallon, *Divided Sun: MITI and the Breakdown of Japanese High-Tech Industrial Policy 1975–1993*. (Stanford, Calif.: Stanford University Press, 1995); Economic Planning Agency of Japan, *Economy-wide Effects of Economic Structural Reforms in Japan: FY1998-2003*. (Tokyo: Government of Japan, 1997); Eisuke Sakakibara, *Beyond Capitalism: The Japanese Model of Market Economies*. (New York: University Press of America, 1993); Robert Uriu, *Troubled Industries: Confronting Economic Change in Japan*. (Ithaca, N.Y.: Cornell University Press, 1996); Kent Calder, *Strategic Capitalism*. (Princeton, N.J.: Princeton University Press, 1993).

5.   Steven Rosefielde (ed.), *Russia's Economic Recovery Potential to the Year 2000 and Beyond*. (London: Ashgate, 1998).

6.   Stefan Hedlund, *Russia's "Market" Economy: A Bad Case of Predatory Capitalism*. (East Orange, N.J.: Uppsala University, Department of East European Studies, unpublished manuscript, 1998); see also Steven Rosefielde, "Klepto-banking: Systemic Sources of Russia's Failed Industrial Recovery," in *The Nigerian Banking Crisis in Comparative Perspective*, edited by Howard Stein. (New York: Macmillan, 1998).

7.   The Russian government claims that GDP grew 0.4 percent in 1997, and the Bank of Finland was forecasting 1.3 percent for 1998, before Victor Chernomyrdin was removed as Prime Minister. See *Russian Economy*, February 1998, Bank of Finland, Institute for Economies in Transition. According to Yevgeniy Gavrilenko and various International Monetary Fund officials, Russia continued to experience negative economic growth in 1997. The official figure was obtained by increasing the estimate of the unobservable component of the Russian economy from 20 to 25 percent and increasing the phantom growth rate. Official institutions have been forecasting rapid Russian economic growth at the beginning of every year since 1992. The sharp decline in oil prices and the Asian economic crisis demonstrated that 1998 was not an exception to the established pattern. Moreover, Russian national currency devaluation and near collapse of the banking and financial systems made the economic situation much worse.

8.   Official Chinese growth rates are even higher than those reported in Table 15.1. See *Historical National Account of the People's Republic of China 1952–1995* (Kunitachi: State Statistical Bureau of the People's Republic of China, and the Institute of National Economic Research Hitotsubashi University, 1997), p. 67, Table A.8; Steven Rosefielde, "Chinese Market Socialism: Managerial Autonomy, State Ownership and Economic Justice," Discussion Paper Series A., No. 336. (Kunitachi: Hitotsubashi University, 1997).

9.   Charles Wolf, Jr., K. C. Yeh, Amil Bamezal, Donald Henry, and Michael Kennedy, *Long-Term Economic and Military Trends 1994–2015: The United States and*

Asia, prepared for the Office of the Secretary of Defense. (Santa Monica, Calif.: Rand, 1995).

10.   The trends used to forecast the reconfiguration of per capita GDP in East Asia have been extremely persistent for the United States, Japan, and China and will probably continue. The Russian projection reflects the author's judgment that the Kremlin will fail in its declaratory effort to create a viable form of market capitalism. There are two plausible possibilities. Russia will install a neo-nationalist managed economy, or the existing system, which gives priority to rent-seeking over production, will be consolidated. In the first instance, per capita GDP growth could exceed 0.5 percent per annum, but with the poor qualitative characteristics that epitomized Soviet economic performance. In the latter case, Russia will be lucky to achieve positive per capita GDP growth.

11.   The use of dollar purchasing power parities instead of exchange rate estimates is highly favorable to both China and Russia. If the choice were reversed, per capita GDP in both these countries in 1996 would be much lower than indicated in Table 15.1. The author believes that the use of purchasing power parities is more justified in the Chinese case than the Russian because the former is a much larger exporter of globally competitive industrial goods, thanks to its overseas Chinese-guided modernization.

12.   Alexander Gerschenkron, *Economic Backwardness in Historical Perspective.* (Cambridge, Mass.: Belknap Press, 1966); see also Takatoshi Ito, Robert Lawrence, and Albert Bresend, *Vision for the World Economy.* (Washington, D.C.: Brookings Institution, 1996).

13.   United Nations, *Human Development Report 1995.* (New York: Oxford University Press, 1995); Steven Vogel, *Freer Markets, More Rules: Regulatory Reform in Advanced Industrial Countries.* (Ithaca, N.Y.: Cornell University Press, 1996).

14.   Paul Krugman, "The Myth of Asia's Miracle," *Foreign Affairs,* 73(6) (1994): 62–78.

15.   Denis Simon, *Techno-Security in the Age of Globalism: Perspectives from the Pacific Rim.* (Armonk, N.Y.: M. E. Sharpe, 1997). The neologism "techno-entrepreneurship" means technology-focused, innovational entrepreneurship.

16.   W. R. Meade, "Roller Coaster Capitalism," *Foreign Affairs,* 76(1) (January–February 1997): 146–52.

17.   Daniel Patrick Moynihan, "Dependency is Our Problem," in *Leading Economic Controversies of 1997,* edited by Edwin Mansfield. (New York: W. W. Norton, 1997), pp. 44–50; President Clinton's Council of Economic Advisers, "Slowing Wage Growth and Widening Inequality," in *Leading Economic Controversies of 1997,* edited by Edwin Mansfield. (New York: W. W. Norton, 1997), pp. 19–25; Michael Sandel, *Democracy's Discontent: America in Search of a Public Philosophy.* (Cambridge, Mass.: Belknap Press, 1996); John Gray, *False Dawn: The Delusions of Global Capitalism.* (London: Granta, 1998).

18.   The term "rent-seeking" means the pursuit of unearned incomes with the connivance of the state. The term "asset-seizing" refers to the unauthorized but officially tolerated insider privatization of state assets and the seizure of other properties on a privileged, non-competitive basis. See Anders Åslund, "Rentoorendrovannoe povedenie v Rossiiskoi perekhodnoe ekonomike (Rent-seeking behavior in Russia's transition economy), *Voprosy Ekonomiki,* No. 8 (1996): 99–108; Anders Åslund, "Russian Banking: Crisis or Rent-Seeking?" *Post-Soviet Geography*

and Economics, 37(8) (1996): 495–502; Steven Rosefielde, "Russian Market Kleptocracy," unpublished manuscript, 1997; Steven Rosefielde, "Forgotten Superpower: Prospects for Reconstituting Russia's Military Might," in Proceedings of the Conference on Russian Military Prospects, FOA, Stockholm, Sweden, March 12–13, 1998.

19.   Anders Åslund, *How Russia Became a Market Economy*. (Washington, D.C.: Brookings Institution, 1995); Joseph Blasi, Maya Kroumova, and Douglas Kruse, *Kremlin Capitalism: Privatizing the Russian Economy*. (Ithaca, N.Y.: Cornell University Press, 1997); Stefan Hedlund, "The Russian Economy: A Case of Pathological Institutions?" Working Paper 25, ISRN UU-OSTUD-AR 97/5-SE. (East Orange, N.J.: Uppsala University, Department of East European Studies, 1997); David Remnick, "Can Russia Change?," *Foreign Affairs*, 76(1) (January–February 1997): 35–49; David Remnick, *Resurrection*. (New York: Random House, 1997); Steven Rosefielde, *Russia's Economic Recovery Potential to the Year 2000 and Beyond*. (London: Ashgate, 1998); William Webster, *Russian Organized Crime*. (Washington, D.C.: Center for Strategic and International Studies, 1997); Organization for Economic Cooperation and Development Economic Surveys, *Russian Federation 1997*. (Paris: Organization for Economic Cooperation and Development, 1997).

20.   Paul Krugman, *Age of Diminished Expectations: U.S. Economic Policies in the 1990s*. (Cambridge, Mass.: MIT Press, 1997).

21.   Richard Bernstein and Ross Munro, "China I: The Coming Conflict with America," *Foreign Affairs*, 76(2) (March–April 1997): 18–32; Gary Jefferson and Thomas Rawski, "Enterprise Reform in Chinese Industry," *Journal of Economic Perspectives*, 8(2) (1994): 47–70; Gary Jefferson, Thomas Rawski, and Zheng Yuxin, "Chinese Industrial Productivity: Trends, Measurement Issues and Recent Developments," *Journal of Comparative Economics*, 23(2) (October 1996): 146–80; Yingyi Quin, "Reforming Corporate Governance and Finance in China," in *Corporate Governance in Transitional Economies: Insider Control and the Role of Banks*, edited by Masahiko Aoki, and Hyuang-Ki Kim. (Washington, D.C.: World Bank, 1995), pp. 215–32; Robert Ross, "China II: Beijing as a Conservative Power," *Foreign Affairs*, 76(2) (March–April 1997): 33–44.

22.   David Hoffman, "A Shrunken and Rusty 'Nuclear Stick': Economic Woes, Obsolescence and Treaties Slash Russia's Arsenal," *Herald Tribune*, March 17, 1998, pp. 1, 6; Steven Rosefielde, *Forgotten Superpower: Russia's Military Revival and the New Global Order*, unpublished manuscript, 1998.

16

Main Events of a New Era
Robert Valliant

The years 1993–98 saw at first a gradual improvement in the relationship between Russia and Japan, and then toward the end a sudden burst of energy as President Boris Yeltsin and Prime Minister Ryutaro Hashimoto decided to move ahead quickly. The following is a year-by-year account of the main highlights of the period.

1993

The year 1993 began with weak governments in both Russia and Japan. Kiichi Miyazawa became prime minister of Japan in November 1992. He was one of a series of weak prime ministers who governed Japan between 1993 and 1998. His government lasted until the summer when Morihiro Hosokawa became prime minister and 38 years of Liberal Democratic Party (LDP) rule came to an end. The new coalition government composed of eight different parties and groups did not even manage to last a year.

In Russia Yeltsin, too, faced mounting political problems. The country's mood was growing increasingly nationalistic. The parliament opposed him at every turn and had forced cancellation of his trip to Japan in the fall of 1992. Public disappointment at the paltry sums of Western assistance fueled accusations of a too pro-Western foreign policy. Yet, Yeltsin managed to weather the spring storm, winning a national referendum on his policy (April 25). The battle, however, continued into the summer and fall.

If Russia's policy toward Japan was mired in nationalistic domestic politics, Japan's policy toward Russia betrayed signs of small change. Japan's policy was to support Yeltsin, provide direct aid only in multilateral efforts, and only humanitarian aid on a bilateral basis. This policy flexed slightly when Japan offered more bilateral aid ($1.8 billion) at the Group of Seven (G-7) foreign and finance ministers' meeting in Tokyo (April 14–15). As a further concession, at the G-7 summit in Tokyo (July 7–9), Japan kept the territorial dispute out of the main meeting and took it up in bilateral meetings. Still the government claimed (April 15) that Japan retained its policy of "expanded equilibrium/balance" and reiterated that claim after the G-7 summit.[1] In the face of the rising conservative storm Russia, too, asserted that its policy had not changed. The Russian opposition and government remained adamant that there would be no concessions to Japan on the islands. A presidential spokesman called the eventual return of two of four disputed islands unrealistic (August 17), and Prime Minister Victor Chernomyrdin even denied the existence of a territorial dispute (August 17, 18). Yet, after discussions with former Yeltsin adviser Gennadiy Burbulis and their own investigations, the Japanese decided that Chernomyrdin's remarks represented his personal opinion and not the views of Russia (Chief Cabinet Secretary Takemura Masayoshi on September 17), and preparations for Yeltsin's visit continued.

Yeltsin made his twice-postponed (October 1992, May 1993) visit to Japan (October 11–13), but only after he had ousted the Congress of People's Deputies, suspended the constitution, announced new elections (September 21), and finally ordered troops to storm the White House (October 4), where the leaders of the opposition were holding out.

In Japan Yeltsin confirmed that Russia adhered to diplomatic agreements concluded by the former Soviet Union, stressed that Russia intended to demilitarize the disputed territories, apologized for the internment and forced labor of some 600,000 Japanese soldiers in Siberia after World War II, and pledged to cooperate in settling problems arising from those acts. The two sides signed 18 documents, chief among them the Tokyo Declaration and the Declaration on Future Economic Ties. They also agreed to hold regular foreign ministers' meetings twice a year, to carry out joint inspections on control over radioactive pollution of the water environment, to set up a working team for drawing up a peace treaty, and to create a system for regular summit contacts between the two countries.

The year ended on a mixed note. On the one hand Russia eased travel restrictions on Japanese residents (November 1), and Japan opened a Consulate General in Khabarovsk (November 11). On the other, the omens from Russia were more ominous. In the December general elections, the Liberal Democratic Party of Russia, one of the most conservative and vocal, captured 43 percent of the vote.

1994

In 1994 the Russian government continued its drift toward conservatism, while the Japanese government just drifted. The strong showing by the ultra-nationalists and other hard-line groups in the Russian elections in December had immediate repercussions. The Russian cabinet changed to reflect the elections. The reformers and their foreign advisers left and were replaced by economic and political conservatives.

Despite the government turnover, the two countries continued to improve their relationship. Japanese Foreign Minister Tsutomu Hata visited Moscow (March 19–21) and got confirmation of the provisions of the October 1993 Tokyo Declaration and agreement to develop contacts among representatives of the defense establishments of the two countries. Hosokawa announced his resignation (April 6). The new prime minister, Tsutomu Hata (April 25), lasted only two months. His resignation opened the way for Tomiichi Murayama, the first socialist prime minister in 46 years (June 30). Murayama was backed by his long-time rivals, the LDP and Sakigake, a small LDP splinter group. He managed to last 18 months. The LDP retained the foreign minister post in the person of Yohei Kono, and progress in the relationship with Russia continued.

Japan continued to loosen the economic purse strings. It agreed to reschedule $753 million in public debt owed by the former Soviet Union (March 1) and also accepted a Russian proposal to shift $500 million, originally announced in October 1991 as humanitarian aid, to investment projects (March 20). The Export-Import Bank of Japan (JEXIM) offered a ¥21 billion ($190 million) credit line (July 6) for construction of a fiber-optic communications line between Moscow and Khabarovsk.

Japan did not insist that the G-7 statement contain a clause on the territorial dispute (July 10), and the Hokkaido prefectural government opened an office in Yuzhno-Sakhalinsk (July 12). A Russian consulate-general, the fourth in Japan, opened in Niigata (September 9). A Japan Center opened in Khabarovsk (October 31) to offer management training to Russian managers.

The economic relationship received another boost when First Deputy Prime Minister Oleg Soskovets visited Japan (November 26–December 1). The two countries signed four documents designed to encourage trade and investment between them and to smooth procedures for Japanese aid: an agreement to set up a cabinet level forum to address various economic issues including trade arrears; an agreement to provide legal advice and other assistance to Russia to help it integrate into the international free trade system under the General Agreement on Tariffs and Trade; an agreement to provide Russia with technical assistance through personnel exchanges in areas such as industrial policy, economic planning, and fiscal and financial policy; and an agreement to reschedule

Russian debt owed to the Japanese government in the form of trade insurance, worth about $180 million.

While Soskovets was in Japan, the Japanese government announced new aid measures (November 28). The Ministry of International Trade and Industry (MITI) offered a three-year productivity improvement program to invite Russian consultants and company executives to Japan to train them in how to manage and restructure firms in a market-oriented economy and an industrial cooperation system to link Japanese and Russian firms to facilitate investment and technology transfer in the private sector. Japan also agreed to provide $530 million for three modernization projects: the Yaroslavnefteorgsintez oil refinery ($240 million), the St. Petersburg–based Impulse plant ($140 million), and the truck-building plant KAMAZ ($60 million).

The timing of Japan's moves was important. Prior to Soskovets' visit a strong earthquake had destroyed most structures on the southern Kuril islands (October 4), and the ruble had collapsed (October 11), losing 21 percent of its value in a single day. The government managed to win a no-confidence vote in the Duma (October 27), but a cabinet reshuffle followed (November 4–9) as Russia went through three finance ministers in four weeks. Then Yeltsin entered the hospital for surgery (December 10), just one day before Russian troops moved into Chechniya.

1995

The increasingly nationalistic tone of Russian politics and the fighting in Chechniya affected Russia's relationship with Japan. *Izvestiya* noted that the patriotic shift that clearly emerged in Russian foreign policy in 1994 left little hope that Moscow and Tokyo would be able to settle the territorial dispute in the foreseeable future (January 12). Foreign Minister Kono warned of an increasing tendency toward "great country-ism" in Russia (January 18), connected with Moscow's intervention in civil strife in Chechniya and the rising influence of conservatives and ethnocentric circles.

The foreign ministries' discussions of improvements in the security sphere began to bear fruit. The Japan Defense Agency (JDA) revealed plans for security dialogues with Russia, China, and South Korea (January 5), and Japan offered to consider the proposals put forth by Deputy Defense Minister Boris Gromov (March 2–4) for invitations to military exercises, exchanges of delegations, demonstration flights of aircraft in each other's airspace, and joint actions of naval forces, including mutual visits of warships.

Russian Foreign Minister Andrei Kozyrev made a few gestures of improvement during his visit to Japan (March 2–4). He agreed to begin official negotiations on fishing rights in waters around the disputed islands, promised to send a group of experts to Tokyo to "explain the difficult aspects" of withdrawing 7,000 Russian military personnel from those islands, and presented Japan with a list of 5,649 Japanese prisoners of war who died while in detention in Siberia. He even surprised the Japanese by offering Moscow's clearest-ever support for Japan's bid to become a permanent member of the UN Security Council.

The framework talks on safety for Japanese fishing around the disputed islands finally got underway (March 13–14). However the two sides did not manage to resolve the issue through four rounds of talks during the year (March, May 29, August 30–31, and December 21–22). For its part, the Russian government released the captains of two boats detained for illegal fishing around the islands in 1994 (March 16). However, Russian border guards remained vigilant, chasing Japanese fishing boats out of the waters around the disputed islands (March 20, 24, April 3) and even firing warning shots when necessary (April 4, September 26).

Economically, 1995 proved to be a somewhat successful year. On May 23, JEXIM announced an agreement with the Moscow-based Bank for Foreign Trade (Rosvneshtorgbank) for a ¥4.2 billion loan to Impulse for a microwave oven project. On November 30, Japan agreed to reschedule part of the Soviet Union's official debt, amounting to about $400 million. The new agreement called for repayment over 13 years, starting in 1998.

The Sakhalin earthquake (May 28) occasioned a strange exchange between the two countries and betrayed Yeltsin's ambiguity toward Japan. He suggested that Japan's offer of "no strings attached" aid for earthquake victims masked ulterior motives (May 31). The matter ended when a Yeltsin spokesman said that the president regretted "his quite emotional statement" (June 2). About a month later (July 11) Yeltsin was admitted to the hospital with a heart attack. He returned to work August 8, only to be hospitalized again (October 26) with a heart problem. He returned to work on December 29, after the elections.

The December 17 elections to the State Duma did nothing to improve Russia's relationship with Japan. The Communist Party made large gains, winning 157 seats out of 450, up from only 45 seats in 1993. The government party, Our Home is Russia, won 55 seats, making it the second strongest party.

1996

The year 1996 brought significant changes in both countries. In Japan, Prime Minister Murayama resigned (January 5), opening the way for the LDP to return to power. Hashimoto became prime minister (January 11), promising a proactive foreign policy, and he was as good as his word. In Russia, Foreign Minister Kozyrev resigned (January 5), and Yevgeniy

Primakov replaced him (January 9).[2] One Japanese action that concerned Russia was the cabinet's decision (February 20) to ratify the UN Convention on the Law of the Sea and establish an exclusive economic zone that would cover disputed islands claimed by South Korea and China and the islands in dispute with Russia. The Diet passed the requisite bills (June 7), the House of Councillors unanimously approved the package, and the cabinet sent a ratification document to the United Nations. The 200-mile exclusive economic zone took effect on July 20.

Japanese Foreign Minister Yukihiko Ikeda visited Moscow (March 19–20) with a dual purpose. The Inter-Governmental Commission on Trade and Economic Cooperation, as agreed during Soskovets' visit in November 1994, met for the first time, and the foreign ministers held one of their regular meetings. Ikeda had three priorities: to get reconfirmation of the 1993 Tokyo Declaration, to get agreement for the strengthening of ties with the Russian Far East, and to step up dialogue on security.

Security talks between Japan and Russia began when JDA chief Hideo Usui visited Moscow (April 27–29). This was the first visit by the head of the JDA. Usui and the Russian Defense Ministry agreed to mutual notification in cases of large exercises, to exchange visits by naval vessels, to joint communications drills, and to exchange information on their armed forces and military doctrines.

The question of Russian troops on the disputed islands came up when Yeltsin and Hashimoto met in Moscow (April 19) at a G-7 meeting on nuclear safety. Yeltsin told Hashimoto things the Japanese wanted to hear: that Russia had cut its troop strength on the Islands to 3,500 and that Russia would accede to the Amendment to the London Convention, which would mean no more dumping of nuclear waste at sea. The meetings went well, and Hashimoto tried a new approach — on the advice of U.S. President Clinton, who had suggested that he establish good personal relations with Yeltsin. This approach would bear fruit later. The two leaders also agreed to revive peace treaty talks, but only after Russia's June presidential election, because Japan wanted to avoid politicizing the issue during the election campaign.

The election campaign proved a very tightly contested one between incumbent Yeltsin and Gennadiy Zyuganov, head of the Communist Party. The vote was close. Yeltsin got just 35.28 percent of the votes cast to Zyuganov's 32.04 percent. General Alexander Lebed, the hero of Chechniya, ran a distant third with 14.52 percent. That threw the election into a run-off (July 3), in which Yeltsin managed to get 53.82 percent of the vote to Zyuganov's 40.31 percent.

After the election, Deputy Foreign Minister Alexander Panov assured Japan that Russia's policy had not changed (July 12). He urged Japan to stop linking economic relations to the return of the disputed islands;

supported Foreign Minister Primakov's statement that the issue should be left to future generations; and noted that Tokyo's "policy of balanced expansion" limited the development of bilateral ties. He also suggested that Japan lift a ban on investment and trade with the disputed islands, noting that economic development would benefit both sides. Two months later Panov became ambassador to Japan.[3]

Panov was generally careful in his remarks about the disputed islands. Others were not, and that made for a discordant approach to policy. Yeltsin, setting out priorities in border policy, averred that Russia had no territorial claims on other countries and denied "any territorial claims on the Russian Federation from other states" (October 9). The Foreign Ministry clarified the statement the following day, announcing that Russia would continue to recognize its territorial dispute with Japan. Less than a week earlier, when the deputy foreign ministers met in Tokyo (October 2–4), Russian Deputy Foreign Minister Grigoriy Karasin reported that for the first time Japan agreed to consider Moscow's proposals on joint economic activities on the South Kurils. However, the Japanese Foreign Ministry quickly responded that Japan's stance on the Northern Territories issue has not changed, and its government does not intend to study the joint development proposal. It turned out that Russia had not made a specific proposal anyway.

The question of joint development came up six weeks later when Primakov visited Japan (November 14–17) for the seventh regular meeting of foreign ministers. Primakov again proposed joint development of the islands but again offered nothing specific. This time, however, in contrast to the previous completely negative response, Ikeda replied that Japan would listen to a concrete proposal. Otherwise, the two foreign ministers agreed that the $500 million originally earmarked as humanitarian aid in October 1991 could be used for projects presented to JEXIM. However, the first *tranche* was not actually delivered until June 1997. During these talks the Japanese believed that they perceived a slight difference in approach. Japan's goal was to advance the territorial issue and to improve the atmosphere surrounding it, while Russia emphasized more the importance of just improving the atmosphere.

As the year drew to a close, the atmosphere showed definite improvement. The framework talks on fishing safety around the Kuril Islands got back on track. There were only three meetings in 1996 — the fifth round (February 19–21), the sixth round (June 4–6), and the seventh round (November 20–21) — compared to four rounds in 1995. The talks were proving difficult. Japanese Foreign Ministry sources admitted a serious policy shift had taken place in Japanese policy: Japan would accept Russia's control of the southern half of Sakhalin Island by setting up a branch office of the Japanese Khabarovsk Consulate General in Yuzhno Sakhalinsk, thus implicitly recognizing Russian sovereignty (December 1).

1997

The year 1997 began with mixed portents. Primakov noted that the territorial issue no longer impeded the development of bilateral ties, but still thought it too early to speak of a breakthrough in relations with Japan (January 8). The three subcommittees of the Inter-Governmental Commission on Trade and Economic Cooperation met and agreed to increase Japanese investment in Russia and enhance bilateral economic relations (January 27–28). Yet, Ambassador Takehiro Togo warned that Russia was not paying enough attention to Asia (January 22), and his warning seemed justified when First Deputy Prime Minister Viktor Ilyushin abruptly postponed a visit to Japan (February 26) only to show up in Switzerland a week later (March 5).

In spite of Togo's warning, security talks continued in a positive vein. Russian Defense Minister Igor Rodionov became the first Russian defense chief to visit Japan since the Soviet era (May 16–18). He and JDA Chief Fumio Kyuma agreed to start a wide variety of defense exchanges, including mutual visits by the chiefs of staff, defense researchers, military academy cadets, and observers to war games and fleets. Rodionov puzzled the Japanese when he said that Russia welcomed closer defense ties between the United States and Japan, because only a few weeks earlier Russia had proclaimed a strategic partnership with China in an effort to counterbalance the United States' growing global influence.

Local level relations received a boost when Foreign Minister Ikeda visited Russia (May 22–24). Russia and Japan agreed to open a Yuzhno-Sakhalinsk office of the Japanese Consulate General in Khabarovsk and a Hakodate office of the Russian Consulate General in Sapporo and on Japanese technical assistance for retraining soldiers transferred to the reserve. Japan also offered relocation assistance to soldiers who would be transferred from the disputed islands. The governors of three Russian Far East provinces (Primorskiy and Khabarovskiy krais, and Sakhalinskaya Oblast) and of Hokkaido signed a five-year Program for Economic Cooperation (September 2). Representatives of five Japanese ports visited Vladivostok to determine if the area could handle increased freight if the Trans-Siberian Railway revived (September 8). On the disputed islands themselves, Deputy Foreign Minister Minoru Tamba, leading a group of 43 Japanese, visited Kunashir (September 30–October 2). Mikhail Lukyanov, chairman of the South Kurils district assembly, told journalists that he himself does not mind if the four islands are recognized as Japanese territories and all or part of them are returned to Japan (October 8). Meanwhile Kyodo News Agency published a poll of 2,200 Russians, including 48 living on Iturup, that showed that 54 percent would accept the return of at least some of the islands to Japan.

Matters moved fastest in the economic sphere. MITI and Russian counterparts met in Tokyo (March 5) and agreed to reschedule Russian debt to the private sector. Russia would repay some $200 million in short-term loans inherited from the Soviet Union to Japanese trading houses over 25 years after a seven-year deferment. MITI also agreed to designate seven more banks to accept export credit insurance. The second meeting of the Inter-Governmental Commission on Trade and Economic Cooperation in Tokyo (June 9–10) seemed more show. First Deputy Prime Minister Boris Nemtsov, the Russian co-chairman, was the showman. The press was filled with such terms as "splash," "personal flare," "wows," but the results were much more prosaic. Nemtsov agreed to take measures to resolve Russia's debt to the Japanese private sector, to improve its tax and legal systems with regard to trade and economic issues, and to set up an office to receive opinions and proposals from foreign companies with regard to its tax and legal systems and carry out measures to improve these systems — all worthy goals, but rather nebulous. The real work was underway elsewhere.

Talks had already begun on restoring container shipments on the Trans-Siberian Railway to the 1980s level; on simplifying customs formalities, accelerating the movement of freight, and lowering tariffs; on the participation of Japanese companies in the modernization of the Yuzhno-Sakhalinsk airport; and to bring the Japanese feasibility studies for the modernization of the port of Zarubino into correspondence with the Russian realities and technical requirements. Representatives of the ruling LDP even passed the Russians a memorandum outlining Japan's approach to cooperation in the sphere of development of energy resources. Russia and Japan also signed the agreement for the first *tranche* of a $500 million loan that Japan originally pledged in October 1991 (June 9). It covered three projects, including an automobile painting factory in Izhevsk and a hospital in Irkutsk.

The Denver G-7 summit (June 20–22) helped open the way for a new type of relationship. Japanese government sources indicated that Japan had reversed its position and agreed to let Russia join the G-7 summit as a formal member (May 18). The apparent reason for the reversal was Japan's fear of isolation. The other G-7 members favored admitting Russia in order to secure acquiescence to the eastward expansion of the North Atlantic Treaty Organization. Russia took part in the summit at every meal and meeting except one. In their bilateral meeting Hashimoto and Yeltsin got on well. Nemtsov had said that Hashimoto wanted to spend a day with Yeltsin and that Yeltsin hoped to communicate with Hashimoto on a personal level (June 10). They agreed to hold regular meetings, to meet unofficially, and to boost Japanese investment in Russia. Yeltsin proposed a telephone hotline between Moscow and Tokyo to improve communication and promised to stop targeting Japanese cities with nuclear missiles.

The incremental changes in Japan's policy culminated in Hashimoto's speech to the Association of Corporate Executives (July 24). Within the context of his Eurasian diplomacy, he spoke of a multi-layered approach to Russia, based on the principles of trust, mutual benefit, and long-term perspective. He also called for "focus on strengthening economic relations with Russia, especially in Siberia and the Far East region, and in particular, in the energy sector." This new approach, founded on personal trust between the leaders, had been foreshadowed in his April 19, 1996, meeting with Yeltsin. Behind it lay the Japanese Foreign Ministry's decision that it was time for Japan to part with old habits and move from a bottom-up to a top-down strategy.

The new approach got off to a fast start when Yeltsin and Hashimoto held their first unofficial meeting (November 1–2) in Krasnoyarsk. Yeltsin gave the Japanese something they had been waiting for: "We have set a concrete deadline for solving the Russian-Japanese problem and reaching a peace accord by 2000." Yeltsin's penchant for exaggeration apparently had gotten the best of him again. His spokesman characterized the concrete deadline as an expression of political will but by no means an obligation (November 4). In spite of the misstatement the two leaders made progress.

The high point of the Krasnoyarsk meeting was a six-point Hashimoto-Yeltsin plan of economic cooperation to be implemented by 2000. The six areas were not new. They had been discussed many times before: investment promotion, integrating the Russian economy into the global economic system, further support for Russian reforms, training of Russian business executives and government officials, dialogue in the energy field, and cooperation in the peaceful use of nuclear energy. However, the two leaders' focus provided new impetus.

Other developments followed swiftly. MITI announced that it would grant long-term trade insurance (two or more years) for projects backed by major Russian commercial banks, even without a Russian government guarantee as required under the current terms (November 4). Foreign Ministers Primakov and Keizo Obuchi, meeting in Tokyo, agreed to head a new bilateral forum to work toward a peace treaty by 2000. Primakov proposed including representatives of Russian provincial local governments in the new forum (November 11–14).

1998

Japan and Russia moved ahead on the Hashimoto-Yeltsin plan. Talks on the peace treaty began at the deputy foreign minister level in Moscow (January 22–23) in preparation for the first meeting of the Joint

Committee on the Conclusion of the Peace Treaty. The joint committee met when Obuchi visited Moscow (February 21–23).

Economic issues occupied a leading position. A Russian delegation visited Tokyo for talks about restoring traffic on the Trans-Siberian Railway (January 26–30). Bilateral energy consultations (January 28) covered Russia's ability to supply Asia, the investment climate as it relates to energy, and energy cooperation between the two countries, in which the private sector will play the major role. Japan and Russia finally signed the framework agreement to ensure safe fishing around the disputed islands (February 21). During his Moscow visit, Obuchi announced Japan's intention to provide an untied JEXIM yen loan (cofinanced with the World Bank) worth $1.5 billion.

The training of Russian managers and servicemen also began quickly. Fifty-five Russian managers visited Japan for training programs in finance, banking, business management, marketing, and so forth (February 15–March 8). They had attended courses held at the Japan Centers in Moscow, Khabarovsk, Vladivostok, and Yuzhno-Sakhalinsk. In Vladivostok 40 officers about to retire from the military in the Far East attended a seminar in automobile sales and service at the Japan Center (February 23–March 10).

From April 11 through 13 Yeltsin visited Japan; in June Obuchi became prime minister of Japan; in September Primakov was nominated prime minister of Russia.

NOTES

1.   Japan adopted the policy of "expanded equilibrium or balance" in 1989. Sosuke Uno introduced it during his visit to Moscow in May. It consisted of five points: solve the territorial dispute and conclude a peace treaty, build up mutual confidence, promote suitable and possible forms of a business relationship, expand and strengthen exchanges of people, and have President Mikhail Gorbachev visit Japan.

2.   Primakov (66) was a man of a different generation, a representative of the Soviet apparatus. He had been closely linked with Gorbachev but had managed to avoid the fate of others with close Gorbachev ties. Yeltsin had even appointed him head of the Foreign Intelligence Service. Primakov found no home among liberals or reformers, but neither was he an ultraconservative. His appointment was expected to assuage the conservatives in the Duma, and he was expected to pursue a more active and less pro-Western policy.

3.   Alexander Panov had served in the Soviet Embassy in Japan from 1968 to 1971 and from 1983 to 1988. He was an assistant to the permanent representative of the Soviet Union to the United Nations from 1977 to 1982. He returned to the Foreign Ministry in 1998, rising from deputy chief of sector to assistant head of the Pacific and Southeast Asia Department. He was ambassador to the Republic of Korea from 1992 to 1993.

NIM

III

DEVELOPMENT, TRADE, AND INVESTMENT

The existing economic basis of the Russia-Japan relationship remains far from its potential in scale and quality. The old system of trade, reliable and predictable, has gone with the dissolution of the Soviet Union, leaving huge unpaid debts, both official and private. Moreover, the crisis in Russia, the protracted decline in industrial output, and shrinking investment stimulated neither trade nor Japanese investment. The Japanese economy also entered a protracted period of stagnation, thus reducing the potential of the private sector to be proactive, particularly in such a difficult environment as Russia. Japan's special attachment to the Far East of Russia and plans to promote closer economic ties with this region did not materialize either. Political constraints on the part of Tokyo combined with the policy of macroeconomic stabilization in Russia prevented closer linkages between Far Eastern industries and Japanese enterprises and investors except in fishery and used car imports by individual Russians.

After Moscow reduced subsidies the economic situation in the Far East began to deteriorate rapidly. A steep decline in the standard of living, enterprise shutdowns, the sudden loss of markets, fewer jobs and federal subsidies, power outages, and rapidly growing tariffs for transportation, electricity, and heat sharply contrasted with the expectations of the early 1990s and hopes that an economic opening toward the Asia-Pacific region would bring prosperity. In contrast, because the Far East of Russia was suddenly cut off from its traditional customers and suppliers in central Russia, trade linkages with Asia and North America became more than simply commercial enterprises; they became a tool for survival.

Japanese businesses seemed disappointed. Their frequent group study tours to the provinces' capitals and enterprises usually had no follow-up in terms of new investment and trade contracts, creating frustration on the Russian side.

Part III examines trade and economic relations between Russia and Japan and provides views on how the bilateral economic relationship progressed in 1993–97, how it can be developed in the future, and what areas can promise new opportunities for economic engagement.

Alexander G. Granberg looks at the problem of provinces-Moscow relations and provides a brief picture of federal-regional budget relations, anti-crisis measures, and development plans. The development of regionalism in a country as big and diverse as Russia is natural. The role of the provinces in Russian domestic politics is growing, but no other group of territories within the Russian Federation equals the strategic value of the Far East. However, in terms of Russia's posture in the Asia-Pacific region and its future relations with its neighbors, including China, Japan, the Koreas, and the United States, the Siberian provinces have to be taken into account as well. The combined economic potential of eastern Russia is significantly larger than that of the Far East alone. Moreover, the *Federal Program for Economic and Social Development of the Far Eastern and Trans-Baikal Region for 1996–2005* already incorporates two Trans-Baikal provinces. Eastern Siberia is the next logical candidate for economic links with the region. The Siberian and Far Eastern provinces are not only rich in resources but also known for their technologically advanced products, such as the *Sukhoi-27* jet fighter. The region has the capacity, human resources, and expertise to support civilian high-tech production.

Pavel A. Minakir continues to analyze this subject from the perspective of foreign trade and investment relations. He begins with an overview of the development plans for Far Eastern Russia, including the one adopted in 1996 and endorsed as a presidential program. The chances for this new program to be successfully implemented are not very good considering declining investment resources under the control of the federal center and dramatic changes in the overall position of the Far Eastern region both within Russia and in Northeast Asia. Economically, the Far Eastern region of Russia always was a remote industrial enclave. However, as a product of the highly centralized planning system and as the strategic outpost in Northeast Asia it was high on the list of priorities for Moscow. The region was shaped economically, industrially, and socially during the decades when the decision-making process was based on economic assessments hardly relevant to such factors as real market costs and efficiency. Moreover, the resource-based industries constitute the backbone of the region's economic structure. Once prices were liberalized, shifts in the relative weight of industries made the regional economy even more dependent on the resource-based industries at the expense of the manufacturing sector, steel making, timber processing, and chemical industry. The competitiveness of local products declined because of hikes in transportation and energy costs. However, exports were growing helping to balance somewhat negative economic trends and linking the Far East closer with the Asia-Pacific region and Japan as a leading market for the resources of the Far East.

Makoto Nobukuni in his chapter analyzes prospects for closer links between the Far East of Russia and Japan, including the problem of economic complementarity, linkages through natural resources, and interindustry relationships. Nobukuni refers to the system of investment guarantees, Japan's involvement in the defense industry conversion, and its support for the *Federal Program for Economic and Social Development of the Far Eastern and Trans-Baikal Region for 1996–2005*. For Japan, potential benefits from closer relations with Russia will be access to its rich energy resources.

If Japan and Russia see one another as partners in Northeast Asia and subregional economic cooperation, they should jointly consider how to create a basis for constructive mutual engagement in the region, how to define potential areas of economic interdependence, what instruments to choose to stimulate mutual interdependence, and how to define a framework for development assistance in Northeast Asia.

Robert N. Ruzanov also addresses prospects for investment links, particularly in the energy sector. Cooperation in this and other sectors benefits from the framework for economic relations that is taking shape on the inter-governmental level. It helped, for example, to manage the problem of the debt settlement. However, in 1997–98 the main target became the implementation of the Yeltsin-Hashimoto plan with large-scale cooperation in the energy sector as one of the key segments of this framework. Complementarity of interests in this area is quite high. By joining their efforts in the area of energy projects, the two governments facilitate the flow of private investment from leading Japanese corporations. Energy development projects also involve the machine-building sector and provide new opportunities for more Japan-Russia co-production linkages.

Nobuo Arai discusses yet another area of business relations central to the interests of Japan and Russia: cooperation in fishery. For more than 30 years cooperation in fishery was a priority item on both Tokyo's and Moscow's agendas. It was not only because the fishery industry had been one of the key sectors in Japan and the Soviet Union (particularly in Far Eastern Russia) but also because annual negotiations on fisheries agreements provided both governments with an opportunity to accumulate experiences on how to deal with each other. Negotiations continued even in the worst periods in the postwar history of the relationship and served as a stabilizing factor in the relationship. Even with the introduction of the exclusive economic zone, which brought in many changes in merits that both countries had received from the cooperation, regular negotiations continued.

If one looks for an analogy, Japanese-Soviet fishery negotiations were playing the same role in the overall context of bilateral relations as did Washington-Moscow negotiations on control and reduction of armaments in the Cold War era. In the Tokyo-Moscow dialogue on fisheries every time each party left the room convinced that the other party could not be trusted, but they were aware of the fact, at the same time, that negotiations must continue. There were many reasons why both Japan and the Soviet Union continued to negotiate their relations in fishery with a great deal of patience and consequently reached agreements: They knew that they had to share the same resource base in the Sea of Okhotsk and the Sea of Japan. Both sides were interested in getting considerable amounts of marine protein in those seas. Moreover, both countries were major consumers and exporters of marine resources and processed goods.

Andrei P. Rodionov provides a broad and detailed overview of economic and trade links between Russia and Japan, emphasizing the task of creating a stronger economic foundation for long-term engagement based on shared interests that are not limited to the exchange of raw materials for processed and manufactured goods.

From 1993 to 1997, bilateral trade remained relatively low in volume with increased Russian exports and a significantly reduced volume of direct import from Japan. There were no significant Japanese investments in Russia (with the exception of the Sakhalin projects). A drop in domestic investment in Russia reduced the demand for machinery, industrial equipment, and materials, while Russian importers of consumer goods looked for cheaper sources of supply. Moreover, a breakdown in the system of payments resulted in debts to many Japanese companies closely involved with Russia before 1991. This damaged the very center of the constituency that was in favor of more economic contacts with Russia.

Diversified economic links, however, are possible and could benefit both sides. Links may include raw materials processing; investment promotion for import substitution in Russia; design, production, and marketing of new products; cooperation in advanced technologies; financial links; and infrastructure projects. Mechanisms creation for contacts at governmental, local, and private levels as well as coordination in multilateral, regional, and international organizations constitute important segments for bilateral relations.

Susumu Yoshida offers a Japanese perspective on the same subject, pointing out that transition from a centrally planned economy in Russia to an economic system based on market principles and the abolition of the state monopoly in foreign trade were among the main factors behind the sharp decline in Japan and Russia trade. In 1992–93, the Japanese trading companies shifted their operations toward imports from Russia and were hesitant to proceed with new deliveries to Russia without guarantees. Since 1993 bilateral trade started to recover. In 1995 its volume amounted to $5.9 billion with Japanese imports amounting to about 80 percent of this trade volume compared with 61 percent in 1991. Considering that prior to 1988 Japan on the average exported 45 percent more than it imported from Russia, this change in balance of trade was among the key features in the changing nature of trade relations. The most recent developments in Japan-Russia trade include the exports of goods made in Japan via third countries, particularly in consumer electronics and motorcars. This indirect trade can be estimated at $1.5 billion and, therefore, the volume of bilateral trade between Japan and Russia exceeds that of the Japan–Soviet Union trade at its peak level.

However, compared with other Group of Eight members, Japan is lagging behind in investment in Russia ($227 million or 0.5 percent of the total volume of Japanese foreign investment). To encourage the inflow of Japanese direct investment Russia needs to make a shift to a policy of protection of domestic producers and manufacturing industries. There are three potential fields for Japanese investors, including manufacturing enterprises targeted at the domestic Russian market, raw material industries of eastern Russia, and high-tech industries. Far Eastern Russia may become a special area for bilateral economic cooperation considering such factors as geographic proximity and huge reserves of energy resources in eastern Russia.

Japan is among the key contributors to this program of economic assistance to Russia. In 1993–98, the total amount of loans extended by the International Monetary Fund to Russia reached $19.8 billion. The total amount of Japan's official commitment is $6 billion, including $5.6 billion in loans and trade insurance. The remaining $400 million was provided in the form of grants. Out of the total amount of $6 billion, $1.5 billion is the untied Export-Import Bank of Japan loan that was offered when Minister of Foreign Affairs Keizo Obuchi visited Moscow in February 1998.

17

(Russia)

H70

RII

The Eastern Provinces and Moscow

Alexander G. Granberg

For a country as big and diverse as the Russian Federation the relationships between the central government and regional authorities are critically important. The development of regionalism in Russia after the collapse of the communist bureaucratic system is a natural phenomenon. Regional authorities, associations, institutions, and industries acquired considerable political and economic authority in their own territories and at the national level.

Popularly elected governors (officially known as heads of administrations), and the speakers (chairpersons) of provincial assemblies belong to the Federation Council and represent a powerful counterbalance to the executive branch and the president. Among all political developments and changes in post-communist Russia this new regional pillar may be the most formidable and significant. The new role of the provinces in Russian domestic politics is vital to the evolution of the federal system, particularly the economic component encapsulated in federal-regional fiscal relations. This problem became central in the aftermath of the financial crisis that unfolded in Russia in August–September 1998.

SIBERIA AND THE FAR EAST

Obviously, regions and provinces differ in terms of their political preferences, economic conditions, size of territory and population, wealth, and geography. However, no other group of provinces of the Russian Federation equals the strategic value and distinctiveness of Far Eastern

Russia. The colonization of Siberia and the Far East over 400 years took different forms and was based on different mechanisms but always retained two specific features. The first was the strong control by the central government and the economic development pattern strongly supported by massive centralized capital flows. The second was uneasy relations with foreign neighbors and a considerable military presence.

The current situation of eastern Russia is unique. The influence of Moscow declined, and new economic forces are at work, including an opening of the Russian market and growing exports. Provinces are gaining more power and economic freedom within an emerging federal framework. Foreign relations are better than ever before and the Far East is replacing its traditional role of a military outpost with that of the springboard to Asian markets.

On the negative side, the role of the federal center as the main provider of investment is decreasing. Rising costs of transportation badly affected Far Eastern enterprises. The end of military tensions and political rivalries with neighboring nations led to significant cuts in defense spending and downsizing, thus limiting the flow of financial resources to the Far Eastern economy. Defense enterprises that constitute the core of machine-building industry in the region experienced much harsher problems compared with enterprises in other sectors of the economy.

However, there are unexplored opportunities for those who live in Eastern Russia and new arenas are emerging for economic engagement with neighbors: Japan, China, the Koreas, and the United States. It would be a mistake to think that only the Far Eastern economic region of Russia is poised for closer economic relations with Asia-Pacific economies. If the current trend toward more economic openness and cooperation prevails, all of eastern Russia must be taken into account as a new economic factor in Pacific Asia.

Eastern Russia includes the Far Eastern economic region (population of 7.4 million), Eastern Siberia, including Angaro-Eniseyskiy and Trans-Baikal regions (combined population of 9.1 million), and Western Siberia (population of 15.1 million). Eastern Russia's territory is two times larger than the Far Eastern region alone, with a population 4.2 times greater and a gross domestic product 5 times that of the Far Eastern provinces alone.

Conceptually, steps toward this broader view have already been taken. For example, the Federal Program for Economic and Social Development of the Far Eastern and Trans-Baikal Regions enacted in 1996 incorporates two Trans-Baikal provinces (Chitinskaya Oblast and Buriyat Republic). A similar approach was taken when the Inter-Regional Association of the Far Eastern Provinces was created in 1990; it includes Trans-Baikal provinces. Eastern Siberia is going to be the next logical participant, while west-oriented Western Siberia, including its industrially developed south and oil and gas rich north can be considered a third frontier to be linked with Pacific Asia.

The problem of definition is important in terms of the Russian domestic political process. In the Federation Council there are only 20 members representing the Far Eastern provinces (11.2 percent of the total number of representatives in the chamber). However, eastern Russia has 58 votes (32.6 percent of the total number of representatives in the chamber). The economic potential of eastern Russia is considerably greater. This super-region has 79 percent of all national reserves of crude oil, 80 percent of the natural gas reserves, 91 percent of coal, 76 percent of gold, more than 90 percent of diamond deposits, 70 percent of copper, and 96 percent of lead ore. Moreover, this super-region contains 78 percent of timber resources, about 75 percent of fish and other marine resources, and more than 80 percent of the national potential for hydroelectric power production. The region was the main resource base for the former Soviet Union and remains a major pillar of the Russian economy, producing 76 percent of coal, 81 percent of aluminum, 49 percent of processed timber, 80 percent of pulp, and 62 percent of fish and marine products. It is also a major exporter of oil, gas, and nonferrous metals.[1]

The Siberian and Far Eastern provinces of the Russian Federation are known for their technologically advanced products, primarily defense equipment and components. Siberia houses many establishments that produce and handle nuclear weapons and fuel for the civilian nuclear power industry. Advanced *Su-27* jet fighter aircraft are assembled in Novosibirsk, Irkutsk, and Komsomolsk-na-Amur. *Black Shark* attack helicopters are produced in Primorskiy Krai, and nuclear-powered submarines were assembled in Khabarovskiy Krai. Even though many defense-related enterprises are now experiencing formidable economic difficulties, the region maintains the capacity, human resources, and expertise to support civilian high-tech production facilities.

Before the mid-1980s, rates of economic growth in eastern Russia were higher than the national average because of the considerable volume of investment, influx of labor resources from western Russia and other former soviet republics, and huge natural resources. The share of eastern Russia in the national industrial output increased from 17.5 percent in 1970 to 27.2 percent in 1990. However, the economic benefits of this growth and the results of the natural resources development were distributed among all republics of the former Soviet Union.[2]

In contrast, these territories were traditionally dependent on capital goods, machinery, equipment, and consumer goods produced in western Russia. Siberian and Far Eastern provinces lagged behind western Russia in housing construction, health care, and the number of universities. Economic problems gradually accumulated; some of them became chronic, such as the lack of investment in social services and inadequate infrastructure, environmental degradation, declining economic efficiency, underdeveloped industry for raw materials processing, and an oversized military production sector.

Economic liberalization complicated this situation mostly because the government retained most key enterprises under centralized control but was ill prepared to manage the transition. Finally, the federal authorities were forced to cut back their economic involvement and withdrew from direct economic management. Moreover, compared with western and central Russia, the Far Eastern and Siberian provinces were less prepared to manage their economic and social affairs under the new economic rules.

In 1992–96, the consequences of the shock therapy were felt more in the Far East and other eastern provinces compared with many other regions of Russia. Life savings kept in bank accounts or in cash were lost as in the rest of Russia, and the sharp reduction in the volume of military orders put the most advanced production and research-and-development centers of the Far East and Siberia in a dismal situation. In some cases, these centers were the key or the only establishments that provided jobs and economic resources for an entire town. Rising transportation tariffs affected the ability of people to travel and, in combination with other economic hardships, forced some of them to move to other regions of Russia. Remote northern areas lost a considerable part of their population. Fortunately, the unique and rich resources of eastern Russia allowed the expansion of exports, thus helping to alleviate the pains of transition to capitalism.

NEW FEDERALISM

The process of forming new federal relations in Russia was strongly influenced by the economic crisis. First, a declining industrial output, new economic limits on the long-distance transportation of products, and the expansion of export-oriented industries put the entire national economy under severe stress. Old economic connections between the regions, industries, and individual enterprises became loose or were broken and new linkages were slow to compensate for these losses. These and other developments led some experts and politicians to warn against the danger of a Russian economic disintegration.

Second, the economic crisis made regionalism not a provincial level but a regional scale phenomenon. Thus, the Association of the Far Eastern and Trans-Baikal Provinces incorporates 13 territories, and the Siberian Agreement association includes 19 provinces. Both associations include the Buriyat Republic, Chitinskaya Oblast, and Aginskiy Buriyat Autonomous District. These associations never claimed a political role and did not pursue separatist goals. However, in their relations with the federal government they were a useful bargaining device and facilitated an essential coordination among the provinces.

The federal center was forced to pay attention to the regions and provinces. Starting in 1992 all annual messages by the president to the Federal Assembly or economic programs issued by the federal government referred to problems of regional policy. In 1996 the president and the government approved a special document on the main directions of regional policy.[3] All these documents refer to the problems of eastern Russia. However, the ability of Moscow to assist the regions in solving their urgent economic problems is limited. By privatizing the state enterprises and other economic assets the federal government has surrendered most of its instruments of administrative control. The non-state sector's share in the gross domestic product now exceeds 70 percent, and a considerable portion of the state property was transferred to the level of provinces and localities. However, the economic tools designed to replace the measures of administrative control are yet to mature.

There are five channels of direct control still available to the federal government, including the transfer of funds to the regions from the Federal Fund for Financial Support of the Provinces (15 percent of the federal taxes collected, but excluding import duties), funds allocated from the federal budget to support federal programs of regional development, state contracts for enterprises, federal support for selected investment projects, and tax and credit benefits and other concessions to particular regions.[4]

However, the effectiveness of these instruments of federal control is in question. For example, the transfers of funds from the Federal Fund for Financial Support of the Provinces was designed to support the regions with emergency needs only. In reality, in 1997 81 provinces of the Russian Federation out of 89 were eligible for such transfers, including all the provinces of Siberia and the Far Eastern and Trans-Baikal regions (with the exception of Krasnoyarskiy Krai, Yamalo-Nenetzkiy, and Khanty-Mansiyskiy Autonomous districts). The share of these provinces in transfers was two times higher than their share in the population of Russia (Table 17.1). For the Far Eastern region the discrepancy in population and the share in federal transfers is particularly marked.

In 1997, the eastern provinces of the Russian Federation were given $3.5 billion or about $100 per capita in federal transfers on average, but the per capita allocations to the Far Eastern provinces were about $200. In addition, in 1997 the Far Eastern provinces received more than $200 million as a compensation for higher electricity rates and about $600 million for fuel shipments to the remote northern areas of the Far East. Nine closed cities and towns of Siberia and the Far East received funds appropriated to support their budgets.

TABLE 17.1
The Federal Fund for Financial Support:
Transfers to Eastern Regions of Russia

Regions	Number of provinces	Provinces eligible for transfers	Total share in transfers, percent	Total share in population, percent
The Far East	10	10	20.60	5.04
Trans-Baikalia	3	3	3.04	1.59
Eastern Siberia	7	6	2.91	4.60
Western Siberia	9	7	13.49	10.25
Total	29	26	40.04	21.48

Source: 1997 Federal Budget Law

Financial resources available for regional development programs were less significant; most regional programs seemed more like political promises than practical plans. For example, all regional programs approved in 1991–95 required 17.9 trillion rubles, including 11.7 trillion rubles from federal sources, but only 0.5 trillion rubles were actually appropriated. In its session on July 11, 1996 (a week after Boris Yeltsin was elected for the second term) the federal government admitted that the economic programs to support the regions are amorphous, not coordinated, and lacking financial resources. Indeed, in 1996 alone the funds required by all these programs were estimated at about $8 billion, but the entire federal investment program for 1996 was set at $6 billion and was fulfilled only by one-fourth.

The problem of nonpayments for government contracts to enterprises in Siberia and the Far Eastern region is well known as is the lack of government support to selected investment projects. Both these factors complicated the financial conditions of the enterprises and in most cases forced them to scrap or postpone their investment plans. In 1994, for instance, the federal government proposed investment tenders among enterprises with 20 percent federal financial backing of the approved projects. In reality, however, this initiative led to the accumulation of federal debts to enterprises.

Finally, the practice of providing certain regions and provinces with tax and credit benefits and other concessions was discontinued in 1994 because of the critical need to balance the budget. Most regional preferences were eliminated in March 1995 with some exceptions made to special economic zones and areas hit by natural disasters. Therefore, the federal budget is now the only tool the federal center has to support the regions. However, this tool, which is subject to political bargaining and lobbying, cannot be applied to all the problems of the eastern regions.

To arrest negative trends in the economy of eastern Russia much closer attention on the part of the federal center to the problems and opportunities of the Far Eastern region is needed. The Far Eastern territories alone cannot combat the decline in production volume in major industrial areas, loss of jobs, massive nonpayments, and problems of energy supplies and transportation services. Urgent measures for economic stabilization requested by the provinces include the elimination of fuel shortages, restraining the growth of tariffs for electric power, federal support for the electric power industry, and anti-monopolistic regulations aimed at transportation tariffs reduction. Without solving these problems it will be impossible to improve the performance of traditional industries, to restore economic links with western areas of the country, and to prevent the outflow of people to other regions of Russia.

ECONOMIC PLANS AND REALITY

The Association of Far Eastern and Trans-Baikal provinces was instrumental in drafting and promoting the development program for the region. The Ministry of Economy served as principal coordinator of the drafting process. Among other main agencies charged with responsibilities to prepare the plan were the Ministry of Labor, Ministry of Foreign Economic Relations, and the State Committee on Industrial Policy. The Council for the Location of Production Forces and Economic Cooperation drafted the final text that was submitted to the government.[5]

Cumulative financial resources needed for the program's implementation are estimated at $74–82 billion. Already adopted federal programs, as far as they are related to the Far Eastern economic region, will contribute $51–57 billion. Additional funds required for 1996–2005 total $23–25 billion, including $11–12 billion provided through the federal budget. Other types of state support will be provided through credit and loan guarantees issued for Russian and foreign banks. Funding is to come from provincial budgets, enterprise funds, and Russian and foreign private investors.

The program was officially approved by the Russian government in April 1996 and was given presidential program status one month later. It is divided into three stages, including urgent anti-crisis measures (1996–97), economic and social stabilization period (1998–2000), and the phase of structural reconstruction that will lead to sustainable development (2001–5). It is expected that the rates of economic growth will exceed the national average and will reach 127 percent and 146 percent in the years 2000 and 2005, respectively, compared with the 1995 base level. The population of the region may reach up to 9.2 million people, although employment in the real sectors may decline.

The program is the product of a consensus between the federal center and 13 provinces. It serves as a coordinating and guiding framework vis-à-vis 68 federal programs developed earlier. However, the leading role of the program and its time span require the adoption of new laws and regulations. It is also important that the program emphasizes institutional changes rather than prescribed investment decisions. A review and correct approach is adopted as the main working feature of the program. The sustainable development of the Far Eastern economic region is the most important long-term goal of the program. Finally, the program is based on the assumption that not only the Far Eastern economic region but also Russia's entire economy should be opened to the Asia-Pacific region.

The two years that have elapsed since the program was approved demonstrate that it is little more than a statement of good intentions. Both federal and local budgets were too tight to help the implementation of the program, and the Russian private sector was still too weak to play a major role in the process. In 1996 4.7 trillion rubles (13 percent of the funds required by the program) were allocated to projects. In 1997 the federal budget had a special clause specifically introduced for the program, but instead of the 40.5 trillion rubles requested by the provincial authorities (half of the funds actually needed to finance all the activities planned under the program for 1996–97) only 1.034 trillion rubles were approved. For example, the most important Bureiskaya hydropower station (Amurskaya Oblast) project was given only 55 percent of financial resources needed in 1996, including only 36 percent of federal funds. In 1997 this project required about 1.5 trillion rubles.[6]

However, the program was not entirely neglected. The federal budget kept its 20 percent share in the investment resources available for the entire Far Eastern economic region — a higher share compared with only 9 percent of funds available to other national projects and development programs from the federal budget throughout Russia.

The weakest component of the program is intimately linked with the previous program-making activities. The Far Eastern program was designed to serve as a coordinating device for 68 federal programs in the region. In 1996, however, 47 programs from this list were half alive, covering only 13.4 percent of the expected investment; others were given no financial resources.

The implementation process also revealed flaws in the Russian administrative system. It was initially planned that the administration of the program would include a program board as a representative body and a program directorate as an executive body. It was also proposed to establish a joint-stock company named the Regional Reconstruction and Development Fund to attract private investment and accumulate and manage financial resources. It took seven months (after the federal government adopted the program) to form the Federal Commission for the Program Implementation and Monitoring. After this body was established there was no single session of the commission for several months. No decision was made either on the directorate of the program or the creation of the reconstruction fund.

CONCLUSION

The Far Eastern economic region of the Russian Federation is undergoing a systemic political and economic transformation. This process is associated with a decline in production volume, inflation, loss of jobs, massive nonpayments, and problems with energy supplies and transportation services. These negative developments aggravate the social and political climate in the region. Among many consequences of the huge economic hardship, three problems have acquired special importance: poor performance of the key traditional industries of the region, collapse of traditional links with western areas of the country, and the outflow of people to other regions of Russia.

In general, the entire system of federal laws and regulations is gradually evolving, while the economic influence of government agencies in Moscow is declining. More powers and greater responsibilities have been transferred to the regions and localities. The federal government was quick to transfer authority in social security, housing, education, and other spheres. Some provinces went further and entered special agreements with the federal center on the division of responsibilities that cover such areas as the ownership, control, and management of land, mineral resources, forests, and others. Among the Far Eastern provinces Yakutia (Sakha Republic), Sakhalinskaya Oblast, and Khabarovskiy Krai reached such agreements.

It is understood both by the federal government and provincial authorities that urgent economic and administrative measures are needed to arrest the negative economic and social developments and stabilize the economic situation in the region. It is assumed also that the Far Eastern economic region will continue to serve as a major source of natural resources and raw materials for Russia, but the geographic location of the region dictates also the development of closer economic ties with neighboring countries. Better access to the markets of Northeast Asia and the Asia-Pacific region can help to overcome current and potential economic difficulties, to facilitate the economic transformation, and to stabilize the economic and social situation in the region. Better relations and closer economic links with Japan can be an important factor in achieving these goals.

Attraction of foreign investment is among the key goals of the program. It will take place through changes in legislation both on the federal and provincial level. Foreign investments are particularly needed for oil and gas fields development, diamonds extraction, gold and tin deposits development, fishery and tourist industry expansion, transport facilities modernization, including those for transit cargo shipments, and telecommunication systems development. The program also looks at some special subregional development projects such as Tumangan, Nakhodka FEZ, and Baikal-Amur Railway economic development zone.[7] It envisages special status provision to frontier territories and proposes adjustments in the regional banking system in order to attract financial resources from other parts of Russia and from abroad. A proposal to create an international Far Eastern Development Bank is now under consideration.

NOTES

1. See E. Kisiliyova, M. Castells, and A. Granberg, *The Missing Link: Siberian Oil and Gas and the Pacific Economy*, Monograph 52. (Berkeley: University of California at Berkeley, Institute of Urban and Regional Development, 1996), pp. 6–9.

2. See Alexander Granberg and Victor Suslov, "Inter-Republican Economic Relations Before Disintegration of the USSR," *Regional Development and Cooperation*, 1 (1997): 17–24 (summary in English, pp. v–vi).

3. See Alexander Granberg, "Regional Issues in the Programs of Economic Reform: 1992-1996" in *Problems of Comprehensive Regional Development in Russia*. (Moscow: Nauka, 1996), vol. 1, pp. 5–46.

4. The Federal Budget Law determines specific shares of the provinces in transfers from the Federal Fund of Financial Support of the Provinces and prescribes such payments only to entities without arrears in taxes to the federal budget. The rules and principles behind such calculations are not entirely formalized and established, allowing negotiations and bargaining between provincial and federal authorities.

5. In 1997, the text of the program was translated into Japanese by the Economic Research Institute for Northeast Asia and published by the Ministry of Finance of Japan (publication division). The short Russian and English language versions of the program were published by the Association of the Far East and Trans-Baikalia in late 1996.

See also Alexander Granberg, "Development of the Russian Far East and Trans-Baikal Region and Activization of Russia's Participation in Pacific Economic Cooperation," paper presented at the Twenty-Ninth International General Meeting of the Pacific Basin Economic Council, Washington, D.C., May 1996; Vladimir Ivanov, Alexander Granberg, and Makoto Nobukuni, "Japan and Russia in Northeast Asia: Prospects and Opportunities," a background paper prepared in conjunction with the Thirtieth International General Meeting of the Pacific Basin Economic Council, Manila, May 1997.

6.   See Y. Ivlev and E. Galichanin, "Economic Reform in the Provinces of the Far Eastern and Trans-Baikalia Region of the Russian Federation, 1991-1996," *Economic Life of the Far East, 1997* (supplement), No. 1 (9–10), pp. 13–15 (in Russian).

7.   A. Granberg and V. Kuleshov, *BAM Region: Current Development Concept.* (Novosibirsk: Siberian Branch of the Russian Academy of Sciences, 1998).

18

The Northeast Asian Drift

Pavel A. Minakir

Economic troubles experienced by the Russian Far Eastern provinces in 1997–98 were usually linked with economic liberalization and reforms initiated in 1992. However, the economy of the Far Eastern region had entered a period of declining investment and output by the end of the 1980s. By 1991 the central government appeared unable to fulfill its obligations and promises given to the Far East earlier. The entire system of close and administratively interdependent relations broke down, and Moscow looked like a bankrupt authority.

In April 1996 the president of Russia signed a decree on the implementation of the *Federal Program for Economic and Social Development of the Far Eastern and Trans-Baikal Regions for 1996–2005*. This federal program was drafted under extraordinary economic and political circumstances. Under pressure from local leaders, the federal government agreed to support the regional economy to ensure investment, modernization of extracting and processing industries, and the region's closer economic ties with foreign neighbors.

The program stipulated that from 1997 to 2005 the regional gross domestic product (GDP) growth rate is expected to be 157 percent compared with 149 percent for Russia's average. Since 1991 investment has fallen faster than output. However, to secure 1 percent of GDP growth the Far Eastern economy requires about a 1.8–2.0 percent increase in investment volume. The total amount of investment during the next 10 years was estimated at $75–80 billion, including 25 percent of expected investment funds coming from the federal budget, 40 percent from regional budgets, 20 percent in the form of commercial loans and credits, and 15 percent in foreign investment. Federal support was expected to facilitate structural changes, launch new industries, and ensure the Far East's reach for new markets, but both in 1996 and 1997 the federal government was unable to fulfill its obligations under the program's provisions.

THE HISTORY

In retrospect this situation is not unusual. There were several programs for the development of the Russian Far East; some of them were only partially implemented, others remained on paper. The first such program was adopted in 1930 and was the most consistent and successful. In the 1930s and 1940s, a huge amount of capital and manpower, including prison labor, was transferred to the Far East. Only Moscow and the Ural economic regions were ahead in terms of the total volume of investment. Before World War II the development of the Far East was a national priority, considering Russia's military weakness in the region, the small population to the east from Lake Baikal, and the history of relations with Japan.

Strategic and security interests also motivated the drafting of the second development program, which was adopted in 1967. In addition to addressing purely economic needs, the program was a response to political tensions and border clashes with China and mounting confrontation with the United States. In 1972 another governmental plan was announced that included plans to channel more resources to the Far Eastern economy. Although neither the second nor the third program was fully implemented, an industrial structure in the region was created, heavily militarized and highly dependent on extracting industries and close ties with western Russia.

After Mikhail Gorbachev announced an opening toward the Asia-Pacific region in 1986 in his speech in Vladivostok, it was hoped that the Far Eastern economic region would move to the forefront of Moscow's foreign and economic policy. The long-term development program called The Long-Term State Program for Economic and Social Development of the Far Eastern Economic Region and Zabaikalie for the Period Up to the Year 2000 was drafted by the central government, declaring significant structural economic changes in the region by the year 2000.

However, the key problem was the basic model on which these relationships were based: the federal ministries were responsible for all the investment programs, but they were taking both the resources produced in the region and the profits of the enterprises under their control. Far Eastern Russia, therefore, was performing the role of a raw material enclave within the former Soviet Union's domestic division of labor with the key industrial ministries playing the role of natural monopolies and owners of resources.

The total cost of this 15-year plan was estimated at 200 billion rubles (in 1987 prices) — an amount equivalent to about $280 billion at the official exchange rate. The program covered a number of large-scale projects in key industries and infrastructure. This plan was aimed also at industrial growth and a population increase in the region to 11 million. Starting from 1989, the key industrial ministries and other government agencies reduced the volume of investment under the pretext that the transition to a market economy had begun. From 1990 the entire system of comprehensive administrative interdependency and Communist Party control became loose. Moscow was struggling with the republics over economic and political issues; the decline of central power symbolized the beginning of the end of the soviet era. With the demise of the Central Planning Agency, responsible for resources allocation, the program was discontinued de facto by 1991.

Moreover, the federal government sharply reduced its responsibilities for supplying the Far East with food and other material resources. The Far Eastern economic region, in general, and its main industries and enterprises, in particular, were totally unprepared to switch to this kind of new relationship with the federal center. The economic consequences of this confrontation were devastating, including the decline of industrial output, inflation, barter transactions, and deficient market.

LOCAL INTERESTS

In the meantime, as a result of internal political changes in Russia, the local administrators and party *apparatchiks* slowly gained self-assertiveness. The Association of Soviet People's Deputies of the Far East and Zabaikalie was established in 1990 to coordinate relations with Moscow. At a meeting held in Khabarovsk in May 1991 the association endorsed the new concept of economic development of the area and its integration into the Asia-Pacific region. The plan proposed that the key development priorities must be supported by economic cooperation with the Asia-Pacific economies.

The goal was set to establish economic and legislative regimes favorable to foreign investment. However, the attempted *putsch* of August 1991 led the economy of the Far Eastern region in a different direction. Since early 1992 the new Russian government, overwhelmed by the unfolding economic crisis, preached macroeconomic stabilization and pursued a unified approach both to regions and industries. Moscow has abolished almost all regional preferences.

The Far East was the first to lose federal support and its economic situation began to deteriorate. The region was suddenly cut off from its traditional customers in central Russia and the nations of the Commonwealth of Independent States while its capacity to export to other markets remained limited. By the mid-1990s, the severe slump in the economy of the Far Eastern provinces demonstrated that indifference to the situation could have serious consequences for all of Russia.

For decades the population growth served as one of the most important indicators of regional development. However, in 1993 the number of deaths exceeded the number of births by 17,600. In 1994 this difference increased to 20,800, and in the first six months of 1995 it reached 11,200. In the five years since 1991, the population of the region has declined by about 1 million people because of these adverse trends and migration to western Russia and the Commonwealth of Independent States.

REFORM, CRISIS, AND DISTANCE

Despite differences among the provinces, there are some main economic trends that are common to the economies of all the Far Eastern provinces. During the first two to three years of economic transformation the Far East looked relatively better compared with the average economic picture of Russia as a whole.

First, extracting industries managed to retain some support of the federal center and displayed some stability. Second, the export earnings of the Far Eastern enterprises remained in the region supporting its economy and people. However, inflation, the decline of the production sector, and emerging commercial and trading businesses led to a shrinking local demand. Investment activities declined faster than the overall business activities of the industrial sector. Financial resources from the federal budget were drying up while interest rates were skyrocketing.

In a way, compared with many regions of Russia the Far Eastern economy performed relatively better during the initial phase of economic reform. However, from late 1992 to early 1993 the crisis became more obvious. Nonetheless, the difference in the pace of decline in the industrial output of the Far Eastern region and that of Russia was not dramatic. The crisis revealed some disparities in the economic performance of the Far Eastern provinces. Before 1993–94, Khabarovskiy and Primorskiy krais were relatively better off because of their diversified industrial structure.

Later on, provinces with resource-extracting and export-oriented industries, such as Magadanskaya Oblast and Yakutia (Sakha), improved their economic situation while Khabarovskiy and Primorskiy krais sank deeper into recession. Among the industries affected by the crisis were timber-cutting, pulp and paper production, machine-building, and construction industries. The decreasing demand for fixed capital goods did not affect the primary industries, and the entire economy of the Far Eastern region became even more resource-oriented. Moreover, there were some modest improvements in the performance of fishery, timber cutting, and non-ferrous metals smelting and refining registered in 1996–97. To a very significant degree this was the result of the export earnings retained by the enterprises.

The economic situation worsened particularly in the energy sector because of a sharp reduction in local coal output. The high cost of transportation of coal from Siberia badly affected prices for electricity and heating. The prices for coal, petroleum products, fertilizers, and grain have grown considerably, forcing almost all key industries into a depression. The chronic shortage of energy resources threatened enterprises, cities, community services, and the population. In 1995, producers and providers of electricity and heat have accumulated about $200 million in unpaid debts for fuel, while the household debt for heat and electricity has reached $500 million.

Local politics became embroiled in the energy crisis, particularly in Primorskiy Krai. The problem of winter heating became the key issue for all administrations of the Far Eastern provinces. Huge unpaid debts for electricity and coal for thermo-power stations were accumulated by enterprises with idle production facilities.

Other types of energy resources became more expensive, too. In 1995, the level of self-sufficiency of the Far Eastern region in coal was estimated at 75 percent, petroleum at 8 percent, diesel fuel at 50 percent, and heavy oil at 50 percent. Provinces of the Far East are, on average, 4,800 kilometers away from East Siberia, 7,300 kilometers away from the Ural region, and 9,700 kilometers from central Russia. By 1996 the investment volume had declined to one-fourth of the 1990 level (Table 18.1).

Average distance for inter-regional transportation exceeds 3,100 kilometers. Under liberalized railroad tariffs the price of coal transported for 1,000 kilometers increased 30 percent and the price for metal goods about 15 percent for the same distance compared with 1990. In addition, new economic barriers were rising between the Far Eastern industries and the domestic market.

Once prices were liberalized in 1992, shifts in the relative weight of industries made the economy of the Far East more dependent on natural resources, including non-ferrous metals production, electricity generation, and food-processing. In 1993 their combined share in value added was 85 percent, but it increased to 91 percent in 1995. The fuel and energy sector surpassed non-ferrous metals production, food-processing, and the fishery industry. This caused a decline in competitiveness of many enterprises and sectors of the economy, particularly the processing industries.

TABLE 18.1
The Far Eastern Region: Industrial Production and
Capital Investment, 1991–95
(1990 level as 100 percent)

	Russia	Far East
Industrial Production		
1991	92	97
1992	75	83
1993	65	72
1994	51	53
1995	49	45
Capital Investment		
1991	85	85
1992	51	47
1993	45	36
1994	36	20
1995	30	18

Source: Compiled and calculated by the Economic Research Institute of the Russian Academy of Sciences using regional statistical data and data published by the State Statistical Committee of the Russian Federation.

A new price structure has resulted in reduction of economic opportunities for the entire Far East and undermined the competitiveness of its industries, enterprises, commodities, and products. In 1993–94 in light industry, for example, the gap between the Far East and the rest of Russia in profitability (production cost-price ratio) increased, making the industry noncompetitive. Then in 1994 the share of capital input increased in all Far Eastern industries, except electricity generation and food-processing. Steel manufacturing, wood and timber processing, and the chemical industry were badly affected. The capital share appeared to be below Russia's average in non-ferrous metal production and food processing (basically the fishery industry), making only these two branches domestically competitive (Table 18.2).

The competitiveness, however, can be estimated more precisely if the cost of transportation is eliminated. If this is done, the competitiveness of the Far Eastern enterprises can be restored in every industry except steel-making. However, even without accounting for the transportation expenses, the capital costs in some industries, particularly in light manufacturing, are significantly higher in the Far East than the national average.

TABLE 18.2
Capital Share in Far Eastern Russia's Industrial Output, 1993–94
(in percent)

Industry	Far Eastern Region Total		Far Eastern Region Without transportation		Russia Total	Russia Without transportation
	1993	1994	1993	1994	1993	1994
Iron and steel	0.855	1.068	0.341	0.331	0.671	0.660
Non-ferrous metals	0.389	0.642	0.350	0.564	0.706	0.611
Fuels	0.690	0.825	0.374	0.359	0.580	0.529
Electric power	0.572	0.354	0.563	0.346	0.491	0.517
Machine building	0.795	0.870	0.584	0.567	0.577	0.501
Chemicals	0.903	0.964	0.522	0.522	0.729	0.677
Logging and timber processing	0.893	1.006	0.599	0.592	0.547	0.528
Construction materials	0.837	0.842	0.523	0.474	0.612	0.590
Light manufacturing	1.475	1.765	1.034	0.947	0.671	0.545
Food processing	0.601	0.576	0.559	0.510	0.741	0.661

Source: Compiled and calculated by the Economic Research Institute of the Russian Academy of Sciences using regional statistical data and data published by the State Statistical Committee of the Russian Federation.

The central problem of the Far Eastern region is the deficit of fixed capital investment. Compared with 1990, the level of investment in 1996 was estimated at only 18 percent (23 percent for the City of Moscow). The share of the federal budget in investment declined sharply. This situation is in drastic contrast with that before 1990 when the investment needs of the region were quite well attended by the central government. As a result, the share of the Far Eastern region in the fixed capital investment for the whole of Russia declined from 7.9 percent in 1992 to 5.2 percent in 1996.

The structural changes in the economy of the Far Eastern provinces revealed the growing role of the service sector and extracting industries, while the share of the manufacturing sector has declined. The gross regional product has declined along with the share of value added, affecting savings and capital formation. In 1995 the fixed capital investment in the Far Eastern regional GDP was higher than the national average, but in 1996 these proportions were reversed. Insolvency and the payment crisis had the most adverse influence on the economic situation in the region. Moreover, the external demand for Far Eastern products is insignificant, and the economic recession of the Far East could continue indefinitely unless there is an external factor powerful enough to reverse economic trends.

NEW MARKETS

Among the outcomes of the economic crisis were a reduction of exchanges among the Far Eastern provinces and decreasing economic contacts between the Far Eastern provinces and other regions of Russia. For example, during January through May 1995, 72 percent of the overall production of the Far Eastern region was consumed within the region itself, 15 percent was exported, and only 13 percent was shipped to the rest of Russia. The dependence of the Far Eastern economy on exports became more obvious and its relations with the rest of Russia weakened. However, this trend is not irreversible, because the growth in domestic demand, normalization in payments, and reduced transportation tariffs can reorient the commodity flows in favor of the domestic market.

The reduction of transportation costs means access to new markets and sources of supply in Northeast Asia. It was hoped that not only traditional industries, such as mining, forestry, and fishery, but manufacturing enterprises as well would be able to form closer economic ties with neighbors and would be supported by external demand and closer investment links with Asia. Such hopes were based on the assumption that Asia-Pacific economies are the major consumers of raw materials and energy resources. To some degree, these expectations materialized but only to the point when in 1992–94 foreign trade was the only factor compensating for the profound economic decline.

Although growing trade volumes were insufficient to balance the destructive consequences of increased production costs and declining living standards, the Far Eastern provinces benefited from finding new sources of supply in Northeast Asia to substitute for sources in western Russia. In 1991–93 this trade reorientation to the Asia-Pacific region, including Northeast Asia, supported production in certain industries and helped to stabilize the food supply and the consumer goods market and to contain inflation. In 1995, for example, processed food, consumer goods, and passenger cars made up almost two-thirds of the total imports of the Far East.

Affected by a deteriorating economy and dismal financial conditions, foreign trade also suffered from the overvalued dollar vis-à-vis the ruble and increased custom tariffs. Shrinking domestic demand for certain products and unpaid debts encouraged manufacturers to sell goods abroad to survive. As a result, there was an 85 percent increase in foreign trade, including 51 percent in exports, and a 170 percent increase in imports over the five years after 1992.

In 1992–93 the Far Eastern provinces were lobbying for their interests to get concessions from Moscow in taxes, tariffs, currency regulations, and export quotas. In those days some preferences were given to enterprises with foreign capital mainly in the form of export licenses for natural resources. This attracted foreign investors in the export sector. The majority of joint ventures created in 1990–93 were trading companies, which were quite active in foreign trade. However, their contribution to regional exports has declined from 25 percent in 1992 to only about 10 percent in 1995.

In 1992 the export share of enterprises with foreign investments in the Far East was more than 24 percent. In 1994, however, there was a sharp recession in trade because of a sharp reduction of re-export (from 20.5 percent in 1992 to 3.2 percent in 1994), growing domestic prices, and increased transportation costs. In contrast, export prices for local exportable goods and commodities fell as a result of a sharp expansion of Russian exports, particularly from the Far Eastern provinces. Despite growth in the physical volumes of exported wood and fish by 1.7 and 1.5 times, the value of exports in constant prices decreased by 26.5 percent and 5.1 percent correspondingly.

EXPORT DRIVE AND NORTHEAST ASIA

In general, foreign trade became one of the major factors in the economic survival of the region. The overall impact of the economic opening on the macroeconomic situation of the region is significant. From 1991 to

1995, the share of exports in regional GDP increased from 1.9 percent to 7.2 percent. In 1990 the region exported only about 5 percent of its industrial output, while the national average was 7 percent. Reforms allowed foreign trade to grow, and by 1996 exports reached 22.3 percent of the total regional output.

The export quota of the timber industry increased from 14 to 56 percent, of fishery from 14 to 64 percent, of the oil industry from 7.4 to 64.8 percent, and of coal from 7.4 to 15 percent. The export share of rolled steel has increased from 14.2 to 50 percent and reached almost 100 percent by 1997. This phenomena can be partially explained by the fall of production volumes, but the export volume growth rates were higher than the rate of decline in production volumes. Moreover, recently export shipments have expanded in parallel with some increases in output.

Northeast Asian and other Asia-Pacific economies now play a significantly more important role in the economic life of the Far Eastern provinces. Traditional industries expanded their exports to Northeast Asia and such commodities as fish, timber, non-ferrous metals, and oil account for about 73 percent of the total export's value. Exports from the Far East to Northeast Asia and the United States reached 60–70 percent of the total regional export, while Russia's exports to the region are only about 20 percent of the total national exports.

Neighboring countries also have become the major suppliers of food and consumer goods. In 1992–93 the share of imports from Northeast Asia in the total regional imports was about 70–80 percent. In 1994–95, it declined by 35–40 percent mainly as the result of increased imports from the United States. By 1995 almost two-thirds of the regional imports consisted of food, consumer goods, and passenger cars.

In 1992–95, the Far East's foreign trade exports exceeded imports. Hard currency receipts from exports were growing, thus indirectly involving more residents in foreign economic relations. Per capita distribution of hard currency is a little lower than the Russian national average level, but some Far Eastern provinces get almost twice as much in hard currency per capita. This reflects a significant input by the Far Eastern provinces in national exports, particularly in certain groups of commodities such as timber (23 percent), fish and marine products (51 percent), and coal (17 percent). However, despite increased export volumes the commodity structure of exports did not change; fuels, metals, wood, and fish accounted for 85.5 percent of all exports (Table 18.3).

The import of capital goods, for example, remained insignificant and was largely confined to equipment for new joint ventures. Institutional barriers, inconsistent and inadequate legislation, particularly in the area of property rights, poor economic performance by key industries, deficient infrastructure, and the attitudes of policy makers and the public

TABLE 18.3
Foreign Trade of the Far Eastern Provinces, 1992–96
(in millions of dollars)

	1992	1993	1994	1995	1996
Exports					
Total	1,539.2	2,048.1	1,610.5	2,426.8	2,236.5
Northeast Asia	1,259.8	1,636.5	1,316.4	1,608.6	1,863.0
Other	279.4	215.1	294.1	817.7	373.5
Imports					
Total	1,189.7	1,190.8	649.8	1,753.4	1,525.7
Northeast Asia	935.7	857.7	306.9	556.3	1,054.6
Other	254.0	333.1	342.9	1,197.2	471.1

Source: Compiled and calculated by the Economic Research Institute of the Russian Academy of Sciences using regional statistical data and data published by the State Statistical
Committee of the Russian Federation.

toward foreign investors were among major obstacles for foreign
investors interested in production activities in Russia. Only fishery ventures and some mining and extracting enterprises were able to attract foreign companies.

FOREIGN INVESTMENT

The only sizable projects that by 1998 attracted foreign investment
were oil and gas extraction in Sakhalin and Yakutia, gold and diamond
mining in Kamchatskaya Oblast, Yakutia, and Magadanskaya Oblast, and
tin ore deposits development in Khabarovskiy and Primorskiy krais. By
1996 there were 2,661 enterprises with foreign investment registered in
the Far Eastern provinces, about 13 percent of the total number of joint
ventures in Russia. However, only one-third of these really function.

High profitability and fast returns became the main driving principles
for foreign businesses in Russia and the Far East. Traditional sectors with
high potential for export, such as timber, fishery, and mineral industries
followed the cut-and-run business strategy. The number of new enterprises created in partnership with foreign companies has gradually
declined together with the scale of activities of existing joint ventures.
This partially explains why the inflow of foreign investment in the Far
Eastern region is estimated only at $500 million. In 1996, for example, in
Khabarovskiy Krai the volume of new foreign investment decreased more
than 14 times compared with 1992. Today, the only remaining option to

attract foreign investment is to grant more freedom to the provinces in decision making, expecting that they will be willing to offer certain preferences to foreign companies interested in the Far East.

Several years ago there was much hope that foreign investment in Far Eastern enterprises would assist post-soviet adjustments in the economy of the region and would support export industries. The Foreign Investment Law was adopted in 1991, and in August 1991 the federal government offered some concessions to foreign companies. Later, however, the government provided neither guarantees nor mechanisms to confirm that the climate for foreign investment would not be amended in a manner that worsens the initial conditions. Skeptics proved to be right when numerous acts and administrative regulations soon followed. These measures made the entire investment environment in Russia complex, unfavorable, and unpredictable, particularly for foreign companies that had a choice of investing in other regions and countries.

Nonetheless, by 1997 many joint enterprises between Russian and foreign companies were created, including 2,648 joint ventures registered in the Far Eastern economic region of the Russian Federation. About 80 percent of all joint ventures were created in southern areas of Khabarovskiy Krai (616 enterprises), Primorskiy Krai (1,174 enterprises), and Sakhalinskaya Oblast (384 enterprises). Investors were attracted by better infrastructure facilities, expectations of the free economic zone regime in Nakhodka and Sakhalin, and numerous opportunities for cross-border trade with foreign neighbors. In 1996 the accumulated volume of foreign investment was estimated by the Institute of Economic Research at $500 million (without oil and gas projects on Sakhalin Island).

There were three distinct stages in the process of the investment links development. In 1989–92, during the first stage, 904 joint ventures were registered in the Far East. About 27 percent of them were active by 1993. Before January 1, 1992, all new joint ventures created in Russia were granted a two-year tax holiday, and those established in the Far East received one additional year of such tax benefits. Some Far Eastern provinces introduced additional benefits such as reduced taxes for reinvested profits and reduced taxation rates for joint ventures in the manufacturing industry, if the foreign capital share in the funds of the enterprise is above 30 percent. In 1992 some special concessions were given only to joint ventures, such as freedom to export their own products without quotas or export licenses.

It seems that during this first stage commercial risks were less critical than concrete benefits and expectations of new profits. About 43 percent of new joint ventures were formed in the service sector, mainly trading operations, and 33 percent were established in fishery. Between 1989 and 1992 their combined share in regional exports increased from about 13 percent to 25 percent and reached 15 percent in import trade from the very low initial level. In 1992 more than 84 percent of the combined exports by joint ventures consisted of fish, marine products, and logs and timber. However, if in 1992 joint ventures were responsible for about 22 percent of all foreign trade, by 1997 this share decreased to only 7 percent. Such redistribution took place mainly because of competition from Russian domestic enterprises.

During the second stage between 1993 and 1995 the national investor regime was introduced for foreign investors, and tax benefits and other preferences were abolished. The List of Strategic Export Commodities was adopted by the federal authorities, affecting the interests of foreign companies in Russia. From February 1, 1993, a wide list of imported goods was subjected to custom duties and value-added tax. Some joint ventures were free to continue the import of capital goods under the previous rules (no value-added tax, no import duties) only if such imports were directly related to production purposes.

The investment climate started to deteriorate. In 1994, the Russian authorities started to charge a value-added tax and a 23-percent special tax was applied to foreign funds already invested in Russia as well as new investment credits. Under the pressure of foreign businesses these measures were abolished, but it took the government three months to correct this sudden deterioration in investment conditions.

The period of 1996–97 can be called a third stage when foreign investment in the Far Eastern region was somewhat consolidated. By January 1, 1997, there were 2,648 enterprises with foreign investment registered in the region, 13 entities fewer than in early 1996. For example, in 1995 there were 460 new joint ventures registered in the Far East, or 10 percent fewer than in 1994. Although the number of new registrations declined, the share of functional joint ventures increased to 33.6 percent in 1996.

For example, many Chinese investors were in a leading position in terms of numbers of registered joint ventures (more than 40 percent), but many of them went out of business. These were mainly small companies; some of them were never really active, others failed to cope with new registration requirements. Out of the 200 inactive enterprises dissolved by regional authorities 123 were formed with Chinese companies.

On the other hand, joint ventures formed with Japanese counterparts were active in export operations. Although the number of joint ventures formed with Japanese companies was only 11 percent of all the registered joint ventures, three-fourths of about 400 joint ventures with Japanese investors were registered in the Far East.

Compared with other investors, Japanese companies made the most significant contribution to the local economy. Most of them are stable commercial entities, support exports, and facilitate the inflow of new capital funds and technologies to the region. The companies from the Republic of Korea are quite active as well, even though they are behind Japan and the United States in numbers. They operate in fishery, the timber industry, and services.

In 1996 the contribution of joint ventures in foreign trade was estimated at $315 million. Since 1992, when it reached its peak, this volume fluctuated at about a 75–80 percent level. The trade activities of joint ventures are indicative of current strategies on the part of foreign investors. The main export items are fish and marine products (about 50 percent of exports), steel and non-ferrous metals (13 percent), and timber (12 percent). Partly because of the activities of enterprises formed with foreign investment, the Far Eastern provinces export more than they import. Joint ventures also help the provinces where they are based. Khabarovskiy and Primorskiy krais as well as Sakhalinskaya and Kamchatskya oblasts are leading in foreign trade and export operations.

However, the overall contribution of foreign investors to the economy of Far Eastern Russia is rather limited. In 1997 only 2 percent of the regional industrial output was attributed to joint ventures and other enterprises with foreign investment. Regional authorities tried to attract more foreign investment by offering a two-year local tax holiday after first profit is announced (available to enterprises with more than 30 percent foreign ownership). Three-year tax holidays were offered to joint ventures involved in transportation and mining (available to enterprises with more than $5 million of foreign funds).

CONCLUSION

The distance between Far Eastern producers and the markets west of Lake Baikal became a formidable obstacle for economic development of the region, particularly its manufacturing sector. The main source of concern, however, is whether the Far East of Russia can develop economically meaningful ties with the Asian-Pacific region, including investment and manufacturing linkages.

The concept of the program adopted in 1996 is comprehensive enough but in general it is an indicative blueprint rather than a real plan for action. It is subdivided into a number of smaller, uncoordinated programs that are not supported by funding. The important feature of the program, however, is the message it sends with regard to Far Eastern provinces–federal center relations. This program is based on the assumption that the Far Eastern economic region is an important part of the unified economy of the Russian Federation even though many vital links were broken or damaged during the first phase of economic reform.

To contribute more to the stabilization of the Far Eastern economy, foreign investors must be given more legal incentives and better opportunities to earn profits, but the current taxation policy allows only 45 percent of all joint ventures to be profitable.

The policy of the federal government is very important for improving the investment climate. First, no amendment must be made at least within the first five years after registration that worsens the initial conditions for joint ventures. Second, the maximum limit (only $17,000) established by the federal government for the local administrations to process the applications for foreign investment must be raised significantly. Third, the registration procedure must be organized as one-stop shopping to save time and reduce paperwork, and, in some cases, simplified allowing investors to apply to establish a joint venture and to wait for approval. Fourth, the licensing procedure for foreign investors requires permission from the Central Bank of Russia; this makes the entire procedure very complex. Finally, the level of taxation is too high.

In addition to numerous administrative and legal problems, the general economic situation remains uncertain and discourages foreign investor interest in the Far Eastern region of Russia. The continuing decline of production, unpaid debts held by many enterprises and insolvency among some of them and the federal government, the relatively small size of the Far Eastern market, and the general economic instability are among the main problems to be solved to improve the investment climate in the region.

19

Japan–Far Eastern Russia Relations

Makoto Nobukuni

The key parameters determining the economic relationship between Russia and Japan in the coming 21st century will be the production factor endowments in the two countries, their complementarity vis-à-vis that in China, Korea, and other surrounding areas, and inter-industrial linkage across national borders.[1] How these parameters will work depends upon policy makers' awareness of the economic development potential, politicians' readiness to provide a favorable politicoeconomic environment for development, and the willingness of the actors to participate in the process and exploit the potential.[2]

COMPLEMENTARITY AND NEW
SOURCES OF ENERGY SUPPLY

Complementarity among the production factors of Japan and Far Eastern Russia can be realized only when they are functionally and physically linked with each other. When they are not brought to the same production site at the same time, the economies suffer from comparative disadvantage.

Currently Far Eastern Russia and Japan are not linked in their endowed production factors. Abundant timber and marine resources on the Russian side are not appropriately utilized because of poor transportation infrastructure and a shortage of processing facilities to meet the specifications of the products demanded on the market, or they are exploited in such a way as to damage the reproductive capacity of nature.

Even the most promising project, Sakhalin oil and gas development, still has some problems in synchronizing the expected production with sales in the most expected market, Japan.

Russia needs the proceeds from Sakhalin energy resources, and as soon as possible, especially to use them for real investment to reverse the downfall of industrial production. However, Japan has already acquired a supply of energy from other parts of the world for the coming 10–15 years. Because of this situation, the response of Japanese energy-related enterprises has been slow, at least relative to expectations on the Russian side. This gap between the Russian expectations of sales and Japanese demand for Sakhalin energy resources will drastically narrow through increased purchases by Japan if the postulated security of energy supply in Japan is considered from a viewpoint of long-term risk management.

Diversification of sources of energy supply in Japan has been neglected, which has led to a high dependency on the Middle East. It is worthwhile for Japanese policy makers to consider, and reconsider, whether Northeast Asia, comprised of an energy rich Russia and the world's leading energy importing countries, should simply be left to develop naturally or should somehow be institutionalized in order to improve Japan's energy security. That is, should a process of institutionalization achieved piece by piece and area by area of activity eventually emerge as an integrated subregion resembling the European Union or the North American Free Trade Agreement?

At present, the economic linkage between Far Eastern Russia and Japan is surprisingly weak. The volume of trade, with the exception of Japanese imports of energy resources, is negligibly small. More significantly, the amount of foreign direct investment is much less than it should be given that the two economies are in close proximity. This is sometimes referred to as an air pocket or even as a vacuum in the midst of the miracle of developing East Asia. All of this cannot be ascribed to the unresolved Northern Territories issue, because basically there is no political hindrance any more to private economic transactions between the two countries. The cause of the slow transactions is, therefore, in the conditions defining the environment for Russia-Japan economic relations.

DIVISION OF LABOR AND
INTER-INDUSTRIAL LINKAGES

The mode of the division of labor[3] is generally governed by the following five factors:

natural resources endowment;

inter-industrial linkage based on an international division of labor;

consumer- or finished goods-market orientation;

technology development; and

competitiveness in factor costs, typically the wage rate (developing country type).

The first, second, and fourth factors or a combination of these will be relevant to Far Eastern Russia. The third factor generally applies to open economies with a large population, such as China, and the fifth one is relevant to developing countries of Southeast Asia, including China, but not Russia.

Linkage through Natural Resources

Eastern Russia has vast energy resources. There are an estimated 330 million tons of oil reserves (0.2 percent of the world reserves), 19.9 billion tons of coal (1.9 percent), and 1.6 trillion cubic meters of natural gas (1.1 percent). Russia as a whole has 47 trillion tons of natural gas (34.1 percent). Siberia certainly has a huge amount of natural gas. The potential relative significance of this area depends, however, on how reserves are counted. According to the amount of present production, eastern Russia has 500 to 700 years' worth of reserves. This seeming abundance is only 2 percent or less of the global share.

However, in terms of incremental demand in the future Asia-Pacific region, particularly Japan, the share of this area will be sizable, if these resources are developed steadily. The significance of this extends to security, because the geographical proximity of Japan and Russia represents an advantage.

Some of the resources included in the Far East Development Program (hereafter referred to as the program) have great potential; timber and marine resources are especially promising.[4] Non-ferrous metals and other mineral resources are still insufficiently developed. In spite of these potentials, Russia has not yet provided strong enough incentives for foreign enterprises to become involved in development. Promotion of Russia-Japan joint activities from the preliminary stage of project surveys will strengthen mutual confidence and accelerate project implementation.[5]

The economic conditions defined by current Russian economic laws and production sharing agreements are only marginally attractive to Japanese businesses. For its part, Japan has not shown a proactive interest in thorough assessment of the economic potential of the region. At this stage, thus, relations between the Russian eastern provinces and the Asia-Pacific region seem to depend more on the will and efforts of the governments of Japan and Russia to activate economic potential, rather than on market conditions.

An international division of labor based upon inter-industrial linkages is determined by their endowments of resources and production factors, the size and development stage of economies, technological standards, and the distance between the countries involved. For industrial linkages to fully materialize, an economy of 15–30 million people closely connected by transportation infrastructure is required. In Far Eastern Russia, 7.4 million people are scattered throughout the region. This prevents the region from forming an industrial linkage. Only Khabarovskiy Krai, parts of the Evreiskaya Autonomous Oblast and Amurskaya Oblast, and Primorskiy Krai may be integrated into one industrial complex based on machine-building and resource-processing industries.

With progress in the Sakhalin oil and gas projects and the adoption of the Local Content Agreement Law, new developments have emerged, such as the shipyard in Komsomolsk-na-Amur, which has already earned orders for parts of an offshore rig. The Local Content Agreement Law of Russia allows the products of a joint venture to be included in the percentage of local content. Closer collaboration with parent companies of joint ventures in machine industries in particular might strengthen the linkage between Far Eastern Russia and the Asia-Pacific region (rather than its traditional linkage with European Russia), and promote the division of labor.

Linkage through Technology

To assess technology from an economic point of view, it should be divided into systems technology and seed technology. Russia still has the old structure of the former Soviet Union; Russian systems technology is weak. However, it seems that all of the advanced technology seeds that can meet international standards have not yet been revealed to foreign countries. The possibility of inter-industrial relationships and the division of labor based on technology cannot be assessed until a systematic survey is conducted.[6]

Division of Labor Based on Technology

The division of labor based on technology depends on whether Japan will choose Russian technology and develop it. An example of such a possibility is aircraft manufacturing. During 1992–96 the Sukhoi Design Bureau in Komsomolsk-na-Amur approached Japanese aircraft-related enterprises seeking possible cooperation. Japanese companies declined, choosing instead to try to expand cooperation with Boeing. In January 1997, however, Boeing announced a freeze in joint development with Japan of a new aircraft that was already in progress.[7]

This does not bode well for the Japanese aircraft manufacturing industry. If Japanese business had a real long-term policy of risk aversion, this might not have happened. Russian technology differs from Western technology in many ways, hence there is a high potential for original technologies. Unfortunately, in the Sukhoi Bureau case, after five years of futile contact with Japanese enterprises, the company is no longer open even to visits by Japanese entities, public or private.

The Extent of Inter-Industrial Linkage

The extent of inter-industrial linkage depends on the Russian business mentality and Japan's evaluation of Russia as a reliable partner. If Russian business entities are ready to disclose with confidence in their foreign counterparts their technologies that can be marketed internationally, Japanese business will respond positively. It is possible, but not probable, that Japanese initiatives will result from the change in the decision-making process of Japanese organizations, including both government and private companies, for: longer-term profit maximization, inclusive of viability and insurance; modest risk aversion from the current extreme risk aversion (well known all over the world as leading to Japanese businesses' astonishingly slow actions); and merit systems that adequately appraise spontaneous actions.

TRANSITION TO A MARKET ECONOMY
IN FAR EASTERN RUSSIA

The economy of Far Eastern Russia is suffering from problems typical in the transition to a market economy. The functioning of a market economy is not yet clearly understood in Russia. It will take another ten years for the market mechanism to be properly understood. It is not unusual for a constitutional system to be in confusion during a transitional period. The lack of transparency in economic regulations, statistics, and information is another problem.[8]

Russia-Japan Economic Cooperation

Russia-Japan economic cooperation can be facilitated through an investment guarantee system offered by Russian local governments. Investment does not necessarily need to rely on guarantees by the Russian central government. At present, the International Monetary Fund's strict contracts on foreign loans are hampering the federal government's ability to provide investment guarantees. The Russian central government, therefore, recommends the use of guarantees or mortgages offered by local governments instead. This option deserves serious consideration by the Japanese government and private enterprises.[9]

Conversion of the Military-Industrial Complex

The conversion of the military-industrial complex needs external support. The military-industrial complex, which occupied more than half of the economy of the former Soviet Union, has been forced to resort to any means available to ensure its survival as the planned economy shifts to a market economy. Military industries are supposed to convert to civil use, but not many military industries are provided with the necessary financial resources, management, commodity development capacity, and manufacturing technology for civil products. A drastic decrease in government orders has forced a revival of exports of military equipment to earn hard currency. If Japan wishes to transcend from Cold War to a welfare-oriented international structure, it should support Russian attempts by the military-industrial complex to find ways to develop non-military products.

Long-Term Development Program of Far Eastern Russia

Healthy development of the Russian Far East is a prerequisite for strengthening the relationship between Russia and the Asia-Pacific region. The regional economy is dependent on natural resources; hence, its labor absorption capacity is small. However, the average education level in Far Eastern Russia is higher than in other Northeast Asian countries.[10] Autonomous growth of the region is difficult because of the weak inter-industrial relationship. Therefore, an increase in labor absorption capacity is not expected. After all, it will even be difficult to stabilize the population of the area, which is one of the aims of the Far East Development Program. Improvement of the program should be fully utilized as a leverage for regeneration and development of the Far Eastern economy. Effective implementation of the program will help strengthen the relationship between Far Eastern Russia and the Asia-Pacific region, particularly Japan. To this end, Japan can contribute to the improvement and prompt implementation of this program.[11]

CONCLUSION

Economic interdependence, as a new and increasingly influential factor of the 20th century, bypassed Northeast Asia, but it affected key countries of the region. A vision for Northeast Asia may serve as a catalyst for cooperation and encourage coordination. It can help ensure that in the 21st century economic interdependence will be strong in Northeast Asia, serving not only development and cooperation but political stability as well.

Countries of the region, including Japan and Russia, are undergoing a transition in one form or another. National economic programs and regional development plans are underway, providing an opportunity to draft a comprehensive overview of these plans and programs. Such an overview can affect planning and assist the decision-making process. If reasonably coordinated, development efforts can ensure better results at a lower cost. Coordination in development plans and programs can positively affect the use of resources, create more business opportunities, and even open new prospects for political cooperation.

There are several contradictory trends in the region. In economics, interests are multiple, including national development priorities, local interests, trans-national developments, and globalization. The interest of nations to maximize their own individual value added may be in contradiction with plans for regional cooperation. Bilateral relations compete with multilateral cooperation processes.

Governments raise barriers to the private sector and cross-border engagement, thus hampering business opportunities. Provincial administrations may be unable to promote regionally oriented policy measures without the support of central governments. A bright spot in this complication is that initiatives have been taken already by the concerned governments, localities, and regional organizations along with assistance by the United Nations Development Program and the Economic and Social Commission on Asia and the Pacific of the United Nations, to ease border crossings for neighboring residents.

Development requires investment, but at present continental Northeast Asia is a capital deficient region. Potential investors — domestic, regional, and from elsewhere — are acting on their own and are considering various investment options. Moreover, investors remain sensitive not only to the current investment environment but also to the prospects of long-term political stability. Another disadvantage for Northeast Asia is that investors have to be prepared to accept such realities as a cold climate that makes industrial activities costly, limiting the profitability of investment there. In some cases, certain industries or economic activities put pressure on the environment.

It is, therefore, important for Japan and Russia to jointly consider the following issues:

how to create a basis for constructive mutual engagement in the region,

how to define potential areas of economic interdependence,

what instruments to choose to stimulate regional interdependence,

how to define a framework for development assistance in the region, and

how to enhance capacity- and institution-building for Northeast Asia.

Strategic elements of the economic security in the region, which are definitely indispensable in national security as well, such as energy resources development and utilization, food security, use and protection of marine resources, protection of the environment, and infrastructure improvement, will be the integrating factors for the Northeast Asian sub-region. An impediment to the realization of long-term, wide stretching economic efficiency in Northeast Asia is the abstention of the major central governments from committing themselves to multilateral schemes in preference to self-retained control over international economic affairs. Remote local affairs are often only a nuisance to central government officials who are loaded with more than enough tasks to pay due attention.

The Japan-Russia economic relationship in the coming century depends on how key actors, not only in Russia and Japan but also in other Northeast Asian countries, envision the future of this subregion. The development potential is high, local initiatives are leading the formulation of multilateral cooperative undertakings of development projects, but central governments' initiatives are weak partly because of the not-yet-normalized diplomatic relationships and partly because of insufficient recognition by authorities of the national significance of local development in shaping the East Asia of the 21st century.

NOTES

1. See Economic Research Institute for Northeast Asia, *Hakuto Asia Keizai Hakusho* (Northeast Asia economic white paper). (Tokyo: Mainichi Shimbun, 1996).

2. Northeast Asia, "Conceptual Infrastructure Master Plan," Report C of the Tumen River Economic Development Area, collected papers, 1994. (New York: United Nations Industrial Development Organization, 1995); Northeast Asia, "Regional Development Strategy for the Tumen River Economic Development Area and Northeast Asia," Report A of the Tumen River Economic Development Area, collected papers, 1994. (New York: United Nations Industrial Development Organization, 1995).

3. See United Nations Economic and Social Commission for Asia and the Pacific, *Trade and Investment Complementarities on North-East Asia*, papers and proceedings of the Roundtable on Economic Cooperation Possibilities through Exploration of Trade and Investment Complementarities in the North-East Asian Subregion, July 10–12, 1995, Seoul. (New York: United Nations, Studies in Trade and Investment, 1996), no. 18.

4. *Russia Kyokuto Zabaikal Chiiki Choki Hatten Program* (Federal target program of economic and social development of the Far East and Trans-Baikal region for 1996–2005). (Tokyo: Ministry of Finance Printing Bureau, 1997).

5. Vladimir Ivanov, Alexander Granberg, and Makoto Nobukuni, "Japan and Russia in Northeast Asia: Prospects and Opportunities," paper prepared in conjunction with the Thirtieth International General Meeting of the Pacific Basin Economic Council, Manila, May 1997, pp. 5–6.

6. See *Technopolicies in Russia and Possibilities and Prospects for International Technological Cooperation* (Tokyo: Japan External Trade Organization, 1996); *New Materials in Russia/CIS*, proceedings for the Fifth Workshop on Advanced Technology in Russia/CIS, Tokyo, October 15, 1997; and *Materials and Mechanics for Space and Aviation in Russia/CIS*, proceedings for the Sixth Workshop on Advanced Technology in Russia/CIS, Tokyo, January 12, 1998, sponsored by Science and Technology Agency of Japan.

7. Ivanov, Granberg, and Nobukuni, "Japan and Russia in Northeast Asia: Prospects and Opportunities," p. 21; *Finansovie Izvestia* reported on February 19, 1998 (No. 12, p. ii), that the recently established Europe-Russia Aviation Consortium will coordinate cooperation of Airbus Industries with Russian enterprises, including all the leading non-military organizations in this sector, particularly in the area of research and development, including the super-jumbo jet project (AZXX). Meanwhile, Russian avionics manufacturers (Rybinsk Motors, for example) are teaming up with the U.S. firm General Electric and the French firm Snekma. See *Finansovie Izvestia*, No. 22, March 31, 1998, p. vi.

8. The system of macroeconomic indicators of the Russian national economy is calculated on the basis of the international methodology of national accounts (System of National Accounts 1993) and is published by the Statistical Committee of the Russian Federation beginning with data for 1989 allowing international comparisons. See *Russian Statistical Yearbook* (Moscow: Goscomstat of Russia, 1996).

9. The Russian government invited Japanese companies to participate in nine major projects in the Far Eastern region, offering to guarantee up to 40 percent of their investment through the federal level insurance scheme.

10. "Although the Soviet centrally planned system failed in many respects, it was reasonably well suited to the task of developing an adequate education system accessible to all. This education system has been severely shaken by the economic crisis of recent years. Indeed, the entire intelligentsia produced by the Soviet era has been in considerable flux because many previously privileged professions have lost their social as well as economic status to the emerging class of entrepreneurs, but, of course, many have managed to join the latter. It has been estimated that about 50% of the entrepreneurial class is made up of former professionals, such as engineers and teachers." *Russia 1996–97: Country Profile* (London: The Economist Intelligence Unit, 1997), p. 23.

11. Ivanov, Granberg, and Nobukuni, "Japan and Russia in Northeast Asia: Prospects and Opportunities," p. 6.

20

Cooperation in the Energy Sector

Robert N. Ruzanov

For Russia-Japan relations the year 1997 was a turning point. Important basic preconditions were created to expand bilateral trade exchange and to reach a new quality of economic cooperation. The informal summits in Krasnoyarsk on November 1–2, 1997, and Kawana on April 18–19, 1998, were particularly fruitful.

The Krasnoyarsk no-necktie meeting resulted in an unprecedented Yeltsin-Hashimoto action plan. Both sides look at the plan as a long-term framework for economic cooperation in several major areas, including investment cooperation and investment protection agreement, dialogue on the energy issues, Russia's integration in international economic institutions, Japan's support for economic reform in Russia, training programs for Russian managers, and bilateral cooperation in peaceful use of nuclear energy.

At Kawana more details with regard to cooperation in the energy sector were discussed. Japan expressed its interest in the Russian energy-saving program and prospects for Japanese private companies' involvement in the projects aimed at environmental protection, including those designed to reduce carbon dioxide emission. It was agreed that feasibility studies will be carried out for 20 projects that can enhance energy efficiency.

THE FRAMEWORK

In 1997–98 an institutional framework for economic relations was further developed. The role of the leading institution in shaping bilateral economic dialogue belongs to the Inter-Governmental Commission on Trade and Economic Cooperation.

According to an agreement this body was chaired by the Russian Vice-Premier (Boris Nemtsov) and Japanese Minister of Foreign Affairs (Keizo Obuchi). At the Commission's meetings in Tokyo (June 1997) a detailed action plan was adopted, and in Moscow (March 1998) important decisions were made on the Yeltsin-Hashimoto plan implementation.

Cooperation with the Export-Import Bank of Japan is progressing; a $500 million credit line was partly used for four investment projects and a $400 million credit line was nearing the completion stage. The two sides agreed that half of the $500 million credit line for humanitarian projects can be used for investment projects.

In 1997–98 the two sides were busy with the issue of debts settlement. As a result of the talks, official $400 million debts left by the Soviet Union to Russia will be repaid over 13 years, starting in 1998. The problem of debts to private Japanese financial institutions was also negotiated. The Hashimoto plan aimed at the development of Russian industry and foreign trade is underway and is carried out by the Ministry of International Trade and Industry (MITI) and the Japan External Trade Organization.

Ministerial level dialogue was launched on energy issues. In September 1997, a delegation of the Japan Forum of Nuclear Power Industry visited Russia, and a protocol on cooperation was signed encompassing various bilateral programs, such as fast-breeder reactors, spent fuel reprocessing, and Japan's involvement in the BN-800 nuclear reactor project designed in Russia. Several high-level Russian delegations representing the energy sector visited Tokyo in 1997–98, including the visit by former minister of energy and fuel industry of the Russian Federation, Sergei Kirienko, in March 1998 (he was approved by State Duma as a Prime Minister on April 24, 1998).

The two private-level, national committees — Russia-Japan Committee on Economic Cooperation and Japan-Russia Committee on Economic Cooperation — continued their regular contacts as well. In November 1997, during their joint session in Moscow the two sides agreed to open a dialogue on cooperation in advanced technologies, in addition to traditional forms and areas of economic engagement.

ENERGY SECTOR

Cooperation with Japan in the energy sector is important for Russia. Energy and fuel production served as the backbone of the Russian economy, and its role has further increased during the years of Russia's economic crisis and transition to a market economy. In 1997 the industry provided 68 percent of all federal budget revenues, including a 25 percent share paid by Gasprom. It is clear that Russian energy and fuel production will serve as the primary basis for industrial restructuring and economic and social modernization.

For Japan, Russian energy resources appear as a strategic asset as well. MITI's energy demand and supply forecast published in 1994 indicates that the consumption of crude oil and oil products will grow at a 1.8–2.0 percent annual rate, and the demand for natural gas will grow much faster. Japan's long-term contracts cover natural gas supplies for the next ten years assuming that consumption holds at the current level. In the year 2010 and beyond an additional annual 20 million tons of liquified natural gas (LNG) will be needed to balance the growing energy needs. New 1998 energy demand and supply forecasts and the changing situation in the energy sector in Northeast Asia and world energy resources markets make Russia a key additional source of oil and natural gas. Meanwhile, according to Japanese estimates, the size of the investment market in energy projects in Eastern Russia is about $90 billion, making Japan a strategic market for the Russian energy sector and an indispensable source of capital investment.

It was not a coincidence that Prime Minister Hashimoto's new policy toward Russia, announced on July 24, 1997, in his speech at the Association of Corporate Executives, emphasized closer economic relations with Russia, particularly its eastern regions, and cooperation in the energy sector. It seems that the long-term economic needs of the two countries in energy resources development and utilization are highly complementary, and that large-scale investment cooperation in the energy sector serves their national interests.

In November 1997, an international symposium on regional cooperation in the energy sector was held in Tokyo with the participation of Russia, China, South Korea, Mongolia, and the International Energy Agency. The meeting was organized by the Asian Energy Community Support Committee and sponsored, among other influential bodies, by the Ministry of Foreign Affairs, MITI, Japan National Oil Corporation, and Export-Import Bank of Japan. The participants discussed how to harmonize energy needs and the interests of the countries of the region and what regional institutions should be created to coordinate activities and projects of regional scale.

KOVIKTINSKOE GAS FIELD

Multilateral cooperation is required for the development of Koviktinskoe gas field near Irkutsk with reserves estimated at 1.5 trillion cubic meters of natural gas and 80 million tons of gas condensate. When implemented, the project will enable Russia to export for 30 years about 20 million cubic meters of natural gas to China, Korea, and Japan through a 3,364-kilometer-long international gas pipeline (1.42-meter diameter) and also switch its nine thermo-power plants in the Irkutsk region to gas, substantially reducing their environmental impact on the Lake Baikal area. It is estimated that the project, including the gas pipeline, requires about $10 billion in investments. In 15–20 years, additional resources of natural gas discovered in Yakutia and Krasnoyarskiy Krai can be linked with this project, making it the largest undertaking in the field of energy resources in East Asia (Figure 20.1).

A semi-governmental organization, Japan National Oil Corporation (JNOC), represents the interests of Japan in the project, and a consortium was formed by the private sector companies including Sumitomo, Marubeni, Nippon Steel, Tokyo Gas, Osaka Gas, and others. The consortium expressed a strong interest in joining all the stages of the project. In December 1997, the JNOC's representatives, along with their potential partners from China, Korea, and Mongolia, discussed the project in Moscow with Russian energy developer Sidanco, which will be represented in the consortium by its subsidiary Russia Petroleum joint stock company. A memorandum was signed regarding a multilateral agreement on a feasibility study, including a gas pipeline location, natural gas marketing, financing, and other issues. An international coordinating committee will be formed to supervise the feasibility study preparation.

Japan is also interested in the resources of the Verkhne-Chonskiy oil field (Irkutskaya Oblast) and Urubcheno-Takhomskoe oil field (Krasnoyarskiy Krai). Japanese companies plan to invest in the oil refinery modernization and construction projects in Komsomolsk-na-Amur and Yaroslavl (Mitsui), Angarsk (Nichimen and Mitsui), and Sakhalin (Nissho Iwai and Mitsui).

SAKHALIN PROJECTS

More than 15 large Japanese companies, including SODECO, Mitsui, Mitsubishi, Itochu, Japax, and the JNOC are involved in Sakhalin-1 (324 million tons of oil and gas condensate and 420 billion cubic meters of natural gas) and Sakhalin-2 (433 million tons of oil and gas condensate and 521 billion cubic meters of natural gas) projects with the total cost of investment estimated at $25 billion. Projects such as Sakhalin-3 and the like can be launched in 1999–2000. With active participation of SODECO, extensive research and exploration work was conducted on the offshore oil and gas deposits of Sakhalin Island. The total amount of oil and gas condensate is now estimated at 1.0 billion tons and the resources of natural gas at 3.5 trillion cubic meters.

The annual production of oil is expected to increase from the current 1.5 million tons to 30 million tons, and the natural gas output will grow

FIGURE 20.1
Prospects for Gas Pipeline Projects Development

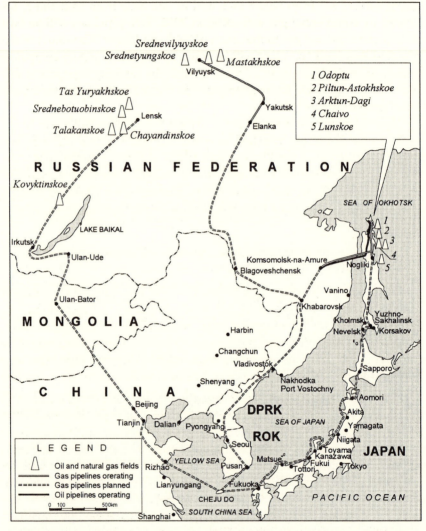

Source: Map drafted by Economic Research Institute for Northeast Asia, Niigata, Japan, 1998

from 1.9 billion cubic meters to 28 billion cubic meters, including 9–10 billion cubic meters for domestic use.

The Sakhalin-1 and Sakhalin-2 projects serve a pioneering role in foreign investment promotion in Sakhalinskaya Oblast and Far Eastern Russia. In 1996 the total amount of investment was estimated at $89 million, in 1997 $420 million, and in 1998 almost $700 million. The first oil is expected in 1999 from Sakhalin-2, and in late 2000 from Sakhalin-1, followed by commercial gas extraction in 2002. Two pipelines will be built to transport oil and gas to the south of Sakhalin Island (Korsakov) where the first Russian LNG plant will be constructed. The Japanese companies led by Mitsui will build an oil refinery with the capacity to process 4 million tons of oil, while Japax is preparing a feasibility study for the household gas production plant.

Japax also drafted a feasibility study on a Korsakov-Hokkaido-Niigata-Tsuruga-Osaka gas pipeline to handle about 7 billion cubic meters (equivalent to about 5 million tons of LNG) of natural gas by 2008. Considering the geographic proximity and sizable and growing demand for natural gas in Japan this project can be implemented provided that the price of natural gas and a long-term export-import agreement are negotiated successfully.

CONCLUSION

Energy projects will play a locomotive role in industrial cooperation, including direct investment by Japanese companies in Russia, joint ventures, research and development links, and transfer of technologies. Some Russian defense enterprises have become subcontractors; Amurskiy Shipbuilding Plant built the sea oil rig foundation, Volzhskiy Pipe Plant supplies pipes for wells, and Voronezh Mechanical Plant produces distribution equipment. More involvement of Russian companies, including those from the defense sector, can be expected as the investment volume in Sakhalin projects grows.

Sakhalin projects also will serve a very positive role in the economic development of Sakhalinskaya Oblast. Once a distant periphery of Russia, Sakhalin is becoming a front runner in international investment and regional economic cooperation. Investors from the United States, Japan, and Europe bring to the local community advanced managerial standards, technologies, and know-how. Sakhalin already has gained from advanced telecommunication networks, new air routes, and opportunities to import both industrial equipment and consumer goods from regional markets. The flow of hard currency from the energy projects will facilitate the industrial restructuring and improvements in social infrastructure.

Considering that more Russia-Japan engagement in the energy sector is expected in the future, the pioneering role of the Sakhalin projects in building professional confidence and problem-solving mechanisms is invaluable. Finally, the energy sector attracts leading Japanese producers and trading houses, thus changing considerably the chemistry of bilateral economic links and contributing to the formation of a constituency in Japan that is keenly interested in Russia as a long-term and reliable partner. One of the central pillars in this partnership relationship can be a joint feasibility study for an energy bridge project between Russia and Japan discussed on the expert level in late 1997–98.

21

Bilateral Trade in Fishery

Nobuo Arai

In the postwar period cooperation in fishery was the most important field in Japan's relations with the former Soviet Union and Russia. Symbolically, the first Japan-Soviet agreement on fisheries was signed in April 1956, about half a year before the re-establishment of diplomatic relatiosn between two countries. For more than 30 years cooperation in fishery was a priority item on both Tokyo's and Moscow's agendas.

It was not only because the fishery industry had been one of the key sectors in Japan and the Soviet Union (particularly in Far Eastern Russia), but also because annual negotiations on fisheries agreements provided both governments with an opportunity to accumulate experience on how to deal with each other. Negotiations continued even in the worst periods in the postwar history of the relationship and served as a stabilizing factor in the relationship. Even with the introduction of an exclusive economic zone, which brought in many changes in merits that both countries had received from the cooperation, regular negotiations continued.

AREA OF STRATEGIC SIGNIFICANCE

If one looks for an analogy, Japanese-Soviet fishery negotiations were playing the same role in the overall context of bilateral relations as did Washington-Moscow negotiations on control and reduction of armaments in the Cold War era. In the Tokyo-Moscow dialogue on fisheries every time each party left the room convinced that the other party could not be trusted, but they were still aware that negotiations must continue.

There were many reasons why both Japan and the Soviet Union continued to negotiate their relations in fishery with a great deal of patience, demonstrating their ability to reach agreements: They knew very well that they had to share the same resource base in the Sea of Okhotsk and the Sea of Japan. Both sides were interested in getting a considerable amount of marine protein in those seas. Moreover, both countries were major consumers and exporters of marine resources and processed goods.

Besides these positive reasons, both Japan and the Soviet Union had some trump cards to prevent the partner from quitting negotiations. Even before the introduction of the 200-mile economic zones the Soviet Union regulated fishing operations by Japanese boats in Soviet territorial waters. In addition, Japan was the only supplier of advanced technology and equipment for the Soviet fishery industry, particularly in Far Eastern Russia in the late 1960s.

It must be noted also for the sake of fairness that Japan-Soviet cooperation in fishery must not be reduced merely to political compromises between governments that in those days considered each other potential adversaries. Fishery was one among the few fields of economic activities where both countries had a possibility to complement each other's needs and interests. Furthermore, fishermen of both countries were helping each other in severe climatic conditions in northern seas.

In the past 40 years, bilateral agreements that have been attained were mutually beneficial. Annual agreements had articles in which both Japanese and Soviet (Russian) fishermen had guaranteed amounts of catch quota in the waters of the partner, that is, so-called quota without compensation. Also, the Japanese side has been getting "onerous quota" in Soviet waters, taking into consideration the fact that Japanese fishermen always asked for more access to marine resources than was possible to provide using the framework of free quota.

Notwithstanding many conflicts around violations of the agreements mainly by Japanese fishermen, the framework was stable enough to keep fishermen within established rules. For the Japanese side it was necessary not to go too far beyond the limits and adopt rules to secure a new quota in the next negotiations. Soviet fishery enterprises in Japanese waters acted strictly within approved production plans and scarcely had a temptation to catch more fish than was allowed. Thus Japan-Soviet cooperation in fishery, based on intergovernmental agreements, had a substantially stable framework. Soviet participants worked in the regime of planned economy and the Japanese were interested to fish in Soviet waters with their own boats. Everything has begun to change since the late 1980s to early 1990s.

PERESTROIKA AND FISHERY

At least in theory the former Soviet Union maintained one of the most effective systems of controlling fishery resources usage. Research institutions provided annual recommendations on upper limits of catch and every object of fishing operations for every major area of fishing. Representatives of the Ministry of Fishery allocated quotas to amalgamations of enterprises on a regional level according to production plans that were drafted by the same ministry. Enterprises were heavily subsidized by the government and had no right to sell the products in foreign markets independently.

One of the first symptoms of changes in the fishing industry in Far Eastern Russian was detected when Gorbachev initiated his reforms. Crews of fishing boats started to make contracts (lease agreements) with enterprises that owned boats. Under these agreements the crew took the obligation to catch the planned amount of fish to be sold through the state network in exchange for the right to sell the surplus on the basis of market prices to any domestic customer. Enterprises that owned boats, in their turn, had to cover only that portion of the cost of operation that was related to the state production orders.

By the late 1980s a substantial part of the fishing trawlers in Far Eastern Russia adopted this system. State-owned enterprises retained ownership of boats and equipment. When the Soviet Union ceased to exist and privatization began, all these lease companies went private, and a great number of small and medium enterprises were created in place of a consolidated and well regulated fishery industry. A powerful production base and management framework were effectively decomposed.

Before privatization began, the fishery industry in the Soviet Union, especially in the Far Eastern region, was highly concentrated and controlled by just a few state enterprises and fishery cooperatives. In fact, it was a substantial disadvantage for the Far Eastern fishery industry because compared with other regional branches it had little connection with the domestic Far Eastern market, selling locally only 2–3 percent of the catch and exporting less than 10 percent of the output. More than 80 percent of raw fish and processed products were transported to European Russia and other Soviet republics with an average distance of transportation exceeding 6,000 kilometers. The entire system, therefore, was based on substantial state subsidies allowing enterprises to grow and guarantee, at least on paper, the economy of scale.

Fishery in the high seas and economic zones of foreign countries were among the most heavily subsidized operations. Under Gorbachev, it became evident that reformers were seriously thinking about how to reduce subsidies for Far Eastern Russia as a whole and for its fishery industry in the region. This idea turned into a concrete policy in 1987–88.

Long-distance oceanic fishing operations were reduced in scale and a shift was made in favor of a Soviet economic zone in order to reduce subsidies. This shift created a qualitatively new situation in the Far Eastern regional fishery, that is, production capacity of the powerful long-distance fishing fleet began to exceed the catch quota limits in the Russian exclusive economic zone. Therefore, newly formed lease companies began searching for catch quota of those species that can be sold not only domestically but also for exports. Notwithstanding many regulations and limitations in the field of foreign trade, from 1989 state enterprises started to establish direct business links with other countries through joint ventures with foreign enterprises.

JOINT VENTURE BOOM

Moreover, shortly before the Soviet Union collapsed, the government of the Russian republic energetically encouraged state enterprises in the territory of Russia to rebel against control by the Soviet ministries. For example, in the summer of 1990, Boris Yeltsin visited Far Eastern provinces and during his meetings in Sakhalinskaya Oblast agitated leaders of regional and municipal administrations and enterprises to take whatever powers they needed to proceed with reforms that people wanted to achieve.

Valentin Fyodorov, then governor of Sakhalinskaya Oblast, was quick to respond. In fall 1990, he issued instructions to redistribute a part of catch quota in favor of new economic structures, that is, small and newly created fishery companies. Newcomers were receiving their pieces of the redistributed catch quota through municipal administrations. Some of the mayors preferred to give some part of the quota to small companies that were able to attract foreign partners (mainly from northern parts of Japan) and to establish joint ventures with them.

For most of these joint ventures the operation strategy was simple enough. Russian partners were to contribute their catch quota as their equity in the joint venture funds, while foreign partners had to take that quota in real terms using their own boats under the Japanese flag. Marine products recovered as a result of such operations were sold in Japanese wholesale markets and, after the deduction of the costs of fishery, earnings were divided between the joint venture partners. Although in their legal registration papers many joint ventures defined fishery operations as the activities that the founders will carry out at sea, lists of activities also usually included some small scale business ventures such as restaurants, hotels, and shops. In other words, joint ventures were willing to announce activities that would meet requests of municipal administrators in charge of quotas for the next year.

This kind of joint venture business suited quite well both Russian and Japanese counterparts and municipal bureaucrats. Still with no direct access to foreign markets, new Russian businessmen had an opportunity to convert their catch quota into hard currency. The established joint ventures also served as a legitimate way to pocket the money. Japanese fishermen using this framework were happy, too, because of an access to marine resources in the Russian economic zone. It was of vital importance because amounts of catch quota allotted to the Japanese by the Soviet side as a result of annual government level negotiations were shrinking.

Local administrations also had a unique opportunity to compel Russian founders of joint ventures to invest in restaurants, hotels, or simply force them to make presents — buses, construction equipment, and other goods needed by their cities and towns. This joint venture fever began to develop intensively in 1991. Sakhalin was the region particularly distinguished in this process. Although it is difficult to estimate the number of such business enterprises, in 1991–92 local newspapers reported about 200 joint ventures with Japanese participation in Sakhalin.

POST-SOVIET ERA

As the Soviet Union collapsed, government policy of the newly independent Russian Federation began to change quickly. The same people in Moscow who made everything possible to limit the authority of the Ministry of Fishery in the area of catch quota distribution and regulation started to reconstruct order, making corrections in the much decentralized system of marine resources distribution.

From late 1992 the State Committee on Fishery of the Russian Federation, a substitute for the ministry, began negotiations with the Far Eastern provinces. As a result, bilateral agreements were concluded between the committee and administrations of the provinces based on mutual compromises. Instead of representatives of enterprises and their amalgamations, under this new system vice-governors were given the right to control the fishery industry, to represent their provinces at the annual meetings of the Regional Fishery Council, and to decide amounts of catch quota for each region.

Under this system each province established its own fishery council, in addition to fishery departments already created within administrations of the provinces. The state committee, however, retained its power to approve the distribution of catch quota both between provinces and within them.

In the process of negotiations between the state committee and the provinces some important decisions were made in the system of allocation of marine resource quotas to joint ventures. Those enterprises registered in Russia with their own fishery fleet are allowed to participate in the deliberations of the provincial fishery council to defend their requests for catch quota in accordance with their technical capacity to use this quota. Companies with foreign participation but without boats had to apply to the State Committee on Fishery in Moscow and to negotiate with its representatives, to whom the regional committee on fishery delegated the right to negotiate with foreign companies and joint ventures without boats.

Bureaucrats based in Moscow, unlike their colleagues from regional administrations, are tough negotiators. Although local administrators agree with requests made by representatives of joint ventures to pay for resources after the operation and for the actual amount of the catch, Moscow requests payment prior to the operation and for the full amount of resources that the joint venture is entitled to.

This change in the system completely altered the environment in which joint ventures were created and operated. For most of the Japanese partners it was not possible to invest in the fishing vessels that make joint ventures entitled to catch quota. Without boats, joint venture partners must go to Moscow for difficult negotiations. As a result of these developments some joint ventures ceased to exist, and others decided not to participate in the management of companies and converted themselves into importers of marine products that their Russian partners bring to Japanese ports.

22

The Russian View of Economic Links

Andrei P. Rodionov

Russia and Japan, long-time distant trade partners, now face new opportunities for cooperation. Soviet Union–Japan trade reached its peak during the Cold War era. Among developed countries, Japan was one of the Soviet Union's leading trading partners. As was the usual practice in the former Soviet Union, trade with developed countries reflected the capabilities of a centrally planned economy, with exports of raw materials and imports of consumer goods, machines, and capital equipment limited by export control restrictions covering some advanced products and technologies.

The task is to create a stronger economic foundation for long-term engagement based on shared interests that are not limited to the exchange of raw materials for processed goods. The political will of leaders and efforts from business communities for close economic engagement are necessary to achieve diversified economic exchanges based on interdependence, coproduction, and joint manufacturing.

TRADE RELATIONS IN 1992–96

After the Soviet Union broke apart, trade between Russia and Japan as well as between Russia and other developed countries was marked by the uneasy process of adjustment to new Russian realities. Gradually this led to new relations and mechanisms for cooperation. A crisis in trade between the two countries during 1992–96 revealed itself in various economic and institutional forms, including the problem of debt to Japanese companies, declining volumes of trade, the loss of traditional links and mechanisms for negotiations, the emergence of new partners, decreasing confidence, the change in geography of trade, financial constraints, and so forth. A lack of positive results during this period in solving serious bilateral problems (especially in debt restructuring, the slow progress in Sakhalin oil and gas ventures, and other major projects credited by the Export-Import Bank of Japan [JEXIM] and insured by the Ministry of International Trade and Industry [MITI]), the absence of a success story, and mutual indifference restrained business contacts between the two countries.

TRADE RELATIONS

Trade between Russia and Japan remains low. Russian exports have surpassed imports but still consist mainly of raw materials. Japan's direct exports to Russia have fallen while the flow of consumer goods through other countries with a made in Japan trademark increased. Some Russian and Japanese companies discuss promising projects, but only a few have entered an implementation stage. There are no significant Japanese investments in Russia (with the exception of the Sakhalin projects in which U.S. and British companies are involved as leaders).

Slow progress in Russia-Japan trade cannot be explained by the current economic transition in Russia only. Many other companies of developed countries, including French, Italian, German, and U.S. firms, have established a more solid presence in Russia, including its Far Eastern provinces. In general, for the first half of the 1990s, Japan-Russia trade was unstable. Its volume decreased sharply in 1992, rose to $5.93 billion in 1995, and fell again in 1996. Russian exports to Japan increased while imports fell, so trade became more favorable for Russia (Table 22.1).

With other developed countries Russia also has a trade surplus. The volume of trade is still extremely small: The share of Japanese exports to Russia forms only 0.26 percent of total exports, and its imports constitute only 1.42 percent.

A drop in domestic investment in Russia reduced the demand for big ticket items from Japan, such as large-diameter pipes for oil and gas projects. For 1996 imports the share of machines and equipment imported from Japan reached 74.6 percent. The share of ferrous metals (pipes and other rolled commodities) fell from 21 percent in 1994 to 5.6 percent in 1996. Chemical products, textiles, and foodstuffs constituted less than 4 percent by 1997 (Table 22.2).

TABLE 22.1
Japan-Russia Trade, 1970–96
(in millions of dollars)

	Total	Exports to Russia	Imports from Russia	Balance
1970	821.9	340.9	481.0	−140.1
1971	873.1	377.3	495.9	−118.6
1972	1,098.1	504.2	593.9	−89.7
1973	1,561.9	484.2	1,077.7	−593.5
1974	2,513.8	1,095.6	1,418.1	−322.5
1975	2,795.8	1,626.2	1,169.6	456.6
1976	3,419.3	2,251.9	1,167.4	1,084.5
1977	3,355.8	1,933.9	1,421.9	512.0
1978	3,943.9	2,502.2	1,441.7	1,060.5
1979	4,372.1	2,461.5	1,910.7	550.9
1980	4,638.1	2,778.2	1,859.9	918.4
1981	5,280.1	3,259.4	2,020.7	1,238.7
1982	5,580.9	3,898.8	1,682.0	2,216.8
1983	4,277.3	2,871.2	1,456.0	1,365.2
1984	3,912.3	2,518.3	1,393.9	1,124.3
1985	4,179.8	2,750.6	1,429.3	1,321.3
1986	5,121.6	3,149.5	1,972.0	1,177.5
1987	4,915.1	2,563.3	1,351.9	211.4
1988	5,895.7	3,129.9	2,765.8	364.1
1989	6,086.2	3,081.7	3,004.5	77.1
1990	5,913.8	2,562.8	3,350.9	− 788.1
1991	5,430.5	2,113.7	3,316.8	−1,203.1
1992	3,479.7	1,076.7	2,402.9	−1,326.2
1993	4,270.0	1,500.8	2,769.2	−1,268.4
1994	4,657.5	1,167.2	3,490.4	−2,323.2
1995	5,933.5	1,170.1	4,763.3	−3,593.2
1996	4,973.5	1,024.7	3,948.8	−2,924.1

Source: Data compiled by the author from Japan Association for Trade with Russia and Countries of Eastern Europe, *Monthly Bulletin on Trade with Russia and Eastern Europe*. (Tokyo: Japan Association for Trade with Russia & Central-Eastern Europe and the Institute for Russian & East European Economic Studies. Data up to January 1992 include trade with the Soviet Union; with the Russian Federation only after January 1992.

TABLE 22.2
Composition of Russia's Trade With Japan, 1992–96
(in millions of dollars)

	1992	1993	1994	1995	1996
Exports					
Fish and seafood	582	710	1,025	1,321	1,221
Timber	465	617	619	770	689
Saw products	42	59	77	108	97
Coal	237	202	212	261	266
Metals	710	880	1,296	1,979	1,484
Steel products	99	127	175	179	117
Non-ferrous metals	609	752	1,120	1,797	1,347
Platinum	223	179	302	402	318
Palladium	116	164	233	319	214
Aluminum	150	335	485	808	691
Total	2,403	2,769	3,490	4,763	3,949
Imports					
Metals	109	376	229	80	57
Pipes	59	222	130	76	42
General machinery and equipment	703	847	288	439	282
Electromechanical goods	235	224	308	311	291
Television sets	27	27	13	64	108
Video tape recorders	43	37	27	42	38
Transport equipment	151	163	88	97	153
Total	1,077	1,501	1,167	1,170	1,077

Source: Data compiled by the author from Japan Association for Trade with Russia and Countries of Eastern Europe, *Monthly Bulletin on Trade with Russia and Eastern Europe*. (Tokyo: Japan Association for Trade with Russia & Central-Eastern Europe and the Institute for Russian & East European Economic Studies. Data up to January 1992 include trade with the Soviet Union; with the Russian Federation only after January 1992.

The economy of the Far Eastern provinces had become more dependent on exports to Japan. This situation has reflected well in trade with Japan. Exports have increased with the growth in deliveries of traditional raw materials, mainly fish and seafood, metals, and timber. However, a further increase in exports of these commodities is limited both by the capacities of the Russian side and the demand on the Japanese side.

Because of the high risks in Russia, starting in 1992 Japanese companies delivered goods to Russia mainly on advance payment terms. The lack of financial facilities and resources of Russian enterprises limited exports from Japan to Russia. Apart from this the high rate of the yen for several years within this period negatively influenced export prices from Japan. In view of the low purchasing power in Russia, local importers of consumer goods looked for cheaper sources.

During the transitional period, so called individual trade boomed in Russia with hundreds of thousands of individual traders traveling abroad to purchase goods for resale in Russian local markets. The volume of such a gray area of imports and exports became quite significant. In Japan's case, with its strict visa entry regime and high consumer goods prices, such forms of transactions were revealed in large volumes. Russians exchanged fish and seafood for used cars and electric appliances when Russian ships called at Japanese ports. However, trade through the barter exchange of fish, metals, coal, and timber from one side and television sets, used or new cars, and other commodities from the other side has its limits.

INVESTMENT LINKS

The new potential of Russian-Japanese economic exchanges can be found in investments and industrial coproduction. In spite of the opening of foreign trade insurance facilities by Japan's MITI and loans by the JEXIM, the existing procedures in Russia are extremely time consuming. Before 1998 it was also difficult for Japan to change the list of projects or transfer new credits before the current trade insurance funds and loans were utilized by the Russian side.

However, both countries should endeavor to achieve a new quality of cooperation in various fields that can serve their national interests, benefit their economic security, and contribute to economic growth. Such an economic partnership can be designed along the following key directions:

diversification of links in raw materials extraction, processing, and exports;

investment promotion in Russia for import-substituting products;

design, production, and marketing of new products;

cooperation in advanced technologies;

financial links aimed at support for joint projects;

infrastructure-building to facilitate trade and joint projects;

mechanisms creation for contacts at governmental, local, and private levels; and

coordination in multilateral, regional, and international organizations.

Diversified economic links could benefit both countries. Japan could benefit from making its products accessible to a sizable Russian market and securing access to reliable and guaranteed sources of energy supplies from Russia. It could benefit from investing capital in Russian enterprises and the creation of new market products. Russia could have better access to financial resources, advanced technologies, management, and know-how from Japan. Energy resources development, raw materials processing, transportation, import substitution, high-tech cooperation, and other areas could become promising areas of cooperation and division of labor creating significant commercial advantages for both nations.

The energy sector is becoming a core area of bilateral cooperation. The Sakhalin projects alone (which have already started) will play a significant role in Russian-Japanese cooperation. In the not-so-distant future, they will lead to an increase in the volume of trade. Recently government and private business organizations have started intensive discussions on the possibility of gas exploration in Irkutskaya Oblast and Yakutia. The implementation of Sakhalin and other Far Eastern and Siberian oil and gas exploration projects will contribute to export earnings and improve energy supplies in the Far Eastern provinces, thus helping their local economic activities. Far Eastern enterprises can also benefit from subcontracts for equipment and construction works leading to more jobs. Japan, by utilizing the advantage of geographical proximity and its own role in exploration and development of the new sources, will enhance its energy security. Both countries with their combined natural, financial, and technological resources could consider the creation of an integrated system of energy supplies in Northeast Asia.

Russia-Japan cooperation will be enhanced by the revival of volumes of transit transportation from Japan to Europe and Central Asia over the Trans-Siberian Railway, which will be modernized along with ports, roads, and other infrastructure. This will contribute to Russia's internal integration as well.

The volume of goods with Japanese major brand names exported to Russia is becoming so large that it may become economically reasonable to consider local production. Japan is continuing to move its industries abroad. Russian enterprises, considering emerging local markets, could become the recipients of Japanese direct investment. The imports of manufactured goods will be eventually replaced by local output supported by foreign companies, including Japanese firms.

There is a need to facilitate cooperation in advanced technology. Governments should support such linkages by special financial and other measures, such as the 1996 Russian high-tech exhibition in Tokyo sponsored by the Association for Trade with Russia and Countries of Eastern Europe. A successful example of such linkage was a contract to supply aluminum cast car wheels. These wheels are especially designed for Japanese cars and produced in Russia from ultralight alloys with the use of unique press equipment.

The total volume of potential joint projects currently under review or at various stages of implementation can be estimated at $12–14 billion (excluding Sakhalin projects). Their implementation will lead to a substantial growth in the volume and structure of bilateral trade. Active and regular contacts at the senior management level of big companies on both sides can help to move these projects forward. However, this requires efforts by business leaders and private business organizations. Russia should also take steps in creating a special investment climate for Japanese investors, including the following possible measures:

mutual support and protection of investment agreements,

effective mechanisms to deal with claims by foreign investors,

information exchanges (within the Hashimoto plan),

the Russian Center for Investments Promotion in Tokyo,

enhanced Japan External Trade Organization activities in Russia, and

joint market research efforts.

The usual concern of Japanese companies in their business contacts with Russia is the limited opportunity to apply their own principles of planning, management, and risk prevention based on collective decision making. Because Japanese commercial banks do not like to finance projects in countries with a high investment risk climate, special efforts must be made by the Russian side to lower the perceived investment risks. Some Japanese and Russian experts propose technoparks, established on the basis of designated Russian enterprises, that will ensure a stable investment microclimate.

FINANCIAL LINKS

Only official financial instruments are currently used in Russia-Japan cooperation. Because of high risks, private banks avoid the extension of financial credits and other facilities to Russian companies and private banks. There are only a few cases of direct Japanese investments in Russia. Official support by Japan is extended in the form of credits by JEXIM and export insurance provided by MITI. The Russian federal government extends guarantees for this assistance, but the volume is limited and has to be approved every year through the state budget.

In contrast, both the JEXIM credits and MITI insurance funds have not been utilized for three years because of defects in the selection procedure of projects and the requirement that enterprises must allocate 15 percent of the required funds in advance. It became clear that practices for opening credit lines and then filling them with projects became outdated.

Instead, the selection of projects with a high level of investment readiness was proposed, as well as changes in the procedure to allow flexibility in decision making.

The Russian government must improve and expand mechanisms for investment guarantees. The so-called Development Budget, designed with reference to the Japanese experience of the early 1950s, offered a maximum 40 percent state guarantee for projects with private investments or credits. It can be seen as an instrument to attract Japanese investments, especially in the Far Eastern enterprises.

The JEXIM extended three credit lines to Russia. The first one is the $200 million credit for telecommunication lines construction to connect Japan and Europe. The second credit line of $400 million is called an investment credit and is used for equipment for the Impulse company in St. Petersburg, the KAMAZ truck manufacturing plant, and an oil refinery in Yaroslavl. The third credit line of $500 million is called a humanitarian credit. It was initially designated for the construction of medical facilities in the Far East, but later was expanded to include the modernization of several industrial enterprises.

Japanese corporations do not accept the guarantees of regional administrations and major Russian commercial banks. However, MITI has taken a step forward by acknowledging the short-term letters of comfort from nine Russian banks as a form of guarantee for projects financed through the MITI External Trade Insurance Fund. Within the first stage of using the $1.1 billion insurance money, steel pipes and machines were delivered to Russia for construction and repair of gas pipelines. The balance is being negotiated. The Japanese side tends to consider big oil and gas projects, where the funds can be quickly recovered.

However, normal mechanisms of commercial financing do not exist. Compared with Japan, other countries more readily accept mixed guarantees including guarantees provided by the consortium of Russian banks, guarantees issued by regional administrations, and accepting shares of the Russian enterprise. In this respect the Japanese companies lack competitiveness. Various approaches should be explored to support projects of different sizes and ranges of implementation.

Private financing is likely to be available only to profitable projects, particularly those in the energy sector. The government has a very significant role to play in this area as well through production-sharing agreements, special legislation on the development sites, participation of local administrations, and active promotion of local subcontractors.

ORGANIZATIONAL IMPROVEMENTS

A network of intergovernmental and private contacts is critically important for progress in economic exchanges. This network can include the formation of working groups when necessary in areas such as international finance, energy projects, transport, technical cooperation, small and medium enterprises, currency and export control, customs, emergency situations, and environmental issues. Energy resources development, processing of raw materials (timber, fish, and marine products), high-tech cooperation, import substitution (audio and video equipment), and transportation could be areas of profitable commercial cooperation and division of labor.

The business communities of both countries, however, should establish direct exchanges and regular contacts if they want to utilize the existing trade and investment opportunities. Both the Russian and Japanese governments are expected to lead the process of exchanges and to facilitate private contacts. In 1995 governmental commissions for economic cooperation were formed. They continue to serve as a main channel for economic exchanges between the two countries. In a memorandum both sides decided on the main functions, structure, and procedures for meetings of these commissions. The chairman of the Russian side is the deputy prime minister; on the Japanese side the minister of foreign affairs is in charge. Three subcommittees were created to deal with terms and conditions of bilateral economic ties, promotion of market reforms in Russia, and economic links with the Far Eastern provinces. The first meeting was held in Moscow in March 1996, during the visit of the Japanese minister of foreign affairs (the joint documents for the first meeting of the commissions were drafted by subcommittees). The second meeting was held in Tokyo in June 1997. Credit agreements for three projects were signed.

Apart from the commissions, regular contacts have been effected between the Russian Ministry of Economy and the Economic Planning Agency of Japan, as well as between the Russian Ministry of Economy and MITI. Consultations are taking place concerning the opening of a representative office of the Russian Center for Promotion of Foreign Investments together with the Russian Chamber of Commerce and Industry. Its main task would be to supply Japanese investors and businessmen with information. However, to attach more significance to their activities the level of commissions should be raised (similar to the Gore-Chernomyrdin Commission).

Unlike in U.S.-Russia relations, private contacts remain underdeveloped. There are many business associations in Russia, but none of them is influential enough to represent the whole business community. Compared, for example, to Keidanren or the chambers of commerce and industries in other countries, Russian business associations are weak. Many practical issues and specific projects are being solved in the framework of government commissions and not by business councils or committees. The organizational support for Russian businesses in Japan is inadequate, too. With the exception of two timber companies, no Russian companies or agencies have opened representative offices in Japan since 1992.

In contrast, Japanese companies have gradually expanded their office network in Russia, both in Moscow and the regions. Practically all big trading companies have opened offices in the Far Eastern provinces. Many well-known Japanese automakers also have established their presence and have formed dealership networks. There are outposts of some Japanese banks in Russia as well.

TECHNICAL ASSISTANCE

The program of technical assistance was initiated by Ryutaro Hashimoto during his term as head of MITI. Hashimoto's plan has three objectives: to support Russian reforms, to raise the productivity of Russian enterprises, and to promote Russian exports to Japan. Various projects are under implementation, including educational centers, assistance to Russian enterprises, the Far Eastern Regional Venture Fund, and others. MITI, Japan External Trade Organization, Association for Trade with Russia and Countries of Eastern Europe, and other organizations are participating in this scheme. In Russia the Ministry of Economy is the coordinator that leads the activities of various ministries, chambers of commerce, and other organizations.

Japanese experts, for example, consulted several Russian enterprises on the problem of restructuring and efficiency (Murom Machine Building Plant, Krasnoyarsk Steel Works, Sharm textile factory, Selenginsk Pulp-and-Paper Works, an electronics factory near Moscow, and others). Seminars on management were conducted and Russian specialists were trained in Japan. Centers to train specialists for medium and small enterprises were opened in Moscow, Khabarovsk, and Vladivostok.

However, technical assistance should facilitate not only informational or educational exchanges or consulting efforts but also Japanese investment in Russia. Joint research and pre-feasibility studies for investment projects, including those of the Far Eastern development program, can be initiated. Plans for the restructuring of selected Russian enterprises can be linked with efforts to attract investment from Japan. Support for small and medium enterprises can also constitute an important area of activities reducing unemployment and supporting local industries.

Experts from both countries can also study and discuss possibilities for applying the experience of Japanese companies in the United States. They can also look at the investment environment in China, their experience in forming joint ventures, and their operations in free economic zones. They may analyze the experience of Russian companies dealing with their counterparts from the United States and Europe, particularly in financing big projects.

CONCLUSION

The progress in economic cooperation between Russia and Japan, in which both countries have a stake, depends upon mutual efforts by the governments and business communities of both countries to improve conditions for trade and investment cooperation. The level and range of contacts between Russia and Japan in the economic field, both at the governmental and private levels, has expanded during recent years. Contacts have become more regular and frequent; they are supported by mechanisms at the working level. Discussions are wider and aimed at facilitating solutions for practical problems.

Through the governmental commissions Russia and Japan can now discuss the problems of development of the Far Eastern region, including projects of the federal development program for the region. They can work out mechanisms for the selection of projects that are eligible for credits by the JEXIM. Working together both governments can better manage the problems of investment risk, financial guarantees, and other forms of support for bilateral projects.

The regional ties between the Far Eastern provinces of the Russian Federation and Japan during the last five years have expanded. There was growth in trade, particularly in fish and marine product exports from Russia. The general conditions and infrastructure for doing business in the Far East of Russia also improved with direct air flights, better hotel facilities, and improved telecommunication services. Leading Japanese companies opened offices in major cities of the Far Eastern region. The Japanese government wants to focus its official assistance and credits on the Far Eastern economic region, and economic cooperation with the eastern part of Russia stands as a separate subject in official bilateral dialogue and private talks. Business organizations and research centers in Japan pay special attention to the Far East.

On the Russian side, regional administrations and organizations want to promote economic cooperation with Japan and other Asia-Pacific nations. There is a network of special relations emerging between some Russian provinces and Japanese prefectures. All these entities play a more active role in the promotion of economic exchanges between the two countries. The activities of the joint commission on economic cooperation between Hokkaido and three Russian Far Eastern provinces (established in 1992) should be noted for its special contribution to bilateral cooperation.

It is quite realistic to expect the expansion of bilateral trade to $20–30 billion by 2005. Diversified investment links and various forms of investments, joint projects in research and development, and technical and financial cooperation are highly possible as well. Both Russia and Japan need to increase the share of processed goods in Russian exports. Moreover, efficient mechanisms for business contacts on various levels are

needed. Both countries should assist contacts and expand existing channels of communication at the private level. Especially Russian leading
companies, commercial banks, and industrial groups should cultivate ties
with their Japanese counterparts and more actively participate in exhibi-
tions, conferences, and other business events in Japan.

Currently Russia-Japan joint projects, especially in the Far Eastern
provinces, target raw materials extraction. Such large-scale and capital
intensive ventures create only a limited number of jobs. Small and medium sized joint ventures must complement current plans. These joint ventures are possible in timber and fish processing, import-substituting products manufacturing, auto assembly, and technical services (considering
the imports of used cars from Japan to eastern Russia). They will improve
the local employment situation and contribute to the restructuring of local
economies.

23

(Russia)

Economic Links from the Japanese Viewpoint

Susumu Yoshida

In his speech on July 24, 1997, Prime Minister Ryutaro Hashimoto launched a new diplomatic concept of Japan's policy toward Eurasia and stated three principles for the relationship with Russia, including trust, mutual benefit, and long-term perspective. As a result of the no-necktie talks in Krasnoyarsk in November 1997, the following two concepts were adopted by the leaders. First, both countries do their utmost to conclude a peace treaty based on the Tokyo Declaration before the year 2000. Second, the implementation of the Yeltsin-Hashimoto Plan was given a high priority. Now, both countries have developed high-level contacts, including regular meetings of the ministers of foreign affairs and discuss a peace treaty agreement using a framework of a special bilateral commission.

COOPERATION WITH NEW RUSSIA

As a result of the breakup of the Soviet Union in 1991 former Soviet republics gained independence. A transition from a centrally planned economy to an economic system based on market principles went on. One of the major elements of this transition was the abolition of the state monopoly in foreign trade. This was among the main factors behind the sharp decline in Japanese and Russian trade. In one year's time during 1991 and 1992 the volume of bilateral trade dropped 36 percent or nearly $2 billion.

The negative impact of the economic transition for bilateral trade, therefore, was larger than expected. Since early 1992 the repayment of loans from the Export-Import Bank of Japan (JEXIM) became delayed, and Japanese trading companies shifted their operations toward imports from Russia and were hesitant to proceed with new deliveries to Russia without guarantees. However, many producers in Russia claimed that they cannot operate on the basis of advanced payment. Therefore, foreign intermediaries became involved in these transactions on a massive scale. This new situation affected the trade in steel products, non-ferrous metals, and chemicals. Since 1993 bilateral trade started to recover. In 1995 its volume amounted to $5.9 billion. Japanese imports from Russia constituted about 80 percent of this trade volume compared with 61 percent in 1991.

Considering that prior to 1988 Japan on the average exported 45 percent more than it imported from Russia, it seems that this change in balance of trade was among the key features in changing the nature of Japan-Russia trade relations. In 1996 the total volume of bilateral trade was $4.95 billion; Japan's exports were $1.02 billion and its imports from Russia were $3.93 billion.

The most recent developments in Japan-Russia trade include the export of goods made in Japan via third countries, particularly in consumer electronics and motorcars. In the case of electronic goods the trade is conducted mainly through Malaysia, Dubai, and Finland. It is difficult to estimate the exact volume of this indirect export, but it could be around $1.5 billion annually. Given these figures, we can estimate that the volume of bilateral trade between Japan and Russia exceeds that of the Japan–Soviet Union trade at its peak level.

JAPAN'S ECONOMIC SUPPORT

From 1993 until February 1999, the total amount of loans extended by the International Monetary Fund to Russia reached $19.8 billion. Japan is among the key contributors to this program of economic assistance to Russia. The total amount of Japan's official commitment is $6 billion, including $5.6 billion in loans ($2.9 billion in trade insurance, and $2.7 billion in JEXIM loans). The remaining $400 million was provided in the form of grants. Out of the total amount of $6 billion, $1.5 billion is the untied JEXIM loan that was offered when Minister of Foreign Affairs Keizo Obuchi visited Moscow in February 1998.

Since 1995 the Ministry of International Trade and Industry has been carrying a set of measures to support Russian exports and manufacturing industries. This program of technical assistance covers three main areas, including promotion of exports, restructuring of Russian industries, and measures to promote high-tech industries in Russia. This plan laid foundations for the Hashimoto-Yeltsin Plan adopted as a result of the no-necktie summit.

INVESTMENT IN RUSSIA

In 1992 the amount of foreign direct investment in Russia was estimated at $700 million. In 1996 it increased to $2 billion, and the total amount of foreign investment in Russia reached $6 billion. In 1997 only the inflow of foreign investment to Russia was $4 billion, or 70 percent more than in 1996. As a result the total amount of foreign direct investment in Russia reached $11 billion.[1]

The city of Moscow received about 75 percent of these investments made by foreign companies in Russia. Moscow was followed by Moskovskaya Oblast (defense enterprises conversion and other high-tech industries), Tumenskaya Oblast (oil and gas resources development), and Magadanskaya Oblast (gold mining).

U.S. companies lead in foreign investment in Russia. By June 1996 they invested $1.66 billion, or 31.5 percent of the total volume of foreign investment. The United Kingdom and Germany followed with $0.46 billion (8.6 percent) and $0.42 billion (8.1 percent), respectively. Compared with these countries Japan lagged behind with only $0.15 billion (2.9 percent) of foreign investment in Russia. In June 1997 the amount of investment by Japanese companies was estimated at $227 million or 0.5 percent of the total volume of the Japanese foreign investment. Among the reasons for a relatively small amount of Japanese investment in Russia, the following five problems should be mentioned.

First, Japan's options for investment are truly wide, including China, Vietnam, and other economies. Russia is only one of these numerous options.

Second, Japanese products, such as consumer electronics and automobiles, could enter the markets of European countries, including Russia, through trade channels and without investment in production ventures.

Third, in the area of import deliveries from Far Eastern Russia, including timber, non-ferrous metals, marine products, and coal, Japanese companies earn profit by investing on a limited scale, only adding to the investment made before 1992.

Fourth, Japanese companies cannot allocate significant funds for investment in Russia because of the domestic economic problems associated with the bubble economy in Japan that surfaced almost in parallel with Russia's transition to a market economy.

Finally, some Japanese medium and small investors who are interested in trade and investment opportunities of Far Eastern Russia failed because of Russia's legal system's deficiencies. The investment environment in Russia is lagging behind other countries in tax, legal systems, and development of infrastructure. Moreover, incentives for foreign investors in general are inadequate.

Russian foreign investment law was adopted in 1991, but the revision of this law was delayed. The law on free economic zones was rejected by the president, and the State Duma continues to deliberate on how to improve it. Only in 1998 was the system of guarantees for investments and loans for large-scale projects finally introduced. It includes a 40 percent share on the part of the federal government, with the remaining part to be covered by Russian commercial banks.[2] However, there were no concrete results achieved by mid-1998 in this area.

At the Japan–Far Eastern Russia Economic Conference held in March 1998, jointly organized by the officials and representatives of business communities, the Japanese side stressed that 100 percent guarantees by the federal government are needed for noncommercial and infrastructure projects that require large amounts of investment and lending.

SAKHALIN OIL AND GAS PROJECTS

In January 1975 SODECO reached an agreement with the Russian side regarding joint exploration in the northeastern sector of the continental shelf of Sakhalin. This project was delayed for a number of years after the former Soviet Union intervened in Afghanistan. However, before it was interrupted, the Chaivo and Odoptu fields were jointly explored and feasibility studies were prepared.

In April 1991, when Mikhail Gorbachev visited Japan, he named the Sakhalin resources development as a priority area of bilateral economic cooperation. In June 1991 Lunskoe and Piltun Astokskoe fields were put forward for international bidding for investment and development. In March 1992 Mitsui Bussan, Marathon Oil, and McDermott (the latter two being U.S. companies) formed an alliance and succeeded in winning the bid for a feasibility study for the project. Later Royal Dutch Shell and Mitsubishi joined the alliance, and McDermott withdrew from the consortium that became known as Sakhalin-2.

In late 1993 the SODECO-Exxon union (Sakhalin-1) acquired from Russia rights to develop Arktun Dagi field and started exploration in 1994. In June 1994 Sakhalin-2 also began exploration after the production-sharing agreement was negotiated with the Russian government. Sakhalin-2 plans to begin oil recovery in 1999, and Sakhalin-1 will reach this stage in 2001. The production of gas is expected to begin in 2005. The total amount of investment in these two projects is estimated at $25 billion. There are problems, however, that need to be solved, including the problem of the compatibility of existing laws and new laws on production sharing and the problem of creating a proper mechanism to refund the value-added tax levied on imported equipment and materials for Sakhalin projects.

In June 1997 the governors of Sakhalinskaya Oblast and Khabarovskiy and Primorskiy krais signed an agreement on the use of Sakhalin natural gas output for the domestic needs of these three provinces. This plan was also included in the federal program on the development of the Far Eastern region.

COOPERATION IN FAR EASTERN RUSSIA

In January 1991, at the thirteenth meeting of the Japan-Soviet joint committee, the Far Eastern subcommittee meeting was held. At this meeting the two sides came to an agreement that they have to pay more attention to the activities and projects that link Far Eastern Russia with Japan.

In July 1991 the second meeting of the Far Eastern subcommittee was held in Vladivostok. In June 1993, after the Soviet Union ceased to exist, the first meeting of the Japan-Russia Joint Economic Conference was convened. In 1994 Japanese members of the Far Eastern subcommittee were dispatched to Primorskiy Krai, Khabarovskiy Krai, and Sakhalinskaya Oblast to conduct interviews and collect data on potential projects. After returning to Japan they chose 4 projects out of 60 in Far Eastern Russia, formed a working group, and started the discussion focused on these selected projects.

In 1995 Jiro Kawage, chairman of the Japan-Russia Economic Committee, visited the Far Eastern region to discuss with Evgeniy Nazdratenko, governor of Primorskiy Krai, prospects for bilateral cooperation. In March–November 1996, a feasibility study for the development of Zarubino Port was conducted, and the results of this research were reported to Nazdratenko.

In March 1997 the first meeting of the Far Eastern Economic Committee was held in Yuzhno-Sakhalinsk, followed by other working level discussions in June and October 1997 and February 1998. In March 1998 the Japan–Far Eastern Russia Economic Committee met for the first time in the history of bilateral relations.

THE FOUR PROJECTS

In 1994, when Japanese members of the Far Eastern subcommittee visited Russia, they held discussions with their Russian counterparts in each province and later organized task forces to discuss the four projects that were selected by the Japanese side. These included expansion of the Vanino port at Sovetskaya Gavan (Khabarovskiy Krai), modernization and expansion of Zarubino Port and improvement of the transportation system in Primorskiy Krai, prospects for development of the Uglegorskoe coal field in Sakhalinskaya Oblast, construction of the seaport at Shakhtersk and a connecting railway, railway construction between

Il'yinsk and Uglegorsk, and development of the medium-size coal field in Primorskiy Krai.

After considering these projects a conclusion was reached that Vanino Port was basically maintained by various private companies that owned the berths and controlled the operation of the port, making this project unsuitable for a single Japan-Russia joint project. Another conclusion was that the development of the coal field project was relatively small in size and the coal highly volatile, making it unsuitable for export. As far as the projects in Sakhalinskaya Oblast were concerned the coal production company was divided into three companies as a result of privatization, and no company was interested in the railway and port construction projects. Therefore, the proposed development projects in Sakhalin were put on hold, and the feasibility study was conducted only for the Zarubino Port project. This project was discussed in March 1998 at the Japan–Far Eastern Russia Economic Committee meeting, and it was proposed to include this project in the Yeltsin-Hashimoto Plan.

OBSTACLES TO ECONOMIC TIES

To promote bilateral economic links both countries need to maintain political and economic stability in addition to a good bilateral relationship. Currently there are obstacles that limit the scope of economic engagement. First, political instability in Russia represents a major challenge. The past several years of Russian history look like a chain of upheavals and crises. Every year, beginning with 1991, Russia was shaken by a major political event, including President Yeltsin's sudden decision to reshuffle his cabinet in March 1998.

Second, during these same years of political instability the Russian economy was shrinking in size. The economic decline began in 1989 because of some measures implemented to relax some rigid regulations of central planning. From 1989 to 1996 the gross domestic product (GDP) declined 48 percent, industrial production decreased 54 percent, and agricultural production contracted by 47 percent. In 1997 there were some first signs of recovery from this protracted economic decline. From 1996 to 1997 the GDP increased 0.4 percent, industrial output grew 1.9 percent, and inflation was 11 percent. We do not know whether this trend will continue.

In his report to the State Duma on April 10, 1998, then acting Prime Minister Sergei Kirienko stated that in March 1998 the GDP did not show any sign of growth. Obviously, it is very difficult to secure private funds or to attract foreign investment for industrial enterprises under the conditions of negative growth.

Third, the legal environment for foreign investment in Russia must be improved. The protection of investment and tax reform are long overdue in Russia. In early 1998 the foreign investment law was in the process of revision by the State Duma along with a new tax code. Nonetheless, the need to protect Japanese investment in Russia was discussed, and the idea of a joint Japan-Russia investment corporation was discussed during an informal summit at Kawana in April 1998. It is important to protect the interests of small and medium Japanese investors in Russia, particularly in the Far Eastern region. The investment protection treaty will help this to a very significant degree.

Fourth, the practice of a relationship between the federal government and regional administrations needs improvement in order to attract more foreign investors to the regions of the Russian Federation, particularly the Far Eastern region. Both the development of the energy sector in Far Eastern Russia and infrastructure improvements require more active involvement of the federal government. The intention of the federal government to guarantee up to 40 percent of investment in such projects is a step in the right direction. However, the commercial banks' participation in such a scheme to cover the remaining part is critically important.

It is unrealistic to expect foreign investors to participate in large-scale infrastructure development projects without full guarantees from the federal government and regional administrations. For example, the administration of Sakhalinskaya Oblast plans to establish a development fund with $200 million in its reserves to support development projects by extending partial guarantees to investors. Also, in the case of the KS-4 project the administration of Khabarovskiy Krai tried but failed to get guarantees from the federal government.

Finally, the trade policy of the Russian Federation must be aimed at the protection of domestic producers. It is very typical of the Russian foreign trade pattern that natural resources serve as a foundation of Russian exports, and imports comprise a wide range of consumer goods from Europe, Southeast Asia, Korea, China, and Taiwan. Also, Russia imports huge numbers of motorcars and consumer electronics from Europe, Japan, and Korea. As a result the Russian textile industry and consumer goods production declined dramatically.

Moreover, the Russian foreign trade surplus cannot be maintained without active promotion of domestic producers. In 1994 the trade surplus was estimated at $19.7 billion, in 1995 it increased to $22.5 billion, and it reached its $34 billion peak in 1996. However, in 1997 the Russian position in foreign trade was affected by the Asian financial crisis, and the total amount of foreign trade increased by only 2 percent compared with 1996, when it was $137 billion. As a result of lower demand for Russian oil and lower prices for raw materials on the international markets, the trade surplus decreased by 6 percent to the level of $30 billion.

The need to shift to a policy of protection of domestic producers compelled Russian leaders and bureaucrats to switch to locally-made motorcars for official use and to strengthen control of imported color television sets. It is likely that an overall change in foreign trade policy in Russia will be implemented to facilitate the shift in investment activities in favor of manufacturing enterprises.

INVESTMENT PROMOTION

Foreign trade is closely linked with foreign investment. In 1971 the total volume of bilateral trade between Japan and the Soviet Union was $870 million. In 1981 this volume increased to $5.28 billion because Japanese private companies and government agencies became closely involved in the timber-cutting industry in eastern Russia and coal deposits development in Yakutia, and significant loans were extended to Moscow to finance these projects. Similar phenomena were observed in Japan's trade with China, one of the primary targets for Japanese investment.[3]

As for investment opportunities, one can think of three potential fields: investment that will target the market of western Russia, raw material industries of eastern Russia, and cooperation in high-tech industries.

Concerning the size of the consumer market in western Russia, Japanese companies can enter Russian industry by investing in enterprises that will produce motorcars, consumer electronics, cameras, and copying machines. Currently Japanese manufacturers sell these products to Russia through agencies in Japan, Russia, and other countries. Sooner or later the Russian government will raise tariffs to protect domestic industries, and that may induce Japanese companies to establish their production subsidiaries within Russia. A majority of the Russian population lives in western Russia (about 115 million in the western part of the country and about 32 million in the part of Russia that lies east of the Ural Mountains). This more populated part of Russia will become a target area for Japanese companies, making their investments closely linked to consumer demand.

Since 1950 Japanese companies have been importing natural resources from eastern Russia, including timber, marine products, coal, oil products, and non-ferrous metals. The effect of investment made by Japan in these areas in the 1970s is being felt even now, but the volume of exports has almost reached its limit. In timber and non-ferrous metals, Japanese trading companies established joint ventures to deepen the level of processing.

In some other cases, Japanese equipment was supplied to Russian enterprises through compensation agreements.[4] However, new investment will be needed to secure the amount of imports or to increase the volume of supplies to Japan. For the present the fields targeted by Japanese companies are the raw materials–processing industries, but in the future these may include mining projects, development of resources on the basis of concessions, and production aimed at highly processed commodities and components.

One of the major trends of the 1990s is the development of the Sakhalin oil and gas fields. Moreover, joint development of Kovyktinskoe gas field in Irkustkaya Oblast by Russia, Japan, China, and Korea will mark a historic shift in energy resources development and trade in East Asia on the basis of multilateral cooperation. Also, significant resources of natural gas and oil have been discovered in northern Khabarovskiy Krai and Magadanskaya Oblast, as well as huge deposits of natural gas in Yakutia. These projects have the potential to be the largest energy projects until the year 2050 and beyond. In this context, improvement of the infrastructure in eastern Russia is gaining critical importance, thus representing one more potential area for investment cooperation.

In January 1998 the federal government and regional administrations discussed progress in the implementation of the Federal Program for Economic and Social Development of the Far Eastern and Trans-Baikal Regions for 1996–2005. As a result 68 projects were selected, and in March 1998 ten projects from this list were presented to Japan for further discussions and evaluation. However, a mechanism is needed to implement these projects, and this will require protection of Japanese investment through a system of guarantees.

Finally, in the high-tech sector Japan-Russia dialogue already includes space research, communication technologies, peaceful use of nuclear power, and semiconductors. Russia welcomes cooperation in this field and proposes to include some defense enterprises in this scheme. There are also some developments in direct linkages among Russian and Japanese research organizations and universities, including a recently established joint program between Akademicheskiy Gorodok of the Russian Academy of Sciences in Novosibirsk, western Siberia, and Tohoku University in Japan. Such exchanges and programs will facilitate and guide investment projects in the area of advanced technologies.

FAR EASTERN RUSSIA AND NORTHEAST ASIA

In 1986 Gorbachev's speech in Vladivostok was welcomed by many people. In this speech Gorbachev emphasized that Far Eastern Russia cannot live without cooperating with neighboring countries. In October 1991 the United Nations Industrial and Development Organization proposed a concept of a greater Vladivostok development zone, but the project failed because it was neither approved nor funded. However, the concept itself did not disappear, being applied to the Zarubino Port development plan and the free economic zone and Nakhodka.

In parallel with these plans and concepts, the development of the Tumen River area was also discussed. This proposal was advocated by the Jilin Province of northeastern China and by the United Nations Development Program. In October 1992 Russia joined this program, and in 1995 coordinating and consultative committees were organized to discuss and direct programs of subregional cooperation in Northeast Asia. Participants of this process paid special attention to transportation and cross-border linkages in this area, including development of the railway and highway routes that link northeastern China with the seaports in North Korea (Hunchun-Rajin and Sonbong ports) and Russia (Suifenhe-Grodekovo-Vostochniy, Nakhodka, Vladivostok, Hunchun-Makhalino-Zarubino, and Posiyet ports).

The improvement and development of infrastructure in this area will facilitate the movement of people and goods. The respective governments should implement measures to allow faster border crossing by simplifying visas and customs regulations and maintaining reasonable levels of taxation and competitive transportation tariffs, thus providing more opportunities for the private sector. Therefore, the Russian government should implement the Zarubino Port modernization project and fully acknowledge its significance for Japan-Russia bilateral cooperation and mutually beneficial economic links in Northeast Asia.

From a long-term perspective this area may constitute a new and growing economic center in Northeast Asia. This demands that Japan and Russia cooperate in a proactive manner to benefit from the potential opportunities of multilateral economic linkages in this promising spot in the Japan Sea Rim.

NOTES

1.   These figures are from the statement made by former Prime Minister Victor Chernomyrdin at the Davos World Economic Forum, January 30, 1998.

2.   Andrei Shapovaliants, deputy minister of economy, was reportedly behind the introduction of this system of mixed guarantees.

3.   In 1992–96 Japanese investment in China amounted to $23.56 billion (in contracts). During the same period the volume of bilateral trade increased from $18.2 billion to $62.4 billion. This illustrates the linkage between investment volume and expansion of bilateral trade exchanges.

4.   In 1994 negotiations on timber resources development (KS project) in eastern Russia (begun during the Soviet era) were discontinued. New talks on the fourth timber resources development scheme resumed in the same year. However, it was difficult for the Russian federal government to maintain this project because it was difficult to extend federal guarantees to ensure that the Japanese companies that will supply the equipment will not be exposed to risks. Private banks also were unwilling to extend their guarantees, which made this project difficult to implement. Therefore, the KS project, launched in 1968, was discontinued in November 1997.

IV

JAPAN, RUSSIA, AND NORTHEAST ASIA

With the Gorbachev era beginning in 1985 and his Vladivostok and Krasnoyarsk speeches delivered in 1986 and 1988, Moscow's ambitions in the Pacific Rim started to diversify. More attention was given to social issues, trade, and economic cooperation with neighbors. The modification and weakening of the post–World War II system of alliances allowed Russia and Japan first to find a common ground in major international and regional issues, then to turn to bilateral political dialogue, and finally to open a discussion on long-term economic engagement.

What form should Japan-Russia relations take in the next 10–20 years? At present there is no clear vision on these prospects. A new framework may include natural resource exploitation, particularly in the energy sector; processing and manufacturing; and linkages in advanced technologies. At this stage energy projects, particularly in eastern Russia, hold great potential. The implementation of oil and gas development projects in Siberia, Yakutia, and Sakhalin would respond to the long-term economic needs of Russia and the energy security needs of Japan. If the energy cooperation linchpin is set it will make Russia and Japan interdependent for decades to come.

There is little disagreement that the future of the entire Asia-Pacific region depends on stability and peace in Northeast Asia. Investment, development, and trade among the economies of this corner of Asia are justly considered to be the cornerstones of new subregional relations. Northeast Asia, however, is approaching the year 2000 lagging behind other subregions of Pacific Asia in promoting such exchanges. As a result, improvement in standards of living, business links, and cooperative attitudes among neighbors are slow and uncertain. This can be changed, but a proper way should be found to promote such changes.

Vladimir I. Ivanov indicates that there is no consensus on how the Northeast Asian economic subregion will evolve. Many people believe that some kind of multilateral framework is needed in this region, in addition to bilateral links between the states, localities, industries, and businesses. Some experts propose that in the long term the goal must be the creation of the Northeast Asian Economic Cooperation Organization similar to the Association of Southeast Asian Nations or, at least, like the less formal nongovernmental Pacific Economic Cooperation Conference. It seems appropriate for those who promote the idea of regional economic cooperation to broaden both geographic and economic definitions of Northeast Asia, thus making politicians and private businesses more interested in the idea. This may also help to map out more areas of converging interests among the neighboring nations.

Ivanov proposes that the multilateral process in this subregion should be issue specific, accommodating different demands and interests and allowing different groups of actors to participate in the processes, depending on the issue and capacity. A dialogue driven by such a concept can help to shape and manage interdependent relations that are emerging in some sectors, such as energy, resources, transportation, and environment. He also looks at the countries of the subregion from the perspective of their differences, modes of transition, patterns of economic strategies, and regional postures suggesting that regional cooperation plans and concepts must take into account political realities. All the players have their specific interests, both converging and conflicting. However, the Northeast Asian countries emphasize economic openness and cooperation. Outward-looking reforms and development programs support national projects of regional importance. Substantial natural resources, a pool of labor, a manufacturing base, and transportation and telecommunication facilities even as they are today can support more intensive economic exchanges growing out of the geographic proximity, economic complementarity, and demand for transit services.

Tadashi Sugimoto and Kazuto Furuta review progress in Sakhalin oil and gas development projects, emphasizing that energy resources are conveniently located in relation to potential markets in China, the Koreas, and Japan. Moreover, in the long term these countries and the entire Northeast Asian subregion may not have alternatives for sources of energy supply. Japan, China, and South Korea have shown an interest in the energy resources of Eastern Siberia and Yakutia. Japanese companies already participate in Sakhalin projects. These will not dramatically change the overall picture of oil and gas production in Russia. When these two projects reach their peak output their combined share will not exceed

8 percent of total Russian oil production in 1994. However, the projects will play a very important role in the recovery of Far Eastern Russia and in strengthening Russia's links with its Northeast Asian neighbors. Sakhalin oil and gas development projects will greatly contribute to the economy of Sakhalinskaya Oblast and the management of the energy situation in Far Eastern Russia. They will create new jobs, improve the business climate, and add to export earnings and foreign trade growth.

Authors emphasize that Japan can benefit from Sakhalin oil and gas resources development in many ways. Foremost is the opportunity to diversify energy supplies and to reduce Japan's current 80 percent dependence on the Middle East. Secondly, a closer look at eastern Russia as a viable alternative has significant economic benefits, such as reduced cost in transportation of energy resources. Thirdly, cooperation with Russia can contribute to the energy security of all of Northeast Asia. If the proposal to build the international gas pipeline between Sakhalin Island and Japan is pursued, the idea to form a gas pipeline network in Japan can be implemented. Moreover, the availability of energy is a key factor in determining the investment climate. If large, reliable energy sources are secured prospects for economic development in Northeast Asia will improve.

Ivanov and Dmitriy L. Sergachev propose another potential area for Russia-Japan cooperation. The Trans-Siberian Railway's modernization and more active international use will facilitate the flow of goods between Europe and Asia-Pacific Economic Cooperation. The world's longest transcontinental railway provides efficient connections between Russian Pacific ports and Siberian provinces of the Russian Federation, Mongolia, all Central Asian states of the Confederation of Independent States , western Russia, Ukraine, Belarus, the Baltic states, all countries of Scandinavia (via Finland), and European states at competitive transit time and rates. However, many Japanese, Korean, or Taiwanese goods consigned for western Russia and even western Siberia are shipped around the world and enter the country either by rail or highway transport through Germany, Poland, Finland, or other Baltic states. Cooperation with Japan in modernizing the Trans-Siberian Land Bridge will help Russia to improve the organization and expand infrastructure to handle in the future up to 1 million containers a year or 25–30 percent of the containerized cargo traffic between East Asia and Europe.

Kazuyoshi Nishikata continues to review the issue of international cooperation in transportation and touches upon trilateral Japan-China-Russia cooperation in border crossing. How cross-border economic contacts proceed depends both on the physical infrastructure and its level of development and the so-called software infrastructure, such as border clearance procedure harmonization. In Northeast Asia discussions have been centered on the physical infrastructure construction or improvement. However, as the flows of commodities and tourists across borders are increasing, issues of software infrastructure become more important.

Jilin and Heilongjiang provinces in northeast China have no seaports in their territories and, therefore, commodity shipment to and from these two provinces has depended largely upon Dalian Port in Liaoning Province. However, as the volume of cargoes went beyond the capacity of Dalian Port and the railroad to the port, the provinces paid more attention to the relative advantage of Russian or North Korean ports in terms of distance.

The change in climate of the China-Russia relationship, Nishikata points out, will surely promote the bilateral talks for transportation cooperation on a practical and scientific basis. Moreover, this will also make the Japanese attitude more positive toward the competitiveness of routes through Russian railroads and ports. The triangle relations among China, Japan, and Russia will lead to the establishment of new transportation, trade, and investment networks in Northeast Asia.

Hisako Tsuji looks at one of the concrete trilateral projects that combines new transportation links between China and Russia, modernization of the Russian port in Zarubino, and access to this facility by Chinese cargo owners. The main reason that this small port is drawing the attention of not only Russia but also China and Japan is China's quest for an outlet to the Sea of Japan and the perceived economic benefits that this outlet can bring to the ports of the prefectures along Japan's western coast, especially Niigata.

The development of Zarubino Port, if realized, will contribute to Northeast Asian subregional economic cooperation not only on a bilateral basis but also on a trilateral or multilateral basis to facilitate economic gains and enhance economic interdependence. Moreover, it may help China in solving its problems. In recent years, freight transportation capacity by railway from the two provinces to Dalian Port (the closest Chinese port in neighboring Liaoning) has almost reached its limit. Therefore, the importance of finding substitute routes for trade has increased. Heilongjiang is developing a route from Suifenhe, a border town in the east of the province, to Russian ports in Primorskiy Krai, such as Vladivostok. Jilin is developing a route from Tumen or Hunchun to the Sea of Japan through other ports in Russia, which will benefit from income from port charges, taxes, and railway transportation fees. In addition, there will be multiplier effects of employment opportunities and income, investment inducement effects, and other macroeconomic spillover effects.

Alexander M. Kurmazov and Igor V. Kazakov examine the significance of fishery and Russia-Japan relations in this area in a regional context. The Northwest Pacific accounts for about 45 percent of the total world catch. Protection measures aimed at the reduction and regulation of fishery must not be solely unilateral or bilateral. Most of the species to be protected belong to straddling stocks, and their fishing areas are exposed to many countries. Fishery activities are particularly intense in the Japan Sea and East China Sea.

They emphasize that difficult bilateral relations between Moscow and Tokyo did not really prevent the two sides from cooperating in this realm. In 1963 Moscow agreed to allow seaweed (*Laminaria*) harvesting near Signalniy Island. However, the agreement on *Laminaria* became void in 1977 after the 200-mile exclusive economic zone was introduced. Intergovernmental agreements were worked out between Japan and Russia on fishery in the 200-mile zones (1984) and on cooperation in salmon fishery (1985). A subsequent reduction in mutual fishing quotas and the discontinuation of drift net fishing by Japan shifted to the Russian 200-mile exclusive economic zone.

Both Russia and Japan participate in international activities on resource management in the Sea of Okhotsk and the Bering Sea. Bilateral cooperation in the sphere of rational use and preservation of stocks of salmon in the northern part of the Pacific Ocean is supplemented by participation in a quadrilateral convention on the conservation of anadromous stocks in the North Pacific. The resources of the Kuril Islands area could serve as a testing ground, a major incentive, and a model for new types of bilateral cooperation in fishery and sustainable development. In this context, productive negotiations on fishery in the waters around the southern Kurils can positively influence both bilateral relations and regional cooperation between Japan and Russia in Northeast Asia. Currently, there is no international body to regulate and manage fishery activities in the Japan Sea. The marine resources of this area remain threatened by overfishing, poaching, environmental pollution, and interstate conflict over fishery rights. Joint management and development of marine resources at the regional level are needed. Necessary conditions for regional sustainable fishery must be created and maintained.

Karla S. Smith analyzes Russia-Japan bilateral cooperation in protection of the environment. Interest in bilateral environmental cooperation remained strong after the collapse of the Soviet Union and into 1992 when Russia published its first environmental white paper and Japan hosted the first formal Northeast Asia conference on environment. However, from 1993 the situation changed rapidly. Immersed in an economic crisis, both official and public interest in Russia in environmental issues waned. The initiatives of the Russian Ministry of Environment from the beginning encountered opposition from energy, industry, and military interests. With decreasing financial resources, its ability to implement new projects and enforce regulations dwindled. On the Russian side, interest in environmental cooperation with Japan might have disappeared altogether had it not become clear that one of Russia's most serious and urgent environmental problems, the disposal of radioactive wastes, has serious implications for Japan as well.

Smith indicates that the priorities of Japan and Russia overlap in nuclear waste management and marine protection. These will likely remain the two most prominent areas for environmental cooperation. Currently bilateral environmental cooperation is most extensive (and expensive) in the area of radioactive waste management, specifically the storage and processing of low-level liquid waste from decommissioned nuclear submarines. However, environmental cooperation in other projects, which can bear quicker and more tangible results, can improve public perceptions and may help pave the way for progress in more difficult areas.

A broader framework for bilateral relations, including the environment, is already emerging. However, overwhelmed by the magnitude of problems they face, Russian officials find it difficult to set priorities and, thus, are unable to make strong proposals for cooperation. Japanese officials previously were also constrained in their approach by the Northern Territories issue. Now the largest obstacles are Japan's own economic reform and limited budget for environmental projects.

24

Russia and Regional Cooperation

Vladimir I. Ivanov

There is little disagreement that the future of the entire Asia-Pacific region depends on stability and peace in Northeast Asia. Investment, development, and trade among the economies of this corner of Asia are justly considered to be the cornerstones of new subregional relations. Northeast Asia, however, is approaching the year 2000 lagging behind other subregions of Pacific Asia in promoting such exchanges. As a result, improvement in standards of living, business links, and cooperative attitudes among neighbors is slow and uncertain. This can be changed, but a proper way should be found to promote such changes.

Although there is no consensus on how the Northeast Asian economic subregion will evolve, many people believe that some kind of multilateral framework is needed in this region, in addition to bilateral links between the states, localities, industries, and businesses. There are attempts to apply models of economic cooperation from other regions and areas and involve international organizations, such as the United Nations Development Program, that support the Tumen River Area Development Program. This project provides a stage for the government officials' regular meetings, but the national governments of the member countries, except the Republic of Korea, do not support this framework financially, and it includes Japan only as an observer.[1]

Some experts propose that in the long term the goal must be the creation of a Northeast Asian Economic Cooperation Organization similar to the Association of Southeast Asian Nations or, at least, the less formal, nongovernmental Pacific Economic Cooperation Conference (PECC), but we do not know when it can be created and what the future building blocks will look like. However, it is realistic to identify potential areas and issues for cooperation as well as problems for joint research and discussions. Obviously, both the scale and the range of these issues and problems will depend on the definition of Northeast Asia. In this context, it seems appropriate for those who promote the idea of regional economic cooperation to broaden both geographic and economic definitions, thus making politicians and private businesses more interested in the idea. This may also help to map out more areas of converging interests among the neighboring nations.

REDEFINING NORTHEAST ASIA

There are problems in defining Northeast Asia. The first one is this subregion's geographical definition.[2] Northeast Asia consists of five countries and six states, represented either in their entirety or by their provinces, territories, and economic regions, including Japan, the Koreas, China, Mongolia, and eastern regions of Russia.[3]

Geographically, a redefined Northeast Asia can mean that its Russian part will not be limited to the Far Eastern economic region (that is, the territory of the Russian Federation to the east of Lake Baikal) only, and will also include Russian Siberian provinces. Similarly, China's involvement in Northeast Asia can be seen in a broader context and may also include both Hong Kong and Taiwan as potentially important sources of investment to Northeast Asian subregional projects in the future.[4]

From the perspective of political geography, it may be practical to see the United States connected to Northeast Asia (through the North Pacific) by the state of Alaska. It is important that the United States already contributes to the stability of Northeast Asia, facilitating subregional ties through its official and private sector connections with the Far Eastern economic region of Russia, economic and technical assistance to Mongolia, and positive influence over North Korea. U.S. companies lead in export trade with the Russian Far East, United States–based multinationals invest in Sakhalin oil and gas development projects, and others investigate opportunities in natural resources development, the manufacturing industry, construction, and services.

The economic boundaries and potential of the subregion must be clarified, too. There are many overlapping economic, geographic, and political images of Northeast Asia. Wider and more flexible economic boundaries will allow Northeast Asia to be seen as linked to trans-Eurasian and trans-Pacific ties with trade flows originated in other regions and transit services provided to out-of-area customers. The shipment of salmon from Norway to Japan by Russian Aeroflot cargo planes is an interesting example of such complex economic links. Similarly, the importance of

Northeast Asia's telecommunications infrastructure cannot be fully appreciated in the subregional context only.

A CONCEPT

Many authors and research groups concentrate their attention on intraregional trade flows and complementarity in trade between the neighboring territories. Some experts are looking at the growth poles phenomena, while others argue that network integration will prevail over spatial integration, that is, regional contacts within and between certain industries will lead over the compact geographical area development.[5]

Moreover, a technological pattern of subregional economic cooperation frequently proposed for Northeast Asia is rather simple and normally represents a triangle with Japan and South Korea serving as sources of capital investment and technologies, China and North Korea offering inexpensive labor, and Russia and Mongolia providing raw materials. It seems that the economic reality is more complex than that.[6]

Northeast Asia's specifics and diversity will influence the shape of the cooperation framework. The multilateral process in this subregion should be issue-specific, accommodating different demands and interests, and allowing different groups of actors to participate in the processes, depending on the issue and capacity. A dialogue driven by such a concept can help to shape and manage interdependent relations that are emerging in some sectors, such as energy, resources, transportation, and environment.

Subregional cooperation should correspond to the global trend toward growing economic interdependence. It seems logical that the principles on which a subregional economic process is based are compatible with those of Asia-Pacific regional cooperation. Some elements of technical and organizational expertise accumulated by existing regional institutions and forums, such as Asia-Pacific Economic Cooperation (APEC), PECC, and Pacific Basin Economic Council, can be borrowed to stimulate subregional dialogue. In this context, prospects for closer economic ties in Northeast Asia improved with Russia's involvement in APEC. This forum's Manila Action Plan for 1996 aimed at measures for liberalizing and facilitating trade and investment may be applicable to the Northeast Asian subregion.

The Manila Action Plan for 1996 integrates the members' individual action plans and their collective action plans. It contains progress reports on joint activities by the members through various APEC forums for addressing different issues of mutual interest. In 1995–96 at their meetings in Osaka and Manila the APEC members agreed to look at several wide-ranging issues as a part of their long-term agenda, including population, economic growth, food, energy, environment, technical cooperation in human resources development, economic infrastructure, and infrastructure projects financed by the private sector. Some of these subjects are highly applicable to Northeast Asia.

APEC's Partners for Progress Program, for example, supports joint activities, such as information sharing, surveys, training, seminars, research, and technical demonstrations, and there is no reason for this mechanism not to involve some projects relevant to Northeast Asia and its specific issues.[7] During preparations for the APEC meeting in Manila the APEC Business Advisory Council came into being and its first report, presented to the leaders of 18 member economies, made ten flagship recommendations for five key areas, including finance and investment, infrastructure, cross-border flows, small and medium enterprises, and regional economic and technical cooperation.

REDUCING UNCERTAINTIES

All countries of the subregion are undergoing a transition in one form or another, demonstrating that no fixed development model or political control over the economy can support economic survival, growth, or international competitiveness indefinitely. Northeast Asian economies differ markedly in their resource endowments, productivity, economic strategies, political orientation, and attitudes toward regional cooperation. There are enormous gaps in their per capita gross national product, economic competitiveness, and openness. Moreover, the subregion has been politically divided for so long that it is not easy to imagine how a subregional community may be formed.

All the players have their specific interests, both converging and conflicting. Because of external pressures, isolation, and its domestic ills, the development strategy of North Korea has been reduced to the needs of preservation of the military-bureaucratic regime and physical survival of the population. North Korea is locked in social stagnation and in a dangerous and economically devastating standoff with South Korean and U.S. forces.

This confrontational survival is paving the way to a national disaster. Some positive developments in North Korea's attitudes toward its adversaries, as manifested by the Korean Energy Development Organization and diplomatic dialogue with the United States, can only delay but not avert the demise of the system. It is critically important for North Korea to maintain economic links with China and to revive some areas of investment and trade cooperation with Russia.

Dual competition and strategic uncertainty may characterize the policy of South Korea. On the economic front, South Korean industrial-financial groups compete worldwide, but the limited potential in technological innovation is one of the reasons for South Korea's chronic balance-of-payments deficit. On the military front, South Koreans are confronted by the

North, and they are still uncertain about their superiority. Some of them perhaps tend to understand that their long-term economic competitiveness strongly depends on reunification with North Korea or at least very close economic ties that will ensure access to labor resources and infrastructure and will allow billions of dollars to be diverted from the defense budgets of both sides for investment and social programs. In this context, such strategic uncertainty is a common feature for both Koreas; their economic futures, international status, and regional roles are hostages of their separation.

Remaining economic barriers and domestic crises reduce trade and investment opportunities for such newcomers to the subregion as postcommunist Mongolia. Its development strategy can be characterized as cooperative survival mixed with a search for a new identity, friends, security protectors, and new sources of economic assistance. Despite some progress, Mongolia finds it difficult to compensate for the major slowdown in economic links with Russia and other traditional partners.

Russia's current position in Northeast Asia is complicated by its decade-long economic decline and the economic transition. The faltering economic influence of the federal government, chaotic liberalization, and physical distance from other Russian economic regions put considerable pressure on the Far Eastern economic region and its people. High transportation costs isolated this part of Russia from the rest of the country. Therefore, it is more dependent on links with Asia and North America. As the Russian Far East finds itself in quasi-isolation from domestic and other western markets and sources of supply, both Moscow and the Far Eastern provinces look at closer links with Northeast Asia as the potential way out of current internal problems.

In China, too, long distances from domestic markets and overcrowded railroads negatively affect large and potentially important northeastern provinces. Lack of economic dynamism in those areas forces their authorities to look for external opportunities to catch up with economically advanced southeastern coastal provinces. Jilin and Heilongjiang provinces are eager to develop closer ties with Far Eastern Russia and explore options for direct links with Asia-Pacific markets using Russian and North Korean ports. Moreover, Chinese and Russian central governments share ambitious plans for economic and technological engagement, which will affect the bordering regions of the two countries and Northeast Asia in general.

The central government in Beijing verbally supports the aspirations of the northeastern provinces and endorses some initiatives by the United Nations focused on the Tumen River (northeastern China) area development. Whether Beijing sees Northeast Asia as a place for multilateral economic cooperation or only as its own political periphery is not clear. China's economic growth and constructive foreign policy can boost regional economic contacts, making the Northeast Asian subregion both economically more dynamic and important for China's own transformation.

Japan is becoming more enthusiastic about the Northeast Asian subregion as its foreign policy shifts further from the priorities of Cold War confrontation to the long-term economic needs and interests that involve both China and Russia. Japan's prosperity, technological edge, and key role in the Asia-Pacific region, however, can be maintained in relative isolation from Northeast Asia; thus, it is not a priority area in Japan's global economic engagement. Local political and business interests are becoming more pronounced, and local administrations are attempting to promote new relationships at the provincial level. However, Tokyo has only recently incorporated the Northeast Asian subregion into its foreign policy agenda because of its political repositioning vis-à-vis Russia and a modified trade and investment outlook of some Japanese businesses for larger the Asia-Pacific region.

The good news is that national development plans of the Northeast Asian countries emphasize economic openness and cooperation. Outward-looking reforms and development programs support national projects of regional importance. Substantial natural resources, a pool of labor, a manufacturing base, and transportation and telecommunication facilities even as they are today can support more intensive economic exchanges growing out of the geographic proximity, economic complementarity, and demand for transit services.

AREAS OF COOPERATION

Keeping in mind these and other impediments, one should not miss the point that for Russia, China, and Japan the emerging regional situation is already beneficial, allowing for discussions, some in a multilateral format, on critical issues, such as long-term approaches to energy resources development and utilization.

Indeed, large-scale investment cooperation in the development of Sakhalin oil and gas resources as well as those of eastern Siberia will promote other projects. Energy use is closely linked to the environment, which represents another concern of the regional states. However, cooperation at an intergovernmental level in environmental protection is still in its infancy.

Northeast Asia is a crossroad currently open to numerous transit flows and elements of transboundary economic activities. Cross-border investment could have a catalytic effect on the bilateral trade of neighboring countries and intraregional trade expansion. As a result, the relative weight of genuinely subregional and transit elements can change over time, but purely subregional exchanges can only benefit if the Northeast Asian economies enhance their bridging role between regions. The

European Union's economic area and the East Asian economies, for example, can be linked through the Trans-Siberian Land Bridge.[8]

Governments of the regional states can improve the investment climate by initiating subregional coordination in national development plans and programs, thus ensuring more business opportunities. Both central and provincial governments must assume greater responsibility for supporting the private sector through national and subregional information networks, micro-level management techniques dissemination, market access information sharing, and small and medium enterprises promotion efforts.

The geographic proximity of the countries of Northeast Asia cannot be fully utilized without reduction of time for travel and visa approval. Customs clearance procedures harmonization is equally important for reducing the transportation time for goods. Efficient production and distribution on the subregional level will strongly depend on customs and immigration services' cooperation. Regional economic cooperation needs fine tuning in immigration and visa procedures to facilitate subregional contacts.

A collective effort is needed to draw up a comprehensive list of issues critical to local and national economies. It is likely that integrating factors for the Northeast Asian subregion will be energy resources development and utilization, use and protection of marine resources, protection of the environment, and infrastructure improvement. The list may also include measures for developing efficient financial markets and subregional institutions for development financing.

Development requires investment, but at present continental Northeast Asia is a capital deficient region. An idea was aired some time ago to bypass existing limitations through a special subregional financial institution — a Northeast Asian Development Bank[9] — to help the private sector manage the investment risks and to finance subregional infrastructure projects.[10] The plan to create a new institution similar to the European Bank for Reconstruction and Development was complicated by the financial problems that emerged in East Asian countries in late 1997.

The financial difficulties associated with creating a new bank would be lessened if the idea were linked to multilateral cooperation schemes in energy resources development in Eastern Russia. Hydropower projects and electricity exports from Russia to China are likely to become important elements in trilateral cooperation among Japan, China, and Russia.[11] There must be more innovation in proposing significant subregional projects of a multilateral nature. What the countries of the region are doing already at the national level can constitute a basis for regional cooperation as well.

NIIGATA CONFERENCE

The Northeast Asia Economic Conference has convened annually in Niigata since 1990. It is a unique process of subregional scale and can serve the role of a prototype of subregional cooperative framework. It provides an opportunity for academics, practitioners, representatives of local and central governments, and international organizations to discuss prospects for cooperation in Northeast Asia and concrete areas for economic engagement. Over the years the Niigata conference has contributed to an improvement in the climate of regional relations, particularly on the provincial level. The conference as an event open to the public and the mass media has served an important social function as well.

It is still difficult to measure the results of these activities, but there is visible progress in the areas that were presented during the meetings in Niigata, including trilateral Japan-Russia-China cooperation on Zarubino Port development, other border-crossing projects and processes, the Trans-Siberian Railway, and the Russian Far East development plans.

In 1997–98 there were several ministerial-level discussions, both bilateral and multilateral, that tackled vital economic problems, such as energy resources development, transportation and cross-border links, environmental protection, and fishery. This means that the topics of previous conference agendas have become a part of the intergovernmental agenda. More concrete developments can be expected with progress in Russia-Japan and Russia-China relations, particularly in their economic dialogues.

However, positive developments at the governmental level and growing practical interest in Northeast Asian regional cooperation have placed new demands on the Niigata process and its role in formulating a practical, relevant, future-oriented, and realistic agenda for regional relations. A proper response to these demands will require more effort, imagination, and expertise. The conference should be complemented by the framework that can be called between-the-conferences task forces, using PECC task forces as a model.

This can help to make the Niigata conference an international working process, in addition to an annual event. Within such task forces framework participants will have more time for professional dialogue, research, and preparation of the reports on specific subjects for the conference. Thus, the goal of exchanging ideas and information and maintaining closer intellectual ties in Northeast Asia will be served more efficiently, helping to identify and select important problems vital for the region and its countries.

Task forces activities can be distributed among research type organizations in the countries of Northeast Asia, so one country, represented by its research institution or similar body, will provide technical support, coordination, and preparation of the working group's report by its own experts and selected international participants. This will help to stay one step ahead of bureaucracies in analyzing key issues for the region and to maintain the high standard of the conference.

CONCLUSION

Significant improvements in Northeast Asian political relationships and ongoing geoeconomic shifts in the region call attention to a number of issues.

First, a step forward must be made in evaluating prospects for multilateral cooperation among major powers in Northeast Asia. In this context, the opportunities for Japan-Russia-China economic interaction need priority attention. Concurrently, changing political and other relationships in the U.S.–Japan–China–Russia quadrangle that ensures stability needed for economic growth and cross-border trade and investment flows must not be forgotten. The future of North Korea and its recovery from the current crisis and isolation can be assured if the four major powers and the Republic of Korea cooperate.

Second, Japan-Russia and Russia-China bilateral economic initiatives must be seen in a broader regional and global economic context. Energy resources development in eastern Russia, for example, is important for all of Russia's neighbors, including Japan and China as the two major consumers of energy resources in the region. Interdependence in energy resources development and consumption in Northeast Asia demand from the countries involved in these projects no less than a truly strategic partnership and a long-term vision that will justify huge investment in the energy sector and its trans-border transportation infrastructure.

Third, with Russia as an APEC member, the Northeast Asian subregion or North Pacific area can gain the recognition of this organization. Therefore, new channels may become available for the governments of Japan, China, Russia, the Republic of Korea, and the United States to discuss prospects and mechanisms for multilateral economic cooperation in the region where the nations are represented by not only central but also local governments.[12]

Finally, an isolated and closed North Korea effectively prevents Northeast Asia from attaining the much needed political predictability required for long-term and large-scale multilateral economic engagement. The inter-Korean crisis must be handled in a subregional context, involving economic initiatives in addition to political and security measures, thus enhancing multilateral cooperation. The international effort to manage the North Korean crisis, including containment of its alleged nuclear weapons program, demonstrates that global concerns and regional issues converge.

Options for coordinated efforts can be actively explored in such areas as upgrading infrastructure, seaport modernization, civil aviation development, railroad and road improvements, use of shipping and navigation facilities, tourism and recreation infrastructure development, and other fields. Informational and educational efforts and diplomacy by localities can make subregional cooperation beneficial not only in commercial or development terms but also in terms of responding to human and social needs. A special effort is required in human networks creation and promotion. These networks that incorporate governments, business people, nongovernmental organizations, and research communities are indispensable for regional cooperation and development.

Currently in Northeast Asia political contacts among regional countries on the problems of subregional cooperation are confined to local governments and business organizations. In a sense, subregional cooperation in Northeast Asia is driven by local efforts, but the role of the central governments is slowly increasing. It is likely that subregional cooperation will develop in natural forms rather than through formal mechanisms.[13] In this context, nonbinding principles, concerted unilateral measures, and careful management of political issues will be required, adding significant specifics to the entire process.

However, subregional initiatives alone will not suffice, and the Northeast Asian subregion cannot be sheltered from the impacts of national and global trends or developments in other regions. The Asian financial turmoil of late 1997 demonstrated how short-term market speculations can instantly deny a country economic stability and even ignite talks about new colonialism, thus weakening the trust and confidence needed for regional cooperation.[14]

NOTES

1. The Tumen River Area Development Program is coordinated and supported by the United Nations Development Program at the request of the five countries that are signatories to the October 1992 Program Agreement: China, Russia, Mongolia, and the two Koreas. The United Nations Development Program is the principal sponsor of the Tumen River Area Development Program; funding is also provided by the Canadian International Development Agency and the governments of Finland and South Korea.

2. Some authors, for example, delineate East Asia and Southeast Asia only, without identifying Northeast Asia specifically. East Asia includes, according to this definition, China (China proper consisting of three great river basins: the Huanghghe in the north, the Yangzi in central China, and the Xijiang in the south), the three Inner Asian components of China (Manchuria, inner Mongolia, and Tibet), outer Mongolia, Korea, Japan, and East Siberia. See Mark Borthwick, *Pacific Century: The Emergence of Modern Pacific Asia.* (Boulder, Colo.: Westview, 1992), pp. 4–7.

3. Economic Research Institute for Northeast Asia distinguishes between a broad definition of the area that includes six countries in their entirety and a more specific area that refers to four countries (Japan, the Koreas, and Mongolia), only territories of China (the three northeastern provinces), and the Far Eastern area of the Russian Federation. See United Nations Economic and Social Commission for Asia and the Pacific, *Trade and Investment Complementarities on North-East Asia*, papers and proceedings of the Roundtable on Economic Cooperation Possibilities through Exploration of Trade and Investment Complementarities in the North-East Asian Subregion, July 10–12, 1995, Seoul (Studies in Trade and Investment, No. 18). (New York: United Nations, 1996), p. 17.

4. "Economic Survey on Northeast Asia," *Far Eastern Economic Review*, 161(9) (February 26, 1998). This published special refers to both Hong Kong and Taiwan. See also Duck-Woo Nam, *Korea's Economic Growth in a Changing World*. (Seoul: Samsung Economic Research Institute, 1997), p. 283.

5. See Jang-Won Suh (ed.), *Northeast Asian Economic Cooperation: Perspectives and Challenges*. (Seoul: Korea Institute for International Economic Policy, 1991); Won Bae Kim and Burnham O. Campbell (eds.), *Proceedings of the Conference on Economic Development in the Coastal Area of Northeast Asia*. (Honolulu, Hi.: East-West Center, 1992); Won Bae Kim, Burnham O. Campbell, Mark Valencia, and Lee-Jay Cho (eds.), *Regional Economic Cooperation in Northeast Asia*. (Honolulu, Hi.: Hawaii Asia-Pacific Institute, 1993); Hiroshi Takahashi and Sumio Kuribayashi (eds.), *Regional Cooperation in Northeast Asia: Assessments and Prospects*. (Tokyo: The Sasakawa Peace Foundation, 1994); Hiroshi Takahashi, Sumio Kuribayashi, and Kap-Young Jeong (eds.), *Trade and Industrial Development in Northeast Asia*. (Tokyo: The Sasakawa Peace Foundation, 1995); Ku-Hyun Jung, *Foreign Direct Investment and Cross Cultural Management in Northeast Asia*. (Tokyo: The Sasakawa Peace Foundation, 1995); Alexander Sheingauz and Hiroya Ono (eds.), *Natural Resources and Environment in Northeast Asia: Status and Challenges*. (Tokyo: The Sasakawa Peace Foundation, 1995); *Prospects of Economic Development through Cooperation in North-East Asia*, compendium of papers presented at the Expert Group Meeting on Development of Transition Economies through Intraregional Trade Expansion and Economic Cooperation with Neighboring Countries, June 30–July 1, 1993, Chungchun, China. (New York: United Nations, 1995); *Trade and Investment Complementarities in North-East Asia*. (New York: United Nations, 1996).

6. A good example is provided by Russia. In the Far Eastern region, the leading exporter is the Komsomolsk-na-Amur Aviation Production Association ($445.5 million or about 20 percent of the region's total exports in 1996).

7. At the Osaka Leaders' Meeting Japan proposed to contribute up to ¥10 billion over several years for projects that support trade and investment liberalization and facilitation. APEC has established a trade and investment liberalization and facilitation special account in the APEC central fund. Projects eligible for support through that account include training programs in trade and investment insurance, programs for simplifying and harmonizing customs procedures, and other topics.

8. In November 1997 at Krasnoyarsk, Japanese and Russian leaders agreed that Japan and Russia would cooperate in modernizing the Trans-Siberian Railroad.

9.   The two proposals were made by Burnham O. Campbell. See Burnham O. Campbell, "Financial Cooperation in Northeast Asia: An Overview of the Case for a Northeast Asian Development Bank," in *Regional Economic Cooperation in Northeast Asia*, Proceedings of the Youngpyeong Conference. (Honolulu, Hi.: Hawaii Asia-Pacific Institute, 1993), pp. 40–53; Hiroshi Kakazu, "The Possible Organizational Structure and Funding Sources of a Northeast Asian Development Bank," in *Regional Economic Cooperation in Northeast Asia*, Proceedings of the Youngpyeong Conference. (Honolulu, Hi.: Hawaii Asia-Pacific Institute, 1993), pp. 52–68.

10.   Stanley Katz, "Establishing the Northeast Asia Development Bank," issue paper for discussion by the Consultative Working Group on the Northeast Asian Development Bank in Tottori, Japan, March 23–24, 1998.

11.   Hydropower resources, for example, in addition to natural gas development projects, can play a particularly important role in the areas along the Russia-China border. For example, Boguchanskaya hydroelectric power station project on the lower Angara River in Krasnoyarskiy Krai is about 60 percent ready (estimated cost $2.9 billion), and it is possible that China will provide the financial resources to complete the project and to build the power grid that will link the site of production with Chinese territory. Russia will pay back with the electricity supply at the proposed rate of $0.07 per kilowatt-hour. The Chinese propose $0.04-0.05 per kilowatt-hour, which, some experts believe, can be accepted by Russia because the cost of the electricity in the region is among the lowest in Russia.

Moreover, in late December 1997 Russia reached an agreement with China to supply $3 billion worth of equipment and expertise for the nuclear light water power plant in Jiangsu Province. The nuclear power plant can be completed by 2005, but before then new agreements that can double the scale of the current contract are likely.

12.   PECC's 1995 Beijing Statement proposed three principles of openness (open regionalism, free trade and investment, transparent and nondiscrimatory decisions), equality (mutual benefit and respect for diversity), and evolution (gradual, pragmatic, sustained, and consensus-based cooperation). See Andrew Elek, *From Osaka to Subic: APEC's Challenges for 1996*, Pacific Economic Papers, No. 255. (Canberra: Australian National University, 1996), pp. 12–13.

13.   Paul S. P. Shu, "Regional Integration: The Asia-Pacific Experience," in *Regionalism and Its Place in the Multilateral Trading System*. (Paris: Organization for Economic Cooperation and Development, 1996), p. 54.

14.   Shoichi Kobayashi, "Hashimoto's Bag of Troubles," *Japan Times*, March 16, 1998, p. 20; Isao Kubota, "Four Points to Consider to Fix East Asia Economic Problems," *Japan Times*, March 16, 1998, p. 17.

25

Sakhalin Oil and
Gas and Japan

Tadashi Sugimoto and Kazuto Furuta

Russia has an advantageous position in Northeast Asia. Its eastern areas, including Eastern Siberia, Yakutia, and Pacific provinces hold huge energy resources and are conveniently located with regard to potential markets in China, the Koreas, and Japan. Moreover, in the long term these countries and the entire Northeast Asian subregion may not have other alternatives   for   sources   of   energy   supply.

Japan, China, and South Korea have shown an interest in the energy resources of Eastern Siberia and Yakutia. Japanese companies already participate in Sakhalin projects. These projects on the continental shelf of the island, both operational and in the planning stage, are expected to provide for export about 27 million tons of oil equivalent (TOE)[1] in 2010. However, Sakhalin alone cannot be expected to cover Northeast Asia's growing demand for energy resources. China, for example, imports nearly all of its oil and its energy shortage may reach 350 million TOE in 2005 and 700 million TOE by 2010. In 2010 China's estimated imports of oil might exceed 130 million tons. The demand for primary energy in China's three northeastern provinces may account for about 50 percent of this estimate, depending on the rate of economic growth and the per capita energy consumption. For Japan, the demand for primary energy by 2005 will grow by 50–70 million TOE compared with 1992. By 2005 the South Korean economy may double its consumption of primary energy compared with 1995 when it was estimated at 149 million TOE.

On the supply side, in 2005 the Far Eastern provinces of Russia are expected to produce about 68 million TOE with domestic consumption not exceeding 45 million TOE. Most of the exportable balance is associated with Sakhalin oil and gas resources development. In addition, natural gas reserves of the Irkutsk region alone are estimated at 7 trillion cubic meters, including Koviktinskoe gas field with proved reserves of 870 billion cubic meters of natural gas. Additional exploration, according to Russian experts, is likely to double this estimate. The entire area of Eastern Siberia and the Far East has 52 trillion cubic meters of natural gas, including 4.2 trillion cubic meters of proved reserves. Eastern Siberia also has more than 2.9 billion tons of oil.

BACKGROUND

The Sakhalin-1 project was launched after Moscow proposed to Tokyo in February 1972 that they jointly explore the offshore oil and gas deposits of Sakhalin Island (Figure 25.1). In 1975 the Japanese joint stock company SODECO and the Ministry of Foreign Trade of the Soviet Union signed an agreement on cooperation. In 1978 the resources of the two fields, Chaivo and Odoptu, were confirmed and work began on development plans. However, the declining prices for oil made the project less attractive, and the two sides resumed their working contacts only in 1991 after SODECO teamed up with Exxon. They each eventually agreed to cover 30 percent of the project costs.

In 1993 Arktun-Dagi oil and gas field was incorporated in the project and two Russian companies, Rosneft (17 percent of the total cost) and Sakhalinmorneftegas (23 percent), joined the consortium in 1995. In June 1995 a production sharing agreement was signed, and implementation of the project began in 1996. The total amount of investment in the Sakhalin-1 project is estimated at $15 billion (Table 25.1).

The first phase of oil production will begin at Arktun-Dagi field in 2000–1 and the first gas will be extracted in 2005. Exxon and SODECO proposed to transport the produced oil through an oil terminal to be built on the eastern coast of Sakhalin Island. Russian participants of the project proposed using the pipeline to De-Kastry Bay, Khabarovskiy Krai, and from there shipping the oil for export by tanker. The rest of the oil will be refined at the Komsomolsk-na-Amur oil refinery. The administration of Sakhalinskaya Oblast wants the oil to be transported to the south of Sakhalin through a 625-kilometer-long new pipeline on the assumption that the same pipeline can be used by the Sakhalin-2 project.

The exploration of Lunskoe and Piltun Astokskoe oil and gas fields (Sakhalin-2 project) began in 1984. In 1986 Mitsui and McDermott formed a consortium (Mitsui's share in the project is 25 percent). In 1991 they were joined by Marathon Oil (37.5 percent of the cost of the project). In 1992 the consortium acquired the rights to develop the fields through tender and two more companies — Mitsubishi (12.5 percent) and Royal

FIGURE 25.1
Sakhalin Oil and Gas Projects

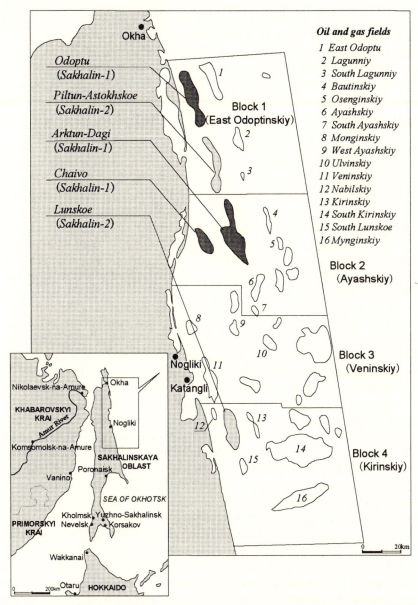

Source: Energy and Mineral Resources of the Far East and Zabaikalye. (Khabarovsk: Inter-Regional Association of Economic Cooperation "Far East and Zabaikalye," 1997), p. 88.

TABLE 25.1
Sakhalin-1: Estimated Reserves and Production Output

	Chaivo	Odoptu	Arktun-Dagi	Total
Reserves				
Oil in million tons	17	28	245	290
Gas in billion cubic				
meters/million tons	97/87.3	41/36.9	287/258.3	425/382.5
Gas condensate in				
million tons	6	1	26	33
Annual Peak Output				
Oil in million tons	—	—	5.3	24.1
Gas in billion cubic				
meters/million tons	—	—	—	19.7/17.7
Planned Output, 2000–5				
Oil in million tons	—	—	—	320
Gas in billion cubic				
meters/million tons	—	—	—	370/333

Source: ROTOBO Monthly Bulletin on Trade with Russia & East Europe, July 1997, p. 12.

Dutch Shell (25 percent) — joined the project. The total amount of investment in the Sakhalin-2 project is estimated at $10 billion (Table 25.2).

In April 1994, Sakhalin Energy Investment Company was formed to operate the project and to enter into a production-sharing agreement with the Russian government. Officially, the project's implementation commenced on April 15, 1996. By that time McDermott had left the consortium. Oil extraction is planned to begin before the onshore infrastructure in Katangly area is complete. From oil and gas terminals at Katangly the gas for domestic use will be transported through a pipeline to Komsomolsk-na-Amur. The oil and gas for export will be transported to the south of the island where a liquefied natural gas plant will be located.

There is a proposed Sakhalin-3 project as well. It will be implemented jointly by Exxon, Mobil, Texaco, and the Russian company Sakhalin-morneftegas. The project consists of four main fields including East Odoptu, Ayashskoe, Veninskoe, and Kirinskoe fields. Total reserves of oil and gas condensate are estimated at about 133 million tons and natural gas reserves in excess of 500 billion cubic meters. The agreement on Sakhalin-3 allows 6 years for the exploratory phase and 19 years for extraction of resources. The implementation of the project will begin in

TABLE 25.2
Sakhalin-2: Estimated Reserves and Production Output

	Piltun-Astokskoe	Lunskoe	Total
Reserves			
Oil in million tons	87	7.7	94.7
Gas in billion cubic			
meters/million tons	76/68.4	379/341.1	455/409.5
Gas condensate in			
million tons	6	31	37
Annual Peak Output			
Oil in million tons	2.1	—	7.9
Gas in billion cubic			
meters/million tons	—	—	16.4/14.8
Planned Output, 2000–5			
Oil in million tons	—	—	90
Gas in billion cubic			
meters/million tons	—	—	322/298.8

Source: ROTOBO *Monthly Bulletin on Trade with Russia & East Europe*, July 1997, p. 8.

the year 2000. In scale the project is very large; geological exploration alone may require about $500 million. A Sakhalin-4 project in Sakhalin Bay may follow soon after Sakhalin-3.

ECONOMIC SIGNIFICANCE

Sakhalin-1 and Sakhalin-2 will not dramatically change the overall picture of oil and gas production in Russia. When these two projects reach their peak output their combined share will not exceed 8 percent of total Russian oil production in 1994. However, the projects will play a very important role in the recovery of Far Eastern Russia and in strengthening Russia's links with its Northeast Asian neighbors. Sakhalin oil and gas development projects will greatly contribute to the economy of Sakhalinskaya Oblast and the management of the energy situation in Far Eastern Russia. They will create new jobs, improve the business climate, and add to export earnings and foreign trade growth. Sakhalin-1 and Sakhalin-2 are the leading projects in Far Eastern Russia in terms of attracting foreign investment.

In 1997 the total investment made in the two projects was estimated at $500 million, and in 1998 Sakhalin-2 investment alone was expected to equal this amount. Total net profit for the Russian side from both projects is estimated at $78 billion. After the recovery of oil and gas begins Sakhalinskaya Oblast alone will gain about $800 million a year. Sakhalinskaya Oblast and Khabarovskiy and Primorskiy krais will gain from gas supplies through existing and new pipelines that will connect their residential and industrial areas with wells on Sakhalin. The domestic network of gas and oil pipelines to be built in connection with Sakhalin projects is likely to exceed 4,000 kilometers at an estimated cost of more than $2.4 billion, but the beginning of work was delayed because of the financial problems in Russia.

In only a few years the two Sakhalin projects will create more than 10,000 new jobs. More than 300 companies, including 30 from Japan, applied for subcontracts related to Sakhalin-1 and Sakhalin-2. Local content requirements of at least 70 percent provide a strong incentive for forming alliances and joint ventures between Russian and Japanese and other foreign companies in order to compete for orders. The first subcontract orders were received by the shipbuilding enterprises at Komsomolsk-na-Amur, Khabarovskiy Krai, and Bolshoi Kamen, Primorskiy Krai.

THE REGULATORY FRAMEWORK

The production-sharing agreement for Sakhalin-1 was signed on June 30, 1995, and for Sakhalin-2, on June 22, 1994. These agreements stipulate that Russia (federal government and administration of Sakhalinskaya Oblast) delegate the right to develop the offshore resources to the investors who will undertake the financing and technical implementation of the projects. It was agreed that profits from the projects will be used first to recover the cost of the investment and royalty payments (6–8 percent of the cost of the product), and only after that initial stage a profit-sharing mechanism will be enacted (Table 25.3).

Under the agreement on Sakhalin-1 the Russian side will receive 15 percent of profits if the internal rate of return is lower than 16.5 percent, but if it is higher the Russian share in profits will increase to 54 percent with the remaining 46 percent going to investors. If this is the case, the total share of the Russian side in profits can be as high as 72 percent, including the share of the two Russian companies participating in the consortium. In the production=sharing agreement for Sakhalin-2 the share of the Russian side will be 70 percent if the internal rate of return is higher than 24 percent. If it is within a 17.5–24.0 range, the profits will be split evenly, but with a level of return lower than 17.5 percent the share of foreign investors in profits will be 90 percent.

TABLE 25.3
Sakhalin-1, 2: Production Output and Sharing Estimates, 2000–25

	2000	2005	2010	2015	2016	2020	2025
Oil and gas condensate in million tons, including							
output	2.7	14.0	25.5	16.6	16.0	7.0	3.5
exports	2.1	9.0	20.5	11.6	11.0	2.0	—
domestic use	0.6	5.0	5.0	5.0	5.0	5.0	3.5
Natural gas in billion cubic meters, including:							
output	—	15.2	19.9	20.6	27.7	28.6	28.6
exports	—	8.0	9.1	9.1	13.6	16.6	13.6
domestic use	—	7.2	10.8	11.5	14.2	15.0	15.0

Source: East & West Report, No. 9739, October 17, 1997.

Within the first five years of project implementation investors must pay $20 million to the Sakhalin Development Fund, which will be used for infrastructure improvement and social needs of the territory. At the beginning of each stage of project implementation investors make bonus payments. For example, *Sakhalin Energy Investment* paid $15 million in bonuses after the production-sharing agreement was signed and $15 million after the implementation was announced. Therefore, the initial payments from the Sakhalin-1 and Sakhalin-2 projects to the Russian side amounted to $60 million, including $32 million to Sakhalinskaya Oblast. More bonus payments are expected after the production phase begins in each of the fields.

The production-sharing scheme serves as an effective mechanism to attract foreign investment and advanced technology for oil and gas resources development. In the future production-sharing agreements for resource development projects will be more attractive to foreign and domestic investors if the federal law enacted on January 11, 1996, on production sharing is adjusted further to serve better the needs of both investors and authorities.[2]

PROSPECTS FOR JAPAN

Japan can benefit from Sakhalin oil and gas resources development in many ways. Foremost is the opportunity to diversify energy supplies and to reduce Japan's current 80 percent dependence on the Middle East.

Second, a closer look at eastern Russia as a viable alternative has significant economic benefits, such as a reduced cost for transportation of energy resources. Third, cooperation with Russia can contribute to the energy security of all of Northeast Asia.

If the proposal to build the international gas pipeline between Sakhalin Island and Japan is pursued, the idea to form a gas pipeline network in Japan can be implemented. In view of the talks on the future use of Russian gas resources discovered in Irkutskaya Oblast and Yakutia for the needs of China, South Korea, and Japan, the Sakhalin-Japan gas pipeline can be seen as a part of a Northeast Asian gas pipeline system. If an integrated subregional network of gas pipelines is formed not only the economic needs of the region will be better served but energy security and political stability in Northeast Asia will also be enhanced.

According to the plans and research proposals of the Japanese Research Society on the problems of gas pipelines and Japan's Gas Association, Niigata Prefecture can serve as the main base and distribution center for Russian gas in Japan. The gas mines of Niigata can be used as natural storage facilities for the gas transported from Sakhalin, and the existing pipelines linking these mines with the Tokyo area and Sendai will ideally fit in the proposed scheme.

Hokkaido can benefit from the Sakhalin energy development projects, too. The geographical proximity of the two islands and the energy intensive industries located on Hokkaido (steel and shipbuilding) make Sakhalin's gas a natural alternative for energy supplies. Moreover, some Hokkaido-based enterprises can fit into the Sakhalin projects as subcontractors and service centers. Regular flights between Hakodate and Yuzhno-Sakhalinsk, the Wakkanai International Sea Terminal project, recreational facilities in Ishikari, and plans to develop Sakhalin projects-related service bases in Otaru and Muroran serve as examples of a new era in economic cooperation between Japan and Russia.

PROSPECTS FOR NORTHEAST ASIA

Energy is directly linked with economic security, and trade in energy resources enhances international stability. Development of energy resources requires a huge capital investment and quite often depends on the public sector and international financial institutions. Energy trade must be based on long-term contracts and long-term cooperation between the supplier and international customers.

The availability of energy is a key factor in determining the investment climate. If large, reliable energy sources are secured prospects for economic development in Northeast Asia will improve, and Japanese enterprises will have more chances to invest in this area. Japan and the Northeast Asian subregion can benefit not only from energy imports from

Russia but also indirectly through changes in energy strategies that put more emphasis on natural gas instead of coal and nuclear power. It is possible in the long term to plan for the use of coal only as a supplementary source of energy for some industries so that the environment is protected. Nuclear energy must be considered carefully, and the safety of the nuclear power plants must be strengthened. Thus, in the long term a cleaner and safer environment can be secured.

In general, trade in energy resources and cooperation in their development can shape the economic and political future of the Northeast Asian subregion and provide a solid framework for subregional cooperation. International cooperation at the governmental level is necessary to promote the development and utilization of Russian energy resources. Through cooperation with Russia, Japan has a unique opportunity to use Russian oil and gas for its own needs and participate in creating pillars of interdependence in Northeast Asia.

NOTES

1. The authors adopted the methodology of Mitsubishi Corporation and Tohoku Denryoku (electric) company in calculating data for measuring natural gas in TOE. Therefore, 1,000 cubic meters of natural gas roughly equals 0.9 tons of oil.

2. Production-sharing agreements on Sakhalin-1 and Sakhalin-2 projects were negotiated before the federal law on production sharing was enacted on January 11, 1996.

26

(Russia
Japan)

Trans-Siberian Land Bridge

Vladimir I. Ivanov and Dmitriy L. Sergachev

Improvement of Russia-Japan relations is important for the future of Northeast Asia and the Asia-Pacific region. Indeed, some Japan-Russia bilateral economic initiatives need to be seen in a broader regional and global economic context. Energy resources development in eastern Russia, for example, is important for all of Russia's eastern neighbors. Bilateral cooperation between Russia and Japan in the transportation sector and modernization of the Trans-Siberian Railway will facilitate the flow of goods between Europe and the Asia-Pacific Economic Cooperation area, creating new jobs and opportunities for businesses in Russia, Japan, and Northeast Asia.

The world's longest transcontinental railway provides efficient connections between Russian Pacific ports and Siberian provinces of the Russian Federation, Mongolia, all Central Asian states of the Confederation of Independent States, western Russia, Ukraine, Belarus, the Baltic states, all countries of Scandinavia (via Finland), and European states at competitive transit times and rates. Ironically, many Japanese, Korean, or Taiwanese goods consigned for western Russia and even Western Siberia are shipped around the world and enter the country either by rail or highway transport through Germany, Poland, Finland, or other Baltic states.[1]

THREE MAIN FUNCTIONS

The Trans-Siberian Railway is a part of Russia's national railway network. What makes it special is that it connects Russia's Pacific and

Atlantic ports and serves as a 9,913-kilometer-long land bridge between European and eastern regions of Russia. The distance between Vladivostok and St. Petersburg by sea via the Suez Canal is about 21,000 kilometers.

This railroad was launched in the late 19th century when Russia's eastward expansion was actively promoted by the government and the economic development of the new territories was high on the agenda. New settlements in the Far East were established, including Khabarovsk (1858), Blagovestchensk (1856), Nikolaevsk-na-Amure (1850), and Vladivostok (1860). However, the transportation links between these new lands and central Russia were extremely difficult to maintain and the cost was very high. For new settlers to move from central Russia to Vladivostok took about one year by land. The sea journey lasted about four months. After the Suez Canal was opened in 1869 the sea route became twice as fast, and it became easier to reach Vladivostok than Blagovestchensk; therefore, the population of the coastal areas rapidly increased.

New economic enclaves demanded new quality of transportation links with the western regions of Russia, and it was in the interest of Moscow not to allow the Russian Far East to transform its economic isolation into a political drift. Thus, a combination of economic, political, and geostrategic interests made the construction of the Trans-Siberian Railway a megaproject of the late 19th and early 20th centuries. After three research expeditions were dispatched to study this route between 1887 and 1890, the construction of the 8,300-kilometer-long railway between Chelyabinsk and Vladivostok began.[2]

The railway's first and foremost function was economic development. Areas close to the construction sites immediately gained economically and the Trans-Siberian Railway became a major factor in the development of the entire eastern Russia. In 1897 Ussuriyskaya Railway between Khabarovsk and Vladivostok was completed, and Khabarovsk's population grew from 5,000 to about 15,000.[3]

Initially the Trans-Siberian Railway was designed as an international project. After train service opened between Chelyabinsk and Sretensk (in Trans-Baikalia, now Chitinskaya Oblast) the option to continue the construction to the east along the left bank of the Amur River was dropped in favor of the Chinese Eastern Railroad (CER) project. This railroad was built between 1898 and 1903, and it linked the Trans-Baikal region (Karymskaya station) with Ussuriysk via Chinese territory and Pogranichnaya station on the Russia-China border.[4] The transportation time between Chelyabinsk and Vladivostok was reduced to a revolutionary six days, and from that moment the long sea route lost its monopoly and strategic value both for trade and new settlers.

In 1898 Russia secured a long-term lease for Port Arthur and Port Dalniy in eastern China and the CER was further expanded to link these ports with Harbin. However, as a result of the 1904–5 war with Japan, Russia lost control over these new enclaves along with unchecked freedom of transportation links with Vladivostok through the CER.

In 1908 these adverse developments induced the Russian government and State Duma to renew the construction of the Trans-Siberian Railway through Russian territory. A train connection between Moscow and Vladivostok was established in 1916. Both the Trans-Siberian Railway and new Russian Pacific ports, particularly Vladivostok, helped the development of Sakhalin Island, Kamchatka Peninsula, and Chukotka and later played a role in establishing military outposts, timber cutting industry along the route, and mining ventures in the remote northeast.

In the 1930s another large-scale railway project emerged as a part of economic development and political plans. The second Trans-Siberian Railway became known as the Baikal-Amur Mainline (BAM). This 3,095-kilometer-long railway construction project was interrupted by World War II and resumed only in 1974. The BAM has operated since the late 1980s, but it will be completed around the year 2000, after the Severomuiskiy Tunnel is finished, allowing the railway (with 145 large bridges) to function more efficiently and 46 settlements along the BAM to grow.[5] In the east, the BAM is linked to Vanino and Sovetskaya Gavan seaports, but in the west it ends up merging with the Trans-Siberian Railway. It is expected that beyond the year 2010 deposits of natural resources will constitute a base for balanced and sustainable economic development of the BAM area. It is likely that foreign investment will be available for the oil and gas projects in the area of the BAM.

The second important function of the Trans-Siberian Railway, particularly after World War II, was to link Russia with the markets of East Asia and North America. Nakhodka port served as an international trading port even during the coldest days of the Cold War.

In 1990 the total cargo turnover of the Pacific ports (Table 26.1) was 65 million tons, including 18 million tons of export-import cargo. In 1995 the total cargo turnover declined to 31 million tons, but 25 million tons was export-import cargo, including 23 million tons handled by the Pacific ports linked to the Trans-Siberian Railway.[6] The three ports in southern Primorskiy Krai (Nakhodka, Vostochniy, and Vladivostok)[7] and one lumber port in Khabarovskiy Krai (Vanino) serve as a gateway to Japan. In 1994 the physical volume of Japanese imports from Russia was 9.98 million tons, including 4.6 million tons shipped between the 4 Russian ports and the 30 Japanese ports on the west coast of Japan.

The third function of the Trans-Siberian Railway is transcontinental transportation of international cargo. Transportation time and costs make the Trans-Siberian Land Bridge (TSLB) a competitive alternative for containerized cargo and general freight. In the future if the northern corridor will link the railroads of the Korean peninsula with Europe through

TABLE 26.1
Russian Pacific Ports Linked with the Trans-Siberian Railway, 1995

	Berths number/length meters	Cargo volume, 1990 million tons	Cargo volume, 1995 million tons	Exports million tons	Imports million tons
Vladivostok trade port	16/2,820	5.08	3.80	3.20	0.350
Nakhodka trade port	22/2,891	7.40	5.20	4.90	0.200
Vostochniy	13/2,295	11.40	8.50	7.90	0.460
Vanino	15/2,326	9.70	5.60	2.40	0.500
Zarubino	4/642	0.20	0.45	0.44	0.005
Posiyet	3/435	1.40	0.73	0.70	0.030

Source: Goskomstat data and *Russian Far East Update,* "Ports of the Russian Far East, A Special Industry Report," Seattle, 1997.

Russia, the TSLB can be directly connected with the largest Northeast Asian container terminal at Pusan in South Korea (Figure 26.1). A new rail link from northeastern China can bring additional possibilities for both trade and transit traffic of containerized cargo for the TSLB. It is unlikely that an alternative route through the territory of China and states of central Asia can offer better conditions in terms of cost and speed because of the different track gauges and several border-crossing points.

TRANSCONTINENTAL BRIDGE

In 1966 an agreement to use the Russian national railway for transit cargo was reached with Japan, test shipments followed in 1967. In 1971 a regular container line was opened between ports in Japan and Nakhodka, replaced by Port Vostochniy in 1975. Port Vostochniy can handle about 250,000 containers a year. In 1981 the total number of containers handled by the railroad (including Soviet exports and imports and return of empty containers) peaked to 138,500. In 1983 the port processed 110,683 transit containers from Japan measured in a 20-foot equivalent unit (TEU), including 82,794 westbound and 27,889 eastbound containers (Table 26.2).

This transit traffic provided significant hard currency earnings, but declined because of two main reasons. First, the demand for Russia's transit services, particularly among Japanese cargo owners, was suppressed by Cold War political complications. Second, the modern sea container carriers outcompeted the railway providing reliable service at a lower and decreasing cost. However, in 1992, the TSLB still accounted for about 68,000 TEU transit containers.

The end of the Cold War did not help the recovery of the land bridge. In 1997 the combined container traffic, including transit, export, import, and empty containers was 55,577 TEU, including 30,013 TEU of transit containers, both eastbound and westbound. In addition, about 31,124 containers processed in Vostochniy Port were of Russian export-import cargo. The decline in the traffic can be explained by decreasing numbers of containers to and from Japan.

As the traffic decreased, Russian providers of services raised tariffs and charges to cover the losses thus discouraging potential clients. In particular, deregulation of railroad tariffs and rigid custom clearing procedures greatly reduced the competitiveness of the TSLB. The time of transportation increased up to 40 days, fees charged at ports were raised, information on cargo location was rare, and its protection inadequate. Vostochniy Port was losing money, and Far Eastern Shipping Company (FESCO), a leading Russian steamship company, reduced its service to Port Vostochniy from weekly to two times a month but reportedly was losing money, too.

FIGURE 26.1
The Trans-Siberian Land Bridge Network

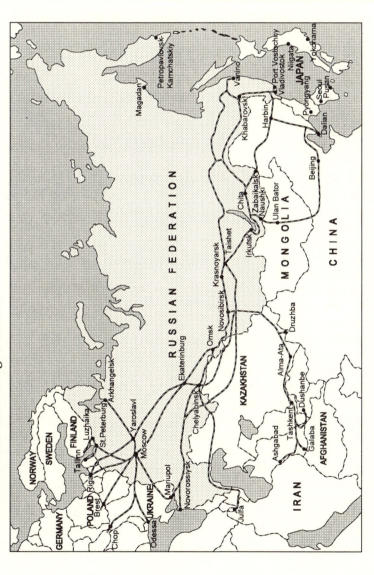

Source: Map drafted by Economic Research Institute for Northeast Asia, Niigata, Japan, 1998.

TABLE 26.2
Containers Handled by Port Vostochniy, 1971–97
(in 20-foot equivalent units)

Year	Total	Export/Import	Transit	Japan's Transit		Korea's Transit	
				Total	Westbound	Total	Westbound
1971	—	n/a	n/a	1,992	1,642	—	—
1976	—	n/a	n/a	79,861	57,684	—	—
1981	138,500	n/a	n/a	103,851	82,794	—	—
1982	100,502	4,992	95,510	78,393	56,901	—	—
1983	121,918	9,670	112,248	110,683	85,962	—	—
1984	118,940	12,657	106,283	88,420	63,084	—	—
1985	118,982	23,887	95,095	85,633	59,053	—	—
1986	110,398	24,601	85,797	77,502	54,980	—	—
1987	111,587	28,107	83,480	77,126	51,694	—	—
1988	132,876	30,851	102,025	86,870	55,566	—	—
1989	127,646	44,950	82,696	72,195	46,325	—	—
1990	126,013	49,196	76,817	67,248	45,131	—	—

1991	134,310	42,445	91,865	66,857	41,607	9,531	5,528
1992	106,371	38,126	68,245	43,150	27,308	11,083	6,459
1993	109,540	56,345	53,195	33,271	16,603	12,705	6,794
1994	86,565	53,041	33,524	16,373	4,174	13,406	5,155
1995	69,407	37,879	31,528	10,360	1,937	17,769	10,685
1996	68,871	31,124	37,049	7,895	2,139	26,731	14,084
1997	55,577	25,564	30,013	6,420	2,802	21,653	12,041

Source: Compiled from data in Department of Russia and Eastern Europe and Nisshin Corporation, "The Siberian Container Bridge," in *Inter-Modal Transportation Handbook* (Tokyo: Japan International Freight Forwarders Association, 1995), p. 173. Data on transit container transportation from and to Japan for the Trans-Siberian Railway was received during an interview with Gennadiy M. Fadeev, October 8, 1998, Moscow. Data on historical statistics, including that of the Container Business & Transport Forwarding Company, was received from Rado Antolovich, December 29, 1997. Data on Japan-Russia and Korea-Russia container flows were received during an interview with Valeriy A. Baranov, August 10, 1998, Vladivostok.

SOLUTIONS

Vostochniy International Container Service is a joint stock company formed by Vostochniy Port, Sea Land Service, and P&O Australia in 1994. Despite Vostochniy International Container Service's efforts to provide a better and more reliable service in terms of the cargo's safety and speed of delivery, until recently the international transit container traffic was declining.

The Nakhodka Free Economic Zone Administrative Committee insisted that urgent decisions must be made by the federal government, local administrations, port authorities, and the railroad administration to improve conditions for transit cargo. As a result, federal and local administrations agreed to introduce a number of economic incentives, and they tried to coordinate the various government agencies involved. A special government commission was created to deal with the TSLB revitalization problem, and an action plan was produced delineating measures to support the TSLB, particularly to regain international container transit as well as general cargo.

First, the tariffs for transit cargo transportation by sea and railroad were reduced. Cargo handling fees by ports were cut. Port call fees for carriers with cargo for the TSLB were cut by 50 percent.[8] FESCO reduced its tariffs by 10 percent.[9] Railroad tariffs were cut by 10 percent for general transit cargo and by 30 percent for transit containers. Vostochniy Port reduced cargo processing fees by 10 percent. Local legislators in Primorskiy Krai and Nakhodka City adopted special regulations to provide tax incentives for all entities to facilitate such cuts in tariffs and fees. Local taxes for Vostochniy and Nakhodka ports were reduced by 50 percent. For example, sea freight of one 20-foot container from Port Pusan, South Korea, to Vostochniy Port decreased from $261 to $235 and the railroad tariff for the transportation to the border-crossing with Finland dropped from $360 to $307.

Second, measures were taken to reduce the time of transportation for transit cargo. The railroad management guaranteed that only rehabilitated equipment will be provided for TSLB service and that containers are moved in unit trains allowing for introduction of a precise schedule. Moreover, 12 days and 6 hours was set as the maximum transportation time between Vostochniy Port and Luzhaika station on the Russia-Finland border (Brest station at Belarus-Poland border: 12 days and 15 hours, Chop station on the Ukraine-Hungary border: 11 days and 15 hours).[10]

Third, the railroad authorities took responsibility for the cargo's physical protection and for the tracing of transit containers. Russian insurance companies now offer their services to cargo owners. Moreover, a demonstration train was dispatched between Vostochniy Port and Brest in April 1998. To promote the route the Ministry of Railway of Russia did not charge the transportation fee for its Russian portion, so the actual cost was reduced to only $50 paid for the railway transit through Belarussian territory.

Finally, the federal government instructed custom authorities to work with transit cargo 24 hours a day, to cancel the practice of customs declarations (reportedly this paper contained up to 50 inquiries) for transit containerized cargo, and to discontinue the practice of charging fees for each processed transit container. It was expected that these measures would help increase transit container traffic by 5–6 times by the year 2000 but in the summer of 1998 the railway was blocked by the coal miners on strike in eastern Siberia.

In theory, transit time through the Russian territory for containers can be reduced to 10 days, and the TSLB can be competitive in terms of cost as well (Table 26.3). Customers from East Asia and Europe can ship a 20-foot container through the territory of the Russian Federation to the border crossing with Finland (or Vostochniy Port) for about $800–900 and the

TABLE 26.3
Trans-Siberian Land Bridge versus Deep Sea Route:
Comparative Cost of Transportation
(US$, Japan-Warsaw, for one 20-foot container)

	Westbound		Eastbound	
Structure of charges	Sea route	TSLB	Sea route	TSLB
Ports, Japan	357	357	353	353
Container lease	180	180	180	180
Insurance	95	95	95	95
Freight, to Europe	800	—	700	—
Ports, Europe	200	—	200	—
Freight, FESCO	—	241	—	241
Vostochniy Port	—	80	—	80
Customs	—	14	—	14
Railroad, Russia	—	377	—	285
Railroad, Belarus	—	67	—	56
Reloading, Brest	—	27	—	27
Railroad, from Brest	—	195	—	195
Railroad, from Europe	620	—	620	—
Others	86	86	86	86
Total	2,338	1,719	2,234	1,612

Source: K. Kholopov, "Trans-Siberian Transit: Is It Good for Russia?" *Ekonomica i Zhisn*, No. 2, January 1998, p. 30.

total cost can be lower by $600 compared with the sea route. However, major customers of the container shipping lines that operate between Japan and Europe are likely to enjoy significant discounts that make the deep sea transportation cost lower than the cost of the TSLB. The sea route tariffs declined over the last 10–15 years by about 50 percent to as low as $1,000 for a 20-foot container and $2,000 for a 40-foot container. Moreover, the Russian railway has only begun operating equipment for 40-foot containers (major portion of shipments from and to Japan), and this reduces its competitiveness.

At this point the problem is not one of profitability; rather the main question is how rationally to use the existing infrastructure without losses. Vostochniy Port, for example, is the largest container terminal in Russia, but by the mid-1990s it was experiencing net losses estimated at $16 million a year. Nakhodka Free Economic Zone, Vostochniy Port, and other entities were affected by high tariffs, customs procedures, and other regulations that undermined the TSLB's attractiveness not only to international transit but also for those who ship their export-import cargo from East Asia to the Moscow region. Ironically, Finland has acquired the role of distribution center for goods exported from Japan and South Korea to western Russia.

PROSPECTS FOR COOPERATION

Cooperation with Japan in modernizing the TSLB will help Russia to improve the organization and expand infrastructure to handle the containerized cargo traffic between East Asia and Europe. Domestic demand for transportation services, export-import operations, and transit cargo will require modernization of port facilities and, therefore, new investment. Primorskiy Krai alone applied to the Ministry of Transportation's department of maritime transportation for an estimated $19 billion to build new ports and to expand existing cargo facilities.

Some of the required financial resources for modernization are expected to come from external sources. Vostochniy Port, for example, will receive about $300 million in credits from Germany and Japan to build terminals to handle timber, coal, and mineral fertilizers, as well as to import grain. Its management looks forward to building additional facilities for the transportation of aluminum from Australia and to handle oil exports in cooperation with Italian investors. There are also two medium-size ports (Posiyet and Zarubino) seen as promising candidates for modernization and expansion and firmer links with the TSLB.

However, as far as transit cargo is concerned, many experts indicate that the TSLB, at best, can only recover to its 1983 peak level with regard to Japanese customers, but its further expansion will be determined by progress in investment and trade links between Northeast Asian economies, particularly Japan, and Russia, Central Asian states, and other members of the Confederation of Independent States. How effectively Russian federal government, national railway, ports, and customs authorities will be able to serve these economic links using the TSLB remains to be seen.

NOTES

1. Rado Antolovich, "Reforms on the Trans-Siberian Land Bridge," *Vedomosti*, No. 29 (152), October 1997.

2. *Railway Transport: An Encyclopedia* (Moscow: Bolshaya Rossiyskaya Entcyklopedia, 1994), pp. 458–59.

3. M. A. Kovalchuk, *History of Transport of the Far Eastern Russia*, vol. 2 (Khabarovsk: Amurskiy Region Geographic Society, 1997), p. 22. For a detailed description of the current status of the Trans-Siberian Railway see A. Sergeev and L. Vinokur, "The Current Situation and the Restructuring Conditions of the Trans-Siberian Railroad," *Monthly Bulletin on Trade with Russia and Eastern Europe*, No. 12 (December 1997): 16–37.

4. *Railway Transport: An Encyclopedia*, p. 185.

5. The cost of the BAM project was estimated at $9.2 billion; it created as many as 130,000 jobs at the peak of construction, with its eastern sector built by engineering troops, prison labor, and North Korean contracted labor. This railroad is not profitable at present and reportedly its maintenance costs the Ministry of Railway about $200 million annually.

6. In 1995 all railways connecting Russia with other countries and ports handled about 6,700 railroad cars with exports daily. The Far Eastern Railroad, which represents the eastern segment of the Trans-Siberian Railway, alone accounted for 3,900 of the cars, and 3,700 of them were designated for the Pacific ports.

7. Nakhodka, Vladivostok, and Vostochniy ports are located within a radius of 70 kilometers and are ice-free. This setting is ideal for inter-port competition and agglomeration because every port is equipped for different types of cargo. Since 1991 these Russian Pacific ports have handled more import-export cargo. On the average, foreign trade cargo occupies about 60 percent of total cargo traffic. For such ports as Vostochniy, Nakhodka, and Vladivostok this share was about 80 percent but increased in the late 1990s to 90–95 percent because of the declining import.

8. Deborah Turnbull, *Ports of the Russian Far East*. (Seattle: Far East Update, 1997), p. 10. Port call fees in the Russian Federation were 30–40 percent higher than in Ukraine or Baltic states. Moreover, in 1992 the Russian government introduced a 40–50 percent tariff discount for railway cargo transportation through western ports, including those of Baltic states.

9. The group of sea carriers in Pacific Russia is the second largest in the country. Four companies operate more than 350 ships with more than 3 million tons capacity. They employ about 50,000 people. The largest, Far Eastern Shipping Company, with its headquarters in Vladivostok, went private in 1992. It

accounts for 28 percent of all cargo traffic, about 68 percent of Russian bilateral trade transactions, and 10 percent of the regular liner cross trade.

The Kamchatka Shipping Company, with headquarters in Petropavlovsk-Kamchatskiy, provides regular line services from the Kamchatka Peninsula to Japan (timber) and the Koreas (cement); however, its main area of operation is coastal shipping on the northeast Pacific.

The Primorskaya Shipping Company, with headquarters in Nakhodka, transports oil, petroleum products, and similar cargoes to Japan, South Asia, East Africa, and Europe.

The Sakhalin Shipping Company, based in Kholmsk, is Russia's key cabotage operator and provides sea-rail ferry services. It also provides regular services to China, Japan, and Southeast Asia.

10. Primorskiy Krai Administration data.

P33, F14, F02

27 (Russia, Japan)
China

Trilateral Cross-Border Links
Kazuyoshi Nishikata

Infrastructure development is the key to the economic development of Northeast Asia. Infrastructure here refers not only to the physical but also to so-called software infrastructure, such as border clearance procedure harmonization. In Northeast Asia discussions have centered on physical infrastructure construction or improvement; however, as flows of commodities and tourists across borders increase, issues of software infrastructure become more important.

NEW TRANSPORTATION ROUTES FROM NORTHEAST CHINA

Jilin and Heilongjiang provinces in Northeast China have no seaports in their territories; therefore, commodity shipment to and from these two provinces has depended largely upon Dalian Port of Liaoning Province. However, as the volume of cargoes went beyond the capacity of Dalian Port and the railroad to the port, the provinces paid more attention to the relative advantage of Russian or Democratic People's Republic of Korea (DPRK) ports in terms of distance.

For example, it is 940 kilometers from Harbin to Dalian and 800 kilometers to Vladivostok. It is 700 kilometers between Changchun and Dalian and 670 kilometers from Changchun through the Hunchun to Zarubino Port. As a result, Jilin and Heilongjiang provincial governments have tried to cultivate the potential of the Hunchun-Zarubino route (hereafter, the Zarubino route) and Suifenhe-Grodekovo-Vladivostok, Nakhodka, or Vostochniy route (hereafter the Suifenhe route).

Suifenhe City is located on the southeastern edge of Heilongjiang Province, and it has a long history as a trade center with Primorskiy Krai. The railroad service was operational at the beginning of the 20th century and Suifenhe Station was designated to be open to the outside world in 1952. The city's border trade with Russia grew significantly in 1996 when the amount reached $3.5 billion, comprising 10 percent of the province's total trade.

Compared to Suifenhe, Hunchun City has a short history of an open-door policy. The city is located on the eastern edge of the Yanbian Korean Autonomous Prefecture. Changlingji Road Customs Office opened in October 1991, and the city itself was designated an open border city in March 1992. The open door policy and the establishment of the Hunchun Border Economic Cooperation Zone in 1992 have resulted in a remarkable change in the city's economy. The growth rate of the population from 1990 to 1996 is 14.4 percent, the second highest rate after the prefectural capital, Yanji City. Reflecting investment promotion in the economic cooperation zone, the share of secondary industry to gross domestic product is the largest in the prefecture (47.9 percent). In contrast, the ratio of primary industry sharply declined from 31.8 percent in 1990 to 19.2 percent in 1996. The amount of foreign trade in 1996 was $54 million, accounting for 25 percent of the prefecture's total.

The economies of both cities depend heavily upon foreign trade and investment. In this sense, it is much more important for Suifenhe and Hunchun to establish new transportation routes using Russian or DPRK ports and to ensure more liberal flows of commodities and passengers.

CURRENT STATUS AND ISSUES

The station consists of two branches, the south station (old station) and the north station (new station). The south station opened in 1903 as a cargo and passengers terminal, and it can now handle 3 million tons annually. The newly built north station is for cargo-handling purposes only, and the planned capacity of cargo handling is 2 million tons annually.

Grodekovo Station, the Russian counterpart, is estimated to handle around 1.3–1.6 million tons annually. The capacity seems much smaller than that of Suifenhe Station. The Russian side plans to improve the facilities to deal with an annual volume of 4 million tons. It is estimated that the improvement cost will be $200 million.

As for road facilities, the class two national road between Harbin and Suifenhe opened to the public in April 1997. The new customs facilities were operational on the Chinese border in June 1997. It is reported that the new customs office can annually handle 1 million tons of cargo and

500,000 passengers. The customs office facilities of the Russian side are less efficient compared to the Chinese side.

The construction of the international railroad between Hunchun and Kraskino commenced in 1993. It was initially planned that the railroad service between Hunchun and Zarubino would be operational by June 1994, but financial shortages and other factors caused a long delay in railroad construction. In October 1996 the rails were connected, but the construction of related facilities, such as signals, cargo transfer facilities, and communication facilities, is not yet completed. Consultations between Jilin Province and Primorskiy Krai are proceeding to complete the construction and commence commercial operations in the first half of 1998.

Road conditions from Hunchun via Changlingzi to Zarubino are rather good. The class three road in the Chinese territory has already been paved, as has the road between the border and Kraskino. Changlingzi Customs Office was constructed in 1990 with a cargo handling capacity of 1 million tons annually. The Russian customs office is underdeveloped compared to the Chinese side.

The above may clarify the problems in China-Russia transportation routes in terms of the physical infrastructure. In addition, there are several obstacles to smooth flows of passengers and commodities in terms of software infrastructure. The problems related to border clearances are: time-consuming procedures in customs clearance, relatively higher transportation costs partly caused by border charges, double cargo checks in the Russian territory by the customs office and the border guard, and differences in hours of operation between the customs offices of China and Russia. Moreover, on the Zarubino route, third country nationals (with few exceptions) are not permitted to cross the border.

The situation is much worse on the Zarubino route because it has a strong competitor, namely the route connecting Hunchun and Rajin Port in North Korea (hereafter, the Rajin route). Although the Zarubino route has an advantage compared to the Rajin route in terms of physical infrastructure such as road conditions and customs office facilities in China, it receives less cargo and fewer passengers because of higher costs, stricter regulations, and less convenient services.

For example, the official grade of Chinese and Russian customs offices is higher than that of China-North Korea customs offices, but even the passage of Chinese or Russian nationals is restricted at the border. In contrast, third country nationals with invitations from North Korea are permitted visa-free entry on the China–DPRK border. On the China-Russian border the time during which cargo and passengers can cross the border is limited because of the differences in working hours of customs offices and the local time differences (only three and one-half hours during summer and four and one-half hours during winter). The demerits of high costs and time-consuming procedures might seriously deteriorate the competitiveness of the Zarubino route.

The feasibility study on Zarubino Port development proposed that the Russian side should reduce tariffs, charges, and fees and simplify the border clearance procedure. However, major progress has not been observed yet. It is often pointed out that there are differences in views between Moscow and Primorskiy Krai and even between the Primorskiy Krai and its Khasan Region as to what measures should be taken for Zarubino Port development.

Some Chinese experts argue that one of the fundamental obstacles to smooth flows is the difference in the levels of open-door policy. They indicate that the Khasan Region is not yet open to foreign nationals. They add that the liberalization of passenger flows, in particular permission for third country nationals to cross the border, should be the first issue to be considered. The Russian side, in contrast, argues that Chinese guarantees for the volume of cargo shipped through the Russian ports should be the first step. The lack of a cooperative partnership seems to hinder the development of new transportation routes.

HARMONIZATION EFFORTS

To enhance harmonization of border clearance procedures, both China and Russia have held frequent meetings at the provincial-territorial level. For example, in September 1997 both Heilongjiang and Primorskiy Krai concluded an agreement concerning cargoes for export-import and transit purposes.

In addition to these bilateral efforts, the United Nations Development Program Tumen Secretariat has provided opportunities for cross-border harmonization. It has organized the Tumen River Area Development Coordination Committee comprised of China, the DPRK, and Russia. In the coordination committee some issues related to border trade or passenger transportation services have been discussed, although major progress has not been observed. In addition to the coordination committee, the secretariat organizes several workshops, some of which are designed to address cross-border harmonization.

Finally, there have also been some efforts made by the Japanese side. Several trading companies in Japan have shown an interest in shipping Chinese cargo through Suifenhe or the Zarubino route. About 10,000 tons of Chinese wood chips were shipped to Japan through Zarubino Port in 1997. Other potential users pay attention to these two routes. Some research reports were published on Suifenhe and Zarubino routes. In addition to the coordination committee, the Tumen Secretariat organized the Consultation Commission including the above three countries,

Mongolia, and South Korea. Japan has been invited to join the commission as a formal member, but it still prefers to remain an observer.

The Niigata Prefectural Government has made some efforts to promote these routes. Niigata maintains a strong interest in establishing new transportation routes across the Sea of Japan and was actively involved in the prefeasibility and feasibility studies on Zarubino Port development. In the fiscal year 1997–98 Niigata sponsored a research project on the cross-border issues between Jilin and Heilongjiang provinces and the Primorskiy Krai. Based on the research, the prefecture organized a Japan-China-Russia trilateral meeting on border crossing in February 1998. Government officials from Jilin, Heilongjiang, and Primorskiy Krai, shipping companies from China, and Japanese trading companies were invited to the meeting. During the meeting, some Japanese participants presented questions and requests on border clearance procedures. The significance of the meeting was to provide an opportunity for China and Russia to learn of the willingness of the Japanese side to use either the Suifenhe or Zarubino route if the route was improved.

CONCLUSION

Because both Northeast China and Far Eastern Russia are remote places from the central governments, they have not been able to draw much attention from Beijing or Moscow. However, some favorable changes were observed that might have an impact on the progress of cross-border harmonization efforts. The Russian government announced that it was prepared to take some measures to revitalize the Trans-Siberian Land Bridge.

Policy measures for this purpose are expected to have a positive effect on the development of the Suifenhe route. As for the Zarubino route, it is reported that research on future commodity flows in the Chinese segment of the Tumen River Economic Development Area will be completed this year. This will be extremely useful for estimating the volume of cargo bound for Zarubino and other ports in Primorskiy Krai.

The change in climate of the China-Russia relationship and the completion of the research project will surely promote the bilateral talks for transportation cooperation on a practical and scientific basis. Moreover, this will also make the Japanese attitude more positive toward the competitiveness of Suifenhe and Zarubino routes. The triangular relationship among China, Japan, and Russia will lead to the establishment of a new transportation, trade, and investment network in Northeast Asia.

28

The Zarubino Port Project: A Case Study

Hisako Tsuji

Zarubino Port is situated 100 kilometers (km) as the crow flies and 180 km by road southeast of Vladivostok, Primorskiy Krai. The port was opened in 1981 as a fishing port, and it was registered as a commercial port the following year. In March 1992 the Khasan Sea Commercial Port Company was founded following the privatization policy of Russian ports. Since then Zarubino Port has been open to foreign ships, customs have been set up, and it has become a commercial port. Although the port's freight-handling capacity is an estimated 1 million tons, since 1992 it has handled only about 500,000 tons.

Why is this small port drawing the attention of not only Russia but also China and Japan? The main reasons are China's quest for an outlet to the Sea of Japan and the perceived economic benefits that this outlet can bring to the ports of the prefectures along Japan's western coast, especially Niigata. The development of Zarubino Port, if realized, represents the future of Northeast Asia, a future in which the countries of the subregion cooperate not only on a bilateral basis but also on a trilateral or multilateral basis to facilitate economic gains and interdependence.

INTERNATIONAL TRANSIT FUNCTION

Zarubino is approximately 60 km from the border between China and Russia and only 80 km from Hunchun, a border town in Jilin (Figure 28.1). Neither Heilongjiang nor Jilin in Northeast China has an exit to the sea. These provinces are important as both production bases and markets. Not only are they expected to be a future granary base for China, but they also have significant natural resources, such as coal and oil, and they have growing industrial production bases as well. However, because of their geographical position, they have been left behind in development, particularly compared to the remarkable success of China's coastal areas. Access to the sea could change that.

Furthermore, in recent years, freight transportation capacity by railway from the two provinces to Dalian port (the closest Chinese port in neighboring Liaoning) has almost reached its limit. Therefore, the importance of finding substitute routes for trade has increased. Heilongjiang is developing a route from Suifenhe, a border town in the east of the province, to Russian ports in Primorskiy Krai, such as Vladivostok. Jilin is developing a route from Tumen or Hunchun to the Sea of Japan through ports in North Korea or Russia. This route envisions the use of Rajin and Chongjin ports in North Korea for transit.

A Hunchun-Zarubino route is another potential transportation route for Jilin to access the Sea of Japan. It is expected that transportation infrastructure will be improved easily, because this route is close to Hunchun, roads in Russia are relatively well equipped, and the railway will open soon. There is a feeling of relief in China, because Russia is more open politically and economically than North Korea. China plans to use both the North Korean route and the Russian route. By playing two cards, China expects to have an advantage in securing reliable transportation services.

A PLAN

A memorandum regarding railway improvement from Hunchun to Zarubino through Changlingzi, Makhalino, and Sukhanovka was signed between China and Russia in December 1996 in Vladivostok, and a joint venture was established. China and Russia agreed that both China's standard gauge (1,435 millimeters) railway and Russia's broad gauge (1,520 millimeters) railway will be extended between Taiyang near Hunchun and Kamyshovaya near Kraskino (18 km of railway from Hunchun to Hunchun transit station and to Changlingzi in China, and 20 km between the junction of Khasansky line, as well as 11 km from Makhalino and Changlingzi on the Russian side). The Hunchun-Makhalino line was completed at the end of October 1996. Kamyshovaya transit station, which was included in the first plan, has not been constructed yet because of a shortage of funds. Only Russia's broad gauge railway has been extended to the Hunchun transit station.

During this time Japan worked closely with both China and Russia. A consensus had been reached in Japan, the Sea of Japan side in particular, that Japan should cooperate both technologically and financially to

FIGURE 28.1
Zarubino Port: Links with China and Trans-Siberian Railway

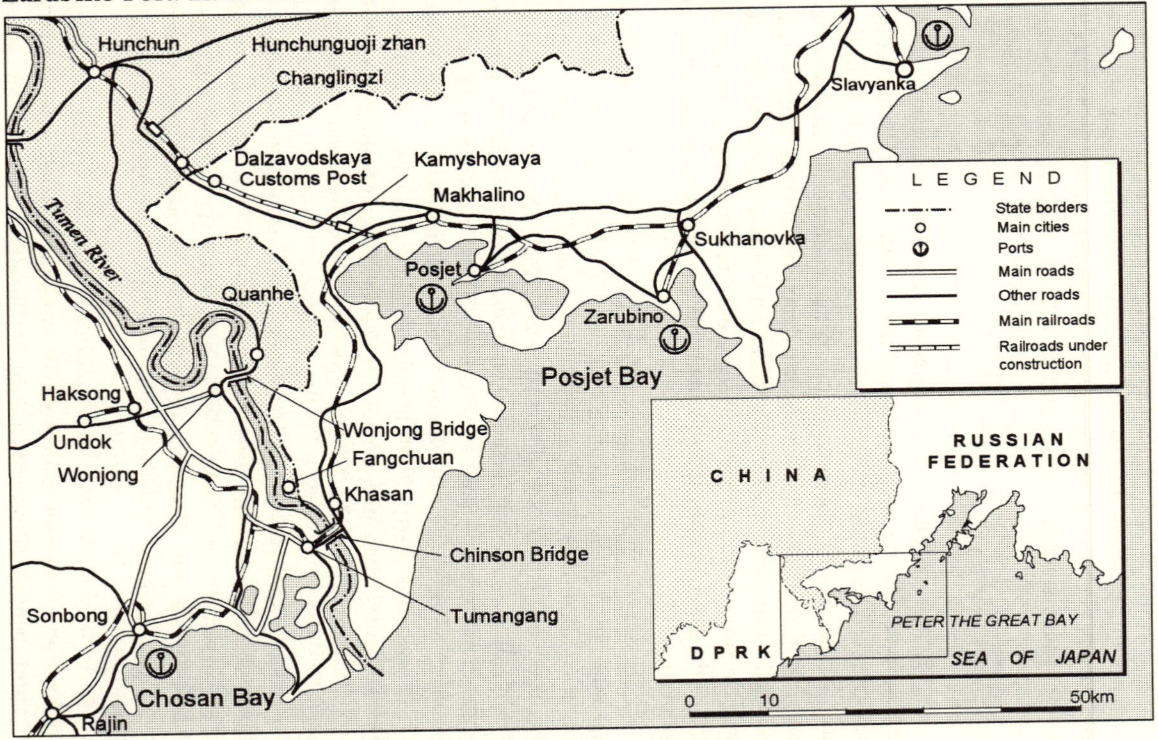

Source: Map drafted by Economic Research Institute for Northeast Asia, Niigata, Japan, 1997.

respond to the initiatives of neighboring countries in Northeast Asia aimed at promoting subregional cooperation and development.

As a gesture of friendship in Jilin-Niigata relations, Niigata Prefecture conducted a preliminary feasibility study for the development of Zarubino Port. The focus of the document was on the conditions for the development of new sea routes to transfer agricultural and other products through Zarubino. Niigata worked closely with China and Russia in the preliminary feasibility study. In September 1994 the document was included in the *Report on the Development of New Sea Routes in Northeast Asia* and was presented to the Primorskiy Krai administration. The study drew attention from both inside and outside Japan as the first official development assistance provided by a local government in Japan.

FEASIBILITY STUDY

In 1995 the governor of Primorskiy Krai sent an official letter to the governor of Niigata and the chairman of the Japan-Russia Cooperation Committee requesting a full feasibility study. In March 1996 the Japan-Russia Business Cooperation Committee together with other organizations established the Committee for Zarubino Port Feasibility Study with financial support from six prefectures on the Sea of Japan side, the Japanese government, and private enterprises. The Economic Research Institute for Northeast Asia conducted the study and published the final report in November 1996.

For Russia the most important element of the feasibility study was the amount of transit freight from China. The total amount of freight was estimated at 1.4 million tons in 1999, when the China-Russia railway was scheduled to be completed. For the year 2002 the estimated amount of total freight was 2.1 million tons. After port improvements the amount of freight could reach 4.3 million tons in 2012. Transit freight from China (primarily grains) accounted for 50 percent in each of the above total freight estimates. From 1994 through 1997 Russia frequently requested Chinese government guarantees for the amount of transit freight or realistic estimates of freight. China, however, was unable to show clear figures.

For the feasibility study the total amount of freight was estimated by utilizing macroeconomic forecasting (Table 28.1).

The working group for the feasibility study twice sent missions to Far Eastern Russia and China to collect information on future commodity flows and economic forecasts. The results of the missions revealed the following:

The Chinese government is expected to continue a policy of restricting grain exports because of forecasts indicating China's food demand and supply will

TABLE 28.1
Forecast for China's Northeastern Region Trade, 1998–2012
(in thousands of tons)

Year	China	Northeastern China	Jilin Province Total	Jilin Province Export	Jilin Province Import	Heilongjiang Province Total	Heilongjiang Province Export	Heilongjiang Province Import	Russia's Own Exports
1998 (estimate)	750	10	10	10	0	0	0	0	730
1999 (forecast)	1,390	620	580	370	220	40	20	20	760
2000	1,770	990	830	520	310	160	100	60	780
2001	1,910	1,120	940	580	350	180	110	70	800
2002	2,060	1,250	1,050	660	390	200	130	80	810
2003	2,220	1,390	1,170	730	440	220	140	80	830
2004	2,380	1,540	1,300	810	490	240	150	90	840
2005	2,560	1,700	1,440	900	540	260	160	100	860
2006	2,760	1,880	1,600	1,000	600	280	180	110	880
2007	2,970	2,070	1,770	1,110	660	300	190	110	900
2008	3,200	2,280	1,960	1,230	740	320	200	120	910
2009	3,440	2,510	2,170	1,360	810	340	210	130	930
2010	3,710	2,760	2,400	1,500	900	360	230	140	950
2011	4,010	3,040	2,660	1,660	1,000	380	240	140	970
2012	4,330	3,340	2,940	1,840	1,100	400	250	150	990

Source: Compiled from Economic Research Institute for Northeast Asia, *Study Report for the Zarubino Port Development Program*, Zarubino Port Feasibility Study Working Group. (Tokyo: Economic Research Institute for Northeast Asia, 1996), p. 4.

be tighter in the future. Therefore, Zarubino Port cannot be expected to be a grain export base.

China's exports of industrial products, building materials, and so forth will increase. Imports to China of capital goods and parts, for example, are also expected to increase.

The ability of Zarubino Port to attract these exports and imports will depend on its competitiveness vis-à-vis ports in North Korea.

To make the Zarubino route more competitive, fees related to transit should be competitive and customs procedures should be simplified.

Freight from Russia will increase only slightly.

The following quantitative estimates of various types of cargo were proposed (Table 28.2).

DEVELOPMENT PROSPECTS

Plans for the development of Zarubino Port and the railway to access the port envision three stages. The main goals of the first stage (Immediate Action Plan) are to use the existing berths and to improve the current facilities to handle freight estimates for 1998. Improvements include conducting electric corrosion-proofing treatment, dredging the front of berths, fixing broken loading facilities and supplementing the shortage, paving storage fields for use as container yards, improving access to the railway and road access to the port, and so forth. The total cost for these improvements was estimated at $28.4 million at 1996 prices.

The second stage (Short-Term Development Plan to the year 2005) includes a complete renovation of existing berths and the construction of two new berths. Loading facilities and container terminals will also be strengthened. Tugboats will be needed because large ships are expected to enter the port at this stage. Facilities for small ships will also be needed because of the increase of small ships for management and operation of the port. The total cost for improvements is estimated at $183.9 million (Table 28.3).

Regarding railway improvement, four-track rail between Hunchun transit station and Kamyshovaya transit station is planned, and it will be extended from Kamyshovaya transit station to Sukhanovka and further to Zarubino. As a result, transportation costs and time will be reduced by eliminating the need to transship. The Zarubino route will then be able to compete with the North Korean route, which does not need transshipment. The final stage (Long-Term Development Plan to the year 2010) requires that two new container berths be built to increase container freight. Transshipment facilities will be improved. New rails in Zarubino

TABLE 28.2
Forecasts of Northeastern China's Trade: Freight Volume Structure
(in thousands of tons)

Year	Total	Agricultural Products	Timber	Wood Chips	Food	General Goods	Metal Products	Containers
1998 (estimate)	750	0	130	10	10	0	600	0
1999 (forecasts)	1,390	120	130	100	10	170	610	240
2000	1,770	210	140	120	10	250	620	420
2001	1,910	230	140	130	10	270	640	490
2002	2,060	240	140	140	10	300	650	570
2003	2,220	260	140	150	10	320	660	660
2004	2,380	270	150	170	10	350	680	760
2005	2,560	280	150	180	10	370	690	880
2006	2,760	300	150	190	10	400	700	1,010
2007	2,970	310	160	200	10	420	720	1,150
2008	3,200	320	160	210	10	450	730	1,310
2009	3,440	340	160	220	10	470	750	1,490
2010	3,710	350	160	240	10	500	760	1,690
2011	4,010	360	170	250	10	520	780	1,920
2012	4,330	380	170	250	10	550	790	2,170
Packaging Origin		Bag, Carton China	Bulk Russia	Bulk China	Carton Russia	Bulk China, Russia	Bulk Russia	Container China

Source: Compiled from Economic Research Institute for Northeast Asia, *Study Report for the Zarubino Port Development Program, Zarubino Port Feasibility Study Working Group.* (Tokyo: Economic Research Institute for Northeast Asia, 1996), p. 5.

TABLE 28.3
Zarubino Port Development Plan: An Outline

	Phase I		Phase II
	Urgent Improvement	Short-Term	Long-Term
Estimated amount cargo	1.77 million tons	2.97 million tons	4.33 million tons
Expected year	1999–2000	2005	2010
Containers	42,000 TEU*	114,000 TEU*	215,000 TEU*
Existing berths	Repair, corrosion-proof	Expand, deepen - 11.5 m	...
New berth	...	2 (240 x 12 m)	...
New container berths	...	...	2 (480 x 12 m)
Open storage	Pave	Pave	Completely pave
Refrigerated warehouse	Maintain	Maintain	Move and construct
Shed	...	2	Behind cargo berths
Container yard	320 slots	690 slots	More than 1,000 slots
Container crane	...	...	2
Jib crane	Repair existing cranes	4	...
Mobile crane	10	5	18
Area for small ships	...	230 x 5 m	...
Central office	Move	Expand	...
Access roads	Improve north road	...	Add a route
Cost†	$28.4 million	$183.9 million	...

*20-foot equivalent units
†Cost includes railway improvement and construction

Source: Economic Research Institute for Northeast Asia.

will be constructed and new reserve lines at Sukhanovka station will be put in place. Costs for this stage have not been estimated.

A financial and economic analysis of the urgent and short-term development plans was conducted to assess the profitability of the project. The purpose of the analysis was to examine the project's financial internal rate of return (FIRR) and the financial soundness of port management. The analysis showed an FIRR of 11.5 percent. This exceeds the expected interest rate of 6.0 percent, assuming borrowing from public financial institutions. Regarding the financial soundness of the port management, indicators of profitability, financial repayment security, and management efficiency are all at reasonable levels. The project is financially feasible, however, the FIRR appears to be slightly low to attract private enterprise investments.

The economic effects were also evaluated (by calculating the economic internal rate of return [EIRR] based on the cost-benefit analysis method). First, transportation costs will be reduced by using the Zarubino route, because the distance of land transportation will be shortened compared to the transportation route through Dalian. Reduction in transportation costs from Yanji, the center of the main user area, is expected to be $613 million for 34 years from 1997 to 2030. The present value of reduction is $188 million, discounted by 8 percent of the annual rate.

Russia will benefit from income from port facility charges, taxes, and railway transportation fees. In addition, there will be multiplier effects of employment opportunities and income, investment inducement effects, and other macroeconomic spillover effects. The net benefit for the Russian Far East is estimated at roughly $150 million. This is 31.1 percent as EIRR, which is very high. If the same spillover effects are evaluated for all of Russia, the net benefit is $178 million, and EIRR reaches 47.6 percent. These figures, however, do not include long-term effects, such as value added from increases of production in port-related industries, direct and indirect economic effects from newly launched industries, and effects on regional development.

The results of the economic analysis show that Russia and other countries will benefit for a long time from the development of Zarubino Port. It can also be said that benefits from the port are too broad to collect directly in the form of user charges and fees. If private enterprises develop the port and try to recover the construction costs by using fees and charges, favorable treatment, such as low interest public loans, will be a prerequisite. Transportation infrastructure is considered a public good. Even in many capitalist countries infrastructure is part of the public sector. In the former Soviet Union ports were owned by the state. After the collapse of the Soviet Union, privatization progressed perhaps too rapidly, and as a result investment in public goods has been insufficient. This is a problem for Zarubino Port.

The Zarubino Port development project should be implemented. However, the project requires improvements. The Zarubino route must have advantageous or at least equal conditions to other routes (Dalian and North Korea routes) to secure the amount of freight estimated in the feasibility study. Improvements include custom duty exemptions for transit freight, abolishment or reduction of charges on transit freight, simplification of customs clearance procedures for people and goods, making railway and port fees more competitive, and raising port management and facilities to international standards.

CONCLUSION

Enthusiasm for Zarubino Port development is palpable in both the Russian Far East and Northeast China. However, to make the improvements mentioned above, the cooperation of the Chinese and Russian central governments is needed. If a project is not given priority by the central government, it is not likely that requests for governmental guarantees for investment, favorable treatment, and foreign aid will be raised. The project has received scant attention in both Moscow and Beijing. For example, there is no reference to Zarubino Port development in Russia's Long-Term Program for the Development of the Russian Far East and Trans-Baikal Region. In China, only 11 words in the Ninth Five-year Plan are devoted to the Tumen River Area Development Program, which includes Zarubino Port. The project is neglected because it involves an area far from the capitals of two huge countries, and development of Zarubino Port is a relatively small-scale project. The central governments in both Russia and China are not yet aware of the multiple long-term social and economic benefits that this small project in a remote border area can bring.

If the Zarubino project is implemented the benefits will be felt throughout the Northeast Asian subregion. The project, therefore, will be promoted best through a multilateral cooperation framework. At a minimum the framework should include Russia, China, and Japan. South Korea, however, may also reap substantial benefits from improved trade potentials with China and the Russian Far East. With the involvement of these four countries, Zarubino project development could become a new model for multilateral economic cooperation in Northeast Asia.

(Russia, Japan)

29   Q22 P33
F14

The Politics of Fishery
Alexander M. Kurmazov and Igor V. Kazakov

Traditionally, for both Russia and Japan fishery has played an important role as an industry and a source of protein. By the end of the 19th century the development of the industry and growing demand for marine resources pushed Japanese fishermen to new areas beyond their coastal waters and made them pioneers in distant water fisheries in the northern Pacific Ocean. In 1899 the central government of Japan introduced the law On Encouragement of Fishery in Distant Waters that gave special attention to development of salmon stocks in northern parts of the Pacific Ocean.

Russian distant fishery in Pacific waters started to increase during World War II after the Russian domestic wartime supply of food was imperiled in the Atlantic Ocean, Baltic Sea, and Black Sea areas. Traditional areas of Russian fishery in the European part of the country were in the war zone. To supply the army with food, including fish, considerable investment was made to expand the undeveloped coastal fishery in the Japan Sea and Sea of Okhotsk.

POLITICAL AND LEGAL FRAMEWORK

Not surprisingly, the first half of the 20th century was a period of difficulty and changing relations between Japan and Russia, intertwined as they were in conflicts and disputes over Sakhalin and the Kuril Islands. There were, however, consistent attempts on both sides to settle fishery interests on the basis of legal arrangements. Bilateral treaties between

Japan and Russia concluded in St. Petersburg in 1875 (article 6, on the transfer of the rights over Sakhalin Island to Russia), in Portsmouth in 1905 (article 11), the intergovernmental convention on fishery signed in 1907,[1] and agreements on fishery of 1928 and 1932 gave Japan extensive rights to fishery resources in coastal areas of the Russian Far East.

The situation has changed radically in favor of Russia after the end of World War II, considerably helping postwar normalization and reopening of diplomatic relations. After the surrender of Japan in 1945, Russian fishery rights and maritime borders were well protected (for the first time in modern history), and new norms in using the resources of the sea were gradually adopted. The 1956 declaration, in fact, was directly linked to bilateral relations in fishery and was followed by the special agreement on fishery with the Hokkaido Fishermen's Association (1963) and the intergovernmental agreement on fishery (1975).

Difficult bilateral relations between Moscow and Tokyo did not really prevent the two sides from cooperation in fishery and related matters. In 1963 Moscow agreed to allow seaweed (*laminaria*) harvesting near Signalniy Island. However, the agreement on *laminaria* became void in 1977 after the 200-mile exclusive economic zone (EEZ) was introduced. Intergovernmental agreements were worked out between Japan and Russia on fishery in the 200-mile zones (1984) and on cooperation in salmon fishery (1985). As a result of a subsequent reduction in mutual fishing quotas as well as the discontinuation of drift net fishing Japan's interests shifted to the Russian 200-mile EEZ.

More recently the level of reciprocal quotas has decreased mainly because of a lack of interest on the part of Russians to fish in the Japanese EEZ, and some extraordinary measures had to be taken to preserve the bilateral fishery agreement. However, this has helped the relations in other areas, such as salmon reproduction based on equipment and supplies from Japan and technical services and training of Russian personnel in Japan. Other forms of compensation included research vessel and simulator transfers to Russia and market promotion for Russian products in Japan. Annual negotiations on Russian origin salmon fishing are complicated. Although the Russian side tries to get higher compensation, Japanese fishermen want to pay as little as possible and to upgrade the composition of the quota by asking for a higher share of expensive species, such as red and chum salmon. For the last 5–6 years prices for salmon were very low to the disadvantage of Russia.

COMPLEMENTARITY OF INTERESTS

The cooperation in fisheries that has gradually developed between Russia and Japan must be seen from the perspective of national interests and needs. Although marine resources are a major part of the food supply in Japan, the economy of the coastal and island regions of Far Eastern Russia also depends on fishery.

In 1996 Russia's total catch in the Pacific was more than 3.2 million tons or 68 percent of the total volume of production in the Russian fishing industry. The share of fish and fish products in the protein supply in Russia was estimated at 28 percent; in Japan this share is as high as 39 percent. Japan's self-sufficiency in fish and fish products is about 59 percent; this naturally creates a demand for imports, including supplies from Russia. Moreover, since 1992 Japan stopped drift net fishing in open areas of the northwest Pacific, and access to the 200-mile EEZ of Russia became more important.

In both Japan and Russia a relative decline in production volumes has taken place since the late 1980s when both countries were the world leaders in fishery with a share in the world output estimated at 20 to 25 percent. In Japan, the cumulative catch in 1996 was about 7 million tons, about 6 million tons less than in 1988 when it reached its peak. In Russia, too, the official physical volume of fishery has declined from its peak of about 6 million tons in the late 1980s.

The factors behind this situation include the rapid aging of the fishermen in Japan. From 1991 to 1995, the share of 60-year-olds and older increased from 30 percent to 38.5 percent, while the 15–38-years age group shrunk from 21 percent to 18 percent. Because of this factor and the 200-mile zone limits introduced by many coastal states, Japanese fishermen had to reduce their operations in distant waters, which had given them about 20 percent of the total catch in the 1980s.

In Russia the distant water fishery (which provided more than 40 percent of the total catch) is facing numerous problems. By 1995 more than 75 percent of the fishery industry was privatized, but without traditional technical and financial support from the state it lost much of its capacity to operate in the open ocean or even in the distant 200-mile zones of other countries. More than 60 percent of the fishing boats need replacement.

The population of the Far East of Russia is only about 7.6 million, and only 4–5 percent of the total catch can be consumed in the region. Remoteness and rising costs of transportation added to the difficulties experienced by the industry and have increased the role of export to Northeast Asia and Japan in particular. However, the decentralization and commercialization of the Far Eastern fishery industry were accompanied by radical changes in the structure of catches in favor of valuable and exportable species, such as salmon, crab, shrimp, and so forth. Japan has benefited from this new situation as the closest and prime market for Russian catches. However, because the expansion of physical volume of exports to Japan is difficult, better market access requires improvement in the range and quality of Russian products. This can be achieved through bilateral interindustry linkages. Fleet modernization, development of processing facilities, and production based on Japanese local standards are needed to compete with other exporters and domestic producers.

MUTUAL CONCERNS

Russian oversight and law enforcement in fishery business need improvement. Irregularities in trade operations with Japan have become quite alarming. According to Russian trade statistics, in 1995 Russia exported to Japan 7,316 tons of crabs and shellfish worth $85.6 million. Japanese data, however, suggest that the actual physical volume was 56,800 tons at an estimated value of more than $600 million.

The discrepancy was created by Russian fishing vessels entering Japanese ports directly from open sea areas in violation of Japanese laws, such as On the Regulation of Fisheries by Foreigners and others. Cooperation with various Japanese agencies, therefore, is indispensable. Procedures in Japan demand that a permit to leave the Russian port be submitted to Japanese customs officers. However, the validity of the documents submitted by Russian crews was not questioned until recently. Furthermore, Japanese customs officers reportedly check documents rather than the actual amount of cargo, and some experts estimate that the total undeclared imports of fish and marine products may be in excess of $1.5 billion. The initial reluctance of Japanese authorities to cooperate with Russian law enforcement agencies recently gave way to first contacts mostly because of growing concern over a rapid depletion of the resource base.

There is no legal framework in Russia to regulate exports of marine products from the 200-mile EEZ. This means that fishing vessels have no obligation to call on Russian ports for customs clearance of loads of fish and marine products for export if they are not caught in territorial waters. Moreover, unlike in many other countries, there is no basic law in Russia that qualifies fishing operations as not only the mere extraction of catches from the sea but also the transfer of products from fishing boats to cargo ships and the transportation of catches. Therefore, a significant amount of fish goes for export undetected by Russian customs. In addition to illegal crab harvesting and trade that threatens the stock, the fishery industry became the most criminalized part of bilateral economic relations.

Currently bilateral activities related to the rational use of biological resources of the sea focus on salmon and crab. Artificial reproduction of salmon is rather well developed and can be considered a success story in bilateral cooperation in fishery and environmental protection. However, in Russia the cost of these reproduction efforts is rapidly rising, which clearly contradicts the interests of Japanese fishermen. In 1983–88 the maximum annual catch of live crabs by Japanese fishermen was only 351 metric tons, but in 1992 the supply of crab reached 2,058 tons mainly because of the rapid expansion of poaching in Russian waters adjacent to Hokkaido and the southern Kurils.

On the positive side, the salmon agreement serves as a key source of financial and technical support for reproduction of salmon of Russian origin. The cost of hatchery equipment delivered from Japan in Russia annually is estimated at $5–6 million. The agreement also provides for leasing Japanese fishing boats, technical modernization of the Russian fishing fleet, and coastal infrastructure. The first fishery joint venture Pilenga Godo (Sakhalinskaya and Kamchatskaya oblasts) serves as an example of mutually beneficial cooperation in salmon hatchery.

Both Russia and Japan participate in international activities on resource management in the Sea of Okhotsk and Bering Sea. Bilateral cooperation in the sphere of rational use and preservation of stocks of salmon in the northern part of the Pacific Ocean is supplemented by participation in a quadrilateral convention on the conservation of anadromous stocks in the North Pacific. The resources of the Kuril Islands area could serve as a testing ground, a major incentive, and a model for new types of bilateral cooperation in fishery and sustainable development. In this context, productive negotiations on fishery in the waters around the southern Kurils positively influenced both bilateral relations and regional cooperation between Japan and Russia in Northeast Asia.[2]

FISHERY AND NORTHEAST ASIAN COOPERATION

The Northwest Pacific accounts for about 45 percent of the total world catch. Protection measures aimed at the reduction and regulation of fishery must not be solely unilateral or bilateral. Most of the species to be protected belong to straddling stocks, and their fishing areas are exposed to many countries. Fishery activities are particularly intense in the Japan Sea and East China Sea. The stocks of major species such as Alaskan pollack, in the Sea of Okhotsk are under pressure from overfishing and tend to decline. In the Bering Sea an international moratorium on pollack fishing has already been announced.

Russia and Japan have to complement their bilateral efforts with a multilateral framework and links within existing international organizations. For example, the problem of illegal fishing and sales is acute not only in Japan-Russia trade. Russian fishery exports to China are close to 500,000 tons, and South Korea is perhaps as important as Japan in terms of sales. To a certain degree the future of regional fishery depends on how closely and effectively Russia and Japan cooperate. Their coordinated efforts could be particularly significant in the context of the United Nations Convention of the Law of the Sea (UNCLOS), which was recently joined by Japan, South Korea, and China and was ratified by Russia in 1997, 20 years after the 200-mile zone was introduced. Japan reciprocated with its own zone in 1977 but applied its regulations only to Russia.

Currently there is no international body to regulate and manage fishery activities in the Japan Sea. The marine resources of this area remain threatened by overfishing, poaching, environmental pollution, and interstate conflict over fishery rights. Joint management and development of the marine resources at the regional level may be needed. Necessary conditions for regional sustainable fishery must be created and maintained.

There is also a potential for conflict and tensions in Northeast Asia arising over fishery issues. The existing treaties between Japan and China and Japan and South Korea were based on the freedom of fishery principle without any limits on catches or quotas. For Japan the situation was not an easy one, because after the UNCLOS was ratified Tokyo was unable to apply new regulations without making changes in national legislation and the bilateral agreements on fishery with China and South Korea based on the freedom of fishery principle.

In 1997 Japan introduced a new system of Total Available Catch for the most important species[3] and introduced limits for each of them, designating certain volumes for Japanese fishermen only. The remaining part can be divided among applicants, including China, South Korea, and Russia. Russia, therefore, has become a competitor for China and South Korea in the Japanese zone and their relationship may become more complex being aggravated by the territorial problems with Japan, on the one hand, and China and South Korea, on the other hand.[4]

CONCLUSION

Well-regulated fishery and sustainable development of the industry should be based on effective national regulations and international cooperation efforts. In this context the Russian government's decision to abolish the State Committee on Fishery and transfer its functions to other ministries and departments was a mistake. The management of the marine biological resources of Russia does not necessarily suit some industrial enterprises that benefit from uncontrolled and unrestricted fishing, especially of crabs and salmon.[5]

This reorganization in Russia took place in parallel with a strengthening of fishing administrations in South Korea and China. In Japan, also, there were changes in the fishery administration aimed at system strengthening and more efficient control over fishery activities, according to the UNCLOS. The decree of the Russian president dated January 17, 1997, and the federal program World Oceans point out the problems of the Russian fishery industry, but new laws are needed to solve these problems.

Another issue is that fishery-related environmental concerns both in Russia and Japan are potentially intertwined with the exploration and development of offshore oil and gas deposits of Sakhalin. The potential damage created by oil and gas development is usually underestimated. Oil and gas development projects may affect large fishing and breeding grounds on the eastern shores of the island. The *Nakhodka* tanker oil spill (January 1997) in the Sea of Japan gave rise to strong negative feeling in Japan. This issue considerably weakened Russia's negotiating position during talks on salmon fishing quotas in March 1997.

NOTES

1.   The convention on fishery adopted on July 15 (July 28 according to the old Russian calendar), 1907, confirmed the rights of Japanese fishing entities to unlimited use of resources in coastal areas of the Russian Far East.

2.   Under the agreement drawn up in December 1997 as a result of 13 rounds of talks, Japanese fishing boats will be allowed to operate within 12 nautical miles of territorial waters of the Russian Federation to catch a total of 2,252 tons of several kinds of fish in 1998 in waters around the islands of Kunashir, Iturup, and Shikotan and the Habomai group of islets. In exchange, the Hokkaido Fisheries Association and local fishing cooperatives will pay about $170,000 to support fishing resources preservation efforts, and they will transfer $120,000 worth of fishing equipment.

3.   The six most important species were covered, including saury, sardine, mackerel, jack-mackerel, pollack, and squid surume, and certain limits on each of these were established.

4.   The territories in dispute are, Senkaku Islands in the East China Sea and Takeshima Islands in the Sea of Japan, respectively.

5.   Concern was expressed by the governments of Norway, the United States, and Japan, with whom Russia is closely connected in the area of fishery.

30

Environment and Cooperation
Karla S. Smith

When Japan and the Soviet Union concluded a bilateral environmental protection cooperation agreement in April 1991, both were readying themselves to take a leadership role at the United Nations Conference on Environment and Development, the Rio Summit. Under the thawing Cold War conditions of the time, the importance of the environment, at least in the rhetoric of Japanese and Soviet politicians, was raised to the level of economic and national security.[1] In practice, however, stated ambitions jointly to tackle environmental threats were pursued through the 1990s only half-heartedly with modest results, except in moments of crisis. At the end of the decade many obstacles to closer cooperation remain unremoved, but the slow steps in earlier efforts have picked up speed encouraged by an acquired experience and ever louder local, regional, and international demands for action.

This chapter reviews Japan-Russia environmental cooperation from early 1991 to early 1998, referring in particular to the political motivations for bilateral collaboration as well as the economic, institutional, and financial obstacles to effective project implementation. The author proposes that environmental cooperation between Japan and Russia can be divided into three phases characterized by well-intended but weak attempts to establish a basis for systematic and proactive cooperation; reactive responses to environmental threats and crises; and new opportunities arising from a favorable political environment, increased capacity of governmental and nongovernmental institutions, and international commitments.

UNEVEN PROGRESS

On the Japanese side, Prime Ministers Nobuo Takeshita, Toshiki Kaifu, and Kiichi Miyazawa kept environmental issues on Japan's international and bilateral foreign policy agendas through the early 1990s. Their enthusiasm was matched first by Soviet President Mikhail Gorbachev, who from the late 1980s devoted special attention to international ecological security,[2] and then by Russian President Boris Yeltsin, strongly influenced by the vocal Alexei Yablokov, state advisor on ecology, and Victor Danilov-Danilyan, minister for Environment Protection and Natural Resources with close ties to reformist Yegor Gaidar.

The backdrop to the environmental agreement of 1991 was, thus, a growing environmental consciousness, the potential for improved political relations as a result of Gorbachev's perestroika, and subsequently, Yeltsin's reformist rise to power. Interest in cooperation remained strong through 1992 when Japan hosted the first ever Northeast Asia conference on environment and Russia published its first environmental white paper. During perestroika the status of environmental institutions had risen suddenly, and the momentum continued in the early years of Yeltsin's first term. Authority over resources management gave the Russian Ministry of Environment and Natural Resources significant power and leverage. The strongly worded Law on Environmental Protection (1992) and the inclusion of three articles (9, 42, 58) relating to environment in the Russian Constitution (1993) provided a progressive legal framework for protection.

However, the initiatives of the Ministry of Environment from the beginning encountered opposition from energy, resources extraction, industry, and military interests, and the legal framework for environmental protection lacked mechanisms and funding for adequate enforcement. As Russia sank deeper in economic crisis, both official and public interest in environmental issues waned. The power of the environment ministry diminished to such an extent that it was stripped of much of its authority over natural resources management, and the budget for environmental protection was reportedly lowered to less than 0.1 percent of the gross national product.[3] (Eventually the environment ministry was abolished and replaced in 1996 with the State Committee for Environmental Protection.) With a dwindling budget the ministry did not have the resources to implement the agreement with Japan on environmental cooperation. Moreover, the chaotic political situation in Russia during 1992 and 1993, dissenting views on Russia's foreign policy, and renewed debate between Japan and Russia over a peace treaty and the Northern Territories precluded progress in bilateral cooperation.

REACTIVE RESPONSES

It was not until January 1994 (after Japan and Russia signed the Tokyo Declaration in 1993) that the first meeting of the Japan-Russia Environmental Protection Joint Committee was held in Tokyo. The meeting discussed potential joint projects to be implemented under the bilateral agreement. By that time, however, bilateral environmental cooperation had already moved from the proactive and systematic to the reactive and crisis-oriented.

Two events pushed cooperation in this direction. First, in April 1993 the Russian government released a report detailing the Soviet and Russian practice of nuclear waste disposal at sea and plans to continue dumping in Far Eastern Seas until 1997 for lack of storage facilities. The report highlighted the need to help Russia secure alternative means of disposal so it could proceed with decommissioning nuclear submarines and fulfill commitments to arms reduction agreements. Thus, during Yeltsin's visit to Japan in October 1993 Japan and Russia signed a bilateral agreement for dismantling nuclear weapons, and soon after a joint committee was formed. Japanese assistance in the management of nuclear waste falls under the general rubric of environmental cooperation, therefore, since 1993 environmental cooperation remains most extensive (and expensive) in this area.

Second, in January 1997 a major oil spill in the Sea of Japan from the Russian tanker *Nakhodka* compelled Japan and Russia to cooperate in the cleanup and to further bilateral and regional efforts for collaboration in marine pollution prevention and response. In the interim the bilateral environmental agreement continued to be neglected, and the joint committee for its implementation has not met again since 1994. Only one small joint research project on the environment of the Sea of Japan was conducted under this agreement.

NUCLEAR DISMANTLING
AND WASTE MANAGEMENT

The Japanese government announced in April 1993 that it would provide approximately $70 million for the safe dismantling of nuclear weapons in Russia. Yeltsin promised at that time and later during his October visit to Tokyo that Russia would refrain from further disposal at sea. Only days after his visit, however, the Pacific Fleet resumed dumping into the Sea of Japan.

Despite the results of bilateral and international studies indicating that the dumping did not have a severe environmental impact in the Sea of Japan, and despite the fact that Japan in the past was censured for its own disposal of radioactive waste at sea, the Russian incident received extensive media coverage and had a strong negative effect on Japanese public opinion toward Russia. Not surprisingly, then, when the Japan-Russia Joint Committee for Cooperation and Assistance in the dismantling of nuclear weapons held its first meeting in December 1993 it determined that finding a solution to the problem of ocean dumping was an urgent priority.

Cooperation in the dismantling of nuclear weapons and nuclear waste disposal have become protracted and complex processes. Japan's original offer to provide a tanker for temporary storage of liquid radioactive waste was rejected in January 1994. A second offer (based on a Russian request) to construct a liquid waste treatment plant in the Russian Far East was also rejected. Both sides eventually signed an implementation agreement in August 1994 for the construction of a low-level liquid waste floating treatment plant that, upon completion, will be moored at Bolshoi Kamen, near Vladivostok. From the point of view of Japanese officials, the project has had to overcome a number of difficulties in Russia, including obtaining parts and government permits; a lack of coordination among central, regional, and local authorities; and insufficient information on the amount of waste to be stored and treated.[4]

To match Japan's assistance with Russia's needs, Japanese officials have repeatedly requested minimal information on the process of dismantlement and the amount of waste. They remain frustrated by the lack of transparency of the Russian military. The situation remains sensitive in light of treason and espionage charges against Russian officers rumored to have exposed potential nuclear and ecological disasters involving Russia's nuclear submarines. Insufficient consideration of local public concerns by central authorities also created project delays. Residents of the Vladivostok area have voiced worries over mooring the treatment plant in their waters. Following a referendum, local authorities finally approved the treatment plant in October 1997. As originally proposed, the project should have been completed by then.

The project itself is subject to commentary in Russia. The facilities are being built by foreign enterprises and, thus, may provide little or no economic benefit or capacity building. There are also worries that an increased ability to store and process nuclear waste may encourage imports of radioactive wastes from foreign countries. These worries, coupled with knowledge of Japan's rapid domestic waste build-up and insufficient storage facilities, have created suspicion over the intentions behind Japan's cooperation, particularly because the Russian government decided in September 1995 to accept spent nuclear fuel from abroad. Furthermore, the Far Eastern Branch of the Russian Academy of Sciences has suggested that its own technologies for low level liquid radioactive waste treatment are more appropriate and cost effective than Japan's.[5] Russian central and regional authorities, however, appear disposed to use Japanese technologies. Finally, both sides recognize that the floating treatment plant may be only the first step in necessary cooperation given that this project does not address the more serious problem of solid waste.

MARINE PROTECTION

Protection of the marine environment was a priority for Japan even before the Russian tanker *Nakhodka* oil spill of January 1997 in the Sea of Japan. However, this accident, the second worst in Japanese waters, kept Japan-Russia environmental cooperation on the crisis-oriented and reactive track it embarked on in 1993. The accident fouled the shores of ten prefectures (from Shimane to Akita), caused a reported $20 billion worth of damages, and again dampened Japanese public opinion of Russia. Russia's response to the accident was not well received in Japan. The Japanese government's chief cabinet secretary, Seiroku Kajiyama, hinted at Russia's irresponsibility, and the Russian report on the cause of the accident was privately described as "ridiculous" by Japan's Ministry of Transport officials.[6] Criticism is partly valid and partly a reflection of lack of faith in Russia's concern.

To a certain degree the censure of Russia may have also served to deflect strong domestic criticism of the Japanese government's delayed and uncoordinated response to the oil spill. Japanese government officials later acknowledged that Japan's emergency response system is unclear, its cleanup capacities neglect the Sea of Japan, contingency plans and equipment are inadequate, and there was a lack of coordination among governmental agencies.[7]

The *Nakhodka* accident thus served as an impetus for Japan to review its own response system, and it underscored the need for greater bilateral coordination with Russia and for a regional system for prevention and emergency responses. Japan's Maritime Safety Agency is already involved in exchange of information and marine pollution prevention activities with the U.S. Coast Guard (since 1990) and the Korean Maritime and Port Administration (since 1994). Russia has bilateral marine protection agreements with Finland, Norway, and the United States. Russia is also party to regional conventions for marine protection of the Baltic Sea (1974) and the Black Sea (1993). However, cooperation between Japan and Russia began only in 1996 when the Russian Marine Pollution Control and Salvage Administration and the Japan Maritime Safety Agency held their first experts' meeting. As of yet, there are no concrete plans for training or joint exercises. However, mechanisms for exchange and cooperation at various levels are being created and strengthened.

At the multilateral level, the Northwest Pacific Action Plan (NOW-PAP)[8] (initiated by the United Nations Environmental Program as part of its Regional Seas Program) has moved to a practical stage. An action plan was adopted by the member countries in 1994, and a detailed program document was approved in 1996. The activities of NOWPAP include prevention of marine pollution, protection of the coastal environments, and harmonization of laws and regulations. NOWPAP's activities have opened channels for exchange of data, experience, and training among administrators and experts. The Japan Ministry of Transport and the Japan Maritime Safety Agency, for example, now have direct contact with Russian counterparts in the Marine Pollution Control and Salvage Administration and with the Emergency Response Department of Vladivostok. The ministries of foreign affairs are no longer intermediaries for all exchange.

From early 1997 the environment began to figure prominently in local Japan Sea rim initiatives for cooperation, largely as a response to the *Nakhodka* oil spill and its effect on the prefectures along Japan's western coast. Shimane, Tottori, Ishikawa, Toyama, and Niigata prefectures incorporated environmental issues into Northeast Asia cooperation plans and conferences. Collaboration with Russia on marine and coastal pollution prevention figured prominently. Toyama is attempting to establish itself as the region's forerunner in environmental cooperation. In 1997 Toyama opened the Northwest Pacific Area Environmental Cooperation Center, held an environmental summit of local governments in the Northwest Pacific Region, and hosted a NOWPAP forum as well as a meeting of Japanese and Russian marine environmental experts. It is Hokkaido, however, that has been most successful in cooperation. In the wake of the *Nakhodka* oil spill, the governors of Hokkaido, Sakhalin, and Alaska reached a voluntary agreement to cooperate in oil spill emergency preparedness and response. The catalyst for this was a common concern for the marine environment (primarily for fisheries) while plans for oil and gas development in Sakhalin progress. This agreement is an excellent example of the ability of local actors to move ahead of national governments in international cooperation. Although for the most part local initiatives for Japan-Russia cooperation are new and progress is slow they represent an important diversification of contacts and a willingness by local governments to experiment with environmental cooperation, an area that until recently was the preserve of the central government.

MECHANISMS AND INSTITUTIONAL ARRANGEMENTS

Despite new contacts and initiatives, some of the greatest obstacles to more and more successful environmental cooperation between Japan and Russia are the limited mechanisms and weak institutional arrangements for exchange. Japanese and Chinese officials from environment and other ministries and agencies meet annually in a joint committee dedicated specifically to advancing environmental cooperation. Japanese and Russian officials, however, met only once in this capacity in 1994.

Project and program selection and promotion are primarily the responsibility of foreign affairs ministries, but the Russian Ministry of Foreign Affairs has shown little interest in proposing environmental projects to Japan. Having lost much of its status, political power, and budget during the 1996 governmental reform, the Russian State Committee for Environment Protection (previously a ministry) is unable to promote its own projects within the Ministry of Foreign Affairs.

The general view is that the greatest potential for Japan-Russia cooperation is in marine environment and resources protection and in forestry resources management. However, the state committee has not developed concrete project proposals, and officials do not yet have strong ties with counterparts in Japan's Environment Agency to consult in proposal preparations. Japan's Environment Agency is also financially weak, and in international cooperation its resources, capacities, and projects are concentrated in developing countries, particularly China and Southeast Asian states. Lacking experience in collaboration with Russia and knowledge of Russia's environmental problems, officials are disinclined to investigate possibilities or propose projects, particularly without prompting from the Ministry of Foreign Affairs.

Even if officials were inspired to initiate projects, cooperation with Russia would be hindered by inadequate and inflexible financial assistance arrangements. Russian scientists and officials participating in small projects with Japan are at pains to find the resources to complete their part of the work and are often unable to meet the standards of their Japanese partners.

Joint projects between Japan and China, for example, are spared similar problems because Japanese official development assistance (ODA) program provisions help cover local costs of cooperation on the Chinese side. In fact, cooperation with China will be further promoted in 1998 through the extension of loans at an interest rate of 0.75 percent for projects designed to address environmental problems. Under Japanese guidelines Russia is ineligible for ODA or the new loans.

Environmental cooperation between Japan and Russia, therefore, would benefit from special ODA financial arrangements similar to those of the U.S. Agency for International Development, which distributes U.S. government money in the form of grants for environmental protection. This type of system allows greater flexibility in the content of projects and the eligibility of recipients. Through similar grants Japan's Environment Agency, for example, could work not only with government counterparts in Moscow but also with regional and local governments, research institutes, nongovernmental organizations (NGOs), and individual experts.

CONCERN AND CAPACITY

A convergence of priorities and a similar level of concern greatly enhance prospects for success.[9] At the bilateral governmental level, both Japan and Russia must be sufficiently interested in addressing an environmental issue and finding specific solutions to make joint action possible and effective. Japan's priorities in international cooperation are climate change, air and water pollution, and the preservation of the natural environment, including forests and biodiversity. Its main geographic focus is the Asia-Pacific region.[10] Water pollution issues include improvement of water and sewage systems as well as coping with marine pollution.

Russia's priorities are biodiversity and forests conservation, climate change, and the protection of the marine environment.[11] Generally, there is a convergence of priorities and the Japan-Russia environment agreement provides a legal basis for joint action. What are lacking are a common approach to these priorities and a political willingness to act, a manifestation of a low level of concern among key political actors.

Forest and biodiversity conservation serve as an example of this. Russia has 22 percent of the world's forests and 50 percent of the world's boreal and temperate forests. Described as "the earth's greatest northern landscape,"[12] Siberia and the Russian Far East are home to most of these forests and their unique systems and species. These vast and relatively intact ecosystems present one of the last opportunities to conserve areas large enough to allow ecological processes and wildlife populations to fluctuate and develop naturally. The forests of Siberia and the Russian Far East also act as sinks for about 40 billion tons of carbon dioxide (half as much as the Amazon) and play a critical and underexamined role in climate stability.[13] The Russian government has issued a series of decrees and laws designed to protect forests and biodiversity, but its capacity to enforce this protection is seriously hindered by the economic crisis.

Japan's Environment Agency has shown little interest in including Russia's forests in its agenda for international cooperation, despite placing forests and biodiversity conservation among its top priorities. Concern and capacity on the Japanese side lie at the heart of the matter. Japan's appetite for tropical timber, particularly Southeast Asian timber, has earned it international criticism. Well aware of this, the focus of its international cooperation in forests and biodiversity is Southeast Asia. Furthermore, the Japanese approach (partly based on experience and capacities) is geared toward technological solutions and reforestation rather than conservation. Japan's forests priority is, thus, narrowly defined, and its approach is inflexible and incompatible with Russia's conservation-focused system of protection.

At the government level on the Russian side, too, the level of concern is questionable. The greatest threat to the forests and biodiversity of Siberia and the Russian Far East is careless timber exploitation. Inefficient and unwise cutting, transporting, and processing practices result in a 40–60 percent waste of all timber cut.[14]

The World Bank and independent experts, citing problems with pricing, taxation, legislation, accounting, and environmental management, have stressed the urgent need to restructure the Russian forest sector.[15] The Russian government, however, has been loath to institute changes, reflecting not only the power of timber interests relative to environmental protection groups but also the government's disposition toward short-term economic strategies at the expense of long-term sustainable economic management.

Japan's indifference to the situation could be overlooked were it not the largest market for Russian wood products (mostly untreated logs). However, a growing international emphasis on the need to protect boreal and temperate forests may capture Japan's attention and increase its concern, especially in connection to the role of Russia's forests as carbon dioxide sinks, their influence on climate change, and Japan's commitment under the third session of the Conference of Parties to the UN Framework Convention on Climate Change (COP3).

There may be sufficient concern on both sides to make joint action in water pollution abatement successful. Through the Japan International Cooperation Agency, an ODA implementing agency, Japan has successfully conducted studies and implemented projects on water supply, sanitation, sewage works, and wastewater treatment in Thailand, the Philippines, Indonesia, and Mongolia. For environmental and health reasons, cities in the Russian Far East, too, greatly need Japan's assistance to replace or improve their water and sewage systems. The poor drinking water quality in Yuzhno-Sakhalinsk, for example, reportedly is the cause of rising cases of intestinal disease.

Marine pollution abatement and prevention are other potential areas for cooperation. Vladivostok bays are seriously polluted by the approximately 500,000 cubic meters of untreated wastewater that flows directly into them (less than 1 percent is treated). Heavy metals, including mercury, and oil also threaten the marine environment and human health. Cooperation in cleanup, pollution abatement, and prevention is well suited to Japan's technological approach and capacities. The main stumbling blocks in this case are the lack of institutional arrangements for financial transfer and the lack of experience on both sides in formulating Japan-Russia projects.

The symmetry of interests between Japan and Russia in marine pollution prevention and their declarations of concern in international forums may induce Japan to diversify and create more flexible financial and technology transfer mechanisms. At the 1997 UN General Assembly Special Session on Environment and Development the Japanese government committed itself to "strengthening measures to cope with significant maritime environmental pollution."[16] In 1997 the Russian president approved the concept of a federal environmental program on World Oceans.

In the Denver Summit of the Group of Eight communiqué (1997), Japan and Russia together with other member nations vowed to "work to ensure an effective and integrated effort to deal with key issues, including sustainable fishing, shipping, marine pollution from land-based and offshore activities, and oil spill prevention and emergency response . . . [and to] enhance cooperation in monitoring the ecology in the North Pacific."[17]

CREATING EFFECTIVE PARTNERSHIPS

Although there is progress, Japan-Russia environmental cooperation continues to be hindered by a weakness in links among relevant agencies, organizations, and individuals. Until the Japan-Russia Environmental Protection Joint Committee is revived, contacts and information exchange among experts and officials at various levels can be developed through new regional initiatives, such as NOWPAP.

At the government level two other regional forums, the Northeast Asia Conference on Environmental Cooperation (held annually since 1992) and the Senior Officials Meeting on Environmental Cooperation (since 1993), provide opportunities for discussion, networking, and project proposals.

Russia's membership in Asia-Pacific Economic Cooperation (APEC) from 1998 will ensure its participation in APEC's environment ministerial meetings, working groups, strategies, and networks, among them the APEC Cleaner Production Strategy, the Strategy for the Sustainability of the Marine Environment, and the Sustainable Cities Program of Action. These regional forums (NOWPAP in particular because it is the more advanced and APEC because it is the most demanding) also act as additional leverage to further bilateral cooperation.

Local government level contacts can lead to a better understanding of the needs and concerns of counterparts and to the identification of common goals. With commitment, local governments can implement projects themselves. On the Japanese side they are encouraged to do so in the national Basic Environment Plan. On the Russian side, given their difficult financial situation, the local governments of the Far East have little alternative than to seek international support to deal with environmental problems. At the Environmental Summit Meeting of Local Governments in the Northwest Pacific Region (1997), the Primorskiy Krai administration proposed the establishment of a Japan Sea rim ecological fund.

Kitakyushu City has proven that cooperation initiated at the local level can be successful. In 1993 Kitakyushu and the Chinese city of Dalian agreed jointly to design a comprehensive environmental plan for Dalian's development. The plan drew the attention of the Japanese central government, which then extended bilateral assistance to implement Kitakyushu-initiated projects. Cooperation with Russia has not reached that level; however, in late 1998 Hokkaido, Sakhalin, and Alaska successfully worked out what is, in essence, a regional government-level agreement to cooperate in an emergency response to an oil spill. In this case regional governments have forged ahead of mutilateral forums (NOW-PAP) as well as national governments. In addition, the Northwest Pacific Environment Cooperation Center of Toyama Prefecture has already started a research project on environmental awareness in Russia and joint projects on water quality monitoring. Ishikawa Prefecture is considering environmental technology transfers to Irkutsk. Hokkaido and Niigata are active in joint monitoring and protection of migratory birds. Musashino and Tama cities cooperated in building a watchtower for a wildlife reserve near Khabarovsk City in an effort to promote sister city relations.

In most cases, however, local government level cooperation between Japan and Russia still suffers from the same shortcomings as central government level cooperation: lack of links and experience in cooperation, limited knowledge of the other's environmental priorities, and lack of mechanisms for financial transfer. By creating partnerships with NGOs these shortcomings can be overcome. Many international and local NGOs already have established links with government agencies, research institutes and experts, private enterprises, and grant-making foundations. NGOs are often in touch with local needs and can work quickly, efficiently, and economically. Their funding mechanisms are more flexible, and they are better able to cross political boundaries in project implementation and policy recommendation.

The work of the Wild Bird Society of Japan (WBS-J) under the Japan-Russia Migratory Bird Protection Treaty provides an excellent example of creating effective partnerships with NGOs. With authority and partial funding from the Environment Agency, in the early 1990s WBS-J teamed up with the Japanese companies Yomiuri Shimbun, NTT, and NEC to conduct satellite tracking of migratory birds (Australia-Japan-Russia route). NEC joined the project because of its interest in using and developing small satellite transmitters. WBS-J succeeded in building a model partnership not only with the government and private sector on the Japanese side, but also with NGOs, scientists, and nature reserve managers in Russia. Well aware of the financial obstacles on the Russian side, WBS-J provided funding (through its own grants) for the local costs of joint research, thereby ensuring the project's success.

Undeterred by political obstacles, the WBS-J is also promoting joint ecological research on Kunashir Island. In partnership with scientists on Hokkaido, Sakhalin, Kunashir, and Alaska, WBS-J has held a series of symposia in Japan on nature conservation on Kunashir. In this way this NGO is promoting dialogue and exchange ahead of government action. WBS-J has presented a project proposal to the Japanese Ministry of Foreign Affairs and requested that the governments of Japan and Russia broaden the scope of visa free exchanges for the Northern Territories to include nature conservation and environment specialists.

THE FUTURE OF COOPERATION

Signs of a new Japan-Russia relationship began to appear in 1996.[18] They include a growing trust between Yeltsin and Hashimoto; a greater emphasis in Russian policy on relations with Asian neighbors; Russian support for a UN Security Council seat for Japan; Japan's support for Russia's membership in Group of Seven summits and APEC; Russia's positive response to the revision of United States–Japan Security Treaty guidelines; the signing of an agreement on the safe operation of Japanese fishing vessels; and cooperation on the conservation, rational utilization, and reproduction of marine resources.[19]

A major turning point in relations came in July 1997, when in a speech to the Japan Association of Corporate Executives in Tokyo, Hashimoto clearly delineated Japan's new multilayered approach toward Russia. This new approach was put to the test at the informal summit of November in Krasnoyarsk to positive results. By January 1998 Hashimoto, then press secretary for the Ministry of Foreign Affairs, declared that "Japan-Russia relations have truly become geared toward a genuine improvement. . . . [Japan is] happy to strengthen cooperation in various fields." Thus, through this multilayered approach a comprehensive framework for bilateral cooperation is being developed that encompasses security, energy, trade and investment, cultural exchange, and environment.[20]

The favorable political conditions of the late 1990s again present an opportunity to move environmental collaboration to the systematic and proactive track envisioned in 1991. The issues of nuclear waste management and marine protection (including marine resources management) will remain the two most prominent areas for environmental cooperation. What began as a crisis-oriented response to prevent further dumping of nuclear waste at sea and to clean up an oil spill has evolved into regular dialogue and new approaches to diplomacy.

Recent and future developments within both countries may induce further cooperation in other areas as well. In Russia a draft State Strategy for Sustainable Development, detailing approaches to solving environmental problems in close connection with social and economic interests is expected to be adopted.[21] This document attempts to bring Russia's policies in line with its commitment to international conventions, and it explicitly encourages cooperation with other countries.

Russia also has adopted specific federal programs on support for reserves and national parks (1995), biological diversity conservation (1996), and the conservation of the Amur tiger (1997). As for internal pressures, a major revival of the Russian NGO movement came about in December 1996 when the All-Russia Protection Society, Socio-Ecological Union, Russian Environmental Union, Russian Green Party, Federation of Independent Unions, and others together formed the Russian Environmental Movement to jointly promote environmental protection and cooperation.

In Japan administrative reform may elevate the Environment Agency to the status of a ministry in 2001. The change would not only raise its image but would also give it greater authority over the administration of environmental issues, including industrial waste management, energy, and climate change. The head of an environment ministry would also be able to make recommendations in the prime minister's cabinet and, therefore, will have a stronger role in domestic and international policy making. NGOs in Japan will also receive a boost from the so-called NPO bill (nonprofit organization) that was passed by the Diet in March 1998. The new law will give corporate status to volunteer and citizens' groups.[22]

A further change that is already affecting Japan-Russia environmental cooperation is Japan's new greenhouse gas emissions reduction commitments under COP3. This represents, in fact, the most promising new area for systematic and proactive cooperation. In accordance with the Kyoto Protocol adopted at COP3 in December 1997, Japan agreed to cut greenhouse gas emissions by 6 percent below its 1990 level between 2008 and 2012. The protocol regulates six greenhouse gases, and it allows emissions trading and the inclusion of carbon sinks, that is, forests and oceans, in the calculation of each nation's total emissions. Joint implementation activities — whereby a nation that provides technologies to help another nation cut its emissions can count the reductions as its own — can also be used to achieve Kyoto Protocol targets.

Emissions of carbon dioxide in Russia declined by 20 percent between 1990 and 1995 because of its economic slowdown; Russia will become a major seller of excess emissions in the envisioned trading mechanism. Japan, thus, is looking toward increased cooperation with Russia to achieve its reduction targets. In January 1998 Japan proposed that the two nations create a partnership to reduce greenhouse gases through emissions trading and joint implementation. Among Japan's proposals for joint implementation were offers of technology transfers to improve the efficiency of natural gas pipelines and thermal power plants. Because the United States is also looking to Russia as a major emissions trading partner, a degree of competition to gain trading rights with Russia may arise. However, a meeting to discuss this issue among the United States, Japan, Russia, and four other non-European developed countries held in March 1998 implies that cooperation rather than competition may prevail.

The inclusion of carbon sinks in the Kyoto Protocol may also provide an incentive for Japan and Russia to cooperate in Siberian and Far Eastern forest conservation and by extension biodiversity and forest resources management. Russia and the United States already cooperate under the U.S. Environmental Protection Agency's Russia–United States Forestry and Climate Change Project. This program foresees the possibility of creating a new market for carbon sinks, and thus forest conservation, as a potential defense against global warming.[23]

The Japanese Environment Agency (or ministry) may initiate its own program for collaboration. If it can succeed in tapping NGO and private sector expertise by forging effective partnerships,[24] it may manage to overcome its own shortcomings and broaden the scope of Japan-Russia environmental cooperation.

A broader framework or a multilayered approach to Japan-Russia bilateral relations will not be complete without the inclusion of environmental issues. There are emerging pressures to further cooperation from below in the form of NGO and local government initiatives and from above in the form of regional forums and international environmental agreements. The lack of success in initiatives of the early 1990s and subsequent crisis-oriented cooperation now represent important experience that can be used in future projects. The main barriers to closer and more successful cooperation — weak cooperative mechanisms, inflexible financial transfer arrangements, asymmetries in concern and capacity — may not be completely removed, but they can be lowered, and more innovative environmental diplomacy can be promoted. What will remain as the greatest challenge is convincing the political leadership on both sides to believe their own environmental rhetoric and to put it to good use.

NOTES

1. Rowland T. Maddock, "Japan and Global Environmental Leadership," *Journal of Northeast Asian Studies*, 17(4) (Winter 1994): 39.

2. See Alexander S. Timoshenko, "Ecological Security: Response to Global Challenges," in Edith Brown Weiss (ed.), *Environmental Change and International Law*. (Tokyo: United Nations University Press, 1992), pp. 413–56.

3. Miwa Ito, "Russia no ecorgi gyosei to kyokuto" (Russia's environmental administration and the Far East), *Roshia Kenkyujo*, No. 24 (April 1997): 65.

4. Personal communication with foreign policy specialist in the Arms Control and Scientific Affairs Foreign Policy Bureau, Ministry of Foreign Affairs of Japan, Tokyo, June 27, 1997.

5. Comments during the Global Partnership Multi-National Workshop on Nuclear Waste in and around the Sea of Japan, Sea of Okhotsk, and the North Pacific Ocean, in Niigata, Japan, June 14, 1996. Organized by the Center for International Security and Strategic Studies, Mississippi State University.

6. Personal communication with officials in the Environment and Ocean Development Division, Ministry of Transport of Japan, July 23, 1997.

7. "Report on Recent Case of Marine Pollution Emergency and Response," submitted by the Government of Japan to the NOWPAP Forum on Marine Pollution Preparedness and Response, Toyama, Japan, July 23–25, 1997.

8. The NOWPAP member states are Japan, the People's Republic of China, the Republic of Korea, and the Russian Federation.

9. For an analysis of concern and capacity and environmental aid institutions see Barbara Connolly and Robert O. Keohane, "Politics Lessons and Opportunities," *Environment*, 38(5) (June 1996): 12–20.

10. Statement by Prime Minister Ryutaro Hashimoto to the Special Session of the UN General Assembly for the Overall Review and Appraisal of the Implementation of Agenda 21, June 23, 1997.

11. Presentation by Dimitri A. Zimin, head of the Department for Ecological Programmes, State Committee for Environmental Protection of the Russian Federation, at the design workshop on global environmental issues, Tokyo, January 28, 1998.

12. Eugene Linden, "The Tortured Land," *Time*, September 4, 1995, p. 45.

13. Josh Newell and Emma Wilson, *The Russian Far East: Forests, Biodiversity Hotspots, and Industrial Developments.* (Tokyo: Friends of the Earth-Japan, 1996), p. 17; Armin Rosencranz and Antony Scott, "Siberia, Environmentalism, and Problems of Environmental Protection," *Hastings International and Comparative Law Review*, 14(4) (1991): 929–47.

14. Newell and Wilson, *The Russian Far East*, p. 19.

15. See World Bank, "New Forest Utilization for Russian Far East and Siberia," *Environment Bulletin*, 7(2) (September 1995): 6–7; Victor Loksha, Ramesh Ramankutty, and Nalin Kishor, "Timber Trade in Northeast Asia: Some Preliminary Analyses," Environment and Natural Resources Division, Washington, D.C.: World Bank, December, 1995, unpublished.

16. "Japanese Position Paper for UN General Assembly Special Session on Environment and Development" (New York, June 23–27, 1997), *Japan Environment Quarterly*, 2(2) (June 1997): 1.

17. *Denver Summit of Eight Communiqué*, Ministry of Foreign Affairs of Japan, January 22, 1997. Available: http://www.mofa.go.jp

18. See Shigeki Hakamada, "Building a New Japan-Russia Relationship," *Japan Echo*, 24(5) (December 1997).

19. For an overview of bilateral cooperation in fishery and sustainable marine resource management see Alexander Kurmazov and Igor Kazakov, "The Politics of Fishery," Chapter 29 in this volume.

20. Compare to the eight committees of the Gore-Chernomyrdin Commission: energy policy, business development, space and technology, defense conversion, health, science, environment, and agriculture.

21. Zimin presentation, Tokyo, 1998.

22. Tax incentives to strengthen the financial base of NGOs were not included in the NPO bill, but a resolution was adopted calling for a review of this matter and a law revision in three years.

23. Newell and Wilson, *The Russian Far East*, p. 27.

24.   The NGO Friends of the Earth-Japan has two ongoing projects on the forests and biodiversity of Siberia and the Russian Far East. It also has an extensive network of international and Russian research institutes, organizations, experts, and officials.

Selected Bibliography
Compiled by Machiko Takahashi

Afonin, Boris M. "V interesakh druzhby i dobrososedstva." *Rossiya i ATR*, No. 1 (April 1994): 76–85.

Afonin, Boris M. "Mezhdunarodnye svyazi." *Rossiya i ATR*, No. 2 (June 1996): 55–57.

Akaha, Tsuneo (ed.). *Politics and economics in the Russian Far East: Changing ties with Asia-Pacific*. London: Routledge, 1997.

Arase, David. "Japan's evolving security policy after the Cold War." *Journal of East Asian Affairs*, 8(2) (1994): 396–419.

Aron, Leon, & Jensen, Kenneth M. (eds.). *The emergence of Russian foreign policy*. Washington, D.C.: United States Institute of Peace Press, 1994.

Banerjee, Jyotirmoy. "Implications for Asia-Pacific security: The Russian enigma." *Asian Survey*, 34(6) (June 1994): 544–55.

"The bear hug." *Far Eastern Economic Review*, October 21, 1993, pp. 12–13.

Berton, Peter. "A New Russo-Japanese alliance?: Diplomacy in the Far East during World War I." *Acta Slavica Iaponica*, 11 (1993): 57–78.

Blank, Stephen. "Why Russian policy is failing Asia." *Journal of East Asian Affairs*, 11(1) (1997): 267-298.

Blank, Stephen, & Rubinstein, Alvin (eds.). *Imperial decline: Russia's changing role in Asia*. Durham, N.C.: Duke University Press, 1997.

Bolyatko, A. V. "Puti ukrepleniya voennoi bezopastnosti v Severo-Vostochnoi Azii." *Problemy Dalnego Vostoka*, No. 1 (1993): 28–30.

Bondarenko, Elena Yu. "Exploitation of Japanese POW labour in the USSR." *Far Eastern Affairs*, No. 1 (1995): 72–85.

Bondarenko, Elena Yu. "Sudby plennykh: Tokiiskii i Khabarovskii mezhdunarodnye protsessy nad Yaponskimi voennymi prestunikami iposledstviya." *Rossiya i ATR*, No. 1 (1993): 117–23.

Bondarenko, Ivan. "Znal li Daikokuya Kodayu Russkii yazyk?" *Acta Slavica Iaponica*, 12 (1994): 205–28.

"Boom in waiting: Sakhalin fights to turn its oil and gas into a better life." *Far Eastern Economic Review*, September 1, 1994, pp. 28–29.

Brown, Eugene. "Japanese security policy in the post–Cold War world: Threat perception and strategic options." *Journal of East Asian Affairs*, 8(2) (1994): 327–62.

Bundy, Barbara K., Burns, Stephan D., & Weichel, Kimberly V. (eds). *The future of the Pacific rim: Scenarios for regional development*. Westport, Conn: Praeger, 1994.

Buszynski, Leszek. "Russia and Japan: The unmaking of a territorial settlement." *World Today*, No. 49 (March 1993): 50–54.

Chu, Shulong. "The Russian-US military balance in the post–Cold War Asia-Pacific region and the 'China threat'." *Journal of Northeast Asian Studies*, 13(1) (1994): 77–95.

Chung, Il Yung, & Chung, Eunsook (eds.). *Russia in the Far East and Pacific region*. Seoul: The Sejong Institute, 1994.

Chuprasova, Svetlana M., & Sovasteev, Vitalii V. "Amerika izuchaet Yaponiyu: istoriografiya SShA o kapitalisticheskoi transformatsiistrana voskhodyashchego solntsa." *Rossiya i ATR*, No. 4 (December 1995): 99–109.

Curtis, Gerald L. (ed.). *The United States, Japan, and Asia: Challenges for U.S. policy*. New York: W. W. Norton, 1994.

Dobrovolski, Vassili N. "The Asia Pacific security dialogue agenda: A Russian perspective." *Korean Journal of Defense Analysis*, 8(2) (1996): 101–16.

Dryzhakova, Elena. "Pervyi obraz Yaponii v Russkoi literature: 'Zapiski' kapitana V. Golovinina (1816)." *Acta Slavica Iaponica*, 13 (1995): 98–109.

Duke, Simon. "Northeast Asia and regional security." *Journal of East Asian Affairs*, 8(1) (1994): 323–84.

Economic Planning Agency of Japan & Ministry of Economy of the Russian Federation (eds.). *Russia keizai ni kansuru nichiro kyodo kenkyu* (Report of the Japan-Russia joint research project on the Russian economic reform). Tokyo: Economic Planning Agency, 1997.

Economic Research Institute for Northeast Asia (ed.). *Japan and Russia in Northeast Asia: Building a framework for cooperation in the 21st century*. Niigata: Economic Research Institute for Northeast Asia, 1997.

Economic Research Institute for Northeast Asia (ed.). *Northeast Asia economic whitepaper*. Niigata: Economic Research Institute for Northeast Asia, 1996.

Economic Research Institute for Northeast Asia (ed.). *Erina Report*. Niigata: Economic Research Institute for Northeast Asia.

Efanov, V. N., Velikanov, V. Ya., & Mikheev, A. A. "Ekologicheskie aspekty promyshlennogo osvoeniya shelfa severo-vostochnogo Sakhalina." *Vestnik Dalnevostochnogo otdeleniya Rossiiskoi Akademii Nauk*, No. 3 (1993): 94–99.

Egorov, Nikita G. "Kaznit nelzya, pomilovat" [Show mercy, never execute (analysis of why the Minsk and Novorossiisk were scrapped)]. *Rossiya i ATR*, No. 2 (June 1997): 90–92.

English, H. Edward, & Runnalls, David (eds.). *Environment and development in the Pacific: Problems and policy options*. New York: Addison-Wesley, 1997.

Faust, John R. "The emerging security system in East Asia." *Journal of East Asian*

Affairs, 8(1) (1994): 56–89.

Fedorov, Valentin Petrovich. *Russia no jiyu keizai: 21seiki e no michi o hiraku* (Free economy in Russia: Paving the way to the 21st century). Translated by M. Takahashi. Tokyo: Simul Publication, 1995.

Fifth Meeting of the Northeast Asia Economic Forum Niigata: Significance and prospects of regional development and economic cooperation in Northeast Asia. Niigata City, Niigata Prefecture, February 16–17, 1995.

"The first 'pancake': Pioneering US oil firm has hits and misses." *Far Eastern Economic Review*, September 1, 1994, pp. 29–30.

Foye, Stephen. "Russo-Japanese relations: Still traveling a rocky road." *RFE/RL Research Report*, No. 44 (November 5, 1993): 27–34.

Fumoto, Shinichi. "Policy toward Ezo and the Sakhalin problem in the closing days of the Tokugawa regime [in Japanese]." *Nihon shi kenkyu*, No. 371 (July 1993): 25–30.

Gaidar, Vitaly. "The South Kuriles: A problem awaiting solution." *Far Eastern Affairs*, No. 6 (1994): 42–52.

Gavrilov, Victor. "Certain new aspects of the run-up to the Soviet-Japanese war of 1945." *Far Eastern Affairs*, No. 4 (1995): 53–76.

Gelman, Harry. *Russo-Japanese relations and the future of the U.S.–Japanese alliance.* Santa Monica, Calif.: Rand Corporation, 1993.

Goodby, James E., Ivanov, Vladimir I., & Shimotomai, Nobuo (eds.). *"Northern Territories" and beyond: Russian, Japanese, and American perspectives.* Westport, Conn.: Praeger, 1995.

Guzanov, V. G. "Rossiiskie kupets na Yaponskoi zemle." *Problemy Dalnego Vostoka*, No. 1 (1993): 120–28.

Hakamada, Shigeki. *Shizumiyuku taikoku: Russia to Nihon no seikimatsu kara* (Sinking great power: Russia and Japan at the end of the century). Tokyo: Shinchosha, 1996.

Hakamada, Shigeki. "Differences should be put aside for now." *Japan Times*, July 7, 1993, p. B3.

Hakamada, Shigeki. *Russia no dilemma: Shinso no shakai rikigaku* (Russia's dilemma: hidden social dynamics). Tokyo: Chikuma Shobo, 1993.

Han, Yong Sup. "Changes in the Northeast Asian strategic environment, and South Korean security in the 21st century." *East Asian Review*, 7(3) (1995): 3–23.

Hanami, Andrew. "Japan and the military balance of power in Northeast Asia." *Journal of East Asian Affairs*, 8(2) (1994): 363–95.

Harada, Chikahito. *Russia and North-east Asia*, Adelphi Papers No. 310. London: Institute of International and Strategic Studies, 1997.

Hasegawa, Tsuyoshi. "Nisso, Nichiro Kankei 50nen to Russia Kyokuto" (Fifty years of relations between Japan and the former Soviet Union, Russia, and the Russian Far East). *Erina Report*, 7 (September 1995): 41–43.

Hasegawa, Tsuyoshi, Haslam, Jonathan, & Kuchins, Andrew (eds.). *Russia and Japan: An unresolved dilemma between distant neighbors.* Berkeley, Calif.: Berkeley-Stanford Program, 1993.

"High cost of field development off Sakhalin Island jolts Russians." *Oil and Gas Journal*, February 22, 1993, p. 30.

Honda, Ryoichi. *Kokkyo o iku: yureru kyokuto Russia* (Traveling to the border areas: the Russian Far East in a state of flux). Sapporo: Hokkaido Newspaper, 1996.

Ijima, Kazutaka. *Shinsei Russia no sugao* (The true face of new Russia). Tokyo: Mainichi Newspaper, 1997.

Ikeshoji, Takanobu. *Utsuriyuku Russia* (Russia in transition). Tokyo: Chuo University Press, 1996.

Institute for Russian & East European Economic Studies. *Russia no boeki kanri taisei no haikei to genjo* (Background and current status of Russia's trade management system). Tokyo: Japan Association for Trade with Russia & Central-Eastern Europe, 1996.

Institute for Russian & East European Economic Studies (ed.). *Russia kyokuto no databook* (Databook of the Russian Far East). Tokyo: Japan Association for Trade with Russia & Central-Eastern Europe, 1997.

Institute for Russian & East European Economic Studies (ed.). *Russia keizai kenkyu nichibei symposium hokokusho* (Japan-US joint symposium on Russian economy), vol. 2. Tokyo: Japan Association for Trade with Russia & Central-Eastern Europe, 1996.

Institute for Russian & East European Economic Studies (ed.). *Russia to rinsetsu shokoku no shin keizai kankei* (New economic relations between Russia and neighboring countries). Tokyo: Japan Association for Trade with Russia & Central-Eastern Europe, 1995.

Institute for Russian & East European Economic Studies (ed.). *Nichiro keizai kenkyu koryu jigyo hokokusho* (Report on Japan-Russia economic research exchange program). Tokyo: Japan Association for Trade with Russia & Central-Eastern Europe, 1995.

Institute for Russian & East European Economic Studies (ed.). *Russia kyokuto kaihatsu no concept* (Concept of the development of the Russian Far East). Tokyo: Japan Association for Trade with Russia & Central-Eastern Europe, 1994.

Institute for Russian & East European Economic Studies (ed.). *Nichiro godo symposium hokokusho: Nihon no taiCIS shien: kanosei to tenbo 1992nen* (Report of Japan-Russia joint symposium: Japan's investment in CIS: Potential and prospects, 1992). Tokyo: Japan Association for Trade with Russia & Central-Eastern Europe, 1993.

Institute for Russian & East European Economic Studies (ed.). *Nichiro keizai senmonka kaigi* (Conference of Japanese and Russian economists). Tokyo: Japan Association for Trade with Russia & Central-Eastern Europe, 1993.

Institute for Russian & East European Economic Studies (ed.). *Russia keizai kenkyu nichibei symposium hokokusho* (Japan-US joint symposium on Russian economy), vol. 1. Tokyo: Japan Association for Trade with Russia & Central-Eastern Europe, 1992.

Ishaev, Viktor I. "Kyokuto Russia to Nihon no Aidano Zenrin Kankei no Isso no Hatten ni Mukete" (Far Eastern Russia and Japan: Prospects for a good neighborhood). *Erina Report*, 24 (October 1998): 16–19.

Ishikawa, M., Komori, G., & Nakatsu, T. *Shinsei Russia keizai no ririku* (Take off of new Russia's economy). Tokyo: Soseisha, 1994.

Ivanov, Mikhail. "Profiles: In memoriam Richard Sorge and his friends." *Far Eastern Affairs*, No. 4–5 (1994): 153-162.

Ivanov, Vladimir I. and Karla Smith. "Hokuto Asia ni okeru Nihon to Russia" (Japan and Russia in Northeast Asia). *Erina Report*, 19 (October 1997): 15–27.

Ivanov, Vladimir I. "Russia and its Far East: Sources of conflict and hope." *Journal of East Asian Affairs*, 8(2) (1994): 482–521.

Japan Association for Trade with Russia & Central-Eastern Europe (ed.). *Russia to Too shokoku no taisei tenkan no keizaiteki cost* (Costs in system transformation in Russia and Eastern Europe). Tokyo: Japan Association for Trade with Russia & Central-Eastern Europe, 1994.

Japan External Trade Organization. *Russia ni okeru Nihon kara no chokusetsu toshi ni kansuru kenkyu: Beikoku kara no chokusetsu toshi to no hikaku* (Japan's direct investment in Russia: Comparison with USA's investment). Tokyo: Japan External Trade Organization, 1993.

Japan Institute of International Affairs (ed.). *Russia no kinrin gaiko: heisei 6 nendo* (Russia's diplomacy towards neighboring countries, 1994). Tokyo: Japan Institute of International Affairs, 1995.

Japan Institute of International Affairs (ed.). *Russia seiji system no tenkan to gaiko ni taisuru impact* (Changes in the Russian political system and their impact on diplomacy). Tokyo: Japan Institute of International Affairs, 1995.

"Japan: G-7 approved Russian aid." *Far Eastern Economic Review*, July 22, 1993, p. 83.

"Japan: Tougher stand." *Far Eastern Economic Review*, September 2, 1993, p. 14.

Jukes, Geoffrey. "Russia's military and the northern territories issue," Working Paper No. 277. Canberra: Australian National University, Strategic and Defense Studies Centre, 1993.

Jukes, Geoffrey. "The Russian military and the Northern Territories." *Acta Slavica Iaponica*, 12 (1994): 24–46.

Kagrlitsky, Boris. *Meisosuru fukko Russia* (The uncertain revival of Russia). Translated by K. Sakuma, A. Mizutani, and Y. Yukawa. Tokyo: Gendai Kikakushitsu, 1996.

Kasyanov, V. L. "V yuzhnykh gavanyakh Sibiri" [In the southern bays of Siberia]. *Vestnik Dalnevostochnogo Otdeleniya Rossiiskoi Akademii Nauk*, No. 5 (1996): 89–95.

Kikabidze, E. "Podkhody Yaponii k razvitiyu malogo biznesa v Rossii." *Problemy Dalnego Vostoka*, No. 5 (1996): 53–57.

Kim, Euikon. "The territorial dispute between Moscow and Tokyo: A historical perspective." *Asian Perspective*, 16(2) (1993): 141–54.

Kimura, Hiroshi, & Okazaki, Hisahiko. "Yeltsin's ice-breaking visit." *Japan Echo*, 21(1) (1994): 72–76.

Kimura, Hiroshi. "Yeltsin's visit and the outlook for Japanese-Russian relations." *Journal of Northeast Asian Studies*, 13(2) (1994): 49–60.

Kimura, Hiroshi. "Money for Moscow: A test case for Japanese diplomacy." *Japan Echo*, 20(3) (1993): 64–76.

Kojima, Terumi. *Russia no energy sangyo to gendai shakai* (Russia's energy industries and modern society). Tokyo: Shindokushosha, 1994.

Kotkin, Stephen, & Wolff, David (eds.). *Rediscovering Russia in Asia: Siberia and the Russian Far East*. Armonk, N.Y.: M. E. Sharpe, 1995.

Kozhevnikova, Irina P. "Vannovskii i Yaponiya." *Acta Slavica Iaponica*, 13 (1995): 149–66.

Kozhevnikov, Vladimir V. "Territorialnyi vopros: k 40-letiyu sovmestnoi Sovetsko-Yaponskoi deklaratsii 1956 goda." *Rossiya I ATR*, No. 3 (October 1996): 45–56.

Kozhevnikov, Vladimir V. "Vopros ostalsya otkrytym: San-Frantsiskii mirnyi dogovor i Sovetsko-Yaponskie otnosheniya." *Rossiya I ATR*, No. 3 (September 1995): 10–23.

Kozhevnikov, Vladimir V. "'I lyubov, i prezrenie': osobennosti vospriyatiya yapontsami Rossii XVIII-XX vv." [in English]. *Rossiya i ATR*, No. 2 (August 1994): 101–9.

Krasnoshchekova, Elena "'Mir i Yaponii' v knige I.A. Goncharova 'Fregat Pallada'." *Acta Slavica Iaponica*, 11 (1993): 106–25.

Kuchins, Andrew (ed.). *Russia and Japan: An unresolved dilemma between distant neighbors* (pp. 161–86). Berkeley: University of California, International and Area Studies, 1993.

Larin, Viktor L. "Dalnii Vostok Rossii i problemy bezopastnosti v Vostochnoi Azii" *Vestnik Dalnevostochnogo Otdeleniya Rossiiskoi Akademii Nauk*, No. 6 (1995): 12–25.

Latyshev, V. M. *Port-Artur—Sakhalin : Kreiser "Novik" v russko-iaponskoi voine, 1904–1905 gg*. Yuzhno-Sakhalinsk: Sakhalinskii Province's Museum of Local History, 1994.

Layard, Richard G., & Parker, John. *Russia wa yomigaeru: Shihon shugi taikoku e no michi* (The coming Russian boom). Translated by K. Tagawa. Tokyo: Mita Press, 1997.

Lee, Min-yong. "Building security regimes in Northeast Asia." *Journal of East Asian Affairs*, 9(1) (1995): 61–85.

Leonhard, Wolfgang. *Taikoku Russia no hyoryu: Gorbachev to Yeltsin no 10nen* (Drifting great power, Russia: 10 years of Gorbachev and Yeltsin). Translated by Noriko Murakami. Tokyo: NHK Publication, 1996.

Mandelbaum, Michael (ed.). *The strategic quadrangle*. New York: Council on Foreign Relations Press, 1995.

McOmie, William W. "The Russians in Nagasaki, 1853–54: Another look at some Russian, English and Japanese sources." *Acta Slavica Iaponica*, No. 13 (1995): 42–60.

Meyer, Peggy F. "Russia's post–Cold War security policy in Northeast Asia." *Pacific Affairs*, 67(4) (1994): 495–512.

Meyer, Peggy F. "Moscow's relations with Tokyo: Domestic obstacles to a territorial agreement." *Asian Survey*, 33(10) (October 1993): 953–67.

Miasnikov, Vladimir. "Security in Northeast Asia." *Far Eastern Affairs*, No. 5 (1996): 18–43.

Morimoto, Tadao. *Samayoeru Russia: hakyoku no keizai kaikaku no moto de* (Bewilderment of the Yeltsin revolution). Tokyo: Nihon Hoso Kyokai Publication, 1993.

Morrison, Charles E. (ed.). *Asia Pacific security outlook 1997*. Honolulu, Hi.: East-West Center, 1997.

Myasnikov, V. "Polozhenie v sfere bezopasti v Severo-Vostochnoi Azii." *Problemy Dalnego Vostoka*, No. 5 (1996): 15–37.

Nakagawa, Hiromasa. *Russia giji shihon shugi no kozo* (Russia's quasi-capitalism). Tokyo: Iwanami Publication, 1993.

Nakatsu, K. *Russia to CIS keizai no henyo to saiken* (Changes and reconstruction of the Russian and CIS economies). Tokyo: Dobunkan, 1996.

Nakatsu, T. *Gendai Russia no shijo keizai: Sono tokushusei to ishitsusei* (A market economy in modern Russia: its peculiarity and heterogeneity). Tokyo: Sagano Shoin, 1996.

Newell, Josh, & Wilson, Emma. *The Russian Far East: Forests biodiversity hotspots and industrial developments*. Tokyo: Friends of the Earth, 1996.

Nihon to Russia kyokuto chiiki to no keizai kankei (Economic relations between Japan and the Russian Far East). Tokyo: Japan Association for Trade with Russia & Central-Eastern Europe, 1992.

Nimmo, William F. *Japan and Russia: A re-evaluation in the post-Soviet era.* Westport, Conn.: Greenwood, 1994.

"No smoke screen: Tokyo uses Central Asia to send a message to Russia." *Far Eastern Economic Review*, December 16, 1993, pp. 46–47.

Ochiai, Tadashi. *Russia to kokusai kankeiron* (Russia and international relations). Tokyo: Bunka Shobo Hakubunsha, 1993.

Ogawa, Kazuo, & Hishiki, K. *Nyumon kannihonkai keizaiken to Russia kyokuto kaihatsu* (Introduction to the Northeast Asian economic sphere and the development of the Russian Far East). Tokyo: Japan Association for Trade with Russia & Central-Eastern Europe, 1994.

Ogawa, Kazuo, & Watanabe, H. *Kawariyuku Russia to Too keizai: Shijoka no shiren to nishigawa no taio* (Russian and Central-East European Economies in transition: ordeals of market economization and response of the West). Tokyo: Chuo Keizaisha, 1994.

Osaki, Heihachiro (ed.). *Taisei tenkan no Russia* (Russia in system transition). Tokyo: Shinhyoron, 1995

Osaki, Heihachiro (ed.). *Konmei no Russia keizai saizensen: keizai gakusha 14nin no kinkyu report* (The front line of the confused Russian economy: emergency reports by 14 economists). Tokyo: Shinhyoron, 1993.

Ota, F., Tanigawa, H., & Otani, T. *Russia no keizai kaikaku to Nihon no sangyo seisaku* (Russia's economic reform and Japan's industrial policy). Tokyo: Research Institute of International Trade and Industry, 1992.

Paik, Keun-Wook. "A Northeast Asian gas grid?" *Geopolitics of Energy*, January 1, 1993, pp. 6–10.

Park, Seon Seop. "Is a joint security system in North East Asia possible?" *East Asian Review*, 5(3) (1993): 3–26.

Pavlov, Dmitrii. "Japanese money and the Russian revolution, 1904–1905." *Acta Slavica Iaponica*, No. 11 (1993): 79–87.

Perras, Galen Roger. "We have opened the door to Tokyo: United States plans to seize the Kurile Islands, 1943–1945." *Journal of Military History*, 61(1) (1997): 65–74.

Petrovsky, Vladimir. "Cooperation-based security in Northeast Asia: Russia's potential role." *Far Eastern Affairs*, 2–3 (1994): 15–26.

Polevoi, Boris P. "Zemlya Rossiiskogo vladeniya: Snova o Kurilskoi probleme, istorii i politike." *Dalnii Vostok*, No. 8 (August 1993): 172–96.

Postel-Vinay, Karoline. "Local actors and international regionalism: The case of the Sea of Japan zone." *Pacific Review*, 9(4) (1996): 489–503.

Rikuguchi, J. *Russia shijo keizai no meiso: kaikaku to konran no 500nichi* (Straying Russian market economy: 500 days of reform and confusion). Tokyo: Kodansha, 1993.

Rimer, J. Thomas (ed.). *A hidden fire: Russian and Japanese cultural encounters, 1868–1926.* Stanford, Calif.: Stanford University Press, 1995.

Rodionov, A. "Problemy i perspektvy Rossiisko-Yaponskogo investitsionnogo sotrudnichestva." *Problemy Dalnego Vostoka,* No. 2 (1993): 15–21.

Rosefielde, Steven S. "Peace and prosperity in the Pacific rim: Optimizing the benefits of Japanese assistance to Russia." *Acta Slavica Iaponica,* No. 12 (1994): 47–61.

Russia kyokuto henkyo chiiki no toshi kankyo (Investment environment in border areas of the Russian Far East). Tokyo: Japan Association for Trade with Russia & Central-Eastern Europe, 1995.

Russia no genjo to tenbo (Current status and prospects of Russia). Tokyo: National Institute for Research Advancement, 1996.

Russia no zaisei (Russia's finance). Tokyo: Research Institute for International Investment and Development of the Export-Import Bank of Japan, 1996.

"Russia: Round, round and round at Sakhalin." *Petroleum Economist,* 60(8) (August 1993): 41–43.

Russian Academy of Sciences Far East Division Economic Research Institute (ed.). *Russia kyokuto keizai soran* (Comprehensive bibliography of economy of the Russian Far East). Tokyo: Toyo Keizai Shinposha, 1994.

Sager, Matthew J. "Prospects for oil and gas development in Russia's Sakhalin Oblast." *Post-Soviet Geography,* 36(5) (May 1995): 274–90.

Sase, Masamori, & Sawa, Hidetake. "Does Yeltsin's Russia deserve our support?" *Japan Echo,* 20(3) (1993): 56–63.

"Sent to Siberia: Japanese city forges own trade ties with Russia." *Far Eastern Economic Review,* October 21, 1993, pp. 20–22.

Shearman, Peter (ed.). *Russian foreign policy since 1990.* Boulder, Colo.: Westview, 1995.

Shimotomai, Nobuo. *Russia gendai seiji* (Modern politics in Russia). Tokyo: Tokyo University Press, 1997.

Sidorenko, Viktor V., & Barantsev, Aleksandr M. "Morskie miny: Istoriya i sovremennost ikh ispolzovaniya v ATR" [Sea mines: history and modern usage in the Asia-Pacific region]. *Rossiya i ATR,* No. 2 (June 1997): 86–89.

Simon, Sheldon (ed.). *Security in the post–Cold war era.* Armonk, N.Y.: M. E. Sharpe, 1993.

Sipols, V. "SSSR i Yaponiya: Dogovor 1941 goda." *Problemy Dalnego Vostoka,* No. 5 (1996): 103–14.

Song, Allan Y. "A half step forward: An assessment of the April 1991 Soviet-Japanese summit." *Asian Perspective,* 16(1) (1993): 103–28.

Stephen. John J. *The Russian Far East: A history.* Stanford, Calif.: Stanford University Press, 1994.

Stolberg, Eva-Maria. "The strategic quandrangle, Russia, China, Japan and the United States in East Asia." *Asien,* (60) (1996): 115-24.

Sugimori, K., Tanbara, T., & Ogawa, Y. *Chugoku to Russia no energy jijo* (Energy situation in China and Russia). Tokyo: Aki Shobo, 1995.

Tanaka, Y., Tsubata, S., & Onishi, H. (eds.). *Saisei ni tenjiru Russia* (Russia, newly born). Tokyo: Tsumugi Publication, 1993.

Task Force on Intellectual Support for Russia, Economic Planning Agency (ed.). *Nihon no economist ni yoru Russia no keizai kaikaku ni kansuru teigen* (Suggestions for economic reform in Russia by Japanese economists). Tokyo: Printing Bureau of Ministry of Finance, 1994.

Tikhvinsky, Sergei L. "Normalizing relations with Japan after the Second World War (conclusion)." *Far Eastern Affairs*, No. 5 (1995): 69–81.

Tikhvinsky, Sergei L. "Normalizing relations with Japan after the Second World War." *Far Eastern Affairs*, No. 4 (1995): 77–91.

Titov, I. "Rossiisko-Yaponskie ekonomicheskie otnosheniya: sostoyanie pti-misticheskogo ozhidaniya." *Problemy Dalnego Vostoka*, No. 3 (1993): 18–26.

Tkachenko, Boris I. "Kurilskaya problema: Istoriya i pravo." *Rossiya i ATR*, No. 1 (March 1996): 10–18.

Tkachenko, Boris I. "Kurilskaya problema: Istoriya i pravo." *Rossiya i ATR*, No. 3 (September 1995): 24–29.

Tkachenko, Boris I. "Kurilskaya problema: istoriya i pravo." *Rossiya i ATR*, No. 4 (December 1995): 21–31.

Tkachenko, Boris I. "Kurilskii vopros (ekonomiko-strategicheskoe znachenie Yuzhno-kurilskogo subregion)." *Rossiya i ATR*, No. 2 (December 1994): 98–105.

Togawa, Tsuguo. "Obraz Rossii v Yaponii nakanune i posle restavratsii Meidzi." *Rossiya i ATR*, No. 1 (1993): 108–16.

Tow, William T. "Reshaping Asian-Pacific security." *Journal of East Asian Affairs*, 8(1) (1994): 90–134.

Tsubata, Satoshi. *Russia keizai, keiei system kenkyu* (Research on Russia's economic and management systems). Tokyo: Horitsu Bunkasha, 1996.

Umezu, Kazuo. *Russia tennen gas sangyo no keiei kozo* (Management structure of natural gas industry in Russia). Tokyo: Koyo Shobo, 1997.

Valencia, Mark (ed.). *The Russian Far East in transition: Opportunities for regional economic cooperation*. Boulder, Colo.: Westview Press, 1995.

Vorontsov, Dmitrii. "The ROTOBO delegation in Buriatia and the Irkutsk Region." *Far Eastern Affairs*, No. 4–5 (1994): 63–69.

Yasko, Tatyana N. "Russkaya emigratsiya v Yaponii (1905–1907 gg.)." *Rossiya i ATR*, No. 1 (April 1994): 56–65.

Yavlinski, Grigori (ed.). *Russia CIS keizai no shinjitsu: koremade nani ga attaka korekara do naruka* (Russian and CIS economies: what has happened and what will happen). Translated by Yukishige Matsumoto. Tokyo: Toyo Keizai Shinpo, 1992.

Yoder, H. S. *Planned invasion of Japan, 1945: The Siberian weather advantage*. Philadelphia, Pa.: American Philosophical Society, 1997.

Yon, Hyon-Sik. "The Russian security interests in Northeast Asia." *Korean Journal of Defense Analysis*, 6(1) (1994): 155–74.

Yonemura, Noriyuki, & Nishimura, Yoshiaki. *Russia no shijo keizaika: Nihon no keiken to chiteki shien* (Russia's transition to a market economy: what Japan's know-how can offer). Tokyo: Simul Publication, 1992.

Zagorsky, Alexei. "The post–Cold War security agenda of Russia: Implications for Northeast Asia." *Pacific Review*, 8(1) (1995): 77–98.

Zimonin, Viacheslav. "Teheran-Yalta-Potsdam: Soviet Entry into the War with Japan." *Far Eastern Affairs*, No. 2 (1995): 40–62.

Zimonin, Viacheslav. "The Soviet-Japanese War of 1945." *Far Eastern Affairs*, No. 4 (1995): 33–52.

Zinberg, Yakov, & Drifte, Reinhard. "Chaos in Russia and the territorial dispute with Japan." *Pacific Review*, 6(3) (1993): 277–84.

Index

List of Contributors

Evgeniy V. Afanasiev, Russian Ambassador to the Republic of Korea, formerly Director of the First Asian Department of the Ministry of Foreign Affairs of the Russian Federation.

Tsuneo Akaha, Professor of International Policy Studies and Director of the Center for East Asian Studies at Monterey Institute of International Studies, Monterey.

Nobuo Arai, Director of the Hokkaido Institute for Regional Studies, Associate Professor at Hokkaido International University, Sapporo.

Douglas Barry, Director of the National Research Center on Education in Washington, D.C., and formerly Professor at the University of Alaska, Anchorage.

Kazuto Furuta, Niigata Prefectural Government office, formerly a Researcher at the Economic Research Institute for Northeast Asia, Niigata.

Alexander G. Granberg, Chairman of the Council for Location of Production Forces and Economic Cooperation of the Ministry of Economy of the Russian Federation, full member of the Russian Academy of Sciences, and President of the International Academy of Regional Development and Cooperation, Moscow.

Tsuyoshi Hasegawa, Professor of History at the University of California, Santa Barbara, and formerly an associate of the Slavic Research Center of the University of Hokkaido, Sapporo.

Vladimir I. Ivanov, Senior Researcher at the Economic Research Institute for Northeast Asia, formerly Head of the Asia-Pacific Region Department of the Institute of World Economics and International Relations of the Russian Academy of Sciences.

Hajime Izumi, Professor of International Relations and Korean Studies, University of Shizuoka, and Chairman of the East Asian Security Study Group, Tokyo.

Hisao Kanamori, President of the Economic Research Institute for Northeast Asia and Advisor to the Japan Center of Economic Research, formerly Chairman of this Center for many years.

Igor V. Kazakov, Deputy Trade Representative of the Russian Federation in Japan and formerly Professor at the Academy of Foreign Trade, Moscow.

Jiro Kodera, Director, First International Economic Affairs Division (Economic Relations with Europe), formerly Director of the Policy Planning Division, Ministry of Foreign Affairs, Tokyo.

Andrei I. Kravtsevich, Director of the Center for Japanese Studies, Institute of Oriental Studies of the Russian Academy of Sciences, and President of the Association of Japanese Studies in Russia, Moscow.

Alexander M. Kurmazov, Deputy Head of the International Department at the Pacific Institute of Fishery in Vladivostok, formerly stationed at the Embassy of the Russian Federation in Japan.

Pavel A. Minakir, Director of the Economic Research Institute of the Russian Academy of Sciences (Far Eastern Branch), and Member-Correspondent of the Russian Academy of Sciences, Khabarovsk.

Kazuyoshi Nishikata, Niigata Prefectural Government office, formerly a Researcher at the Economic Research Institute for Northeast Asia, Niigata.

Makoto Nobukuni, Professor of Economics at Nagoya City University, formerly Director of the Research Division, Economic Research Institute for Northeast Asia (1993–97), and Advisor on Economic Planning and Development to the government of Indonesia (1990–93).

Andrei P. Rodionov, until 1997 was stationed in Japan as a representative of the Chamber of Commerce and Industry of the Russian Federation, and now works at Maximov Publications, a private information and research organization, Moscow.

Steven Rosefielde, Professor of Economics at the University of North Carolina, Chapel Hill.

Robert N. Ruzanov, Trade Representative of the Russian Federation in Japan, formerly Trade Representative of the Russian Federation in the United States.

Konstantin O. Sarkisov, Director of the Center for Japanese Studies, Institute of Oriental Studies, Professor of International Relations, Hosei University, Tokyo.

Robert A. Scalapino, Robson Research Professor of Government Emeritus, the University of California, Berkeley, formerly Director of the East

Asia Studies Institute and editor of *Asian Survey*, Berkeley.

Dmitriy L. Sergachev, Researcher at the Economic Research Institute for Northeast Asia, Niigata.

Nobuo Shimotomai, Professor of Political Science and Russian Studies at Hosei University, Tokyo.

Nodari A. Simonia, Deputy Director of the Institute of World Economics and International Relations of the Russian Academy of Sciences and full member of the Academy, Moscow.

Karla S. Smith is Visiting Researcher at the East-West Center, Honolulu.

Tadashi Sugimoto, Chief Economist and Secretary-General of the Japan-Russia Business Cooperation Committee, Keidanren, Tokyo.

Machiko Takahashi, Administrative Officer at the Research Division of the Economic Research Institute for Northeast Asia served as technical coordinator of this book project.

Georgiy D. Toloraya, Ministry of Foreign Affairs of the Russian Federation and formerly Minister-Counsellor, Embassy of the Russian Federation in Seoul, Korea.

Ivan S. Tselitschev, Professor at the Niigata University of Management and Resident-Representative of the Institute of World Economics and International Relations of the Russian Academy of Sciences.

Hisako Tsuji, Senior Researcher at the Economic Research Institute for Northeast Asia, Niigata.

Robert Valliant, Director of the Center for Russia in Asia at the University of Hawaii at Manoa, Honolulu.

Susumu Yoshida, Senior Advisor at Nissho Iwai and Deputy Chairman of the Japan-Russia Business Cooperation Committee of Keidanren, Tokyo.

ISBN 0-275-96382-9

90000>

EAN

9 780275 963828